Russian Military Reform

This book examines reform of the Russian military since the end of the Cold War. It explores the legacy of the Soviet era, explaining why – at the time of the fall of the Soviet Union – radical reform was long overdue in the wake of changing military technology, new economic and political realities, and the emergence of new threats and challenges. It discusses the problems encountered by Gorbachev in his attempts to promote military reform in the late 1980s, and goes on to analyse in detail the mixed fortunes of the policies of his successors, Yeltsin and Putin. It describes how the onset of war in Chechnya in 1994 provided clear evidence of the weaknesses of the Russian military in modern conflicts, and shows that although the Chechnya debacle did provide some impetus for reforms in the Armed Forces in 1997–98, the momentum was not continued under the Putin government. It argues that Putin's policies of bolstering central control over all aspects of decision making has left untouched many key problems facing the Russian military, including infighting between different force structures, lack of transparency and independent scrutiny over defence spending, and absence of consensus on the main threats to Russia and optimum force posture. Moreover, it argues that in his attempts to concentrate all means of control in a corrupt and inefficient Kremlin bureaucracy, Putin has deprived himself of all alternative channels of independent scrutiny, control and oversight, thus exacerbating the problems that continue to plague the Russian military.

Carolina Vendil Pallin is a research fellow at the Swedish Institute of International Affairs and has authored a number of publications on Russian domestic, security and military policy. She was previously deputy research director at the Swedish Defence Research Establishment.

Routledge Contemporary Russia and Eastern Europe Series

Russian Military Reform

A failed exercise in defence
decision making

Carolina Vendil Pallin

Taylor & Francis Group

LONDON AND NEW YORK

First published 2009
by Routledge
2 Park Square, Milton Park, Abingdon, Oxon OX14 4RN

Simultaneously published in the USA and Canada
by Routledge
270 Madison Ave, New York, NY 10016

Routledge is an imprint of the Taylor & Francis Group, an informa business

© 2009 Carolina Vendil Pallin

Typeset in Times New Roman by
Taylor & Francis Books

British Library Cataloguing in Publication Data
A catalogue record for this book is available from the British Library

Library of Congress Cataloging in Publication Data
Pallin, Carolina Vendil.
  Russian military reform : a failed exercise in defence decision making /
Carolina Vendil Pallin.
    p. cm. – (Routledge contemporary Russia and Eastern Europe series ; 14)
Includes bibliographical references and index.
  1. Russia (Federation)–Armed Forces–Reorganization. 2. Civil-military
relations–Russia (Federation) I. Title. II. Title: Russian military reform,
a failed exercise in defense decision making.
  UA770.P226 2008
355.30947–dc22   2008006926

ISBN 978-0-415-44744-7 (hbk)
ISBN 978-0-203-89239-8 (ebk)

Contents

Illustrations

Figures

Tables

Boxes

Preface

This book started in 2002 as a short paper on explanations as to why military reform was failing in Russia. As so often is the case, the more I studied the question, the more absorbing it became as the different facets of military reform and decision making on defence forced their way into the analysis. Gradually, the paper grew into a more comprehensive study where the link between decision making and the progress of military reform was at the centre of the analysis. The first draft was written while I was deputy research director at the Swedish Defence Research Agency (FOI), which carries out analyses on commission from the Swedish Ministry of Defence.

A note of gratitude is due to the ministry, and especially to Jörgen Cederberg, for granting me the opportunity to develop this study and for kindly allowing me to rewrite it into a monograph. It could not have been written without the in-depth knowledge of Russian military affairs of my colleagues at FOI (formerly FOA, the Swedish National Defence Research Establishment), from which I have profited greatly. This is reflected, not least, in the frequent references to the biannual FOI reports on Russian military capability. Regrettably, these reports (published in May 1999, November 2000, February 2003 and 2005) are only available in Swedish. Short English summaries of the 1999, 2003 and 2005 reports were published in 1999, 2003 and 2005, respectively. The 1999 summary was also translated into Russian in *Nezavisimoe voennoe obozrenie.*[1] In a way, therefore, this book contributes to making some of these reports' findings available in English. A number of other FOI reports and publications, for example, on the Russian military–industrial complex, also provided important background for the present book. I joined the Swedish Institute of International Affairs (SIIA) in June 2006 and my new employer has been as forthcoming as FOI in providing encouragement and material support in the writing of this book.

I have benefited greatly from a number of colleagues' comments on the text as well as from their analyses of individual areas of reform. They include Jan Leijonhielm, Jakob Hedenskog, Dr Ingemar Dörfer, Dr Jan Knoph, Robert Larsson, Ingmar Oldberg and Wilhelm Unge, and Fredrik Westerlund, to mention but a few. Per-Olof Nilsson was a main source of reference on early Russian military reform. Outside FOI, a number of people generously shared their expertise and delivered incisive and helpful comments on drafts of the book. Professor Stephen Blank pointed out, among other things, the need to take account of the strategic aspects throughout the book. Dr Anna Jonsson provided advice on the judicial aspects of defence decision making. In addition, Dr Maria Hedvall, Ulf Thorsson, Dr Lena Jonson and Dr Gudrun Persson and Professor Steven Rosefielde all contributed comments that I have incorporated into the text. Finally, I was in the fortunate position of having the opportunity to discuss military reform with three authorities on the development of the Russian military – Aleksandr Golts, Vitaly Shlykov and Professor Dmitri Trenin – as a result of which my thinking on the topic developed considerably.

A special note of gratitude is due to Professor Pavel Baev who kindly agreed to read a first version of the manuscript and to present his critique at a seminar at FOI in May 2005. The text profited greatly from his suggestions and scrutiny. As a direct result of his critique and encouraging comments, the structure of the text changed drastically. Needless to say, neither Pavel nor anyone else should in no way be criticized for any mistakes or transgressions that still remain in the text. Eve Johansson tidied up the language of the text and the footnotes. Deeply felt thanks for this effort. Finally, I dedicate this book to my husband who in the first place encouraged me to 'make a proper study' rather than just a paper. He provided advice on military terminology and endured the at times towering presence of this book during what has been a very happy but often demanding time in our life together, since our children were born between 2003 and 2007. Thank you for your support and advice, Krister.

A note on spelling and Russian terminology

Throughout the book Russian words and names have been transliterated using the Library of Congress system. However signs for the Russian ь and ъ have been omitted. Exceptions have also been made in the main text for names that begin with e, ё, й, ÿ or ý. The letter 'y' then starts the name as in the case of Yeltsin (rather than 'Eltsin'). Likewise, in the case of geographical and personal names such as Chechnya (rather than Chechnia) and Tolstoy (rather than Tolstoi) I have adopted the spelling most commonly used.

I have endeavoured to keep the number of abbreviations to a minimum. However, it proved impractical to use the full name of institutions and organizations, especially those with long, cumbersome names that are referred to frequently. I have, in the main, opted for the Russian abbreviations of the different institutions that are discussed in the text. However, in certain cases – such as MoD for the Ministry of Defence, CIS for the Commonwealth of Independent States and MIC for the military–industrial complex – I have opted for the established and easily recognizable English abbreviations rather than the Russian MO (*Ministerstvo oborony*), SNG (*Sodruzhestvo Nezavisimykh Gosudarstv*) and VPK (*voenno promyshlennyi kompleks*).[2] All abbreviations are explained the first time they are used and a list of all abbreviations is provided below after this note.

In the main, the NATO–Russia glossary has been used for the translation of military terms such as 'formation' (*soedinenie*) and 'services of the Armed Forces' (*vidy Vooruzhennykh Sil*).[3] Certain words and expressions proved central for the understanding of the Russian framework for military reform. A word that occurs frequently in Russian sources on military reform is *stroitelstsvo*, here normally translated into 'development' (or more rarely 'development and deployment'). In a Russian–English dictionary, the translation is 'building, construction' or figuratively 'organization, structuring'.[4] However, further discussion of the term is called for when it is used abstractly as, for example, in *voennoe stroitelstvo* or *stroitelstvo vooruzhennykh sil*. It is clear from the way the term is used that it may refer to a state or condition of the Armed Forces (for example, the organization and deployment of the Armed Forces) as well as a process (the development of the Armed Forces). Consequently, *stroitelstvo* has been intermittently translated as, for example, 'developing and structuring forces', 'military development' and 'military organization'.[5] A Russian military dictionary specifies the development of the Armed Forces as the most important constituent of *military* development. 'Military development [*voennoe stroitelstvo*], a system of economic, social-political, strictly military and other measures undertaken by the state in order to strengthen its military capability.'[6]

Another word that often causes certain confusion is 'professionalization' or the 'creation of professional Armed Forces'. Usually, this designates the Russian efforts to switch from a conscript army to one manned by soldiers recruited on a voluntary or contract basis. The word 'professionalization' (or 'professional army') has been avoided for two reasons. First, the word suggests that the Russian military was not professional before, which is hardly true. Its officers were far from amateurs. Second, the term 'professional soldier' is closely connected to Huntington's theory on civil–military relations and refers to something other than simply the way soldiers are recruited and appointed.[7] In Huntington's terminology a 'professional army' could definitely include conscripts in its ranks. For these two reasons, this study designates the Russian attempts to move away from a conscript army as moving towards 'recruitment on a voluntary basis' or 'on a contract basis', thus avoiding the word 'professional' in this connection (except, of course, in direct quotations).

Russia experienced a number of political crises and power struggles during the 1990s. This frequently resulted in changes of names of political institutions such as the parliament and the security services which succeeded the KGB. The names and abbreviations of the different 'power ministries', as well as a definition of this elusive term, are provided in Chapter 3. A short explanation is also called for when it comes to the names of the Russian parliament during the 1990s. Two parliaments, which existed in early 1991, are mentioned in this book since the Russian Soviet Federative Socialist Republic (the RSFSR) had a Congress of People's Deputies (of the RSFSR) at the same time as there was a Congress of People's Deputies of the Soviet Union. Out of these congresses, which were the highest decision making organs at the republican and federal level respectively, smaller working parliaments were elected – the Supreme Soviet of the RSFSR and the Supreme Soviet of the Soviet Union. As the Soviet Union crumbled, so did its parliament. The Russian Congress of People's Deputies and its Supreme Soviet, however, lived on until September 1993, when Yeltsin decided to dissolve the parliament. In December 1993, a new constitution was adopted at the same time as a new parliamentary assembly was elected. According to the Russian constitution of 1993, the Russian parliament, the Federal Assembly, consists of two chambers – the State Duma, the deputies of which were directly elected, and the Federation Council, formed by the constituent parts of the Russian Federation. The reader should find that all the other institutions as well as the twists and turns in Russia's political life are explained in the text.

Acronyms and abbreviations

ABM	Anti-ballistic missiles
AFV	Armoured fighting vehicles
AVN	Akademiia voennykh nauk (Academy of Military Science)
BBC	British Broadcasting Corporation
CFE	Conventional Forces in Europe
CIS	Commonwealth of Independent States
CPSU	Communist Party of the Soviet Union
CSTO	Collective Security Treaty Organization
DPA	Dvizhenie v podderzhku armii (Movement in Support of the Army)
EU	European Union
FAPSI	Federalnoe agenstvo pravitelstvennoi sviazi i informatsii pri Prezidente RF (Federal Agency for the Protection of Government Communications)
FOA	Swedish National Defence Research Establishment
FOI	Swedish Defence Research Agency
FPS	Federalnaia pogranichnaia sluzhba (Federal Border Service)
FSB	Federalnaia sluzhba bezopasnosti (Federal Security Service)
FSK	Federalnaia sluzhba kontrrazvedki (Federal Counter-intelligence Service)
FSO	Federalnaia sluzhba okhrany (Federal Guard Service)
GKO	Gosudarstvennyi komitet oborony (State Committee for Defence)
Glavpur	Glavnoe politicheskoe upravlenie (Main Political Administration)
GNP	Gross national product
GOSPLAN	Gosudarstvennyi planovyi komitet (State Planning Commission)
GOSSNAB	Gosudarstvennyi komitet po materialno-tekhnicheskomy snabzheniiu (State Supply Committee)
GRU	Glavnoe razvedyvatelnoe upravlenie (Generalnogo shtaba Voennykh Sil) (Main Intelligence Directorate of the General Staff of the Armed Forces)

GUMVS	Glavnoe upravlenie mezhdunarodnogo voennogo sotrudnichestva (Main Directorate of International Military Cooperation (of the Ministry of Defence))
GUO	Glavnoe upravlenie okhrany (Main Guard Directorate)
GUSP	Glavnoe upravlenie spetsialnykh programm Prezidenta Rossii (Main Directorate for Special Programmes)
ICBM	Intercontinental ballistic missile
INF	Intermediate nuclear forces
KGB	Komitet Gosudarstvennoi Bezopasnosti (Committee of State Security)
KPRF	Kommunisticheskaia Partiia Rossiiskoi Federatsii (Communist Party of the Russian Federation)
LRA	Long range aviation
MChS	Ministerstvo Rossiiskoi Federatsii po delam grazhdanskoi oborony, chrezvychainym situatsiiam i likvidatsii posledstvii stikhiinykh bedstvii (Ministry of Civil Defence, Emergency Situations and Liquidating the Consequences of Natural Disasters)
MD	Military district
MIC	Military–industrial complex
MID	Ministerstvo Inostrannykh Del (Ministry of Foreign Affairs)
MoD	Ministry of Defence
MVD	Ministerstvo Vnutrennykh Del (Ministry of Internal Affairs)
NAK	Natsionalnyi antiterroristicheskii komitet (National Anti-Terrorist Committee)
NATO	North Atlantic Treaty Organization
NCO	Non-commissioned officer
NGO	Non-governmental organization
PONARS	Program on New Approaches to Russian Security (Center for Strategic and International Studies
PVO	Protivo-vozdushnaia oborona (Air Defence Forces)
R&D	Research and development
RFE/RL	Radio Free Europe/Radio Liberty
RKO	Raketno-kosmicheskaia oborona (Missile Space Defence Troops)
RSFSR	Russian Soviet Federative Socialist Republic
RVSN	Raketnye voiska strategicheskogo naznacheniia (Strategic Rocket Forces)
SLBM	Submarine-launched ballistic missile
SORT	Treaty on Strategic Offensive Reductions
SVOP	Sovet po vneshnei i oboronnoi politike (Council on Foreign and Defence Policy)
SVR	Sluzhba vneshnei razvedki (Foreign Intelligence Service)
UN	United Nations

UVKR	Upravlenie voennoi kontrrazvedki FSB (Directorate of Military Counter-intelligence of the Federal Security Service)
VDV	Vozdushno-desantnye voiska (Airborne Troops)
VPK	Voennaia promyshlennaia kommissiia (Military–Industrial Commission)

1 The Kremlin and military reform

The political development in the Soviet Union and Russia from the late 1980s and onwards has been nothing short of breathtaking. An empire crumbled and fell, bringing fifteen independent states into existence. Russia in particular went from being the centre of an authoritarian, socialist Soviet Union to building a new Russian state and introducing democracy and a market economy. All these changes could not but lead to momentous changes within the Russian military establishment. The Russian military found itself within an entirely new strategic environment. For example, the country had fourteen new neighbouring states and had lost most of its military allies that were tied to the Soviet Union through the Warsaw Pact. Meanwhile, innovations in the field of military technology and warfare had long pointed to the need for military reform. This was brought home to the Russian military not least after the Gulf War in 1991.

Relations between the military and society underwent change as well. The Soviet military officer had been a respected member of an elite that enjoyed much sought-after privileges. He was the outpost against aggressive Western imperialism and warmongering. The heavy burden that the Soviet military imposed on society was seldom, if ever, questioned. This state of affairs changed drastically with the fall of the Soviet Union. Starting under Gorbachev and accelerating in the 1990s, there was less consensus on the need to prioritize military spending in the way it had been prioritized throughout most of the Soviet era. The West was no longer the enemy it had been. Instead, the lifestyle of the West was increasingly seen as something to aspire to. Living a good life, *zhit normalno*, became the main concern of most Russians at the same time as the prestige and authority once enjoyed by the Russian military rapidly eroded. Russian military personnel were left with a feeling of having been bitterly abandoned and let down by an ungrateful society and political leadership. It was thus hardly surprising that the changes that Russian society underwent, starting in the late 1980s, would lead to tensions between the military and civilian sectors of society.

The challenges that resulted from these changes would have to be met by the political leadership. It would have to provide a new list of threats that the

Russian military was to prepare to meet. No less important, the political leadership had to decide in no uncertain terms which threats were no longer relevant. Moreover, the Kremlin had to provide the guidelines for how to meet these threats, and this involved difficult questions such as which force posture Russia should have, which threats were to be handled by the military as opposed to the police, what would be the role of the strategic nuclear forces compared to conventional forces, and so on. In other words, military know-how was of the essence if political circles were to be able to decide these questions. Finally, the political leadership needed to hammer out a new place for the military organization within a rapidly changing Russian society. This was by no means an easy task, but was essential if questions of manning and financing were to be resolved in the long term.

Why another study of Russian military reform?

The volume of books and articles on Russian military reform is daunting. The question whether another study of Russian military reform is really needed is therefore a real one. There are at least three justifications for approaching the subject again.

First, coming to grips with reforming the military system is an essential challenge to Russian policy makers. It plays a central role in the development of Russian politics as a whole. Russia's military reform raises fundamental questions about how civil–military relations should be organized. It is not the much-discussed question of whether or not the generals will be involved in a military coup that is at the centre of attention here; rather it is the question within the field of civil–military relations that has come to the fore in recent years – of how to impose political will on a military system.[1] This has proved urgent not only for Russia but for other post-communist countries as well. In the Russian case, a precondition for the reform was that the monopoly over defence spending and planning was wrested from the military. As will be evident below, this proved to be a prolonged and arduous process that may not come to fruition for another ten years. This study will add to the existing literature in these fields.

Second, even a cursory glance at the problems faced by the Russian political leadership reveals that many of the dilemmas it faced and the experiences it gained were far from unique to Russia. The fall of the Soviet Union and the drastic changes of international society that it brought about more or less coincided with major changes in military technology and doctrine. Together these changes prompted radical reforms of most, if not all, Western armed forces – reforms that often met with considerable resistance. The Russian experience, with all its specific preconditions and problems, provides an interesting backdrop for other studies on military reform. It is worth pointing out, though, that the Russian case has a number of unique specifics – an ongoing war within its own borders in the republic of Chechnya, Russia's possession of nuclear weapons, and a national identity crisis, to mention but a few. Certainly, the magnitude of the tasks ahead for anyone wishing to reform the Russian military was impressive.

Finally, there exists a purely selfish motive for studying military reform: to anyone interested in security policy decision making, studying the Russian military reform process presents an irresistible challenge. It spans several security policy areas and engages key institutions within the executive, the legislative and the judicial sphere. Moreover, there are few studies that focus on Russian defence decision making and military reform, and especially on the institutional framework.[2] The present study aims to fill this gap.

Argument and structure

This book was born out of an interest in security decision making – and when it comes to Russian security decision making, few decisions (or the lack thereof) have sparked more interest and debate than the military reform. The very way in which military reform has been managed by fits and starts, with intense activity one month only to be followed by long periods of inertia, cannot but arouse interest. This is therefore not a systematic comparison with military reform in other countries or previous centuries. Nor will the reader who is interested in order-of-battle descriptions in chronological order find this book satisfying. Rather, the focus is on defence decision making and its relationship to the progress (or lack thereof) of military reform.

Only the Russian political leadership could decide and provide the military organization with the guidelines for military reform. When the Russian Armed Forces were created in 1992, a significant perception gap had opened up between society at large and the Russian military. The military needed to change its outlook on the world to become more in tune with the society it was supposed to serve. Even more importantly, the politicians had to assert authority over military policy. This required both political courage and a good grasp of military matters. In a longer perspective, the political leadership also needed to develop an effective institutional framework for defence decision making. This book traces the evidence of, first, the politicians' determination to change the military system; second, the dissemination of military know-how outside the military sphere; and, finally, the development of a framework of efficient institutions through which to carry out reform.

It should be clear to most people by now that the Russian military organization will not be comparable with, for example, that of the USA in the foreseeable future. This book proceeds from Russian definitions of military reform and evaluates progress primarily against these definitions. This is then combined with Western theory on defence decision making and civil–military relations in order to provide guidelines for analysis of the political level and the decision-making framework. The underlying argument is that when political will and know-how were present, as well as an institutional framework for defence policy making, there was some progress in military reform as well. However, the main tendency was for energetic policy making to peter out after a short, intensive period of activity. The Kremlin lacked perseverance in pushing through the much-needed military reform. Instead, its reform proposals became bogged down by bureaucratic resistance the minute the political leadership wavered in its determination.

Many of the problems in conducting a military reform in Russia were precisely those that one might expect. Money was scarce and the military bureaucracy was reluctant to implement reform. However, a strong political leadership with a clear vision of why and how it wanted to conduct a military reform would have overcome such difficulties. Instead, Russia's political leadership tended to get embroiled in political turf wars. It never made the strategic analysis that was necessary if it was to develop a goal and a plan for military reform. Nor did it build the necessary defence decision-making machinery and recruit the experts who could have acted on its behalf when other policy issues took precedence over military reform in the Kremlin. Military reform in Russia was hindered by the lack of political will, decision-making structures and know-how on the political level. This is true of both the Yeltsin and the Putin era, contrary to the impression that Putin pushed military reform forward significantly.

Chapter 2 starts with an account of the different explanations that have been advanced as to why military reform has been so slow in materializing in Russia. Most of them can be divided into three main categories: economic explanations; explanations that focus on threat perceptions; and explanations that identify the absence of political leadership as critical. Although all three reflect important factors, the chapter concludes that there is a good argument to be made for exploring further the third, which centres on the dearth of political leadership in military affairs. Chapter 3 examines defence decision making in general. It then goes on to explore the Soviet legacy that Moscow was left with. The different Russian institutions for defence decision making are described and an 'ideal' structure for Russian defence decision making is suggested. This chapter can be read as part of the overall study, but also separately as an overview of Russian defence policy making.

Chapter 4 goes on to explore the Russian definition of military reform and the reasons for conducting a reform in 1991. In Russia, military reform embraces not only the Armed Forces of the Russian Federation. A number of other armed troops are also included in Russia's military organization. The chapter thus discusses and defines what should be regarded as the military organization of the Russian Federation. Finally, it defines the political leadership that was responsible for military reform.

Chapter 5 looks into the early record of Russian military reform during the Yeltsin era. It finds that very little was done and that the defence decision-making structures hardly evolved at all during this period. Meanwhile, the political leadership showed little or no interest in military reform since it was busy consolidating its own position of power. Some of the main problems facing the Armed Forces and the military organization are discussed.

The war in Chechnya was a vivid reminder to Moscow that the need for military reform was extremely urgent. This is illustrated at the end of Chapter 5, since there was a flurry of political activity on military reform following the defeat in Chechnya. However, this intense defence decision-making activity petered out before some of the most significant challenges to the Russian military organization had been met.

Chapter 6 deals with the advent of Putin to power and examines whether his commitment to creating a strong Russia has resulted in military reform. The chapter explores Putin's so-called power vertical against the record of reform. The conclusion is that this decision-making structure will do little to address the basic problems within the military organization.

The closing chapter concludes that military reform in Russia has still moved forward relatively little. Although a number of decisions have been made that affect the Armed Forces, there is little evidence that Russia's military organization as a whole has made great strides in meeting its military policy challenges – even in the long-term future. Putin's power vertical appears to give him more power, but in practice makes him hostage to his circle of closest advisers and to bureaucratic politics. Instead of a system of checks and balances, Putin has created a fragile structure where all levers of power are concentrated in the Kremlin.

2 The debate on Russian military reform

Military reform is a process where goals and means change over time rather than a set of fixed end goals to be reached at a given point in time. It is in the very nature of a major reform project that adjustments are called for along the way as domestic and international conditions change. Perhaps this sense of longevity and moving targets helps to explain the intensity of the debate on Russian military reform. Different Russian actors blame each other and enumerate a multitude of reasons for the failure of military reform. Outside observers, mainly in the West, have provided equally long lists of impediments to reform and of culprits who either willingly or by their sheer incompetence undermined the reform process. Nor is there any consensus on where military reform ought to be heading. Most analyses tend to converge on one conclusion, though: Russia's military reform record has been dismal and the future seems to hold few promises of radical improvement.

One way of explaining the poor record of the military reform could be simply to point to the Soviet legacy as crippling and effectively preventing radical reform measures. However, the Soviet legacy explains close to nothing unless one goes on to pinpoint which aspects of it are the problems. All reform processes must build on a legacy of some kind, and in the Russian case it had to be of Soviet descent. In addition, an explanation that roughly says that Russian military reform failed because it is impossible to reform the Soviet/Russian legacy is tautological. Nor should the main reason why Russian military reform has been slow in coming be sought in pre-Soviet legacies such as the Mongol yoke, tsarist authoritarian practices or, as has been suggested, the fact that Russian officers have read Tolstoy's *War and Peace*.[1] While these kinds of historical analogies and comparisons are certainly useful in putting the present situation in perspective, they provide less convincing explanations of progress (or lack of progress).

The different explanations that have been suggested as to why Russian military reform has proved an insurmountable task can be roughly divided into three categories. In the first are the explanations that concentrate on economic factors – particularly the poor state of the Russian economy in general in the 1990s and the degree to which the Russian economy was militarized during the Soviet era. The second category contains explanations that centre on old threat evaluations that lived on within the military sphere. The focus is on the reluctance Russian generals have shown to abandon old conceptions of what Russia's place in the world is and the tendency to continue to regard NATO as the main enemy. Finally, the third category focuses on the lack of political leadership and the inability to control and scrutinize the Russian military. This last category is also the main focus of this study. Evidently, most explanations tie into and reinforce each other and most of the writing on Russian military reform refers to more than one explanation, as will be evident below.

Economic obstacles

The start of Russian military reform coincided with a sharp downturn in the Russian economy in general. From independence and throughout the 1990s, Russia struggled with a severe budget deficit. The economy showed few signs of growth and the positive signs that were visible in 1996–97 disappeared from sight as Russia tumbled into a deep economic crisis in August 1998. These economic problems could not but affect the Russian defence budget and, thus, the funding of an intended military reform since even simply downsizing usually proves expensive.[2] A military reform would require either significant increases of the defence budget as a whole or a radical redistribution of funds within it. Neither of these occurred in Russia, and military reform was stalled almost immediately by lack of funds.[3] In addition, evidence suggests that the political leadership seriously underestimated the costs associated with military reform. In other words, the economic assumptions were flawed from the very start.

Instead the defence budget decreased while the Russian Ministry of Defence (MoD) proved reluctant to make the redistribution of funds that would have been necessary.[4] Russian military participants in the debate usually overlooked the need for a reallocation of the available resources and concentrated their critique on the political leadership's failure to understand that reforms cost money. In short, they called for an increase in the defence budget.[5] This view existed already in the Soviet Union under Gorbachev when the military – far from accepting the need for reduced spending on defence – demanded increased funding.[6] In the late 1990s, the chairman of the Duma Committee on Defence and former head of the Federal Border Service, Andrei Nikolaev, lamented that instead of focusing on improving the defence and security of Russia, the political leadership was concentrating only on bringing the size of the military into line with the financial resources available. In his view, military reform demanded more spending rather than the reverse.[7] He reiterated this point in 2001: 'Our leaders and many politicians hold, ever since the Soviet times, the mistaken idea that the military should be getting less money once military reform has been launched.'[8]

The root of these officers' view on how much military spending Russian society was able to carry is to be found in the degree to which Soviet society was militarized. As Russia became independent in 1991, it inherited an economy and society where military needs had always taken precedence over private consumption and even over achieving overall economic growth.[9] The size of the Russian defence budget was notoriously hard to estimate throughout the 1990s. This was due in part to the difficulty of establishing the size of the Russian national budget overall. However, in the case of the defence budget, the difficulty of estimating its size was compounded by the fact that it was impossible to determine the share of the economy that directly or indirectly produced for the military.[10] This legacy from the Soviet era, a 'structural militarization', permeated not least the industrial sector and hindered conversion that could have freed resources and yielded increased welfare for the rest of Russian society.[11]

In the 1990s the military found itself in a position of having to pay for things that it had previously received for a price that did not reflect the market value. On top of this, contractors no longer prioritized military orders in the way they had done in the Soviet era. The financial difficulties were aggravated by the fact that the Armed Forces had to provide housing and other benefits to their personnel. Since there was a chronic shortage of housing, the Ministry of Defence was rarely able to do this. Still more pressing was the obligation to provide housing to those officers who were dismissed from the Armed Forces. This obligation overrode that of housing the remaining personnel. Consequently, this provided little incentive for the MoD to reduce its forces, since reducing the Armed Forces could prove more expensive than keeping them at the existing level.[12]

Meanwhile, on a personal level, Russian military personnel struggled to make ends meet, especially those with a family to support. The military was one of many categories of state personnel who were forced to wait for months on end for their wages. This was probably one of the reasons why the level of corruption increased within the Armed Forces.[13] Indeed, as officers found themselves compelled to increase their incomes by means other than regular wages, the situation approached a point where profitable corruption within the military made many officers reluctant to see changes in the system.[14] In this connection it is worth mentioning that, although the war in Chechnya cost the Russian state considerable sums, it is equally true that it has proved a valuable source of income to a number of officers there.[15] In other words, in certain cases the level of corruption removed the incentives for getting reform under way.

Considering the magnitude of Russia's economic and financial difficulties, it is natural that many observers regard the economic situation and the unrealistic defence budget as the main reason why Russian military reform was poorly implemented during the 1990s. Indeed, the economic factors ought not to be disregarded; but it is important to remember that the struggle between the Ministry of Finance and the Ministry of Defence over the size of the defence budget is far from unique to Russia.[16] Nor is a situation where diminished national financial resources put limits on defence budgets unique. Other states have struggled with difficult economic constraints while restructuring their armed forces. The difference in scale and the magnitude of the problem faced is considerable, and this makes comparisons between Russia and other countries difficult. However, in the Russian case it was the need to strike a balance between economic goals and defence goals that was the critical factor rather than budgetary constraints as such. Deciding this balance was always first and foremost a political decision.

For example, the increases in the American defence budget in 2003 took place under conditions when the USA was experiencing an economic downturn. One criticism levelled against this increased spending was that simply providing more financial resources would not force the military sector to prioritize, innovate and reform.[17] Indeed, the main problem for the Russian military was not the cuts that were made in its annual budget. Rather it was the fact that the military continued to wear a costume that was much too large for its present needs and out of proportion to the available resources that proved central. The Ministry of Defence failed to draw the inevitable conclusions from the new situation it found itself in. The Soviet military had gradually gained a position where defence policy had become the preserve of military officers and the political leadership lacked the necessary skills to provide guidelines and goals, let alone ensure that these were fulfilled. This made it possible for the MoD and other power ministries to ignore the exhortations to make drastic structural changes of the military system. Reductions were forced on the military by the political leadership, but without providing clear goals for the military reform process. In other words, it was the lack of political guidelines and vision, coupled with an inability to enforce political decisions upon the military, that resulted in the economic crisis within the military organization rather than lack of money per se.

Old threat perceptions dominated military planning

The Russian Armed Forces were created in the midst of great confusion. There were, for example, few clear signs as to where the Commonwealth of Independent States (CIS) was heading as an organization. Initially, Russia had championed the transfer of the armed forces of the Soviet Union to a joint CIS command. Only when all the other CIS states had formed their own armed forces or announced their intention of doing so did Russia create its own Russian Armed Forces, in May 1992.[18] Russia also found itself having to bring home troops from the former Warsaw Pact states and the Baltic states – something that impaired the implementation of military reform.[19] This complicated the process of building new national armed forces.

At the same time, Russia found itself within entirely new borders and with a new set of neighbouring states. Quite apart from the practical problems that this created when it came to organizing border controls and so on, there was a lingering confusion as to whether these were indeed the proper borders of Russia. Although the Kremlin never advanced revisionist claims regarding its borders with the former Soviet states, this policy line was not always consistent with public sentiment.[20] Certainly, within the military there was a growing consensus that the former Soviet republics should constitute Russia's sphere of influence. For example, in 1993 Colonel-General Andrei Nikolaev claimed that Russia's declining defence potential was the reason why 'many of its neighbours feel free to encroach on its national interests and infringe the rights of its citizens'.[21] The conclusion was that Russia should have a strong military in order to be able to exert pressure on its neighbouring states. In 2003, Igor Rodionov, former minister of defence, echoed a similar concern when it came to NATO enlargement, which had seriously limited Russia's 'independence in making domestic and foreign policy'.[22]

Russia also displayed a certain degree of ambiguity as to who were its enemies and what represented the main threats to Russia. During the first few years after the fall of the Soviet Union, the Kremlin experienced something of a honeymoon with the USA. Yeltsin and the minister of foreign affairs, Andrei Kozyrev, were the main proponents of this line. At the same time, local conflicts erupted within several of the newly independent CIS states. For example, the Russian Fourteenth Army in Moldova became embroiled in the conflict between the Russian-speaking minority in Transnistria and the Moldovan authorities in Chisinau. Later, Russia became involved in the conflict between the secessionist republic of Abkhazia and the Georgian authorities in Tbilisi, and in the civil war in Tajikistan. This list of conflicts within the CIS is far from exhaustive, but it suggests that local conflicts ought to have become important focal points when the Kremlin constructed its new armed forces. In other words, local and perhaps regional wars (or limited wars) rather than total war was the kind of conflict that Russia's military system was most likely to become embroiled in.[23] Preparing for a large-scale NATO attack under these circumstances stretched the scarce resources available to breaking point.

Nevertheless, it was clear that many within the defence and foreign policy bureaucracy retained the view that the USA and NATO remained Russia's main enemies. That threat perceptions are hard to change overnight is hardly surprising (or, for that matter, unique to Russia). Ideological education had featured as a regular part of all officers' education and, partly proceeding from this base, the Soviet military had always put stress on military superiority and on preparing for worst-case scenarios.[24] Although Russian military education no longer included lessons in Marxism-Leninism, many aspects of it remained unchanged in the 1990s.[25] Closely connected was the view that Russia must remain a great power. Thus, in 1993 vice president and former military officer Aleksandr Rutskoi warned against Russia losing its 'historic role':

> In order for Russia to fulfil her historic role to ensure peace on Earth and to retain a fitting position in world civilization and the status of a

great power worthy of respect, she must first and foremost take measures to overcome domestic instability, and preserve access to surrounding water space, something that was severely limited as a consequence of the republics achieving sovereignty.[26]

Analysts have focused on this contradiction between Russia's great power ambitions and its actual power as one of the main contradictions in its defence policy.[27] Leading generals continued to live in the realities of the Cold War and exuded 'traditional anti-Western conservatism'.[28] It was then hardly surprising that the conservative strand of the Russian debate on military reform regarded NATO expansion as a factor that prevented the implementation of reform.[29]

Like the problem of reduced financial resources, the difficulty in changing perceptions of threats is hardly unique to Russia or to the military. However, in Russia this lack of flexibility was aggravated by the fact that the Russian military had acquired a monopoly on defining the basic threats and dangers to the state. Thus, in 1996 the head of the Main Directorate of Operations of the General Staff, Colonel-General Viktor Barynkin, stated that Russia's Armed Forces ought to have the personnel and modern military technology 'that corresponds to the status of a great power'.[30] There was a reluctance to accept the primacy of the political leadership in formulating the threats to national security. Although the military frequently stated that it needed the political leadership to formulate a threat against which to prepare, when this threat did not correspond to the threat perception of the military it was simply ignored.

The problem was compounded by the fact that the chain of command was unclear and that the political leadership often provided conflicting directives. The Russian dash for Pristina Airport during the Kosovo crisis in 1999 was a clear example of how Russian generals broke the chain of command, albeit with the tacit support of Yeltsin.[31] During negotiations between Russia and the USA, it became obvious to the American deputy secretary of state, Strobe Talbott, that neither the Russian minister of foreign affairs nor the minister of defence had been provided with accurate information about the Russian deployment in Kosovo by their subordinates – most notably by the chief of the General Staff and deputy minister of defence, Army General Anatolii Kvashnin, and the head of the Main Directorate of International Military Cooperation (GUMVS) of the Ministry of Defence, Colonel-General Leonid Ivashov. Sergei Stepashin, prime minister at the time, later admitted to Talbott that 'there had been a serious breakdown in discipline and bureaucratic order'.[32]

Aleksei Arbatov, as deputy chairman of the Duma Committee on Defence, was one of the few people outside the military establishment with insight into the defence budget.[33] His conclusion in 2002, from looking at the items included in the budget, was that the Ministry of Defence pursued a foreign policy line completely at odds with official Russian foreign policy:

As we know, President Putin has declared the principal goal of Russia's foreign policy to be integration with the West, primarily with the European nations. However, decisions taken behind closed doors suggest that even at this late date, 90 per cent of our military budget goes into the training and maintenance of those forces that are intended for a big war with NATO.[34]

The scenarios played out in most Russian military exercises during the fifteen years of military reform reinforced this impression. The Russian military establishment continued to regard themselves as being able to make autonomous decisions on fundamental issues of international security. Evidently, the Russian political leadership had failed to impress its foreign policy goals upon the military establishment.

Dearth of political leadership and control

Thus, another explanation that has been advanced is that the political leadership abdicated its primacy in decision making on military reform.[35] Political will is a necessary precondition for any successful reform. In the Russian case, a number of factors influenced the degree to which the political leadership displayed (or failed to display) initiative in military reform. First, other political developments during the 1990s tended to distract Yeltsin's attention from military policy issues. Possibly, a degree of gratitude towards some of the military for their role in the preventing the 1991 August Coup and later for their role in the October Events in 1993 also played a role. Second, there was an acute lack of knowledge of military affairs outside the military establishment, since the latter had gradually come to monopolize this policy area. Finally, the political leadership did not possess the necessary institutional levers to exercise effective control over the military. The necessary coordination between the different ministries and agencies concerned was lacking.

Just before the fall of the Soviet Union, political power struggles drained energy from necessary (including military) reforms. To a considerable degree, military reform was 'held hostage to the twists and turns of Soviet politics'.[36] After Russia became independent, the situation hardly improved. Yeltsin signed the decree that created the Russian Armed Forces, but the attention he paid to the issue seemed to wane immediately. He did not seize this unique opportunity to radically reform the leadership of the Armed Forces and the functioning of the Ministry of Defence. Instead, he more or less left it to the military bureaucracy 'to set its own guidelines'.[37] This was in spite of the fact that Yeltsin initially combined the posts of president, prime minister and minister of defence.

Undoubtedly, this lack of attention to military matters is partly explained by the fact that Yeltsin was embroiled in a fierce power struggle with the parliament from January 1992 to October 1993. However, the lack of interest in military reform continued even after a new constitution was introduced – a constitution that vested the president with supreme power over security-related issues. Formal authority was thus not lacking, but Yeltsin continued to dedicate military reform limited attention at best. Although he spoke out on a number of occasions in favour of a renewed effort at military reform, it stopped at rhetoric and he swiftly lost interest in the issue, handing it over to a committee or to the MoD.

The lack of civilian insight into military affairs also explains why Russia's political leadership devoted only limited attention to military reform. The Soviet tradition of leaving defence matters to the Ministry of Defence (or rather the General Staff) persisted.[38] There was a culture of exaggerated security concern that complicated any attempts to expand the debate on military affairs outside the walls of the MoD. Dissatisfaction with this state of affairs, which was present under Gorbachev, increased in strength under Yeltsin. For example, a former colonel and professor of military science complained in 1991 about the way independent scholars or observers were kept out of the process of developing a new military doctrine and the framework for military reform. He contrasted this to the way military policy was widely discussed before being adopted in the USA.[39]

Closely related to the dearth of knowledge outside the military sector was the Kremlin's lack of institutions and mechanisms to control the military. It was difficult for the civilian political leadership to control the decisions and activity of a military establishment into which it had little insight. For example, the Duma was inherently weak when it came to scrutinizing the military budget and the Ministry of Defence did not make inventories on a regular basis. One of the means Yeltsin resorted to in order to control the military was to favour other power ministries at the expense of the MoD. This may have increased Yeltsin's sense of leverage over his subordinates, but did little to enhance military reform. Instead, infighting between and inside different power ministries complicated defence decision making. There were fierce conflicts over resources, the allocation of conscripts and prestige between different ministries and ministers. During most of the 1990s, the units of, for example, the Ministry of Internal Affairs (Ministerstvo Vnutrennykh Del, MVD) and the Federal Security Service (Federalnaia sluzhba bezopasnosti, FSB) were strengthened both qualitatively and in terms of numbers, draining resources from the Armed Forces.[40]

An additional reason why the Kremlin was slow to implement military reform was fear of entirely losing control of the military. Some analysts claim that the Kremlin feared a military coup.[41] These fears were exaggerated. The Russian military did not have a history of coup-making and loathed the fact that it had become involved in domestic political struggles in 1991 and 1993.[42] However, there may have been a strong fear of alienating the military too much.[43] Another related explanation is that Yeltsin hesitated to start a radical military reform process because he felt indebted to the military after the different power ministries (including the Armed Forces) had helped him out in August 1991 and October 1993.[44] In the case of Yeltsin's successor, there were speculations that Putin was indebted to the military after his election in 2000. His victory in the presidential election was attributed by many to the initial Russian successes in the second war in Chechnya in 1999. In particular, the chief of the General Staff, Anatolii Kvashnin, has been identified as the military planner behind the second Chechen military campaign.[45]

In complete contrast to the shortages in political leadership enumerated above, what was really needed in order for military reform to be successfully implemented was a keen interest in the issue on the part of the Kremlin, the presence of knowledge in military affairs outside the General Staff, civilian control over the military establishment and smooth coordination of decision making and implementation between the authorities concerned. In other words, reform of civil–military relations was of the essence. Although there were many important lessons to learn in this respect from the literature on Russian civil–military relations, until recently it has focused mainly on how to prevent military coups,[46] while the problem in Russia consisted in coming up with a model for exercising civilian control over the military on a daily basis. 'It is not merely a matter of the military withdrawing from politics. Civilians must take the initiative, step into leadership roles and equip them-selves with the knowledge and expertise necessary to oversee and monitor the military establishment effectively.'[47]

Thus, rather than the risk of the military taking control of civilian politics, the issue was one of enabling the political leadership to take control of defence policy making. This was the main challenge when it came to carry-ing out military reform. Only the Russian political leadership should decide what resources to devote to the military, which were the main threats that Russia faced and which defence policy priorities were pivotal. The policy level also had to acquire the ability to check that its policies were imple-mented in the manner intended. However, precisely at the time when the Russian Armed Forces most needed strong and informed political decision making, it was hopelessly lacking.

3 Defence decision making

At first glance, there could not have been a better time to carry out a military reform than in 1992. The turmoil that followed the fall of the Soviet Union complicated matters, but also created a unique opportunity for Russia to start reforms. Although Yeltsin's popularity within the Armed Forces petered out quickly – not least as a result of the role he played in the implosion of the Soviet Union – his popular mandate was strong after his decisive role in suppressing the August Coup in 1991.[1] There was a surge of support for democracy in the country while the Armed Forces, like many other institutions, were at a loss, trying desperately to adapt to the new situation. Most importantly, there were no significant large-scale external threats to Russia.[2] At the same time, several of the newly independent neighbouring republics grew increasingly unstable after the fall of the Soviet Union. Although this did not result in a direct external threat to Russian territory, it did involve new challenges for the Russian military organization as it took on tasks in the former Soviet republics. For the time being, however, Russia enjoyed a period of relative international calm and a benign environment. The conditions for planning and implementing a thoroughly thought-through military reform were thus quite favourable. In spite of this, military reform came to a standstill almost at once.

Defence decision making and civil–military relations

In analysing the development of military doctrines between the world wars, Barry R. Posen found that when there was an overshadowing threat of war, balance of power theory tended to explain the policy outcome best.[3] In this case, the decision-making process is explained in terms of the government as a rational actor who selects 'the action that will maximize strategic goals and objectives'.[4] The external threat results in a situation where infighting and bargaining gives way to concerted action. 'Fear of disaster or defeat prompts statesmen to question long-standing beliefs, to challenge service preferences, to alter budget shares, and to find new sources of military advice and leadership.'[5] By contrast, during periods of 'relative calm, when statesmen and soldiers perceive the probability of war as remote, the organizational dynamics' dominate decision making.[6] In other words, the government is then no longer best analysed in terms of being a rational actor. Decisions are rather the output of organizational process and bureaucratic politics as well as the result of a political process.[7]

In the seventeenth and early eighteenth centuries, kings like Peter the Great or the Swedish Gustavus Adolphus were often able military commanders as well as being the top of the political hierarchy in their respective states. However, the era when political leadership was intrinsically linked to military expertise has gone.[8] Increasingly complex societies have demanded increased specialization, resulting in bureaucracies that possess exclusive expertise in their field of activity. Political leaders' dependence on the expertise of specialized bureaucracies followed. Bureaucracies – and the military is arguably a bureaucracy, albeit of a special kind – tend to want to increase their power and autonomy or independence from 'civilian interference'.[9]

> Under normal conditions, the power position of a fully developed bureaucracy is always overtowering. The 'political master' finds himself in the position of the 'dilettante' who stands opposite the 'expert,' facing the trained official who stands within the management of administration.[10]

According to Posen, there are two situations in which innovation or reform tend to occur even when a major external threat is absent. First, a major failure or defeat may induce the military to innovate. Second, civilians can interfere to achieve change and reform.[11] However, civilian intervention in military affairs is fraught with difficulties. The civilian leadership lacks the necessary knowledge at the same time as the military will 'try to increase this power by mystifying their art, and concealing that art from civilian authorities'.[12] Finding military knowledge elsewhere or getting the military sector to provide different options for actions are avenues that the civilian leadership could try in order to rectify this problem. At the same time, the military will probably try to avoid changes that are initiated from outside and do its utmost to hinder potential competing bureaucracies from gaining the upper hand.[13]

In other words, there were plausible explanations for the failure to move the reform agenda forward in 1992. Following Posen's predictions above, there was, first, no enemy that threatened the very existence of the Russian state. In other words, the Russian leadership did not act according to the rational actor model. The institutional level is a better place to start when analysing military reform during this era. Second, there was no perception of a major military defeat. Although the Soviet Union had lost the Cold War, it had not done so on the battlefield. Within the military the perception reigned that it had been betrayed by its political leadership rather than lost a military battle. In other words, the military establishment did not feel that it was to blame and felt little in the way of urgent need to reform itself.

The last possibility, according to Posen, would have been the 'civilians' – the political leadership – interfering in order to achieve reform. However,

Yeltsin's overarching priority after coming to power was market rather than military reform. He did not even prioritize the need for a new constitution – something he would come to regret as the antagonism between the executive and legislative branch grew immediately in Russia after the Soviet centre had disappeared. Knowledge of military affairs was lacking on the political level or among the 'civilians', and Yeltsin was probably lulled into a false sense of security when it came to the state of Russia's Armed Forces by his minister of defence, Pavel Grachev.[14] There is also every reason to suspect that Yeltsin feared antagonizing the military after the events in August 1991 and later, after securing its vital support during the October Events in 1993. Nor did Yeltsin try to build the institutional framework that might have rectified the lack of scrutiny and military expertise outside the military sphere. As will be evident below, the institutional framework for defence decision making was left largely unreformed. Yeltsin certainly found himself in a position vis-à-vis the military whereby military experts dictated policy while the political level had little in the way of independent analyses to rely upon. There was no pressing external threat and, in accordance with Posen's predictions, the military bureaucracy, most notably the General Staff, expanded its administrative preserve over defence decision making.

Civil control existed over the Russian military in the sense that the military leadership showed little inclination for taking over the political leadership of the country. The officers who did go into politics did so after they left active service. Nor can the August Coup in 1991 or the October Events in 1993 be designated as military coups, although the military did play an important part. However, there is little evidence of civil control when it comes to civilians making inroads into the sphere of defence decision making.[15] The Kremlin was very much the hostage of the 'expert problem' in civil–military relations. The MoD still considered itself the sole possessor of the necessary knowledge in this field and did little to disseminate knowledge of military affairs outside the defence establishment. The ministry's ability to maintain a monopoly on defence decision making was considerably facilitated during the Yeltsin era by the fact that the Kremlin lacked a coherent defence policy most of the time. Initially, reductions in the defence budget were the only thing resembling a defence policy emanating from the Kremlin; and, even if it had developed a defence policy, the political leadership lacked the necessary levers to verify that this policy was implemented by the military.

In Russia, applying prescriptions for handling civil–military relations must take into account the fact that the minister of defence, by tradition, usually came from the military. This should not necessarily be interpreted as evidence of Russia's militarization. Most ministries in Russia are managed by ministers who have made their career within the same bureaucracy that they become head of.[16] In other words, the practice of the prime minister appointing ministers from his party has not taken root in Russia. This makes it necessary to adapt the theory of civil–military relations somewhat to the

Russian case – at least up until the appointment of Sergei Ivanov, formerly of the Foreign Intelligence Service (Sluzhba vneshnei razvedki, SVR) to head the MoD.[17] With this caveat in mind, it is possible to apply a number of prescriptions from theories of civil–military relations for civil control of military affairs.

First of all, it is necessary to ensure that the political leadership has the ability to direct the activities of the military organizations. To do so it needs access to military knowledge in order to make informed choices. The information should come from different sources: from the military organization, from defence research institutes outside the military sector, from civil experts on defence issues. In order to receive good advice from the military, the policy makers should 'involve themselves in the defence decision making process early and continually'.[18] Civilian involvement is of key importance as is a ministry of defence that integrates civilians with military officers.[19] This, of course, makes it easier for the minister of defence to control the process, but it also 'connects officers to the political dimensions of policy making'.[20] With time, the military will probably experience that civilian involvement in policy making and understanding of these issues is beneficial.[21] Since the political leadership should seek advice outside the military as well, it is essential that there exists a community of think tanks, defence interest groups and academics to consult. These will all provide their own specific expertise as well as an outside view.

The choice of minister of defence is also critical. In the Russian case, a civilian (and even then a civilian with a past within another power structure, the SVR) was not appointed to the post until 2001. When a civilian is appointed it is important to choose ministers 'who are in some sense experts in their own right'. They should also enjoy strong support from their own superiors and peers (i.e. from the prime minister, president and fellow ministers). The officers within the military bureaucracy 'tend to judge the minister first as a politician, noting the minister's skill, success, and power relative to his colleagues'.[22] In the Russian case, he would be evaluated as an administrator and according to the degree of support he enjoyed from the president and the Presidential Administration. However, in budgetary terms it may even be more critical to enjoy a good relationship with the prime minister and his administration, the minister of finance and the minister of economy.

One of the main levers for defence management is without a doubt the defence budget. However, this tool must be used with caution since 'defense expenditures are usually integrated into the national economy in many ways and sudden alterations to the defense cash flow may have unintended and surprising consequences'.[23] This was something the Russian leadership experienced when it reduced defence spending without taking into account, for example, the fact that the military had in reality funded large sections of the science community. The budget instrument for directing the military is nevertheless a potent one, not least when it comes to questions of procurement and the military–industrial complex (MIC). This is evidenced by the experience of former first deputy minister of defence Andrei Kokoshin. In his view, the Ministry of Finance had a critical role in managing defence, and not only in deciding the size of the defence budget, but also in actually disbursing the funds. Meanwhile, the Ministry of Economy played a central role in procurement.[24]

Just as important as issuing directives and distributing funds is a 'strong accountability element that includes statements of responsibility, firm milestones, and rigorous expenditures procedures'.[25] This includes two elements. First, there must be a unity of command and accountability, which presupposes lucid legislation and written regulations on the division of responsibilities.[26] Second, there must be a system for scrutinizing defence policy and expenditure.

> It is important, therefore, that politicians and officers understand that military leaders will be held accountable to the government for their responsibilities and for the faithful execution of the government's policies. Ministers must put accountability mechanisms in place and they should be as open as national security will allow, which means that in camera accounting will be the exception. ... Public accountability also serves the armed forces because where errors can be clearly attributed to political decisions, military leaders might make that point obvious to the citizens and, perhaps, retain their support in turbulent times.[27]

In the Russian case, the accountability function (or scrutiny) should be performed mainly by parliament (the Federal Assembly), the Audit Chamber and the judicial branch (the General and Military Procuracy).[28] In reality, this did not take place, and other accountability functions (such as those within the Ministry of Finance or Ministry of Economy) were equally weak. Without these sources of independent scrutiny and in the absence of political will, military reform tended to fall victim to bureaucratic politics and inertia, and the exaggerated security concerns that continued to plague the military bureaucracy further undermined outside scrutiny.

The Soviet legacy

Without the Soviet background it is difficult to understand many of the institutional choices made by the Russian leadership when it created its Armed Forces and Ministry of Defence. The Soviet Union's system for defence policy making had evolved gradually over several decades. The political leaders of the Russian Federation more or less inherited this system for the new state that they were creating. After a feeble attempt at keeping the Soviet forces under unified command within the CIS, Moscow had to come up with solutions in order to save whatever parts of the Soviet military machine it could. With this in mind, there is every reason to start with a short description of how defence policy was made in the late Soviet era.

The degree to which the Soviet military was able to make decisions autonomously of the Kremlin varied over time. In the early 1920s, the Soviet leadership exercised a high degree of political control over the military and defence policy making. This control began to subside somewhat in the late 1920s, only to become rigorous again under Stalin. After Stalin's death, the Soviet military was able to wrest a certain degree of autonomy over decision making on military matters, such as doctrine and force structure, from the Kremlin, while adapting to the cuts that Khrushchev forced through. Khrushchev also created a system of non-military institutes which studied military affairs under the aegis of the Soviet Academy of Science in order to break the military's monopoly on know-how in this sphere.[29] Under Brezhnev, however, 'most civilians were excluded from involvement or even knowledge of what was going on in these areas'.[30] This was the case not only regarding questions of force posture and so on but also concerning details of the defence budget. Such matters were simply not discussed outside the military. In fact, not even the military itself knew the overall size of defence spending.[31] At the same time, it is worth emphasizing that, while the military establishment enjoyed considerable autonomy in deciding military matters, party control continued to be exercised through political officers at all levels. There was a complicated web tying the Communist Party in with the military. This was the case at the local level in the military districts and at the very apex of the Soviet decision-making structure.[32]

> Party members within Soviet state structures, therefore, received two sources of direction, formal direction from their state bureaucratic superiors and informal direction from their party organizations. The informal party direction, of course, was more important, and when the party was functioning properly, that direction was so strong and uniformly understood that the two sources of direction seldom conflicted.[33]

There was also a system of political control handled through the Main Political Administration (the *Glavpur*). Each commander within the military (down to the level of battalion) had a political deputy, a *zampolit*. These political deputies were responsible for political indoctrination and for discipline and morale within the military units. They reported to the Main Political Administration, which was subordinated to the Central Committee Secretariat of the Communist Party of the Soviet Union (CPSU).[34] During the final years of the Soviet Union, one of the tasks of the Main Political Administration became agitating against Yeltsin in the elections. At that time, however, Yeltsin's popularity ratings within the military were quite impressive.[35]

In writings on the Soviet military, much attention was devoted to the Soviet Defence Council (Sovet oborony), which appeared in the Soviet constitution for the first time in 1977. The Defence Council was an heir to the Council of Labour and Defence (STO), which was established during the

Civil War and disbanded by Stalin in the 1930s. A successor, the State Committee for Defence (Gosudarstvennyi komitet oborony, GKO) was formed again during the Second World War.[36] Stalin disbanded this body after the end of the war. Khrushchev later created a Defence Council again in the 1950s. Assessments of the role of the Defence Council vary considerably. On the one hand, there is the view that the Politburo of the CPSU was likely to 'endorse whatever was recommended by the Council of Defence'.[37] However, William Odom claims that by the 1980s the Defence Council tended to confirm whatever the Politburo had decided.[38] The truth is probably that the influence of the Defence Council varied over time and with the people at the helm in the Politburo.

The general secretary of the CPSU headed the Defence Council, which had no secretariat or apparatus of its own and met only five to six times a year. For expert advice, it depended on the General Staff. The party did not possess its own civilian military-technical expertise to rival that of the General Staff.[39] By the time Gorbachev took over as general secretary, the role of the Defence Council had diminished considerably.[40] He enlarged its membership to include both more civilians, such as the minister of foreign affairs, Eduard Shevardnadze, and military commanders, such as chiefs of the services of the Armed Forces.[41]

Apart from the party, its Politburo and the Defence Council, the government played a significant role in, above all, procurement policy. GOSPLAN (the State Planning Commission, Gosudarstvennyi planovyi komitet) was responsible for developing the country's five-year plans, which decided the main directions of the economy. Furthermore, GOSSNAB (the State Supply Committee, Gosudarstvennyi komitet po materialno-tekhnicheskomy snabzheniiu) decided who would be first in line when resources were handed out. In a system were shortages were endemic, this was an important institution. In practice, the military was prioritized by both GOSPLAN and GOSSNAB. A number of ministries also played a procurement policy role. To further coordinate and facilitate the military procurement process there was an inner circle of government ministers, the Military–Industrial Commission (Voennaia promyshlennaia kommissiia, VPK).[42] The VPK coordinated the different ministries with a military industrial connection and was responsible for seeing that the production goals of the defence industry were met.[43]

Another organ that became very influential in defence decision making in the late Soviet era was the special commission on disarmament, which was formed in November 1969. It was formally called the Commission of the Politburo of the CPSU, Observing the Negotiations about Limitations of Strategic Arms in Helsinki. However, because of the secrecy that surrounded it, it was also known under names such as the 'Political Commission' or simply the 'Big Five'. The latter name derived from the fact that soon after it was created it came to include five members – the defence secretary of the Central Committee, Dmitrii Ustinov; the minister of defence, Andrei Grechko; the minister of foreign affairs, Andrei Gromyko; the head of the Committee of State Security (Komitet Gosudarstvennoi Bezopasnosti, KGB), Yurii Andropov; and the deputy prime minister and head of the VPK, Leonid Smirnov.[44]

The Ministry of Defence and the General Staff, which formally constituted a part of the MoD, were the most important executive organs of the military system. The responsibility of the ministry was 'to design, equip, and staff the services of the services'. The minister of defence had a number of deputies. Among these were the chief of the General Staff, the head of the rear services, and the commanders in chief for each of the five services of the Armed Forces. Within the MoD there was also a collegium. This collegium consisted of the minister of defence, his deputies and a small number of additional senior officers.[45]

The General Staff was charged with managing operations. In the 1970s and 1980s, its area of responsibilities grew substantially. Among these responsibilities were a number of administrative functions and it soon became evident that the General Staff had more or less eclipsed the Ministry of Defence of which it was a part.[46] There are also indications that by the time of the fall of the Soviet Union the military establishment had developed its own security policy which at times differed radically from that of the Ministry of Foreign Affairs. For example, Colonel-General Matvei Burlakov, responsible for the Soviet Group of Forces in Europe in 1991, stated in an interview in 2005 that his forces were ready to use nuclear weapons first. That the minister of foreign affairs repeated that the Soviet Union had no intention of being the first to use nuclear weapons was of no consequence. 'He said one thing, but the militaries were of a different mind. We were responsible for the war.'[47]

The above organs of party and state power were central in defence policy making in the Soviet Union. Although formally the Supreme Soviet was responsible for passing legislation, in practice its influence was non-existent. It met only for a few days a year and its deputies did not have their own staffs to study the questions on which they were supposed to legislate. Scrutinizing the defence budget was, of course, out of the question for the Supreme Soviet deputies. Nor was there an independent judiciary to control the military.[48] Similarly, individual citizens had no way of influencing defence decision making through elections or draft evasion (although this occurred, it was certainly more rare in the Soviet era) and independent organizations or think tanks were non-existent.

Russian institutions of decision making

The institutions of Russian defence decision making and the actors that inhabited them will be examined in more detail in the following chapters. This chapter provides the overall structure. The influence of the different institutions involved in defence decision making in Russia after 1991 varied considerably over time. Moreover, additional commissions, committees, councils and other bodies were created and abolished. The outline that follows is thus a description of the main actors and institutions of the defence policy-making system in Russia. It is based on the situation after the introduction of the 1993 constitution, unless stated otherwise.

The Presidential Administration

Defence decision making after 1991 was mainly the realm of the executive branch. Formally, however, the parliament (the Supreme Soviet and the Congress of People's Deputies) had more of a say in security policy before the 1993 constitution. Yeltsin delayed introducing a new constitution after 1991 and the country was left with the constitution of the Russian Soviet Federative Socialist Republic (RSFSR), which was largely modelled on the Soviet constitution. Even with the amendments introduced in the late 1980s, the constitution was riddled with inconsistencies and struck a discordant note with the dominant mood in Russia after the eventful year of 1991. In essence, the Congress of People's Deputies was the highest decision-making institution of Russia and whatever powers Yeltsin had acquired could be taken away by a simple majority vote in the Congress. At the same time, Yeltsin had a strong popular mandate, partly as a result of his strong showing in the election in 1990 and because of his prominent role in suppressing the August Coup in 1991.

Decision making in general was in disarray during much of the first two years after the Soviet Union had ceased to exist. A virtual tug of war broke out almost immediately between the executive and legislative branch. This concerned most questions, among which the appointment of prime minister became the most visible bone of contention. Needless to say, the legislature and executive found it impossible to agree on the basic provisions for a new constitution. During this period there existed rival foreign and defence policies proposed by the two competing branches of government – the legislature, represented primarily by the Supreme Soviet, and the executive, represented first and foremost by President Yeltsin. The situation was at best confusing and at worst outright detrimental to the international standing and internal stability of Russia and its military organization.

The situation culminated in the October Events of 1993, when Yeltsin dissolved parliament and put forward his own constitution. It was adopted in a national referendum in December the same year. The formal structures for defence policy making became more defined and were concentrated within the executive branch. The president gained control of the main levers in all security policy making while the role of the parliament was considerably reduced. According to the 1993 constitution, the president is the supreme commander of the Armed Forces (article 87:1). When the Russian Federation is threatened by aggression, the president has the power to declare a state of war on the whole territory of Russia or in certain regions. He must then immediately inform the Duma and Federation Council of this (article 87:2). The president can also introduce a state of emergency and must then inform the Federation Council of this (article 88). Although the main responsibility for developing the military doctrine was vested with the Ministry of Defence during the 1990s, the constitution prescribes that it is the president who signs and thus confirms the doctrine (article 83:z).

The president also forms and leads the Security Council (Sovet bezopasnosti), as well as appointing and dismissing the high command of the Armed Forces (articles 83:zh and 83:l of the constitution). He nominates the prime minister, who – upon being confirmed as prime minister by the Duma – suggests a government to the president (article 112). However, the so-called power ministries are excluded from this rule. These are ministries and agencies that are closely related to security policy, such as the Ministry of Foreign Affairs, the MoD, the SVR, and the FSB, and they are all directly subordinated to the president.[49] In other words, the president's power within the military policy sphere is considerable. In addition to deciding who is appointed to the most prestigious positions, the president also awards honorary titles and the highest military ranks (article 89:b of the constitution).

To help him in deciding on military and other policy issues, the president has a Presidential Administration. This institution is only mentioned briefly in the constitution, but has grown to become a sizeable machinery for executive decision making. In practice, it took over many of the functions that the Communist Party Apparatus had once carried out as well as its army of bureaucrats and even its offices on the Old Square (*Staraia plosh-chad*) in Moscow.[50] The areas of responsibility of the departments, councils, committees and commissions within the Presidential Administration have varied. However, the main elements of the Presidential Administration have remained more or less intact and it is possible to identify certain sections that have been involved in defence policy making in one way or another for most of the time (Figure 3.1).

Within the Presidential Administration there has been a team of a dozen or so presidential advisers (*sovetniki*) and aides (*pomoshchniki*) on different policy areas. A handful of these have specialized in defence, security and foreign policy. Initially, there was an analytical centre of the Presidential Administration that was concerned with developing 'a social–economic policy for the Armed Forces'.[51] Gradually, however, mentions of such specialized military centres within the Presidential Administration disappeared from Russian newspapers. As a rule, advisers have less influence than aides within the administration. At times, this position seemed little more than an honorary post for former ministers of defence and there is little evidence of them having an analytical staff at their disposal. The Apparatus of the Presidential Advisers was probably of limited help in this area. Instead, military advisers relied on analytical resources located inside the General Staff to the extent that they had any influence at all.

In 1994, a presidential aide on military–technological cooperation was appointed and given responsibility for a newly created State Committee on Military Technological Cooperation. This state committee was not included

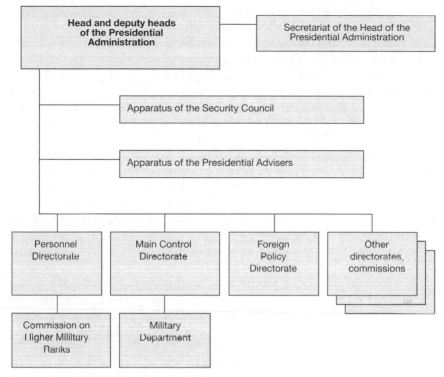

Figure 3.1 Defence policy-related sections of the Presidential Administration

in the Presidential Administration, but became one of the committees that were directly subordinated to the president (see the definition of 'power ministries' below). The president has also had a national security aide and a foreign policy aide. Their influence has fluctuated over time. For example, Yurii Baturin came came to occupy a central position in formulating defence policy as a national security aide before he was forced to leave this position. The foreign policy aide has usually been the head of the Foreign Policy Directorate within the Presidential Administration.

Yeltsin inherited the embryo of a Security Council from the Soviet Union. Formally, the Russian Security Council was founded by presidential decree in June 1992, but its first meeting had already taken place on 20 May 1992. Although it is mentioned in the 1993 constitution, a separate law regulating its activity was never adopted. Instead its role was determined through a number of different laws – most importantly the Law on Security (*O bezo-pasnosti*). The Russian Security Council was very much modelled on the National Security Council of the United States. It would be misleading to compare its role to that of the Politburo. The explicit focus of the activity of the Security Council is security policy making. (Table 3.1 lists the secretaries of the Russian Security Council.)[52]

Membership in the Security Council is ex officio, but the posts associated with membership have varied over time. The inner circle has usually consisted of, at least, the president, the prime minister, the minister of defence, the minister of foreign affairs, the secretary of the Security Council and, often, the head of the FSB (or its predecessors). All in all, the membership of the inner circle of the Security Council was almost the same as that of the Soviet Defence Council. In addition, there is an outer circle of members. Here the membership has varied even more. The minister of justice, the minister of internal affairs and other heads of power structures have regularly featured among these, but also, at times, the chief of the General Staff, the head of the Academy of Science and others. In contrast to the Soviet Defence Council, the Russian Security Council has its own apparatus. Its influence has varied with the influence wielded by its secretaries. In the mid-1990s, the Apparatus of the Security Council, which forms part of the Presidential Administration, developed considerably. At about this time, a commission on military security was created under the aegis of the Security Council.

There are military branches of two of the largest directorates of the Presidential Administration – the Main Control Directorate and the Personnel Directorate.[53] The Main Control Directorate in many ways stepped into the shoes of the Communist Party Control Committee, even inheriting its premises on the Old Square. It is the president's instrument for enforcing issued laws and decrees upon the bureaucracy and constituted a first attempt at instituting a presidential 'power vertical'. Its officials turn up at ministries, agencies and in the regions to conduct check-ups. In essence, its function is to enforce pliability within a bureaucracy where respect for legal norms and official policy is often lacking.[54]

The president wielded considerable influence when it came to deciding staffing within the military sphere. The Commission on Higher Military

Table 3.1 Secretaries of the Russian Security Council, April 1992–July 2007

The Russian Security Council		
Secretary	Yurii Skokov	April 1992–May 1993
	Yevgenii Shaposhnikov	June 1993–September 1993
	Oleg Lobov	September 1993–June 1996
	Aleksandr Lebed	June 1996–October 1996
	Ivan Rybkin	October 1996–March 1998
	Andrei Kokoshin	March 1998–September 1998
	Nikolai Bordiuzha	September 1998–March 1999
	Vladimir Putin	March 1999–August 1999
(acting)	Vladislav Sherstiuk	August 1999–November 1999
	Sergei Ivanov	November 1999–March 2001
	Vladimir Rushailo	March 2001–March 2004
	Igor Ivanov	March 2004–July 2007

Ranks was formed in March 1994 and Yeltsin's trusted security adviser, Yurii Baturin, appointed its chairman. As mentioned above, the constitution stipulated that the president appoints and dismisses all higher commanders and this commission became a powerful institution for the review of cadres under the purview of the president. Until 1996, the Presidential Commission on Higher Military Ranks formed part of the Personnel Directorate of the Presidential Administration and was an important lever of control at the president's disposal. A sign of this was the fact that Yeltsin was reluctant to let potential competitors for power gain influence or control over this commission.[55]

In 1996, Yeltsin also created a Defence Council, which according to official statements was to play a central role in planning military reform. The Defence Council was probably created in part to offset the colourful Aleksandr Lebed who, as secretary of the Security Council at the time, made less and less of a secret of his ambitions to succeed Yeltsin as president.[56] Contrary to Lebed's ambitions, he was not made chairman or even secretary of the Defence Council. Under the deputy chairmanship of then prime minister Viktor Chernomyrdin, the Defence Council lingered on for almost two years. Another reason for creating the Defence Council was the fact that Yeltsin's illness made it impossible to push through policy initiatives in the Security Council, where his presence in the capacity of chairman was required.[57]

Additional measures to enable the president to scrutinize the activities of the Ministry of Defence were instituted in November 1996 when Yeltsin decreed a State Military Inspectorate into being. The State Military Inspectorate was to become an independent division of the Presidential Administration (although one of its departments was a branch inside the government).[58] A formal decree and statutes on the State Military Inspectorate appeared only in September 1997. The decree specified that the head of the State Military Inspectorate was to combine the offices of state military inspector and secretary of the Defence Council.[59] Formally, the State Military Inspectorate received considerable powers.[60] As usual, however, practical work proved more difficult and its ability to scrutinize independently was circumscribed. For a start, the majority of the personnel were recruited from the Armed Forces and other force structures. Figure 3.2 shows the structure of the State Military Inspectorate.[61]

In 1997, the Presidential Administration had thus begun to acquire a certain degree of military know-how within its own structures – not least within the Security Council and Defence Council. The problem was, of course, that it was still dependent on the military to fill many of the newly created posts rather than relying on a new cadre of civilian experts on military affairs. The few civilian experts on security matters and, to a certain degree, military affairs who existed found it difficult to deal with the military. Experts like Yurii Baturin suffered from a severe lack of clout within military circles, where he was despised and hated.

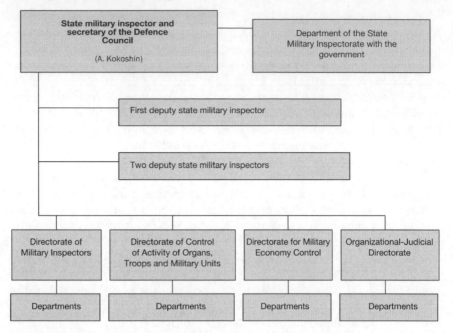

Figure 3.2 Structure of the State Military Inspectorate in July 1997

The government

At first glance the role of the prime minister and his government in defence policy making appears considerably less prominent than that of the president and his administration. Certainly, when it comes to overall force levels, military organizational and pre-deployment questions, the government has very little say. However, the prime minister and his ministers play an important role when it comes to the defence industry and deciding the size of the defence budget. Often, one of the deputy prime ministers has had responsibility for the defence industry. For example, Ilia Klebanov, as deputy prime minister in Putin's government, was responsible for the defence industry until February 2002.[62] There is, furthermore, a Military–Industrial Department within the Apparatus of the Government,[63] which is best described as the apparatus of the prime minister – a cabinet office of sorts. Figure 3.3 shows sections of the government related to defence policy. Table 3.2 lists heads of government of the Russian Federation up to September 2007.

The ability of the MoD to push through important decisions on defence policy was often dependent on getting access to the prime minister. Often, the prime minister has had his own military adviser, but probably lacked an independent staff to analyse and evaluate complicated issues such as defence procurement. One of the government organs that had the potential to play a role in defence policy making was the Administrative Department of the prime minister's apparatus. This depended very much on who headed the

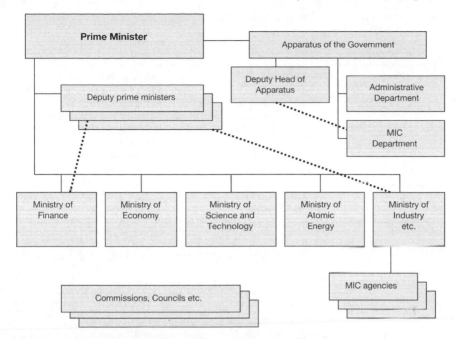

Figure 3.3 Defence policy-related sections of the government
Note: The description above is schematic. The name and function of the different
components have changed over time, as has the degree to which deputy prime ministers and deputy heads of the government apparatus have exercised influence over
defence-related policy (the latter is indicated by the dotted lines in the Figure above).

Administrative Department. For example, Sergei Stepashin, with a past in
Soviet and Russian power structures, became head of the Administrative
Department in November 1995 and played a role in military affairs.[64]
   There are also a number of ministries that have been involved in various
aspects of military industrial policy, such as the Ministry of Atomic Energy
and the Ministry of Industry, Science and Technology. The Ministry of
Finance has the main responsibility for the budget and has played a major
role in deciding the share of resources that the military is allotted each year.
The defence budget was a constant bone of contention between the Ministry
of Finance and the Ministry of Defence. The MoD wished to retain its right
of precedence in formulating military policy and regarded the budget
restrictions that were imposed as uninformed. However, the Ministry of
Finance was central not only when it came to deciding the overall size of
the defence budget. It also controlled the actual disbursement of money
to the MoD. Between 1995 and 2000 the word 'sequestration' became part
of the everyday vocabulary at the MoD since it rarely received even the
funding it had been promised in the defence budget. When it came to procurement, the Ministry of Economy took over the role previously played by

Table 3.2 Heads of government of the Russian Federation, January 1992–September
2007

Head of government		
Prime minister	Boris Yeltsin	January 1992–June 1992
(acting)	Yegor Gaidar	June 1992–December 1992
	Viktor Chernomyrdin	December 1992–March 1998
	Sergei Kirienko	April 1998–August 1998
	Yevgenii Primakov	September 1998–May 1999
	Sergei Stepashin	May 1999–August 1999
	Vladimir Putin	August 1999–May 2000
	Mikhail Kasianov	May 2000–February 2004
(acting)	Viktor Khristenko	February 2004–March 2004
	Mikhail Fradkov	March 2004–September 2007
	Viktor Zubkov	September 2007–

GOSPLAN in this area. The MoD often found it difficult to gain hearing within these ministries.[65]

Initially, the main concern of the government in the defence policy sphere was reducing defence spending. Thus, neither the Ministry of Finance nor the Ministry of Economy were inclined to listen to calls for increased defence spending from the Ministry of Defence. As mentioned above, the defence budget decreased at a steady pace and large parts of it were even sequestered. In a way, the MoD was paying the price of having almost exclusive rights on defence expertise. The lack of military expertise outside the MoD made it difficult for the military to find any understanding for its demands on the budget – whether those demands were justified or not. According to former first deputy minister of defence Andrei Kokoshin, it was the Ministry of Finance rather than the Ministry of Defence that insisted that the defence budget be secret with very few details provided on how the money was to be spent.[66] To a degree, the MoD went along with this in exchange for retaining its autonomy when it came to deciding how to use the money it received.[67]

The policy-making framework for deciding on military–industrial questions and procurement underwent constant reshuffling from 1992 and onwards. Initially, there was a Ministry of Science and Technology Policy. Its minister was also deputy prime minister. In 1993, the minister of science and technology policy lost the rank of deputy prime minister and another deputy minsister divided his attention between this and other policy areas. In 1996, the ministry was degraded to a state committee[68] and a Ministry of Defence Industry was created by presidential decree. This ministry replaced an earlier arrangement whereby a State Committee on the Defence Branches of Industry had supervised these policy areas. The creation of a new ministry was accompanied by a decree on measures to improve conditions within the military–industrial complex.[69] The Ministry of Defence Industry was disbanded in March 1997 and the policy area transferred to the Ministry of Economy. Meanwhile, the Ministry of Science and Technology Policy was resurrected and a deputy prime minister was made responsible for research policy until April 1998.[70] In 1999, furthermore, the defence industry was reorganized into five agencies, which were coordinated by a deputy prime minister.[71] In May 2000, a Ministry for Industry, Science and Technology was created again,[72] only to be subject to further reorganizations during the Putin era (see Chapter 6).

The tendency to want to solve problems within the military–industrial complex by creating and disbanding ministries and agencies illustrates very well the disarray that plagued efforts at Russia's military reform. There were concerted efforts to kick-start it, and much activity was concentrated in the government, representatives of which were included in commissions on military reform and related issues. The overall impression, however, of defence policy making within the government is one of inconsistency, with ever-changing ministries responsible for different areas of military reform. The prime minister had a weak institutional framework at his disposal for developing his policy on military affairs in spite of his central role, and the situation in the other ministries concerned was hardly better.

The Ministry of Defence and the General Staff

The Russian Armed Forces and a Russian Ministry of Defence were created in May 1992. The ministry was constructed basically on the basis of that of the armed forces of the CIS, which in turn differed only in minor details from the MoD of the Soviet Union.[73] The structure and practices inherited from the Soviet era continued to prevail within the ministry.[74] The president formally retained tight control of the MoD. For example, the minister of defence was not allowed to designate the areas of responsibility of his own deputy ministers This remained the prerogative of the president, who had the final say over the central structure of the ministry.[75] In addition to the deputy ministers of defence in the Soviet era, two new deputy ministers of defence were appointed, one in charge of peace operations and the other with responsibility for negotiations on the withdrawal of troops from other states. The Russian MoD also inherited a structure consisting of five defence services for its Armed Forces. In contrast to the practice in the Soviet Union, the chiefs of these five services were not made deputy defence ministers.[76]

According to both the law on defence that Russia inherited and the one issued in 1996, the Ministry of Defence is vested with overall responsibility for the organization and pre-deployment (*stroitelstvo*) of the Armed Forces. However, in practice influence remained concentrated in the General Staff, which is both separate from and an integral part of the MoD. In fact, it is difficult to exaggerate the role of the General Staff within the MoD. In describing the role of the General Staff within the Soviet MoD, William Odom concluded: 'In sum, the Soviet General Staff without the MoD is conceivable, but the MoD without the General Staff is not. The General

Staff was the key organization for handling technical military affairs, without parallel in Western military establishments.'[77]

The structure of the General Staff, in turn, was kept almost entirely unreformed. Of its major directorates it lost only one – the directorate in charge of international military cooperation. This was made into the Main Directorate for International Military Cooperation of the ministry and was subordinated the first deputy minister of defence.[78] In other words, the General Staff retained its influential position. Indeed, in late 1996, the Kremlin announced that the authority of the General Staff should be increased.[79] Vital directorates of planning, analysis, intelligence and so on remained the preserve of the General Staff, and the minister of defence was dependent on these resources in his decision making. Even more daunting than the position of the General Staff in the formal structure of the Ministry of Defence inherited from the Soviet Union was the informal influence the General Staff had acquired. In practice, the MoD was a military administration rather than a ministry and there was little in the way of integration of civilian and military officials.

> In some ways, the term ministry of defence is misleading because it implies the existence of a bureaucratic structure that acts as a buffer between the armed forces and the state authorities whereas in actual fact no such buffer exists. Indeed the distinction between political, administrative and operational command functions loses its meaning in a ministry where there are virtually no civilian decision-makers.[80]

After an initial period when Yeltsin combined his duties as president with those of prime minister and minister of defence, Pavel Grachev became head of the MoD and was awarded the rank of army general (*general armii*), the second highest (after marshal) in Russia.[81] No doubt Grachev's loyalty during the August Coup in 1991 played a role when Yeltsin settled on him for the top job in the newly created Ministry of Defence of the Russian Federation.[82] Yeltsin apparently became convinced that the time was not ripe for a civilian minister of defence in Russia.[83] Grachev argued that military officers would oppose a civilian at the helm of the MoD. Only 'someone who had breathed its air all his life' could deal with the many problems that faced the military.[84] In contrast to many other former Soviet and Warsaw Pact states, Russia had a strong candidate for the job in Andrei Kokoshin, who became first deputy minister of defence. His task was above all to oversee procurement. This proved a difficult task. Kokoshin found himself surrounded by military officials with low opinions of civilians' abilities to handle defence policy, and his own staff was notably small.[85]

The main problem, however, was not that Yeltsin failed to appoint a civilian as minister of defence: it was that the Ministry of Defence also needed a civilian bureaucracy. A civilian minister of defence would probably have been able to achieve next to nothing in the ministry without a sizeable staff comprising civilian administrators and experts who had clout and considerable military knowledge. Ministers of defence and chiefs of the General Staff from 1992 to 2007 are listed in Table 3.3

The Centre for Military Strategic Research of the General Staff was created in 1985 in the Soviet era and comes under one of the deputy chiefs of the General Staff. Its three main directorates are charged with studying military security, military planning and organization (*stroitelstvo*) and how to deploy the Armed Forces.[86] When it comes to penning military doctrines, officials of this centre claim to have wielded a certain influence as well, since it undertakes studies of military operations such as those in Chechnya and Operation Freedom in Iraq.[87]

Other power ministries

The term 'power ministries' (also sometimes referred to as 'power structures' or the 'presidential bloc') is a Russian way of designating ministries and agencies that are directly controlled by the president, are related to security policy making and/or have armed personnel at their disposal. The exact meaning of the term is often difficult to define. Different analysts stress different criteria for the designation of 'power ministry' and the very popularity of the term is no doubt partly to be found in the fact that it refers to a rather amorphous set of authorities. Usually, however, when an author refers to 'power ministries', the emphasis is on security policy issues, and most of the power ministries are represented in the Security Council.

Here, power ministries or 'power structures' are defined as the ministries and other state executive authorities that are under the direct control of the president, in other words, the 'presidential bloc'. The president decides who is to become head of these bodies of power as well as their statutes. This

Table 3.3 Ministers of defence and chiefs of the General Staff, 1992–2007

Ministers of defence	
Boris Yeltsin	Yeltsin initially combined the presidency and post of prime minister with that of minister of defence.
Pavel Grachev	May 1992–July 1996
Igor Rodionov	July 1996–May 1997
Igor Sergeev	May 1997–March 2001
Sergei Ivanov	March 2001–February 2007
Anatolii Serdiukov	February 2007–

Chiefs of the General Staff and first deputy ministers of defence	
Mikhail Kolesnikov	December 1992–October 1996
Viktor Samsonov	October 1996–May 1997
Anatolii Kvashnin	June 1997–July 2004
Yurii Baluevskii	July 2004–

definition centres on the fundamental point that these are the bodies of power that the president wishes to keep a close eye on and will not leave to the authority of the government even in details.[88] The ministries and other state agencies that fall under this description are specified in two presidential decrees.[89] There have been changes in the authorities that are included in these two decrees. However, together these decrees give a good approximation of which ministries, services and agencies should be considered power ministries.

The presidential decree issued in March 2004 was a direct result of the administrative reform which resulted in only three levels of executive authority – ministries, services and agencies. Under this decree, a number of committees and commissions were abolished or reorganized. In addition, a number of bodies of executive power that had been directly subordinated to the president became subordinated to ministries instead – probably in an effort to streamline the system of executive power. As a result, the number of authorities directly subordinated became substantially fewer (12 as opposed about 20 before) (see Table 3.4).

An unprecedented number of power ministries and agencies sprang up and flourished together with those that were already present in 1992. In a way, their experience was the reverse of that of the MoD.[90] The power ministries treated here are those which have troops relevant to military reform and those that had an impact on defence policy making. In defence policy making, Yeltsin tended to adopt the same strategy he used in other policy areas to keep control of his subordinates: he created parallel institutions in order for all ministries and agencies to feel that they had to compete for the president's attention. After the fall of the Soviet Union the notorious KGB (Committee of State Security) was split into a number of different agencies and services. Many of these were subsequently reorganized and renamed during the 1990s. All the heirs of the KGB became so-called power ministries and some of them had their own armed formations, which would be subordinated to the General Staff in the event of war – most notably the FSB, the Federal Border Service (Federalnaia pogranichnaia sluzhba, FPS), the Federal Guard Service (Federalnaia sluzhba okhrany, FSO) and the Federal Agency for the Protection of Government Communications (Federalnoe agenstvo pravitelstvennoi sviazi i informatsii pri Prezidente RF, FAPSI) (see Figure 3.4). Furthermore, a Ministry of Civil Defence, Emergency Situations and Liquidating the Consequences of Natural Disasters (Ministerstvo Rossiiskoi Federatsii po delam grazhdanskoi oborony, chrezvychainym situatsiiam i likvidatsii posledstvii stikhiinykh bedstvii, MChS) was created in 1994. It controlled its own civil defence forces, and the MVD had its own Interior Troops.

The emphasis that the Russian definition of military reform places upon its having to span the whole spectrum of defence – not just the Armed Forces – directs attention to the role played by these ministries, services and agencies. A number of defence-related tasks are carried out by structures other than the Armed Forces and this has led to a tug of war between the ministries

Table 3.4 The power ministries, 1991–2007

Power ministries		Note
MVD	Ministry of Internal Affairs	
MChS	Ministry of Emergency Situations	
MID	Ministry of Foreign Affairs	
MoD	Ministry of Defence	
	Ministry of Justice	
SVR	Foreign Intelligence Service	Federal service from March 2004
FSB	Federal Security Service	Federal service from March 2004
FPS	Federal Border Service	Abolished and its responsibilities transferred to the FSB in March 2003.
FAPSI	Federal Agency for the Protection of Government Communications	Abolished and its responsibilities transferred to FSO, FSB and SVR in March 2003.
GUSP	Main Directorate for Special Programmes	Federal agency from March 2004
FSO	Federal Guard Service	Federal service from March 2004
	Federal Service for Control of Drug Traffic	Created in March 2003 as a directorate within the MVD.
	Federal Courier Service	Federal service from March 2004
	Federal Service of the Tax Police	Abolished in March 2003 and its responsibilities transferred to the MVD.
	Federal Service of Railway Troops	Abolished and its responsibilities transferred to the MoD in March 2004.
	Federal Service for Special Construction	Reorganized into the Federal Agency of Special Constructions and subordinated to the MoD.
	State Technological Commission	Reorganized into the Federal Service for Technological and Export Control in March 2004 and subordinated to the MoD.
	Committee for Military-Technological Cooperation with Foreign States	Reorganized into the Federal Service for Military-Technological Cooperation in March 2004 and subordinated to the MoD.
	Committee for Financial Monitoring	Reorganized into the Federal Service for Financial Monitoring in March 2004 and subordinated to the Ministry of Finance.
	Directorate for Administrative Affairs of the President	Federal agency from March 2004

concerned over resources. The Ministry of Defence claimed that the other power ministries have grown at an unprecedented rate during the 1990s, draining the Armed Forces of resources. There was some truth in this, but the picture was more complicated.[91] Moreover, the struggle was not only over resources, but also over influence and the related questions of which organizations were to perform which tasks and which were the main threats facing Russia.

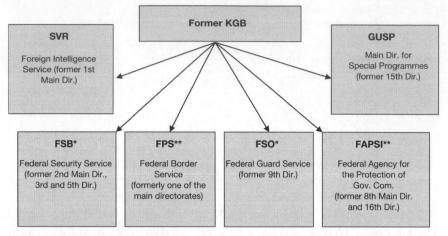

Figure 3.4 The heirs of the KGB
Notes:
* The FSB from 1995. Previously the Ministry of Security until 1993 and FSK (Federal Counter-intelligence Service) until 1995. The FSO from 1996. Previously the GUO (The Main Guard Directorate).
** The FPS was merged with the FSB while FAPSI was abolished and divided between the FSB, SVR and FSO in March 2003.

The Ministry of Foreign Affairs (Ministerstvo Inostrannykh Del, MID) has a role in formulating and implementing security policy and is one of the ministries that are directly subordinated to the president. This ministry did not increase its influence under Yeltsin and Putin. Instead, it tended to lose the power over foreign policy formulation to other organs – such as the Presidential Administration or, more specifically, to the Security Council – leaving it only to deal with the implementation of foreign policy. Its influence has varied over time and with the different ministers of foreign policy. Yevgenii Primakov was probably the minister of foreign affairs with the greatest leverage. Other ministers found themselves under the thumb of the Presidential Administration, part of which has been referred to as a kind of 'mini-MID' headed by the presidential adviser on foreign policy.[92] However, this point should not be overstated. The MID is still a formidable bureaucracy specializing in foreign affairs and the Presidential Administration probably relies on its analyses and expertise to a considerable degree when making decisions.[93] Moreover, the minister of foreign affairs is a permanent member of the Security Council.

The MChS was formed in January 1994 on the basis of a committee headed by Sergei Shoigu (the Russian Federation State Civil Defence and Emergencies Committee). Shoigu is unique in that he has occupied the position of MChS minister ever since. Even before the MChS formally came into being, Shoigu was made a member of the Security Council.[94] The

MChS even made a bid for organizing peacekeeping troops. The Ministry of Defence managed to thwart these costly plans with the support of the Ministry of Finance.[95] However, the MChS and its minister kept expanding its influence during the 1990s and it was not until the administrative reform in 2003–4 that the limits of its areas of responsibility became somewhat more defined. Even then Shoigu's continued good relations with the Kremlin were evidenced by the fact that the MChS was allowed to keep whatever saved funds the administrative reform resulted in to augment the wages of MChS employees.[96] Shoigu has attained the rank of army general and remains a member of the Security Council, albeit not a permanent member.

The MChS controls Russia's Civil Defence Troops. By 2002, the Civil Defence Troops numbered 70,000 men.[97] According to the MChS, they have participated in operations in Southern Ossetia (in Georgia) and Northern Ossetia (in Russia), Abkhazia (in Georgia), Transnistria (in Moldova), Yugoslavia, Tajikistan, Chechnya and Afghanistan.[98] Although information provided by the MChS emphasizes the humanitarian work done by its forces, there have been allegations that the MChS mission to Afghanistan provided cover for representatives of Russia's intelligence community. The MChS also commands its own special units (so-called *spetsnaz* units), probably intended primarily for combating terrorist attacks.[99] The regional organization of the MChS follows that of Russia's federal districts (and military districts). It is thus divided into six regional centres (the Central, the North-West, the Southern, the Volga–Ural, the Siberian and the Far East Regional Centre).[100]

The MVD has certainly experienced more turbulence in its development than the MChS. At times, the influence of the MVD has expanded together with that of the Interior Troops.[101] At other times, the MVD has suffered criticism – not least as a result of its performance in Chechnya and the far-reaching ambitions of its ministers (most notably Anatolii Kulikov in 1998).[102] The ministry has a wide remit ranging from the Russian police force to the Interior Troops. It is mainly the Interior Troops that are of interest from the viewpoint of military reform. These have varied in size over time from about 180,000 to 329,000.[103] There are also special units (*spetsnaz*) of the Interior Troops that are trained for combating terrorism.[104] In Chechnya, the MVD was charged with coordinating the troops there, but its Interior Troops were poorly prepared for the mission.[105] The Ministry of Internal Affairs that Russia took over in 1992 was a ministry with many problems. The role of the Interior Troops within the ministry appeared to grow during much of the 1990s at the expense of crime fighting – a serious development in a country that saw the incidence of crime rise at an unprecedented rate during the same years. In spite of frequent rumours of imminent all-embracing reforms of the MVD, its basic structure and functioning are very similar to those it had in 1991. The minister of internal affairs is a permanent member of the Security Council.

The main heir of the KGB was the Ministry of Security, which was Yeltsin's response when the Constitutional Court ruled against his creating a joint Ministry for Internal Affairs and Security. It was reorganized into the Federal Counter-intelligence Service (Federalnaia sluzhba kontrrazvedki, FSK) in December 1993. In April 1995 the FSK became the Federal Security Service (Federalnaia sluzhba bezopasnosti, FSB). Until Putin's administrative reform in 2003, the FSB enjoyed the status of a ministry. The loss of this status did not lead to reduced leverage. Instead, the FSB has steadily increased its influence since Putin came to power. Apart from the fact that many of its employees were recruited into presidential and government structures, the FSB was the main winner from the reorganization of the power structures that took place in March 2003. As a result, the FSB took over parts of the disbanded FAPSI and the entire Border Troops organization from the FPS, also disbanded. At a stroke, the FSB tripled its personnel and budget. Its director is a permanent member of the Security Council.

The FSB controls a number of units that are included in the Russian military organization and some of which have played a prominent role in the second war in Chechnya and in much-noticed anti-terror operations. Even more importantly from a military reform perspective, the FSB is responsible for military counter-intelligence, which in the Russian case has involved everything from preventing military secrets from trickling out of the military organization to the prevention of theft and misuse of financial resources. In other words, significant parts of the FSB's military organization fulfil tasks that in many other countries would be the responsibility of the military police within the armed forces.

The Foreign Intelligence Service, the SVR, came into being in 1991 and was essentially based on one of the main directorates of the KGB. The SVR managed not to become too embroiled in political intriguing and the president has at times relied on foreign policy analyses from the SVR rather than from the MID. Its director is a member of the Security Council's inner circle of permanent members. However, there is no evidence that the SVR has significant troop resources at its disposal, although it probably embeds its personnel in military operations.[106] Its influence in defence policy making is thus exercised mainly through the information and analyses it provides the political leadership with.

In common with the MChS, the Border Troops started as a committee, the State Border Committee, during the first tumultuous months after the fall of the Soviet Union. The Federal Border Service was created in December 1993 and became an independent body in December 1994.[107] Its main component, the Border Troops, came from the KGB. It got an influential head in Andrei Nikolaev, with a career in the Armed Forces and the General Staff. Not only was Nikolaev one of the most promising young officers in the General Staff, but his father (a colonel-general) had known Yeltsin from the time when they were both members of the Urals Military District Council.[108] Under Nikolaev, the FPS was more successful than the Ministry of Defence in getting access to Yeltsin. In November 1995, Nikolaev was awarded the rank of army general. There were also demands that the FPS be given responsibility not only for the guarding (*okhrana*) but also for the defence (*oborona*) of the borders – something that would have involved extensive investment in new and heavier equipment (probably at the expense of the Armed Forces).[109] This dispute was settled in March 2003, when Putin disbanded the FPS and subordinated the Border Troops to the FSB.

FAPSI came into being in December 1991. Its basis was two directorates of the KGB and FAPSI became responsible for signals intelligence, for communication systems within state structures and for information security.[110] It also controlled armed units that formed part of the military organization. However, for many years it was surrounded by rumours of high-level corruption and in March 2003 it was disbanded and its component parts incorporated in the FSO, the FSB and the SVR. The head of FAPSI became a member of the Security Council only in 1998 and remained so until the agency was abolished in 2003. The heads of the ministries above and of the agencies (FSB and FPS) have all been members of the Security Council since 1992 (or whenever the respective ministry or agency was founded).

The Federal Guard Service, the FSO, was created in 1996. Earlier its functions had been performed by the Main Guard Directorate, the Glavnoe upravlenie okhrany (GUO), which was an offspring of the former KGB (its ninth directorate). The main responsibilities of this agency are the protection of government buildings and establishments, most famously the Kremlin, and after 2003 also the communication systems used by government structures.[111] The Presidential Regiment is subordinated to the FSO and more or less constitutes a full military regiment. The Main Guard Directorate rose to prominence during the period when Aleksandr Korzhakov was head of the Presidential Security Service, which was part of the GUO. Korzhakov gained an influence over Russian policy making that in no way reflected his formal position. He lost this position in 1996 and the GUO was reorganized into the FSO. In common with FAPSI, the head of the FSO was a member of the Security Council only for a short period – between 1996 and 2000.

The last power structure to be treated here, the Main Directorate for Special Programmes (Glavnoe upravlenie spetsialnykh programm Prezidenta Rossii, GUSP), was created on the basis of the KGB's 15th directorate. According to its regulations, issued in 2004, GUSP handles preparations for mobilization for central state organs of power such as the Presidential Administration and the government. Among its responsibilities are securing alternative command posts for the state leadership and the Armed Forces in the event of a major crisis or war. One of the main components of GUSP's organization is the Presidential Service for Special Establishments. It employs sixty of the central GUSP's total personnel of 232 within its central administration.[112] The GUSP has troops at its disposal and forms part of Russia's military organization. Its head has never been a member of the Security Council and, overall, it is a very reticent agency. It has come directly under the president ever since it was created.

The influence of the different power structures varied after 1991 and some of them were involved in security policy rather than specifically in defence policy. However, the fact that many of them grew substantially and were allowed to create their own separate rear services during the 1990s diverted scarce financial resources from the defence sector. Many of the power structures were also dependent on conscripts to fill their ranks, a resource that became increasingly scarce during the 1990s. Most of the ministers and directors of the respective power structures were members of the Security Council and many were permanent members. This gave them a voice when defence issues were discussed and voted on in the Security Council.

Parliament and the judicial branch

After the fall of the Soviet Union, the parliament played a limited role in defence policy making. There were no broad debates on military reform in the Supreme Soviet. The head of the Supreme Soviet Committee on Defence, Sergei Stepashin, and his deputy Aleksandr Piskunov, tried, unsuccessfully, to include these questions on the agenda.[113] The situation hardly improved with the introduction of the new parliament, the Federal Assembly (consisting of an upper house, the Federation Council, and a lower house, the State Duma).

Initially, the Federation Council consisted of the directly elected heads of the 89 'federation subjects' – the constituent parts of the Russian Federation (the presidents of the autonomous republics, governors of the regions, etc.) and the chairmen of the parliaments in the subjects of the federation. In effect, the members of the Federation Council met in Moscow only for a few days a month and it is safe to assume that their main concern was their respective constituencies rather than the work in the upper house of parliament. Putin changed the rules for appointing members to the Federation Council in 2001 and as a consequence his influence over its composition increased. According to the constitution, it is the Federation Council that votes on whether to approve the use of the Armed Forces abroad, the introduction of martial law and the granting of emergency powers. In sum, however, the scrutiny that the Federation Council exercised over military affairs was negligible and its Committee on Defence and Security was considerably less active in the debate than that of the Duma. There was no party structure in the Federation Council similar to that in the Duma through which cooperation could take place between the two chambers of parliament. In practice, negotiations between the Duma and Federation Council on specific policy issues took place between the respective committees.[114]

The Duma became the most active of the two chambers in the defence debate and wielded influence, at least in theory, over the defence budget. However, the Duma deputies were not allowed access to the secret sections of the defence budget that they were supposed to vote on. In other words, the Duma could vote on the overall level of defence spending, but not on how the resources were to be used and divided within the military organization. In addition, the Duma Committee on Defence lacked its own analytical staff and thus often depended on analyses prepared by the Ministry of Defence.[115] Although the Committee on Defence used outside expertise, the lack of permanently employed expertise within the Duma hampered its ability to assess the defence budget and other laws pertaining to defence matters. The dearth of independent expert advice and the fact that deputies, apart from those with a military background, lacked in-depth knowledge of military affairs made the Duma susceptible to pressure from the MoD.[116]

Under Yeltsin, the Duma possessed the power to frustrate in this policy area, as it does in others. This could be achieved, for example, by delaying vital legislation. Overall, however, the Duma's position even on legislation was extremely weak. Although in theory it had the power to legislate on defence matters, the laws could not contradict the military doctrine, which, of course, was decreed by the president.[117] Despite the sometimes fervent rhetoric in favour of defence reform from Duma deputies courting the military, there has been no concerted effort from parliament to push through military reform.

A number of former high-ranking officers were elected deputies of the Duma during the 1990s. Some of them, like Lev Rokhlin and Eduard Vorobev, made their way into the Duma Committee on Defence. However, any fears that this might amount to a creeping military takeover of civilian politics were duly abated. In the event, the military deputies did not constitute a coherent and unified group. They were divided among themselves as to how military policy ought to be formulated and implemented.[118] Their views on politics in general differed even more. Thus, there were deputies like Albert Makashov, Valentin Varennikov and Vladislav Achalov – reputed for their role in the August Coup of 1991 and in the October Events of 1993 – who belonged to the ranks of the Communist Party of the Russian Federation (KPRF). There were deputies like Lev Rokhlin, who started out a centrist Our Home Is Russia deputy only to gravitate towards the KPRF towards the end of his short political career. Finally, there were deputies like Eduard Vorobev, situated in the liberal camp.[119] In addition, officer-deputies rarely performed the expert role that the respective power ministries might have expected. They proved to be less effective lobbyists than civilian experts in military affairs like Andrei Kokoshin and Aleksei Arbatov.[120] It is worth underlining that these officers in parliament had been transferred to the reserve when they became members of the Duma. Nevertheless, it is notable that all chairmen of the Committee on Defence were former high-ranking officers (see Table 3.5).

There is an additional parliamentary institution which, at least in theory, could fulfil an important role in scrutinizing defence policy. The Federal Assembly appoints the auditors of the Audit Chamber of the Russian Federation (*Schetnaia palata Rossiiskoi Federatsii*). The Audit Chamber is responsible for control of the implementation of the federal budget. Before it began its work in 1995, there was a Committee for Budget Control that was

Table 3.5 Chairmen of the Duma Committee on Defence, 1992–2007

Chairman	Date (Supreme Soviet/Duma)	Background (party affiliation)
Sergei Stepashin	1992–3 (Committee on Defence and Security of the Supreme Soviet)	Colonel-general, MVD (–)
Sergei Yushenkov	1993–5 (1st Duma)	Colonel (ret.), lecturer at the Military-Political Lenin Academy (Russia's Democratic Choice)
Lev Rokhlin	1995–20 May 1998 (2nd Duma)	Lieutenant-general (ret.), Armed Forces (Our Home Is Russia until September 1997)
Roman Popkovich	20 May 1998–1999 (2nd Duma)	Major-general (reserves), Armed Forces (Our Home Is Russia)
Andrei Nikolaev	1999–2003 (3rd Duma)	Army general, director of the Federal Border Service (Narodnyi deputat)
Viktor Zavarzin	2003– (4th Duma)	General, Armed Forces (United Russia)

Notes: The Russian party system was not well developed and some of the parties above were not even formally registered. It is worth noting, however, that the chairman of the Committee of Defence has always represented the 'party of power', that is, the party closely affiliated with the president and/or prime minister. Russia's Democratic Choice was started by then prime minister Yegor Gaidar. Our Home is Russia was headed by then prime minister Viktor Chernomyrdin. Narodnyi deputat was a Duma fraction closely affiliated with the party of power. United Russia, in turn, was closely associated with Putin, although formally he never became part of its leadership or even a party member.

originally formed by the Supreme Soviet of the Russian Federation in February 1992. The staff at the Committee for Budget Control comprised about 150 people. After the October Events in 1993, this committee was transferred to the government and later, in April 1994, to the newly formed State Duma. It was abolished in December the same year when the federal law 'On the Audit Chamber of the Russian Federation' was adopted.[121] The Audit Chamber led a rather obscure life; by its own admission very few cases of improper use of government property resulted in prosecution (even fewer in a conviction – one in 1999).[122] This changed somewhat under Putin when Sergei Stepashin was appointed its chairman and the Audit Chamber began to play a more prominent role in, among other areas, defence policy.

Within the judicial system, the General Procuracy (Generalnaia prokuratura) plays a certain role in scrutinizing the military since the Main Military Procuracy (Glavnaia voennaia prokuratura, GVP) is subordinated to the former (see Figure 3.5).[123] During the Soviet era, the military prosecutors were formally subordinated to the General Procuracy. However, they were dependent on the MoD for material support and this undermined their independence and even led to corruption among the military prosecutors.[124]

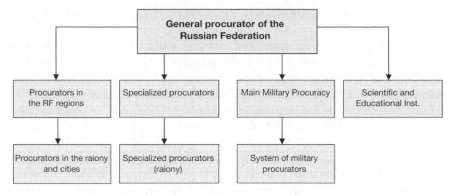

Figure 3.5 The military procuracy within the General Procuracy
Source: General Procuracy of the Russian Federation, *Struktura organov prokuratury Rossiiskoi Federatsii*. Online. Available HTTP: www.genproc.gov.ru/ru/about/structure (accessed 22 March 2005).

Although this changed in the 1990s, there is an argument to be made for regarding the General Procuracy (and therefore the Military Procuracy) as a political institution rather than a part of the judicial branch.[125]

The General Procurator's Office is tasked with overseeing the legality of all actions within the Armed Forces and other power structures: the Main Military Procurator's Office performs this task. In practice, this section of the judicial system is responsible for scrutinizing the legality of the actions of the civil and military officials within the Ministry of Defence and other power structures. Over time it has developed close cooperation with the Audit Chamber in order to be able to fulfil these tasks, with a number of corruption cases as a direct result.[126]

With the new law, 'On Military Courts of the Russian Federation' in 1999, the military courts became answerable to the Supreme Court of Russia.[127] There are more than 100 military courts in Russia active in garrisons, military districts and fleets. Their verdicts are open to scrutiny of the Military Collegium of the Supreme Court. They are subject to the same regulations as other courts in Russia according to the 1996 law 'On the Judicial System of the Russian Federation'.[128] Cases aginst a military serviceman or someone doing military service are referred to the military courts. In cases where a group of people is prosecuted, if one of them is within the ranks of the military organization a military court can take over. Among the cases tried by military courts the majority are concerned with desertion, 'non-statutory relations between servicemen' (the terminology favoured for *dedovshchina,* or harassment, within the military) and failure to comply with weapons regulations. Many servicemen also seek justice through the military courts when their rights have been violated, for example when they have not received the social benefits they are guaranteed in connection with leaving military service. The Military Collegium of the Supreme Court delivers opinions on the legality and constitutionality of military legislation and regulations – mainly on regulations emanating from the Ministry of Defence.[129]

Although the entire Russian court system is riddled with problems, the military courts have stood out for their failure to pronounce a verdict against high-ranking officers. A well publicized case was that of Colonel Yurii Budanov, who raped and killed an eighteen-year-old woman in Chechnya.[130] There was public and international outrage when Budanov at first was freed from the charges and later deemed by a military court as not answerable for his actions on grounds of temporary insanity. The case was therefore tried again in the Supreme Court. Budanov was sentenced to ten years in prison in the end, but the case was an example of political use of the court system rather than of justice being administered.[131] However, it is safe to assume that the majority of cases of *dedovshchina* escape prosecution, as do many charges of corruption within the military and other power structures.[132] Although this is not unique to the military sector, it is clear that the judicial branch is very weak in exercising control over the military.

Other actors in defence policy making

There is undoubtedly a grey zone between government and non-governmental actors in defence policy making. Most of the actors who belong to independent think tanks, for example, are deeply involved in government policy making or maintain close contacts with the Russian leadership and government institutions. Furthermore, the degree to which journals, think tanks and other organizations have been connected with the government has varied over time. The first half of the 1990s saw a surge of independent newspapers and organizations. Market conditions tended to take their toll among these and only a few survived into the Putin era, and they were much less independent than before. It is difficult to provide an exhaustive description of the defence community outside government structures. What follows below is thus an overview and a rough outline of how this community has developed since 1991.

During the Soviet era, media concentrating on defence matters were exclusively under the aegis of the Ministry of Defence. Examples of defence publications were the newspaper *Krasnaia zvezda* and specialized journals such as *Armeiskii sbornik, Morskoi sbornik* and *Voennaia mysl*. These found themselves suddenly challenged by glossier journals such as *Military Parade* and newspapers such as *Nezavisimaia gazeta*.[133] In February 1995, the latter started its own weekly military supplement, *Nezavisimoe voennoe obozrenie*. In 1997, *Nezavisimoe voennoe obozrenie* ceased to be a supplement in the newspaper *Nezavisimaia gazeta* and became a weekly broadsheet in its own right. By the late 1990s this publication set the tone in the debate on military affairs. At the same time, the publishers behind *Nezavisimaia gazeta* and *Nezavisimoe voennoe obozrenie* lost some of their earlier independence. Nevertheless, *Nezavisimoe voennoe obozrenie* continued to play a role as a forum for defence debates. Other journals and newspapers also gradually improved their reporting on defence affairs and developed a cohort of journalists with military matters as their designated speciality.[134]

As in the case of publications, there were virtually no military think tanks outside the realm of the General Staff in 1992. The Council on Foreign and Defence Policy (Sovet po vneshnei i oboronnoi politike, SVOP) became one of the most influential think tanks on military affairs. It was founded in 1992 and came to influence the debate on military reform. This was in no small way due to the fact that the members of SVOP were recruited within the Russian military and foreign policy establishment. In July 1997, SVOP presented its theses for a military reform in a large article in *Nezavisimoe voennoe obozrenie*.[135] It also presented its own suggestions in connection with the publication of what was sometimes referred to as a new military doctrine, the policy document published by the Ministry of Defence in October 2003, *Priority Tasks of the Development of the Armed Forces*.[136] SVOP's suggestions tended to be considerably more radical than anything trickling out of the Russian MoD. For example, Vitalii Shlykov recommended that the role of General Staff within the MoD should be reformed partly with an eye on the US Joint Chiefs of Staff.[137]

The Academy of Military Science (Akademiia voennykh nauk, AVN) is another organization that wielded influence over the public debate on military reform. However, it is dominated by retired military officers. Its chairman, Army General Makhmut Gareev, is a prolific writer on military issues – often in direct opposition to members of SVOP. Gareev was deputy head of the General Staff in the Soviet era and the links between the AVN and the Ministry of Defence are strong. For example, at its annual meeting in February 1998, the Academy discussed the military reform. Among those who took part in the annual meeting were the minister of defence, Igor Sergeev, the minister of internal affairs, Anatolii Kulikov, and other representatives of the military leadership. Both ministers were members of the Academy.[138]

There are a number of independent organizations whose aim is to influence military policy.[139] The most famous of these is probably the Committee of Soldiers' Mothers (*Komitet soldatskikh materei*).[140] It started its activity in the late Soviet era and was in many ways unique in that it was a non-governmental organization (NGO) that managed to make something of an imprint on Soviet politics.[141] In September 1990, the first all-union congress was held for conscripts and their parents. The Committee of Soldiers' Mothers played a dominant part at this congress – a congress that was promptly branded in *Krasnaia zvezda* for its 'anti-militarism'.[142]

The main aim of this organization is to improve conditions for conscripts undergoing active service in the Armed Forces and in the forces of other power ministries. As part of its activities it documented the deaths of conscripts and actively helped bereaved relatives to demand justice.[143] It has put the perennial problem of hazing (harassment) firmly on the political agenda. At the same time it is clear that the Committee of Soldiers' Mothers frequently has met with little or no understanding from the military.[144] In a typical outburst in October 2004, the Duma deputy and former officer, Viktor Alksnis, requested that the Military Procuracy investigate whether the Committee of Soldiers' Mothers received money from abroad in order to undermine Russia's defence capability. The Military Procuracy dismissed this. On the other hand, there is also evidence of cooperation between the Committee of Soldiers' Mothers and the military. Thus, according to a source at the Moscow District Military Procuracy in 2004, the Committee of Soldiers' Mothers was an organization with which they cooperated closely.[145]

On the other half of the spectrum of the military policy debate is situated the notorious Officers' Union. Because of its name this organization was often treated – not least in Western press – as if it indeed represented Russia's officers. In reality, it was never a professional union but rather the political vehicle for Lieutenant-Colonel Stanislav Terekhov, a former officer who moved rapidly towards the lunatic fringe of Russian politics.[146] In the Duma election in 1999, Terekhov joined the Stalinist bloc, 'For the USSR'.[147] In comparison with Terekhov's organization, the political movement of, for example, Lev Rokhlin, the Movement in Support of the Army (Dvizhenie v podderzhku armii, DPA), came across as positively moderate.

An alternative defence policy machinery

The Russian state took over the defence policy-making institutions more or less unreformed from the Soviet Union. Perhaps even more importantly, Russia inherited the people and the practices present within those institutions. In other words, the policy-making machinery was not subject to major changes while the society as a whole and the geopolitical position of Russian had changed fundamentally. At the same time, the powerful instrument that the Communist Party had been for exercising control disappeared with the fall of the Soviet Union. This, coupled with Yeltsin's failure to take a consistent interest in formulating a clear direction for military reform and putting in place the necessary mechanisms for implementing it, could not but have dire consequences.

Proceeding from the different sections of this chapter, it should be possible to compose a picture of how civilian control over military reform could look in Russia. There are at least three components in the decision-making machinery that deserve special attention. First, the decision-making structure at the top must have the ability to coordinate the constituent parts of the military organization, and this is done through information that it receives, preferably from different sources that are independent of each other. Second, the machinery for implementing defence policy should be integrated with military and civilian experts working side by side. Finally, there should be independent functions of scrutiny built into the system.

These three components of 'ideal' decision making are, of course, interrelated. For example, the executive's ability to receive independent analyses presupposes indendent scrutiny functions such as a non-political judicial system. Another precondition is unity of command and a clear divison of responsibility between politicians and the military, as well as within the military. The executive branch should be mainly responsible for issuing directives and for coordination of the different parts of the Russian military organization. This is done by using advice from a military bureaucracy as well as from civilian defence bureaucrats and policy advice and debate articles from outside the government sector (society). The executive branch also uses the defence budget to exercise control within the parameters decided by the legislative branch (see Figure 3.6).

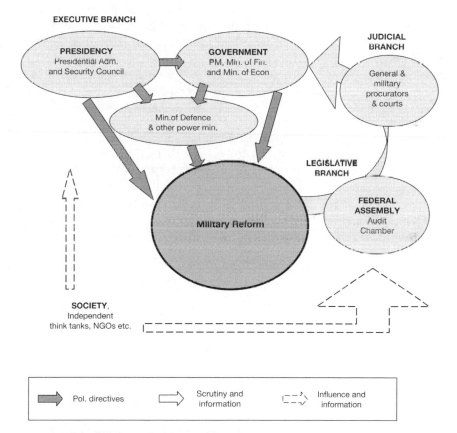

Figure 3.6 'Ideal' defence decision making
Source: General Procuracy of the Russian Federation, *Struktura organov prokuratury Rossiiskoi Federatsii*. Online. Available HTTP: www.genproc.gov.ru/ru/about/structure (accessed 22 March 2005).

Note: The Figure illustrates how defence policy making could work in Russia. In real life, the influence of, for example, the Duma is neglible. The presentation is, of course, only schematic. The executive branch could very well try to influence society and there are significant functions of scrutiny within the executive branch, etc.

In order for defence policy to be implemented in the way the executive wishes, there is a need for control and scrutiny. The immediate accountability function should be mainly performed by the legislature, that is the Federation Council and the Duma with the aid of the Audit Chamber, and the judicial branch consisting of procurators and courts. Its scrutiny of how directives have been implemented will form a new basis for further decision making by the executive branch. In the long run, society could play a role here as well, for example, in general elections to the executive and legislative branch – a precondition for such a role being, of course, that the accountability mechanism is public. On a more subtle level, society may also influence the process by the mere threat of not re-electing the incumbent politicians. In the Russian case, society has influenced military reform if nothing else by the widespread draft evasion. Furthermore, independent think tanks, NGOs and the media could feed additional information into the decision-making machinery.

In this ideal picture of defence policy making, the accountability element really presupposes a degree of democracy. The threat of not being re-elected would constitute a strong incentive for the political level to manage all policy areas effectively. In addition, 'ideal' Russian defence policy making presupposes free access to and dissemination of information in order for the accountability process to function properly. Although in theory it would be possible to imagine a Weberian system, where control was exercised within the executive branch by honest, zealous officials, this choice was not available to Russia. The level of corruption within government authorities coupled with an almost institutionalized level of inefficency barred the Weberian option more or less from the start.

4 Russian military reform

Definitions and goals

At this point a number of definitions are called for, as well as an approximation of what a Russian military reform should reasonably be expected to contain. Below, the Russian definition of military reform is explored. It is specific in its requirements of what constitutes a military reform and what it should involve in order to qualify as genuine reform. The reasons why Russia had to embark upon reforming its military organization are then outlined and the object of reform, Russia's military organization, is defined, as is the agent of reform, the political leadership. Finally, an inventory is provided of the goals that a Russian military reform should reasonably aim to reach.

The Russian definition of military reform

The Russian theoretical approach to military reform could strike an outside observer as overly formalistic and rigid. Russian theoreticians often create the impression that one is dealing with a law of nature, not to be discussed or questioned.[1] However, the Russian definition of military reform, when analysed in a less rigid manner, has distinct merits. Not least, it illustrates what a military reform according to the Russian view should involve. It also precludes the application of strictly Western concepts without due consideration to the special conditions and perceptions inherent in the Russian military organization. As will be evident below, the Russian terminology is useful as an analytical tool since it does take into consideration a multitude of aspects of military reform (economic, societal, geopolitical) and puts emphasis on the policy level as well as the need for reform to embrace the entire military organization rather than just the Armed Forces. All in all, it provides a comprehensive tool for analysis as well as providing a Russian perspective.

Many states experienced the need to reform their military after the Cold War. With the implosion of the Warsaw Pact and the Soviet Union, the international security arena had changed drastically. Simultaneously, major changes in the military technologies available for warfare had made defence planners sit down and think seriously about how these new circumstances ought to affect future planning. Each state chose its own way of designating the changes that were made within its defence sector. For example, the Ministry of Defence of the United Kingdom carried out a Strategic Defence Review in the late 1990s; Swedish defence underwent thorough restructuring and downsizing during the 1990s – usually referred to as the 'Redirection of the Defence' (*Ominriktning av försvaret*). These names for the planning processes were all innovations, whereas the Russian term, 'military reform' (voennaia reforma), had historical roots and its own entry in Russian military dictionaries. A dictionary compiled during the Soviet era provides the following definition.

> Military reform, significant transformation of the mil. systems of the state, undertaken after decision by the highest organs of state power. Military reforms are brought about by new political tasks of the state, the emergence of new kinds of arms, economic considerations, or a change in the level of production, the means and methods of warfare etc.[2]

It is only reasonable to ask whether this Soviet definition from 1983 has any relevance when military reform in the Russian Federation in the 1990s is the topic at hand. Indeed, Marxist-Leninist ideology and rhetoric is noticeably present in many of the explanations provided in the same dictionary. Nevertheless, there is every reason to assume that officers trained during the Soviet era continued to apply the terminology they had become used to even in the 1990s, albeit purged of the most obvious elements of ideological parlance. A quick survey of the definitions provided in a later *Russian Military Dictionary* supports this assumption, as do definitions of military reform used in Russian military journals and newspapers.[3] The way military reform was defined on the websites of the Russian president and the Ministry of Defence in 2002 also echoed many of the thoughts expressed in the definition of military reform above.[4] A new entry on 'military reform' appeared in volume 7 of the *Russian Military Encyclopaedia* in 2003. Although some of the text is new, the basic framework for and definition of military reform remains the same. The 2003 definition and description emphasize roughly the same aspects of military reform as the Soviet definition, but the entry is longer and enumerates details in a way that the Soviet definition did not. It starts by stating that military reform is 'the sum of substantial quantitative and qualitative transformations of the *military organization* of the state, intended to raise its effectiveness and to bring it into accordance with changed domestic and international conditions; a special stage in *military development*'.[5]

The definition then goes on to list the different aspects of the military organization that should be involved in a military reform. The Armed Forces are singled out as an especially important part of the military organization. Military reform should involve transformation of 'the country's defence command system, modernization and conversion of the military industrial complex, optimizing mobilization training of the population, the economy and organs of state command, and changing the manner in which the Armed Forces and other forces are manned and provided for'. The 2003 definition also calls for specific time frames to 'bookend' the reform.[6] Like the 1983 edition, the 2003 edition lists changes that bring about the need for military reform.

> The carrying out of a military reform is as a rule caused by objective circumstances associated with defeat in war, radical changes in the societal–political structure of the state and the means of production, and also fundamental achievements in the scientific–technological process, the appearance of new means, forms and methods of armed conflict, the appearance of new military threats and so on.[7]

Proceeding from these definitions, the Russian leadership was unwise in the early 1990s (and the Soviet leadership in the late 1980s) to claim to have launched a 'military reform'.[8] Although the Russian Armed Forces were formally established on 7 May 1992, they were essentially a continuation of the Armed Forces of the Soviet Union. The changes made in the early 1990s mainly consisted of force reductions and in taking home troops from the former Warsaw Pact countries and former Soviet republics. It is obvious from the definition above that military reform ought to constitute more than mere downsizing. The creation of mobile forces, an initiative cherished by the minister of defence, Pavel Grachev, does not qualify as military reform either. It is hardly surprising that Russia's military policy during the early 1990s has been referred to as 'pseudo-military reform'.[9]

Although the Russian definition above is far from exact, the insistence on 'significant transformation' together with the historical examples rules out the possibility of piecemeal reform under the banner of 'military reform'. The historic examples of military reforms enumerated in the *Russian Military Encyclopaedia* are those of Ivan IV (the Terrible), Peter I (the Great), the tsarist military reform of 1860–70 under Dmitrii Miliutin, those in 1905–12, and Mikhail Frunze's reform in 1924–25.[10]

According to the Russian definition, military reform should, moreover, include all military formations, the military–industrial complex (MIC) and other institutions connected to the national defence. A multitude of paramilitary forces constitute important building blocs of the Russian military system. To guard its borders, for example, the Russian Federation is dependent on its Border Troops. These are not part of the Armed Forces. However, according to the Law on Defence adopted in 1996, the Border Troops, Interior Troops (under the Ministry of Internal Affairs), the Railway Troops, the troops of FAPSI and the Civil Defence Troops were all part of the military organization. Other troops such as the technical engineering troops, the road-construction military units, the SVR, units within the FSB, the border service, and the FAPSI and other special units were included 'in order to fulfil separate tasks within the defence field'.[11]

Since these military units are included in the Russian military organization, there is a significant difference between 'military reform', which affects the military as a whole, and 'reform of the Armed Forces', which pertains only to transformations of the forces that are under the control of the MoD.[12] Although the distinction would appear clear at this point, it is much more difficult to make in practice. Often, authors on Russian military reform will start their articles by making this distinction only to make it clear that they intend only to discuss the reform of the Armed Forces. As will be evidenced below, however, the distinction usually becomes muddled when the details of reforming the Armed Forces are discussed. It is, for example, impossible to discuss the problems of conscription for the Armed Forces without taking into account that the armed units of other ministries and authorities also use conscripts.

Reasons for Russian military reform

In the autumn of 1991 the then head of the Soviet General Staff, Army General Vladimir Lobov, claimed that he had become aware of the need for military reform as early as the late 1970s.[13] By the early 1990s, the reasons for carrying out a military reform had multiplied. Proceeding from the Russian definition in the previous chapter, there were three kinds of changes that should lead to military reform. Adapted to a less ideologically framed parlance, it is possible to divide the incentives for military reform into three categories: (a) intra-military incentives such as new military technology and new methods of warfare; (b) new threat perceptions resulting from a radically transformed international environment and, thus, new tasks for the defence system; and (c) a fundamental transformation of society. This transformation could involve everything from a changed system of values (which in turn leads to a different perception of what role the military should play) to strictly economic considerations. All these categories applied directly to the Russian military system after the fall of the Soviet Union, as the debate on Russian military reform reflects.

New military technology and demands on military capability

Changes within the military sphere, such as 'the emergence of new kinds of arms' and 'means and methods of warfare' together with 'fundamental achievements in science and technology', are specified as conditioning military reform in the Russian definition.[14] To a considerable extent, the discussion of the need for military reform in Russia started with the realization that changes were called for within these fields already under Gorbachev. As will become evident below, the need for new technology was not an overly controversial issue, although debaters differed on which new weapon systems and equipment the military organization needed most. However, other aspects of military changes prompting reform compounded the question. Which organizational changes in manning and command systems did new technology and new methods of warfare require? And, even more important in conditions of scarce economic resources, which technology should be prioritized and what changes in organization would such prioritization lead to? Inevitably, different services and arms of the Armed Forces favoured different solutions – usually pointing to an increased role for their own respective forces. This is far from unique to Russia. However, the debate also mirrored the fact that NATO and the USA were still regarded as the main antagonist that Russia needed to keep up with.

As is evident from General Lobov's comment above, the first seeds of military reform were planted before the fall of the Soviet Union. To the Russian military the need for new technology was further evidenced during the Gulf War. 'This will make war "supertechnological", with informatization and automation systems playing a decisive role in achieving victory', concluded Colonel-General Andrei Nikolaev in 1993.[15] For the military analyst, retired colonel and professor of military science Ivan Yerokhin, the overall conclusion from Operation Desert Storm was that the military doctrine and military reform must be geared to creating a stronger air defence. He still considered the USA and NATO the enemy against whom the Soviet Union should prepare itself. A strong air defence, preferably as a separate service of the Armed Forces, was needed to counter a NATO attack. 'Such a way to build the Armed Forces will benefit the strengthening of our ability to defend the country and its authority in the world.'[16] Another lesson was how weak a static defence could prove against an opponent like NATO. Mobile forces thus quickly became a priority for the Russian military.[17] Andrei Kokoshin, then first deputy minister of defence, emphasized that high-precision weapons were expensive. In his view, one important effect of high-precision weapons was the psychological effect on the opponent. In spite of the costs, Kokoshin stated that developing high-precision weapons was a priority of Russian military-technological policy.[18] Overall, the military establishment tended to put great emphasis on the technological aspects of military reform and the need for new weapon systems.[19] Closely linked, however, was the question of what education and training officers and privates would need in order to handle the new technology. This in turn could mean a need to introduce a less hierarchical command culture within the Armed Forces – something that appeared to receive less attention in the debate.

Military reform has historically implied both a qualitative and quantitative change of the armed forces, and the recruiting system has undergone changes as well as the military training and education system. Thus, Vladimir Lobov, who was chief of the General Staff for a short period in 1991, proceeded from the historical use of the term and stated that military reform should transform 'both qualitative and quantitative parameters'.[20] The need for change in the education and manning system does not necessarily imply that the Russian Federation would transform its conscript army into a volunteer army, although this became increasingly probable during the 1990s. In the Russian case, the age structure of the Armed Forces was a cause for concern and needed rectifying as junior officers left its ranks and the army became increasingly top-heavy. Also closely connected were questions of order of battle – which battle groups were to form the basis of the new Armed Forces? Furthermore, a 'significant transformation of the military system' will also imply a qualitative and quantitative change of the weaponry and military technology actually procured – an aspect of military reform that many of the Russian military debaters focused on the most in connection with, for example, the wars waged by the USA against Iraq.[21]

The Soviet and later the Russian Armed Forces suffered military defeats in the 1980s and 1990s. It was evident from the Soviet experience in Afghanistan that Russia would have to prepare itself for new kinds of war. Kokoshin was convinced – wrongly, as it turned out – that the presence of veterans from Afghanistan in the military leadership would prevent a repetition of the experiences made there.[22] The inability of the Soviet Union to force its will upon Afghanistan was evident for everyone to see after ten years of war. Whereas Soviet military force had been able to bring mutinous East European states back to the fold, Afghanistan proved more difficult. The decision to invade Afghanistan proved momentous to Moscow, costing needless suffering and, of course, draining much-needed resources from other sectors of the defence and the society as a whole. After ten years in Afghanistan 'the Soviet military's image of invincibility' was lost beyond a shadow of doubt.[23]

The dismal performance of the Russian military in Chechnya in 1994–96 provided further fodder to the conviction that military reform was of the essence. Aleksei Arbatov considered the war in Kosovo and the Russian experience in Chechnya as reasons to revise both the national security concept and the military doctrine.[24] Clearly, the Russian Armed Forces remained poorly prepared for the new kind of local wars they found themselves embroiled in. Both the equipment and the practical conduct of warfare needed revising. In spite of this, however, low-intensity conflict did not really enter the agenda as a separate type of warfare.

Another glaring failure for the Russian Armed Forces was the *Kursk* disaster in 2000. It made it clear that the Russian military was grappling with several shortcomings, and not only in the field of technology. The way the Russian military leadership handled the crisis ought to have alerted Putin to serious deficiencies in the highest military command system. Although the *Kursk* disaster was not a defeat in war, Russia's loss of prestige internationally could hardly have been more evident. Its failure to help its own seamen, to organize a rescue operation or even to treat the bereaved relatives with respect left Russia again looking a poor, backward nation in the eyes of the world at a point when Putin was trying to change this image.

The second war in Iraq, Operation Iraqi Freedom, spurred a debate on Russian military reform yet again. From the very forms the debate took, it was obvious that there was still little in the way of consensus on the purpose of the military reform.[25] Furthermore, the technological supremacy of the

USA increased the level of urgency of many partial reforms, and the General Staff announced that it would revise its procurement plan as a direct result of the war. An example of this – closely connected with information technology on a wider scale – was the need for a Russian satellite navigation system. The Russian Glonass system was bogged down by financial difficulties and could not compete with the America's Navstar.[26] An article in *Nezavisimoe voennoe obozrenie* concluded that the political and military leadership had failed to establish the right priorities.[27] Overall, the war in Iraq made it obvious that military reform had not resulted in the technological boost for Russian arms and warfare that the initial calls for reform had foreseen.

New political tasks and military threats

The Russian definition of military reform mentions 'new political tasks of the state' and 'new military threats'.[28] Translated into Russia's conditions it was clear in 1992 that the political tasks that the Soviet Union had wanted its Armed Forces to perform were not the same as those the Russian Armed Forces would have to carry out. The Russian Federation did not have the far-reaching ambitions of the Soviet Union and was not a member of a military alliance of the kind that the Warsaw Pact had been. Russia managed to conclude a military alliance with a number of former Soviet republics, the 1992 Collective Security Treaty (Dogovor o kollektivnoi bezopasnosti, DKB), but from a Russian perspective this was a poor substitute for the Warsaw Pact.[29] At the same time, new tasks came to the fore for the Armed Forces as local conflicts erupted and low-intensity warfare, even within the borders of Russia, entered the agenda. In spite of this, the political leadership was notably slow in formulating what it considered to be the new main threats that its military organization was to handle. A new military doctrine came only in 1993 and was largely written within the walls of the General Staff. There is also reason to suspect that even had the political leadership been able to define the new threats, it would have had to enforce its view upon a recalcitrant military organization.[30]

In the late 1980s, as military innovations prompted reform, the situation on the international arena started to change drastically. The new general secretary in the Kremlin, Mikhail Gorbachev, began talking of reforming the Armed Forces, albeit mainly for economic reasons. Within the political leadership the realization had begun to dawn that the costs of the Soviet military were slowly but mercilessly stifling the country's economy. Gorbachev's 'new political thinking' initiated a change of the geopolitical map that culminated in the end of the Cold War and the implosion of the Soviet Union. This changed the entire security situation on a worldwide scale.

Russia was far from being the only country to experience the need to change its military system on account of this. As mentioned above, most states carried out sweeping reorganizations of their armed forces during the

1990s. However, in the Russian case the situation was further compounded by the fact that the Russian Federation faced a radically changed geopolitical situation. As early as in October 1991, it was obvious that the position of the Soviet Union had changed as a result of the collapse of the Warsaw Pact. This prompted General Lobov to call for a radically new military doctrine.[31] However, by 1992 the very territory that the Armed Forces were supposed to defend had changed. Overnight, the Russian Federation had acquired new neighbouring states as well as losing former neighbours.

The threat of total war with NATO and the USA was no longer imminent and Russia was keen to become a respected cooperation partner internationally. Moscow also appeared eager to take part in international peacekeeping operations, although Bosnia remains the only example of Russia actually taking part in such an operation on any significant scale. Peacekeeping was costly and involved new demands on the Russian forces. Russia also coveted membership in exclusive clubs such as the Group of Seven industrialized countries (G7) and sought deeper cooperation with, for example, NATO. All these ambitions made it necessary to change official documents and rhetoric, but the main task was to change the force posture, military education and training, and the personnel's perceptions of which wars to prepare for. However, the military exercises that were staged showed little or no evidence of such an ambition. The fact that NATO was no longer an imminent threat ought to have released scarce resources for reform. Instead the Russian military remained large and costly at the same time as it had additional tasks to perform and a bloody war in Chechnya to manage.

While the threat of total war with NATO abated, limited wars and low-intensity conflict became a reality that Russia had to face. Local (or limited) wars and conflicts erupted on the borders of the Russian Federation and Moscow soon found itself involved in a number of military conflicts within the CIS. Among these were the conflicts in Transnistria (Moldova), in Abkhazia (Georgia) and in Tajikistan. In late 1994, Russia was even fighting a war on its own territory – the war in Chechnya. Gradually, Russia also became the target of large-scale terrorist attacks (mainly as a result of the war in Chechnya). Initially, the region bordering on Chechnya suffered, but in 1999 the very centre of Russia, Moscow, was subject to terrorist attacks. This was a new and potent threat that the Russian military organization proved poorly prepared for. The situation again called for new definitions as to what were the main threats to the Russian Federation, but low-intensity conflict remained a neglected topic in official documents emanating from the Russian MoD.

New economic realities

Not only military innovations and changes in Russia's external environment prompted military reform. Economic, political, social and other reforms in Russia brought about radically altered domestic conditions for the military organization. However, even in the late 1990s it was obvious that the Russian military had remained almost untouched by the great transformations that had been going on in the rest of society. The barrier between military life and civilian society seemed to remain almost impenetrable. High-ranking military officers who went into politics – like Aleksandr Lebed and Lev Rokhlin – continued to speak in a way that made it clear that they had spent 'much of their lives outside civilian society'.[32] Whereas Russia's civilian society became a largely pluralist one, where perceptions and modes of actions adopted from the West coexist with aspirations to go back to traditional Russian values, the Russian military by and large remained a bastion of conservative values. To its personnel, it was natural that military needs should take precedence over 'other' needs in society.

According to the Russian definition, 'economic considerations' and 'a change in the level of production' prompt military reform.[33] Undoubtedly, the economic conditions had changed considerably by 1991, as had the level of production. The economy had been in a state of decline long before the collapse of the Soviet Union. However, the fall in production and the increasing Russian foreign debt during the 1990s changed conditions drastically. In addition to a large defence budget, the military burden on society also consisted of hidden costs. For example, the military education that all Soviet young people went through in school was financed through the budget of the Ministry of Education, not through the defence budget.[34]

The most important change was that the new leadership in the Kremlin had a stated ambition to cut military spending and to reduce the overall level of militarization of the Russian economy. This necessitated a new way of managing the economy as a whole and drastic cuts in the military budget. Although the defence budget increased again under Putin, it was not likely that Russia would become militarized on a Soviet scale. A remilitarization of society and the reconstruction of a Soviet-type mass army were clearly no longer possible.

> While the top brass could grudgingly accept the fact that Russia is not able to reproduce even half the size of the Soviet army, the real problem is that no amount of political will can reinstate the old model of military-society relations.[35]

By 2002, public opinion in Russia was strongly in favour of military reform and moving towards contract service rather than a conscript army.[36] It was equally obvious that the Russian public was hostile to the use of Russian conscripts in Chechnya.[37] Although there were public promises that only voluntary soldiers, *kontraktniki*, would be sent to Chechnya in 2003, conscripts were still serving there in 2004.[38] Meanwhile, the democratization process put new demands on the political leadership as regards control of the military.

In a broader sense, Russian society was less inclined to devote resources to the military. This relates to 'changes in societal–political structures' listed as a reason for reform in the 2003 definition. Whereas sacrifices for the sake of the national defence had been silently suffered by the Soviet population for decades, the late 1980s and the early 1990s saw increased concern about human rights issues. It was inevitable that attempts at democratization and the introduction of the rule of law would entail changes in the military organization as well. In practice, society displayed its unwillingness to participate in developing the Armed Forces through draft evasion on a massive scale, and this became one of the main reasons for military reform.[39] Draft evasion coupled with a declining demographic pattern that will drastically reduce the number of eligible young men for military service, and a military bureaucracy that refused to abandon conscription produced one of the most pressing circles for the political leadership to square.

Not least the activity of human rights activists prompted a new attitude to conscription and hazing.[40] In this context it is worth mentioning again the Committee of Soldiers' Mothers which demanded security guarantees for their sons while they were going through military service. Its influence grew in the late 1980s and early 1990s.[41] As a reaction to the numerous 'non-combat deaths' within the Armed Forces, draft evasion was already increasing in the late 1980s. Many of the deaths were apparently the result of ethnic violence in the Soviet Armed Forces. The dominance of Slavic officers together with the principle of extraterritoriality, which dictated that conscripts never did their military service in their own republic, made non-Slavic conscripts easy targets for *dedovshchina*.[42] Leaders of the individual Soviet republics also started to oppose 'their' conscripts being used to quell ethnic disturbances in other republics. Calling up young men was thus already a major problem before the Russian Armed Forces formally came into being, and the problem only grew during the 1990s. There were greater demands on the Armed Forces to be able guarantee the safety and health of conscripts.[43] Clearly, significant sections of Russian society were no longer ready to sacrifice their sons.

Resistance to this within the Armed Forces remained strong. In an article in *Nezavisimoe voennoe obozrenie* in December 2002, two former officers of the Armed Forces claimed that the only 'cure' against *dedovshchina* was harsher discipline and greater authority for the commanders. Military training, they wrote, was hard work and the 'absolute majority of people' will not go through it unless they are forced to.

> This coercion is the main function of the commanders, mainly of the officers. There is no one else in society or the state who can do this thankless work. No prosecutors, soldiers' mothers or parliamentarians can take upon themselves the whole responsibility for discipline within the troops.[44]

The lack of concern among officers for the welfare of their soldiers could not but further reduce the inclination of young Russian males to be conscripted.[45]

Nor did the measures taken by the MoD to curb public concern prove very successful. By the time of the autumn call-up in 2003, the Ministry of Defence publicized the fact that it had established a hotline and reception office for worried conscripts and their next of kin.[46] However, the problems of draft evasion continued, as did the military complaints that the conscripts that it did get were 'of lower quality'.

Russia's military organization

An approximation of what constitutes the 'military' or 'military organization' is called for. The Law on Defence cited above gives clues as to which forces should be included, but is not specific. Although officials of the SVR could be called on to assist the Armed Forces in specific tasks, this does not make the entire SVR subject to *military* reform. Nor is it enough only to include the Armed Forces or even the troops under the direct control of the Ministry of Defence. As discussed above, troops such as the Interior Troops and the Border Troops constitute important elements of the Russian military organization. For the purpose of this report the troops listed in *Military Balance* by the International Institute for Strategic Studies have been taken to represent the 'military' or 'military organization' that is the main object for military reform (see Table 4.1).

Military reform will, of course, entail changes in the military–industrial complex as well. However, the military organization, as defined here, centres upon troops, while the defence industry is interesting mainly in its capacity as supplier of weaponry, equipment and military technology. Similarly, only the troops of certain power ministries are included in this definition of the military organization. Nevertheless, they are also relevant as a whole when discussing military reform since they often, through their growing influence and budgets, drew attention and resources away from military reform. The wide array of power ministries also tended to confuse defence decision making on a general level when decision making on military reform was forced to give way to bureaucratic infighting.

The Russian leadership – principal agent of reform

One additional requirement in the definitions of military reform above deserves attention. The 1994 definition states that reform should be undertaken 'after decision by the highest organs of state power'. The 2003 definition is even more specific as it insists that military reform 'is carried out after a decision by the highest organs of state power on the basis of laws or other normative–legal documents on corresponding programmes and plans'.[47] In other words, military reform must emanate from a decision taken by the Russian political leadership.

This may seem to be a statement of the overly obvious, but in the context of this study there are two reasons for emphasizing it. First, it has consequences

Table 4.1 The military organization of the Russian Federation

Forces of the Russian Federation	Troops	Note
Ministry of Defence (MoD)	Armed Forces	Army, navy, air force and Strategic Deterrent Forces
	Railway Troops	(under the MoD since 2003)
	Special Construction Troops	(under the MoD since 2003)
Federal Security Service (FSB)	Special units	E.g. Alpha, Beta and Zenit commando units. Also Vympel
Federal Border Service (FPS)	Border Troops	These troops were incorporated in the FSB in 2003.
Ministry of Internal Affairs (MVD)	Interior Troops Special units	OMON (Special Operations Police Detachments) and SOBR (Rapid Reaction Special Police Detachment) are also subordinated to the MVD.
Federal Protection Service (FSO)	Elements of the Ground Forces	
Federal Communications and Information Agency (FAPSI)	Signal Troops	Agency disbanded and divided between the FSB, FSO and SVR in 2003.

Source: International Institute for Strategic Studies (IISS), *The Military Balance, 2004/2005*.

for when it is possible to say that the Russian military reform was initiated. Different criteria for what constitutes reform will lead to different dates. If the criterion is that the military system undergoes fundamental change, then it is obvious that a leadership decision is called for, since more sectors of society than the strictly military sector will become deeply involved in the process. Although the Russian Ministry of Defence undertook a number of measures to change the Armed Forces already in 1993, it would be difficult for these measures to qualify as military reform when the state leadership did not become involved in prescribing the parameters of reform.[48] Second, one of the main explanations that have been proposed for why military reform has become bogged down has been the absence of political will, that is, the will to take the necessary decisions and the perseverance see them carried through. Indeed, this is part of the explanation that emerges from this book. Political will in connection with military know-how outside the MoD and a well oiled decision-making machinery for implementing and controlling military reform stand out as basic requirements.

Perhaps most importantly, the political leadership has to decide the balance between defence spending and other needs in society; it has to reach a position of 'equilibrium' between domestic and military policy goals.[49] The US administration made a critical decision in the 1950s. It decided that, although it perceived the threat of a major war with the Soviet Union as the principal concern, the amount of resources spent on the military could not exceed a level beyond which economic growth would be threatened in a long-term perspective. The argument was not only that the civilian sector should not suffer because of excessive spending on defence. There was also a realization that in order to keep up military spending in the long term, economic growth was of essence. Of course, this did not solve all the problems of deciding resource allocation between the civilian and military sectors. There were still heated debates as to what constituted a critical level. However, in contrast to the Soviet Union, there was a conscious decision on how military spending was to be ensured in the long term.

On the whole, it was obvious that the Russian military organization found itself out of balance in the three main areas identified in the Russian definition of military reform: (a) military technology and doctrine; (b) threat perception and geopolitical change; and (c) the transformation of society. There were essentially three main options for the Kremlin. First, the political leadership could close its eyes to the problem and leave the imbalances unattended to. This would leave the country with a defence that was unsuited for the new demands it was likely to face and fundamentally out of touch with the rest of society. Second, the Kremlin could try to adopt the Soviet approach and let the military dictate what kind of defence the country should have. This would involve huge costs to society and a militarized economy – an option that was really no longer open to the Russian state. Russia would also run the risk of finding itself unprepared for new types of war, such as low-intensity conflict, since it was evident that the Russian military contintued to regard armed confrontation with NATO as the main threat. Finally, the political leadership could choose the arduous path of adapting the military organization to the new geopolitical, military technological realities and to the society that it formed a part of. Clearly, the last option was preferable in the long term. However, the worst solution would be to try and straddle all of the options at once. In other words, political decision making was urgently called for.

All in all, it is difficult to arrive at a strict definition of Russian military reform. However, the examination above has provided a number of clues as to which aspects of reform are important to look at further. The many aspects involved suggest that military reform ought to be studied as a political process[50] where the goals and means of reform may change over time rather than as a strict document where certain targets should be met by a specific date. Indeed, a successful military reform is probably the reform that changes as the process matures or external and internal conditions alter. As stated above, military reform is prompted by major changes in the domestic and/or international arena which result in a disequilibrium, and there is every possibility of new imbalances arising during the course of reform.

The political leadership must initiate the reform process in order to redress these imbalances. Only when a new equilibrium is present is it possible to talk of having successfully implemented a military reform and because of the multitude of factors involved this will probably only be evident from a historical perspective. History will decide whether or not Vladimir Putin enters the encyclopaedia as a military reformer together with names such as Peter the Great (in the early eighteenth century), Dmitrii Miliutin (in the nineteenth century) and Mikhail Frunze (in the twentieth century). However, it should be possible to arrive at a first tentative evaluation of the reform record at the close of Putin's second term in office as elected president of the Russian Federation.

The goals of Russian military reform

The emphasis on studying Russian military reform as a political process rather than an endgame does not rule out a discussion of which goals the reform should reasonably arrive at. If nothing else, an inventory of the main problems that need rectifying provides an idea of which approximate goals should be formulated by the political leadership. First and foremost, the political leadership has to strike a balance between the resources devoted to the military organization and other policy goals such as economic growth, spending on social welfare, and so on. This can only be a political decision and involves tricky questions such as as determining which are the main threats that Russia must be able to meet in the immediate and near future. Including all possible threats on this list is hardly the best solution. Not only will available resources never cover the expenses for such a list, but the military would still have to prioritize among the threats according to the wishes of the political leadership. Clearly, not all threats are best met by military means, and political measures such as clever negotiations and building alliances could reduce military threats, as could other means of statecraft.

Furthermore, the political leadership must provide guidance as to how the threats should be met. This involves difficult decisions on force posture, the structure of the military organization, military education and training, and the division of responsibilities between the different power ministries. In other words, downsizing and eliminating the duplication of functions only goes part of the way in meeting these requirements. Closely connected to the questions above is the question of manning the military organization. What kind of officers and soldiers should the military organization employ and what qualities should they have? Should Russia have a mass army or a smaller military organization tasked with local wars? How many men should Russia be able to mobilize? These became some of the main problems facing the Kremlin. The question of conscription or manning by means of contract employment has often been the focal point here, but the question is no less pertinent when it comes to the officer corps.

Apart from personnel, the military organization needs to be furnished with weaponry, equipment and different kinds of military technology. Again, this question is intimately related to finding solutions to all the questions above. Procurement is dependent on what the main threats are, how much money is available, force posture, and the education and quality of the soldiers and officers destined to handle the weapons and equipment.

In the Russian case, moreover, civil–military relations needed redefining. This embraced questions of how the political leadership was to be able to impose its decisions upon the military – an interesting aspect of military reform, not least since it involves some reform of the agent of reform, the political leadership, as well as of the military organization as a whole. Civil–military relations also raise questions about the role the military organization is to play in society as a whole. Depending upon the kind of society, the conditions for military activity change. A democratic society is bound to demand a greater degree of transparency and accountability from the military organization that it is funding through the state coffers and lending its young men to. A repressive society will put quite different demands upon its military organization, although they will not necessarily be easier to comply with.

5 The Yeltsin era
Virtual reform

When Yeltsin took over Gorbachev's office in the Kremlin, he also took over the habit of Soviet leaders of having the rush-hour traffic along his route to work blocked off every morning. Just before entering the Kremlin through the Borovitskii tower, Yeltsin usually travelled along Znamenka Street with the Ministry of Defence on one side of the street and the General Staff on the other. In other words, there was every opportunity to be reminded of the urgency of military reform each morning.[1] In spite of this, he displayed only a faint interest in building a military organization that could answer to Russia's national security needs. His initial main concern in this area seems to have been to retain the loyalty of the Armed Forces and other power ministries, while the military security of Russia remained a low priority.

In December 1993 Yeltsin, as president of the Russian Federation and the supreme commander of its Armed Forces, gathered all the formal decision-making power on defence affairs into his own hands only to quickly turn his attention away from the problem of military reform. He failed to put mechanisms in place for achieving a rational defence decision-making process and instead used the system to cement his own position of power. The situation was further exarcerbated by Yeltsin's failing health and preoccupation with political intrigues. He proceeded to create a plethora of parallel and rival institutions and offices. Whatever groundwork and plans had been made for military reform during the Gorbachev era and whatever political capital Yeltsin initially had in order to force through reforms were rapidly and thoroughly squandered.

Gorbachev's push for military reform

While it is perfectly possible to claim that no serious efforts at military reform took place in the early 1990s, there is also a reasonable case to be made for a military reform process having started by the mid-1980s – well before the Russian Federation came into being.[2] Russian military thinkers had already been writing of a revolution in military affairs for years. However, their emphasis on new technology was bound to lead to budget increases rather than reductions. In 1985, Gorbachev entered the arena and by 1987 he had formulated his new foreign policy under the banner of 'new political thinking'. He wanted to cut back defence spending significantly. Domestic economic needs were to be given precedence to a degree not seen since Frunze's reforms in the 1920s.[3] To underscore his sincerity, Gorbachev declared a unilateral moratorium on nuclear tests. He also signed the Treaty on Security and Confidence Building Measures in 1987, which allowed inspections on Soviet territory. Both measures met with resistance within the General Staff.[4] The Soviet Union also signed both the Intermediate Nuclear Forces (INF) treaty with the USA in 1987 and the Conventional Forces in Europe (CFE) treaty in 1990, neither of which received the wholehearted support of the General Staff.[5]

In order to carry through his policy of new political thinking, Gorbachev aimed to curb the dominant influence of the military in defence affairs. At the twenty-seventh Party Congress in February 1986, he formulated his new foreign policy goals and made clear his resolve to reduce defence spending. A key term was 'reasonable sufficiency'. The military quickly became wary of what this new policy would involve. Would it, for example, entail radically new force structures?[6] The goal of cutting defence expenditure was certainly perceived as a threat by the Russian military.

By the end of the 1980s, two rival drafts for military reform were circulating in Moscow. One was authored by military officers who had been elected to the Congress of People's Deputies of the Soviet Union. This reform proposal was radical and very unpopular within the military establishment. For example, it contained demands for greater civil control over the military, and calls for the creation of a contract-based army and reductions in defence spending. The leader of this group of officers was Vladimir Lopatin, who also headed a temporary subcommittee of the Supreme Soviet of the Soviet Union. In April 1990, this subcommittee approved Lopatin's military reform programme. The Soviet Ministry of Defence quickly proceeded to develop a military reform draft of its own – a considerably more conservative programme. Force reductions were modest in this draft and it demanded increased budget spending on the Armed Forces even in the face of the severe financial difficulties that the Soviet Union was facing.[7]

In August 1990, Gorbachev delivered a speech while visiting the Odessa Military District and expounded upon his policy of perestroika and new political thinking. He also outlined the main content of the military reform he perceived as necessary.[8] However, Lopatin complained in the same year that military reform had stalled.[9] Indeed, military reform soon became a victim of the political battle around Gorbachev's entire perestroika reform programme, in which military reform played a subordinate role.[10]

Clearly, a situation of disequilibrium developed rapidly as a need to prioritize between domestic and military policy goals developed. Perestroika had set in motion ideas and aspirations for human rights, democracy and private consumption which became incompatible with a militarized society. At a time when the military wanted more funding in order to keep up with the developments in military technology and warfare, the rest of society was willing to yield less. Meanwhile, Gorbachev's new political thinking was changing the international scene beyond recognition. The 1991 Gulf War made it obvious that a new technological era had dawned, but it also heralded a new setting for international relations.[11] The USA received support for waging war against Iraq from the Soviet Union – something that enraged significant sections of the military establishment.[12]

After the August Coup in 1991, Gorbachev did his best to hold together the Soviet Union even after accepting that the Baltic states were on the road towards independence. However, Yeltsin held the upper hand in his power struggle with Gorbachev. Both leaders were located in Moscow, but, whereas Gorbachev represented the Soviet centre, Yeltsin represented Russia. On 8 December 1991, Yeltsin met the leaders of Belarus and Ukraine, Stanislav Shushkevich and Leonid Kravchuk, at the Belovezhskaia Pushcha outside Minsk. Here were signed the Belovezha Accords that signalled the end of the Soviet Union. Gorbachev was forced to resign his office in the Kremlin and all that went with it, such as the control of the nuclear weapons, to his nemesis, Boris Yeltsin.[13]

The Belovezha Accords became one of the reasons why Yeltsin's previously favourable popularity ratings plummeted within the military. Not only had he signed away what many perceived as eternal 'Russian lands', but there were widespread rumours that he had done so on a drinking bout. Even before the Belovezha Accords, Yeltsin had encouraged the different regions of the Soviet Union and Russia to grab as much freedom as they could – an exhortation that did not go unnoticed within the military and would return to haunt him with the onset of the war in Chechnya.

Between August and December 1991, military reform had been mired in uncertainties as to the future of the Soviet Union as a state entity. Both the chief of the Soviet General Staff, Vladimir Lobov, and the Soviet minister of defence, Yevgenii Shaposhnikov, regarded it as essential that the Soviet Armed Forces were kept under unified command. This view should not be discarded out of hand as mere military conservatism. There were purely technical reasons for keeping the Soviet Armed Forces together, but decades of secrecy made it impossible for the military to explain this point to the politicians at the helm – let alone to a public in the grips of nationalistic fervour.

> The Soviet military's obsession with secrecy meant that virtually no civilian understood the structure of the USSR-wide PVO [air defence] system of radar, air control systems, centralized communications, and control networks. They were like a 'public good,' in that for one republic to have the PVO system, it also had to be able to defend all the others. Dividing it would virtually destroy the system. The space program and early warning system against missile attacks were also in this category.[14]

Indeed, the vision of military reform that Vladimir Lobov outlined during his short spell as head of the Soviet General Staff in the autumn of 1991 in certain areas stands out as more radical and foresighted than the reform ideas that emanated from the Russian General Staff between 1992 and 1996.[15] Possibly, the wish to keep the Armed Forces united under the banner of the CIS made Lobov more open to discussing the demands of civilian control and economic efficiency that the newly independent republics were bound to put upon a central CIS General Staff.[16] Shaposhnikov and Lobov proposed, among other things, that the paramilitary forces, such as the Interior and Border Troops, should be stripped of their military tasks and insignia. Instead, these troops should assume 'guard and militia functions'. Only these troops would be allocated to the new republics. The Union army was to be divided into corps and brigades rather than armies and divisions. In Lobov's view, this would increase the effectiveness of the Armed Forces.[17] Both Shaposhnikov and Lobov also advanced the opinion that the Ministry of Defence should be a civilian institution subordinated to the supreme commander-in-chief and that the ministry's personnel could be reduced by 20–30 per cent. The General Staff should, according to Shaposhnikov, limit itself to 'an operational and command role' and shed all tasks that were not of a purely military nature.[18] The intense activity of Shaposhnikov and Lobov came to naught when the Armed Forces of the Soviet Union were dismantled in 1992.

Consolidating the Presidency, 1992–93

With hindsight, many would hesitate to call the measures taken between 1992 and 1996 a military reform in the true sense of the word.[19] Initially, there were two basic political reasons why military reform was slow to materialize. First, there was considerable confusion as to whether the Soviet Armed Forces were to be divided between the newly independent republics or become the CIS Armed Forces. Second, the Russian Federation continued to live with a constitution written in the Soviet era, albeit amended significantly during recent years. This, among other difficulties, resulted in an unfortunate lack of clarity when it came to determining who in fact the main arbiter on security issues was. Although Yeltsin had a strong popular mandate, after having won the presidential election by a large margin in June 1991 and after his role in quelling the August Coup, the constitution stated that the parliament, the Congress of People's Deputies, was the highest decision-making body in the country. The power struggle that ensued paralysed much of policy making in Russia, and military reform was no exception. On a practical level, the Herculean task of bringing back personnel and equipment from the former Warsaw Pact and former Soviet republics further complicated the reform process.[20]

There was only a small military circle around Yeltsin to advise him on defence policy. From his time as president of the RSFSR, Yeltsin had a military adviser, Dmitrii Volkogonov, who had headed a commission on military reform in 1991.[21] On 4 April 1992 Yeltsin appointed him head of the State Commission on Forming a Russian Ministry of Defence. Pavel Grachev, Andrei Kokoshin, Yurii Skokov and Konstantin Kobets became deputy heads of the commission, which in all comprised twenty-eight politicians and military commanders. At its first meeting on 8 April 1992, the commission was divided into working groups on such matters as military doctrine, the structure and organization of the new ministry, social security for servicemen, military development and logistics.[22] At this point, there was a clear political goal to civilianize the Ministry of Defence. Yeltsin expressed as much in a speech to the Congress of People's Deputies on 8 April 1992.[23] Volkogonov claimed that there would be 'decisive staff reductions and rationalizations of the military-bureaucratic structures and also the involvement of a growing number of civilians in the military ministry'.[24]

Volkogonov went on to become head of the Russian Commission on Military Reform.[25] On the whole, however, Yeltsin's institutional framework for defence policy making was still only developing and it did so in the shadow of his most immediate concern – his duel with the Supreme Soviet. The Security Council had to define its role and develop its own apparatus – a process in which it became very much dependent upon its secretaries and their respective policy priorities. Its first secretary, Yurii Skokov, concentrated much of his attention on foreign policy and successfully wrested much of the responsibility for foreign policy formulation from the Ministry of Foreign Affairs during his tenure as secretary of the Security Council. However, Skokov quickly lost his favoured status with the president after he refused to endorse Yeltsin's attempt to disband the Supreme Soviet in March 1993. Yevgenii Shaposhnikov made what almost seemed like a reluctant guest appearance as secretary of the Security Council. Just before finally disbanding the Supreme Soviet in September–October 1993, Yeltsin replaced Shaposhnikov with the trusted Oleg Lobov, who went on to direct much of the attention of the Security Council towards economic security.[26] In other words, military reform was not high on its agenda during these years.

One of the additions to Yeltsin's presidential administration just before the showdown with parliament was Yurii Baturin. He was a doctor of law by training and became one of Yeltsin's advisers on legal matters, initially, but in January 1994 he became presidential national security adviser. He was charged with penning the famous presidential decree no. 1400, by which Yeltsin dissolved the parliament on 21 September 1993.[27] This decree ended in a bloody confrontation in early October 1993 between the executive branch and the legislative chamber – a battle won by Yeltsin and resulting in a new constitution in December 1993 that prescribed a strong presidency.

It is hardly surprising that Yeltsin prioritized his own political survival at this stage. The power ministries were not to be antagonized by unnecessary meddling in their affairs and were left to handle military reform as best they saw fit. Yeltsin made every effort to ensure that his power ministries remained loyal in the forthcoming showdown with parliament. The director of the Ministry of Security, Viktor Barannikov, was dismissed in July 1993 –

ostensibly on suspicions of corruption and for the failure to prevent an attack by Afghan extremists on Russian Border Troops on the Afghan–Tajik border. The real reason was that the Kremlin had grown increasingly unsure whether Barannikov would prove loyal in a showdown with parliament.[28] Nikolai Golushko became the new minister of security on the proposal of Sergei Stepashin, who at the time was chairman of the Committee on Defence and Security of the Supreme Soviet as well as deputy minister of security. Stepashin, who was one of Yeltsin's loyal supporters, was promoted to become first deputy minister of security.

The two most important people within the Ministry of Internal Affairs – the minister, Viktor Yerin, and the commander of the Interior Troops, Anatolii Kulikov – proved reliable and no changes on these posts were required. On 1 September 1993, Yerin was promoted to the rank of army general (and after the October Events he received Russia's most coveted military award, 'Hero of Russia').[29] The Ministry of Defence proved more reluctant. The commanders of the Armed Forces were wary as a result of their experience of being used in domestic conflicts and made scapegoats of. The MoD promised Yeltsin support only at the very last moment after he had visited the ministry in person.[30]

In the October Events in 1993, the Ministry of Security, FAPSI, the MVD and the Alpha and Vympel elite units, subordinated to the Main Guard Directorate (the GUO, later to become the FSO), all played pivotal roles. FAPSI cut off telephone communications between the Supreme Soviet and other potential opponents of the Kremlin; military counter-intelligence within the Ministry of Security ensured that army units did not join the ranks of the opposition in the Supreme Soviet; the MVD patrolled Moscow and other major cities; Alpha and Vympel were the units ultimately responsible for detaining the leaders who had barricaded themselves in the White House (the official premises of the Supreme Soviet).[31] From Yeltsin's point of view, his strategy of not antagonizing the power ministries had paid off.

Yeltsin and the Ministry of Defence

Initially, in 1992, Yeltsin assumed the post of minister of defence, which he combined with those of president and prime minister. This was partly a result of the power struggle between Yeltsin and parliament, but was also dictated by the unclear fate of the CIS Armed Forces. After the August Coup in 1991, Pavel Grachev and Yevgenii Shaposhnikov both appeared as good candidates for the post of minister of defence as it gradually transpired that Russia would have to form its own armed forces. Shaposhnikov, as commander in chief of the CIS Armed Forces, seemed to be Yeltsin's initial choice for the post of Russian minister of defence, but was reluctant to accept it.[32] In the end, Grachev was appointed instead. With the creation of the Russian Ministry of Defence, two additional deputy minister posts were introduced. Colonel-General Georgii Kondratev became deputy defence minister in charge of peace operations and Colonel-General Boris Gromov deputy defence minister with responsibility for negotiations on the withdrawal of troops from other states.[33] Few other changes were made.

The issue of reform of the Ministry of Defence itself quickly disappeared from Yeltsin's agenda as he concentrated on winning his battle with the Supreme Soviet. There was a certain feeling of optimism and new impetus for reforms after October 1993. After a new constitution was approved in a national referendum and a new parliament, the State Duma, elected on 12 December 1993, there were rumours that Yeltsin intended to reorganize the MoD drastically and make it into a 'civilian department'. However, Dmitrii Volkogonov dispelled these rumours. In his view, it was impossible to carry out such a reorganization in the unstable situation that the country was in. Such a ministry of defence was possible only in 'three to four years or five years, maybe at the end of the century'.[34]

Nor did Grachev envisage a civilian Ministry of Defence on a Western model – not even in a long-term perspective. According to Grachev, work on building the Russian Armed Forces would be finished by the year 2000. Only then it would be possible to divide the MoD in two – one civilian authority and one strictly military. The civilian section would decide military policy, develop the Armed Forces, be responsible for cooperation with other ministries, and decide on weapons procurement but would not influence the operational command of the army and fleet. The General Staff would take over the functions of the present MoD and in peacetime lead military training, be responsible for mobilization readiness, conduct inspections and deal with manning issues (*zanimatsia komplektovaniem*).[35] All in all, though, the MoD remained largely unreformed and very little in the way of civilian influence was introduced. One civilian gained an important post in the ministry when Andrei Kokoshin was appointed first deputy minister of defence. Alone, however, in a predominantly military ministry, the limits of Kokoshin's influence were obvious.

Trying to maintain the scientific potential of the military–industrial complex became one of Kokoshin's main areas of responsibility. He initiated a discussion on these issues in the Security Council and at one of the first meetings of the Collegium of the Ministry of Defence. In the end, the decision was made to concentrate on developing single test editions in order not to lose the competence to develop complex systems. Serial production would have to wait.[36] In other words, retaining competence for potential future projects was prioritized at the expense of rearming the Armed Forces at this stage. Consequently, little in the way of new technology actually reached the military units. In December 1993, Kokoshin summed up the troubles facing the Armed Forces in this area. There was simply no money to provide new military technology or even repair old equipment. Therefore the units would have to keep the equipment they had and 'try to find their own reserve'.[37]

The unreformed Ministry of Defence made plans for reform something of a prerogative of the ministry and the General Staff. Meanwhile, the Russian leadership displayed only intermittent interest in military reform and reform of the Armed Forces while the deadlock between the executive and legislative branch was requiring its direct attention. Public debate on reform was also poorly developed in 1992. Grachev claimed that the Ministry of Defence wanted an open debate on military reform. 'One of the special features of the activity of the present Ministry of the Defence is that all our plans will be subject of broad discussions in the Supreme Soviet and in Russia's government.'[38] He invited an even broader debate in the media. Nevertheless, it was clear that this debate should take place only on certain terms. He hoped for support and would not allow 'emotions and populist sentiments' to gain the upper hand. 'We will openly explain and defend our intentions for organizing the Russian Armed Forces and are ready for a constructive dialogue with all interested parties.'[39] Clearly, the basic tenets of the plans developed by the MoD would not be subject to discussion. In a speech later the same year, Yeltsin concluded that the information provided to the Russian population about how military reform was proceeding had been lacking. 'Here there are clear failings.'[40]

Grachev's plan for reform of the Armed Forces

In July 1992, Pavel Grachev presented a plan consisting of three stages for reforming the Armed Forces (see Box 5.1). In his view, three major changes had taken place, which guided the plans on how to reform the Armed Forces. He pointed to the geopolitical changes such as the end of the Cold War, the fall of the Soviet Union and the disappearance of the Warsaw Treaty Organization. He went on to conclude that the Russian Armed Forces were created on the basis of those of the Soviet Union, a structure that was unsuitable for the Russian Federation.[41] In his view, the development of its Armed Forces would have to go ahead in spite of the fact that the Russian Federation lacked a military doctrine.[42] Interestingly, Grachev did not mention innovations within military technology and warfare as a reason for reform. It would become clear that his main thoughts on innovation revolved around rapid deployment forces or mobile forces (*mobilnye sily*). Nor did Grachev refer to the changes that were happening within Russian society as underpinnings for his reform plan.

Consequently, Grachev saw four main tasks ahead and these guided the planning process: (a) creating the Russian Armed Forces; (b) ensuring that all Russian troops were transported back to Russia; (c) significant reductions of the Armed Forces; and (d) reforming the Armed Forces of the Russian Federation.[43] In other words, Grachev's reform plan started with what hardly amounted to military reform – troop transports and reductions.

Early on, Yeltsin also singled out developing mobile (or rapid deployment) forces as a priority.[44] Meanwhile, few other guidelines were provided and a new military doctrine was still to be adopted. It is then hardly surprising that Grachev's reform was limited to creating mobile forces and carrying out

Box 5.1 **Defence Minister Grachev's reform programme as presented in July 1992**

Phase 1 (during 1992)

- Make an inventory of all weapons and military equipment.
- Decide the status of Russian troops outside Russian territory and bring them home.
- Reduce military personnel, weapons and military equipment.
- Develop a legal framework for military development.
- Recreate the Ural Military District (MD) and reform certain MDs.

Phase 2 (before 1995)

- Form the structures of the Armed Forces. At this stage, the intention was not to change the overall system of services since this would entail heavy costs for new communication systems, infrastructure, etc.
- Create 'New operative-strategic forces', the mobile forces, starting during the second phase and to be concluded after 1995.
- Create groups of forces that answered to the needs of the Russian Federation, that were in line with international treaties and able to fulfil their missions. Reduction of the number of units in order to equip and find personnel for the remaining ones.
- Introduction of a mixed way of manning the Armed Forces (conscripts and voluntary contract service).

Phase 3 (after 1995)

- After 1995 – 'radical transformation of the structures of the Armed Forces' and changes in the military-administrative division of the territory. Operative and administrative command was to be strictly divided. One possibility was to give operational command of groups of forces to special and territorial commands. A Council of Commanders of Special and Territorial Commands would be created under the chief of the General Staff.
- The Ground Forces were to go from a structure of armies and divisions to corps and brigades. A concept of a mobile defence would be developed. Changes in military-technological and procurement policy. The number of the Armed Forces would be reduced to 1.5 million men.
- Restructuring of the MoD. The chief of the General Staff would be first deputy minister of defence and in charge of the highest executive organ of military command. The General Staff would implement strategic and operative planning as well as command the Armed Forces

in peace and war. Another first deputy minister of defence would develop a cohesive military-technological and procurement policy. The remaining four deputy ministers of defence would be in charge of (a) rear and medical services and housing of troops, (b) bringing troops home and force reductions, (c) training and relocation of cadres, and social protection of servicemen and their families, and (d) operationally deciding in so-called 'hot spots', peacekeeping troops, etc.

Source: *Krasnaia zvezda*, 21 July 1992, p. 2.

reductions. He argued that Russia was unable to maintain forces all along its extended perimeter. Instead, mobile forces would be an efficient way of accomplishing this task and 'by the end of 1993 the idea of establishing rapid-deployment forces had become one of the central points in the discussions of military reform'.[45] Late in 1992, the first plans for fully developed mobile forces were outlined in *Krasnaia zvezda*. According to these, in 1995 the mobile forces command would be directly subordinated to the General Staff. The forces would consist of two parts – immediate reaction forces (*sily nemedlennogo reagirovaniia*) and rapid deployment forces (*sily bystrogo razvertyvaniia*). The latter would only be subordinated to the mobile forces command operationally and the airborne forces (Vozdushno-desantnye voiska, VDV) and naval infantry would constitute the core of the immediate reaction forces. The basic structure of five services of the Armed Forces was to remain intact at this stage. Altogether these plans amounted to a transformation of primarily the ground forces. For example, three army corps would be included in the rapid deployment forces.[46]

Mobile forces proved slow to materialize – not least because the plans would have demanded considerable resources to be spent in retraining and regrouping formations and units. In May 1993, Grachev announced that the Ministry of Defence had strengthened the North Caucasus Military District (MD), where five combat-ready motorized rifle brigades (*boesposobnye motostrelkovye brigady*) had been created 'practically from zero'.[47] (The plan from December 1992 called for six 'light motorized rifle brigades' to be included in the mobile forces.)[48] According to Grachev, the newly created units were 'highly mobile', small but highly effective, and armed with the most modern weapons and military equipment.[49] Plans were announced in December 1993 for mobile forces in each MD consisting of fully manned and well trained units that could be sent to any part of Russia at short notice. This also involved prioritizing the development of air transport forces.[50] In real life, however, the mobile forces remained somewhat of a chimera. In addition to the lack of funds for such plans, the Ground Forces would have been reduced to little more than an organization of mobilization reserves since a full-scale development of mobile forces would have robbed it of its top units.[51] As might be expected, Grachev's plans met with resistance from the Ground Forces.

The military districts that Russia inherited within its own borders from the Soviet Union were essentially kept intact, although their functions within the military system were changed according to the new geopolitical realities. Thus, both the Leningrad and the Moscow MDs were strengthened as forces and military equipment brought home from, above all, Germany became concentrated here. The North Caucasus Military District went from being a rather unprioritized district to one of central importance. However, this upgrading of the North Caucasus MD to a front line against threats from the south proved mainly to have been a paper tiger once the war in Chechnya broke out.[52] The Volga and Ural MDs had formerly been rear districts. They became districts of 'the second strategic echelon'. In addition, the Volga MD became a base for the mobile forces and the military transport aviation they depended upon.[53] There were also plans to develop a new regional command structure, leaving the military districts as mobilization districts. However, these plans were slow to materialize.[54]

The strategic context after 1991: theory and practice

At a time often referred to as the 'honeymoon' in Russian–American relations, the Russian military proved markedly less ready to embrace its former foe than the Ministry of Foreign Affairs under its new minister of foreign affairs, Andrei Kozyrev. In many ways, Russia was still struggling to define its national interest. It was clear that new threats had emerged while others had abated. Russia's relations with the West were of an entirely new nature and military conflict with NATO or the USA appeared highly unlikely. Still, Russia was left a military heritage from the Soviet Union, a force posture that was almost entirely geared to the threat of a large-scale war with the West and an officers' corps that was geared to meeting this threat. Russia also inherited the Soviet nuclear arsenal, which was overdimensioned for the new strategic context.

More problematic, from a Russian point of view, was the fact that new threats were emerging – threats for which its military was poorly prepared. Above all, this was the case in Russia's borderlands; in many of the former Soviet republics inter-ethnic conflicts erupted and Russia often played a role in these. In spite of having been involved in counter-insurgency warfare in Afghanistan only a few years earlier, the Russian military organization seemed ill adapted and unprepared for handling such conflicts. Thus, such 'low-intensity conflict was also understood predominantly in state-centric terms – as limited political or military action taken by a state and aimed at supporting other friendly states'.[55] In practice, the adversaries in these local wars were mainly irregular units representing a specific ethnic community rather than a state. On a more practical level, the Russian military organization did not possess the units that would have been most suitable for these kinds of conflicts. The force posture inherited from the Soviet Union proved cumbersome. Rather than mobile, independent units, the military organization was made up of large formations trained to act in unison and wait for orders from above. The different services of the Armed Forces were unable to communicate and cooperate on a tactical level. Their equipment and training were simply not intended to facilitate this. Needless to say, the units of other power ministries, for example, the Border Troops of the FPS, were also unable to operate together with the troops of the MoD on this level.

The draft military doctrine produced by the General Staff and published in May 1992 still regarded NATO, although it was not mentioned explicitly, as the main enemy and its military section mainly discussed how to meet this threat.[56] Meanwhile, Russian military units still remaining in newly independent states such as Moldova and Tajikistan found themselves embroiled in armed conflicts.[57] This, if nothing else, inspired new thinking about which conflicts were the most likely to occur in the near future and about Russia's relations to the so-called 'Near Abroad'. Indeed, local and regional conflicts on the close periphery of Russia's borders moved up the agenda of the Ministry of Defence and the Ministry of Foreign Affairs during this period. The development of both a foreign policy concept and a military doctrine went ahead even in the absence of a national security concept, which should have set the paramenters for and coordinated foreign and military policy in the respective documents.

In April 1993, a new foreign policy concept was adopted at a session of the Security Council. The secretary of the Security Council, Yurii Skokov, who was mainly interested in foreign policy formulation, had played a significant part in penning the concept[58] as he chaired the Security Council's Interdepartmental Commission on Foreign Policy. The main tenets were presented by the deputy head of the Directorate of Strategic Security of the Security Council, Vladislav Chernov, in an article.[59] The military threats were defined as mainly those arising from armed conflicts near Russia's new borders and consequent on the disintegration of the Soviet Union. The threat of proliferation of weapons of mass destruction was specifically mentioned. Closely related to this was the Russian commitment to take control over all the nuclear weapons in the former Soviet Union and concern for the fact that the disintegration of the Soviet Armed Forces had severed especially the strategic defence system. NATO and the USA were not mentioned as threats to the new Russian state, but it was clear which threat the strategic defence system had been designed to protect against.

The military doctrine appeared only after the October Events in 1993. Addressing the Collegium of the Ministry of Defence in November 1992, Yeltsin stated that developing a new military doctrine was one of the most important tasks ahead. In his address, Yeltsin started by emphasizing that Russia had been and remained a great power. 'As president and supreme commander I do and will continue to do everything possible in order for

Russia to have a modern army that corresponds to its place in the international community.' The new structure of the Armed Forces would transpire from the new doctrine.[60] Work on developing a new military doctrine proceeded. In an interview in *Nezavisimaia gazeta* in June 1993, Andrei Kokoshin expounded on the basic tenets and problems of such a doctrine. Russia had no enemies at the gate. Rather, the majority of states were real or potential partners and economic and democratic goals were overarching. 'All efforts to safeguard the security of Russia from a military point of view in the end must be focused on benefiting a stable development of Russia as a democratic and economically flourishing state.' He also criticized the fact that Russia was ill prepared for limited wars.[61]

> An analysis of the development of the armed forces of the Soviet Union demonstrated that for decades it was directed mainly towards being ready for the least likely form of war – a Third World War with massive use of nuclear weapons. We were less prepared for local, comparatively small wars, which are more likely.[62]

The outline of a new military doctrine was reviewed at a meeting in the Security Council in the immediate aftermath of the October Events of 1993.[63] In November 1993, the 'main theses' of a new military doctrine were published in *Krasnaia zvezda*. These had been discussed and adopted by the Security Council in October and November 1993. The document was very much in line with the domestic and foreign policy goals as proclaimed by the Kremlin. The preamble stressed that it was a 'document of a transition period – the period of the establishment of Russian statehood'. The threat of military aggression against Russia had become significantly lower, according to the document. Among the threats listed were international terrorism, local wars, the proliferation of nuclear weapons, violation of the rights of Russian citizens abroad and 'the enlargement of military blocs and unions that damage the military security interests of the Russian Federation'.[64] This was an obvious reference to NATO and the prospect of new members joining the alliance. The Armed Forces were also given increased responsibility in the domestic arena.[65] However, the policy formulation process was in disarray and a national security concept was not adopted until 1997.[66]

Due to Russia's weakness in fighting conventional wars, the nuclear component came to the fore in Russia's new military doctrine and in statements made by prominent officers and politicians. Contrary to early misgivings, the process of concentrating the Soviet nuclear arsenal in Russia went smoothly. It was clear that Russia was determined to preserve its status as a nuclear power. In the new military doctrine, not only did Russia omit the standard 'no first use' formula; it became clear that Russia would emphasize nuclear weapons in order to compensate for its relative conventional weakness. However, at a press conference given to present the new military doctrine, Grachev stated that nuclear weapons should be regarded 'above all not a means of warfare, but as a political means of deterrent from aggression'.[67] Perhaps even more important at this stage, Russia's nuclear status was its main claim to great power status (apart from pointing to its sheer size and permanent membership in the United Nations (UN) Security Council).[68]

On the whole, these early official documents were now more or less in line with one another. The Ministry of Foreign Affairs and Ministry of Defence had approached each other's positions. This was, no doubt, partly achieved under pressure from the Kremlin. More interestingly, however, the difference between the draft military doctrine published in May 1992 and the actual military doctrine that was finally adopted in November 1993 mirrored a discrepancy in world outlook that existed within the MoD between the minister and the General Staff.[69] There were signs that the military establishment was far from ready to dismiss the possibility of total war.[70] On a rhetorical level, moreover, there was a discrepancy between the emphasis on strategic nuclear weapons and the assertion that most states were partners or potential partners.

The new threats and the new geopolitical situation led to only marginal adaptations of the overall force posture and military organization. Although both Yeltsin and Grachev emphasized mobile forces as the main solution to most of Russia's military security problems, these proved difficult to create in practice. The military districts were in the main kept intact, as was the organizational structure of the Armed Forces.[71] There was no clear plan for adapting the military organization to new threats. Nor did the emphasis on local wars and terrorism lead to new investment in technology or education and training to counter such threats. This became obvious when the war in Chechnya began. At a press conference in November 1995, after almost a year of war, Grachev claimed that the main efforts in training the Armed Forces were focused on handling local (and regional) wars.[72] If this was indeed the case, results were slow to materialize in Chechnya.

War in Chechnya: Yeltsin and the military

During 1994, Yeltsin's machinery for security policy making had started to develop somewhat. However, the emphasis seemed to be primarily on acquiring levers for controlling the power ministries rather than on devising a strategy for Russia's national security. A presidential adviser on foreign policy, Dmitrii Riurikov, exercised a certain influence on security policy making in general.[73] In June 1994 Yeltsin also appointed Boris Kuzyk presidential adviser on international military-technological cooperation.[74] In December the same year, the Commission on Military-Technological Policy was created by presidential decree.[75] Kuzyk became responsible for this commission, which was directly subordinated to the president. Meanwhile, Yurii Baturin was rapidly becoming one of the Yeltsin's most trusted advisers on security policy. Highly irregularly, the head of the Presidential Security Service, Aleksandr Korzhakov, also played a role in security policy as well as other policy areas from 1994 until 1996.[76] Yevgenii Shaposhnikov, mean-while, became Yeltsin's military adviser. This plethora of security-related advisers with unclear mandates and overlapping areas of responsibility was bound to complicate defence policy making within the Presidential Administration in the absence of a strong political will and mechanisms for coordination.

The Commission on Higher Military Ranks was formed in March 1994 and Yurii Baturin was appointed its chairman. The intrigues around the commission started almost immediately. The heads of almost all the power ministries signed a letter to Yeltsin protesting that the commission put the authority of commanders in question. One important task for this commission was to reduce the number of generals. The commission also thwarted the attempt of Sergei Shoigu to create an MChS with no less than 122 generals – a rather excessive number for a newly created civil defence authority. Even Shoigu had to acquiesce to the rank of major-general rather than that of army general, which he had proposed for himself.[77] There were a number of attempts to wrest this commission from Baturin's hands. Aleksandr Lebed succeeded in doing so briefly in 1996, when he became Yeltsin's national security adviser and secretary of the Security Council, but on the whole the president resisted this, well aware of the political capital the commission represented.[78]

The natural centre for coordination of civilian defence policy would have been the Security Council. It is unlikely that it performed such a function during this period. However, the decision to go to war in Chechnya was formally taken in the Security Council on 29 November 1994.[79] At this time, Oleg Lobov was secretary of the Security Council. On 30 December 1994, he maintained that the operation in Chechnya would last for one more month – maximum. He also praised the war efforts of the Russian forces and commended the 'high morale and psychological spirits of the army'.[80] This involvement in a decision to go to war – a war that quickly became a political liability to the president and a national trauma – could not but affect the standing of the Security Council in central decision making. While it continued to play a role in handling security matters related to Chechnya, its influence on other security questions became marginal. Still, according to Andrei Kokoshin, it was during Lobov's time at the Security Council that it started to cooperate with the Ministry of Defence on defence development. A number of Security Council commissions were created, one of them on defence security. In his capacity as first deputy minister of defence, Kokoshin headed this commission.[81] On the whole, however, it is difficult to pinpoint an institution in the Kremlin that was responsible for military reform at this time. The impression is rather that Chechnya was the main concern and that the different power ministries were left to their own devices.

On the eve of the war in Chechnya, Pavel Grachev declared at the annual evaluation of the Armed Forces that they were 'able to guarantee the national security of Russia, that they were under control and battleworthy'.

President Yeltsin, who was also present, noted in his address that the withdrawal of troops from abroad had been concluded and that the Ministry of Defence was coping well with peacekeeping missions. The Armed Forces had been reduced by 385,000 men and by 1 January 1995 the manpower level would be at 1,917,000. Yeltsin ended his address by stating that the 'appearance of the Armed Forces was becoming increasingly worthy of the Great Russia'.[82] The hollowness of these exhortations and Grachev's promises of effective mobile forces became obvious within the first weeks of the war in Chechnya in December 1994. One of the reasons for the poor tactical performance was that the MoD found itself compelled to use so-called 'composite units' drawn from several units that were not fully manned and had never trained together.[83]

When it became obvious that the war in Chechnya was not going to be the swift, successful operation first promised by Grachev, there were rumours that Yeltsin was considering the possibility of subordinating the General Staff directly to the president.[84] This could be evidence of Yeltsin's search for effective means of controlling the Armed Forces. True to his predilection for bombastic statements followed by inertia, however, Yeltsin did nothing to change the basic mechanisms within the Ministry of Defence. This suggestion, put forward in January 1995, came to naught, as did many of Yeltsin's other ideas and proclamations. If nothing else, the frequent outbursts from Yeltsin kept his generals on their toes, since his lack of concern for reforming the MoD was outweighed by a propensity to play the power game by sacking and appointing people.

The feeble attempts by the judicial branch to scrutinize the decision to go to war in Chechnya are a vivid example of its inability to exercise scrutiny and control. The war started as a covert operation, but quickly escalated into an armed conflict. Soon the dreaded 'cargo-200' started to arrive, carrying the bodies of servicemen and young conscripts in metal boxes. Eager to seize the opportunity, the opposition in the Duma initiated an investigation into whether the war had been initiated according to the constitution and federal laws. The Federal Council should have approved the operation, and the case was tried by the Constitutional Court. In the end, however, the political and military leadership got away with a warning. The Constitutional Court criticized certain formal routines, but did not dare go against the Kremlin in the question that really mattered.[85] At a lower level, the failure to expose corruption scandals within the military and bring the guilty to justice for human rights violations in Chechnya was ample evidence of the weakness of the judicial branch vis-à-vis the Ministry of Defence.

Nor did the military leadership suffer any consequences. The minister of defence, Grachev, had signed the order to intervene, and the chief of the General Staff, General Mikhail Kolesnikov, had been responsible for planning the operation together with a group of officers from the Main Directorate of Operations of the General Staff, Viktor Barynkin, Anatolii Kvashnin, Leontii Shevtsov and others.[86] Indeed, Kvashnin took over as commander of the federal forces in Chechnya – something that did not impede his future career.[87] According to the deputy minister of defence at the time, Colonel-General Boris Gromov, the military board of the Ministry of Defence had not been involved in the plans for the operation in Chechnya, which were made in secret.[88] Of course, Gromov had every reason to disclaim any involvement in any of the preparations for a war he was openly critical of. However, there is ample evidence that the military operation was poorly planned. Preparations were inadequate and intelligence insufficient.[89]

The Committee of Soldiers' Mothers contributed to forming a public opinion against the war in Chechnya in 1994–96 and it became difficult for the Ministry of Defence to ignore its demands, not least because of the increase in draft evasion. Heartbreaking television images of young Russian conscripts lying dead and abandoned in the muddy streets of Groznyi reinforced the position of the Committee of Soldiers' Mothers since it arranged for mothers of conscripts reported missing to go to Chechnya to search for their sons.[90] The Committee of Soldiers' Mothers also intensified its work against hazing (or *dedovshchina*) by, for example, informing conscripts and their families of their legal rights. The MoD preferred to call the problem 'non-statutory relations' (*neustavnye otnosheniia*), but it became increasingly important for it to be seen to be doing something about it.[91]

In late 1995 and early 1996 the Kremlin was eager to find a way out of the war in Chechnya. It was obvious that the war would prove an enormous burden in the forthcoming presidential campaign. In May 1996, Yeltsin issued a decree stating that by April 2000 the Russian military would be manned entirely on a contract basis. The decree was entirely unrealistic, but well in tune with the public outrage against the war in Chechnya. 'It is a measure of how weary the Russian public had grown with the waste of young lives in military service that a patently hollow promise to end the draft could still be thought to generate votes.'[92]

Military reform in the shadow of Chechnya

The level of manpower is a blunt instrument for measuring the progress of military reform. In addition, the figures are difficult both to interpret and to confirm.[93] Often, they are intentionally blurred by the representatives of the Ministry of Defence and other power ministries, where resistance against manpower reductions is firmly entrenched, since radical reductions in manpower should, at least in theory, lead to reductions in the number of high-ranking officers employed as well.[94] Sometimes the figures include all personnel employed by the relevant ministries, sometimes only military personnel (civilians are excluded). Another source of confusion is whether the manpower numbers include vacant positions.[95] Nevertheless, the numbers of people employed in the different military forces indicate changes that would be difficult to spot in other ways (Table 5.1).

Table 5.1 Level of manpower within the military organization, 1991–1997

Year	MoD Armed Forces		MVD	KGB etc.	Tot. paramil.	Total*
1991/2	Total	3,025,000	350,000	230,000	580,000	3,605,000
	Ground	1,400,000				
	Air def.	475,000				
	Navy	450,000				
	Air force	420,000				
	RVSN	280,000				
1992/3	Total	2,720,000	170,000	220,000	520,000	3,240,000
1993/4	Total	2,030,000	120,000	100,000**	220,000	2,250,000
1994/5	Total	1,714,000	180,000	100,000**	280,000	1,994,000
1995/6	Total	1,349,000	180,000	100,000**	280,000	1,629,000
1996/7	Total	1,270,000	232,000	100,000**	352,000	1,622,000
	Ground	460,000				
	Air def.	175,000				
	Navy	190,000				
	Air	145,000				
	RVSN	149,000				

Sources: The Military Balance 1991/1992, *1992/1993, 1993/1994, 1994/1995, 1995/96 and 1996/97.*

Notes:
The totals of the services of the Armed Forces and the different paramilitary forces do not always add up. The totals presented are those given in *The Military Balance* except for the totals in the last column.
*   Total calculated from Armed Forces plus paramilitary forces total – not given in *The Military Balance.*
** The Border Troops belonged to the KGB during the Soviet era. The FPS, the Federal Border Service, was created in 1994. The apparent reduction from 220,000 men in 1992/3 to a mere 100,000 in 1993/4 probably results from the fact that only Border Troops are included in the figure from 1993/4 and onwards.

The main source for figures on manpower within the Russian military organization is *The Military Balance* for the relevant years. There are problems inherent in these figures as well. In particular, the figures for paramilitary troops are difficult to interpret. However, these figures are often quoted in other texts on Russian military reform and there is an advantage in being able to use the same source for the entire period under investigation – even taking into account that *The Military Balance* has used different methods for counting force levels during this period. The latter problem will be addressed by commenting the figures and comparing them with other numbers stated in, for example, the statistics provided by the Russian Ministry of Defence.

Early on, the political goal was to reduce the size of the Armed Forces to 1,500,000 and later to 1,250,000.[96] At that point there was little talk of the structure and numerical strength of the rest of the military organization. In late December 1993, Pavel Grachev summed up 1993 for the Armed Forces and spoke of the future at a press conference. He stated that the numerical strength of the Armed Forces was just over 2,300,000 men and that there were plans to carry out further reductions to 2,100,000 men during 1994. According to Grachev, specialists had spoken against reducing the numerical strength to 1.5 million men as recommended by the Supreme Soviet, and in favour of it exceeding 2 million men.[97] Nevertheless the overall trend is clear: reductions of the Armed Forces continued as the defence budget grew steadily smaller.

Table 5.1 does not reflect the relative development of the power ministries very well. If the figures relating to the troops subordinated to the Ministry of Defence are sometimes problematic, those relating to other power ministries are often misleading. Certainly, the fact that troops belonging to FAPSI, the Railway Troops, the FSB and the FSO are not included at all distorts the picture. Moreover, the sudden jumps back and forth in the numerical strength of the Interior Troops are difficult to explain, and the even number of 100,000 men belonging to the Border Troops in successive years only to jump to 220,000 in 1997/98 (see Table 5.4) appears dubious. Some of the power ministries probably grew at a steady pace. This growth is often exaggerated, but military reform was clearly failing in this regard.

A clear sign that military reform was going nowhere in the field of developing the military operational art was the absence of large-scale exercises. Starting in 1992, exercises at divisional level ceased entirely.[98] A year after the creation of the Russian Armed Forces, Pavel Grachev summed up the achievements he considered had been made so far. 'After a four-to-six-year break, the forces have again during this year started to do what they should mainly be doing – military training instead of painting fences etc.'[99] In fact, the few exercises that were conducted during 1993 struggled with a number of difficulties and deficiencies. The only exercises that took place at higher command levels were command staff exercises (*komandno-shtabnye ucheniia*).[100] When the chief of the General Staff, Colonel-General Mikhail Kolesnikov, summed up the year at the annual evaluation session in December 1993, he was critical of a number of factors. For example, a number of commanding officers were poorly trained for the exercises and were not familiar with the procedural guidelines and instructions. Some of the exercises had been superficial and new technology was only slowly assimilated in the units. The latter was especially true for command and control systems. The number of flying hours within the air force had been drastically reduced, as had the number of missiles launched within the Naval Forces. Overall, however, there was an optimistic note in the evaluation of 1993 at the session. The initial difficulties were over and now the time had come to try out the new concepts of the military doctrine.[101] However, it would become obvious that the tide had not changed yet for the Armed Forces.

With the break-up of the Soviet Union many factories, research institutes and construction bureaux ended up outside the borders of the Russian Federation. For example, Russia lost 80 per cent of the Soviet repair facilities for armoured fighting vehicles (AFVs), with the result that only about 20 per cent of the AFVs that Russia inherited from the Soviet army were still serviceable by 1994.[102] In addition, the cutbacks in defence spending resulted in a drastic decrease in the funding going to research. During the Soviet era, up to 70 per cent of research conducted under the aegis of the Academy of Science was defence-related.

For the period 1994–96, the government had already decided to finance the procurement programme at the same level as in 1993.[103] According to the deputy commander of the Ground Forces, Colonel-General Anton Terentev, the overall share of modern equipment in the Ground Forces was about 30 per cent in November 1995.[104] Summing up the situation in November 1995, Pavel Grachev acknowledged that the Armed Forces were not receiving necessary new weapons system or military technology and that they lacked the ability to repair and maintain much of the existing equipment.[105] In spite of this, Grachev stated that the second phase of his reform plan had been completed.[106] It was obvious, however, that, for example, the goal of mixed manning was far from being fulfilled.

Support among the political establishment for Grachev's plans was weak. During his tenure, the forces of the Ministry of Defence were subjected to drastic cuts in personnel and resources at the same time as other power structures grew.[107] Perhaps the MoD was being punished for hesitating to support the Kremlin in the turmoil during the October Events.[108] However, an equally convincing explanation is that other power ministries and agencies were more effective lobbyists than the MoD.

Overall, it was clear that the Ministry of Defence during this period was finding it difficult to understand how best to influence the Kremlin and the government. The limited clout of the Duma did not prevent Grachev from attempting to improve his ministry's position by getting officers elected to the Duma in 1995. More than 120 candidates were selected as representatives of the MoD for the election. The plan proved a failure for the MoD even compared to its modest goal of reaching thirty-five officer-deputies (enough to form a Duma faction). In the end, only two of the ministry's candidates were elected.[109] Most probably, the whole exercise was staged in an attempt to achieve more funding for the MoD. This was, yet again, indicative of the poor grasp the ministry had on how to work the system. Given that the Duma had little influence, even an officers' fraction in the Duma would have been able to achieve little in the way of increasing the defence budget or improving the military's prestige. The other power ministries proved more politically agile and moved to influence the Kremlin and government directly instead.

The Ministry of Internal Affairs experienced mixed fortunes between 1993 and 1996. It was in relatively good favour after the October Events, but after it took over responsibility for the war in Chechnya this changed. The Interior Troops were not trained to fight even a small war or a low-intensity conflict. In addition, the MVD's relations with other power ministries, especially with the Ministry of Defence, were poor.[110] The security service was slightly more successful. With Sergei Stepashin at the helm, Yeltsin had assured himself a loyal service. Consquently, Stepashin was able to convince Yeltsin that the FSK needed more than just information-gathering powers.[111] However, the FSK was also subjected to cuts in personnel. In July 1995, it was renamed the Federal Security Service, the FSB, and Mikhail Barsukov was made its director – partly as a result of the bungling of the hostage crisis in Budennovsk in June 1995.

Two power ministries that started to grow at about this time were the MChS and the FPS. Both started as committees. The State Border Committee was subordinated to the Ministry of Security during the first tumultuous months after the fall of the Soviet Union. However, exactly how the Border Troops were to be organized and managed remained undecided for a long period. When Yeltsin created a Federal Migration Service as a civilian organ for border control, the exact function and mission of the State Border Committee became somewhat blurred. This confusion hardly alleviated the difficult situation the Border Troops found themselves in as new borders had to be demarcated, new border crossings established and troops brought home from some of the former Soviet republics.[112] They were plagued by some of the same problems as the Armed Forces. The FPS found it difficult to recruit conscripts and lost many of the graduates of its schools.[113] The Border Troops played a limited role in the first Chechen War. They were already involved in Tajikistan when they were given responsibility for guarding the Chechen border with Ingushetia and Dagestan – formally not an external border of the Russian Federation. However, they proved fortunate in receiving the influential and capable Andrei Nikolaev as director of the newly founded Federal Border Service in 1994. In this the FPS was similar to the MChS: Sergei Shoigu would become unique in holding on to his ministerial post at the MChS for more than a decade and a half, and was very successful in lobbying for his new ministry. For example, Anatol Lieven claims that the MChS employed about 120,000 men in 1996 and wished to enrol 20,000 more.[114]

Apart from being better able to work the political system, these power ministries all had the indisputable advantage over the Ministry of Defence that they could point to how their troops were being used in practice. Although the Armed Forces were being used in, for example, Chechnya, the main mission of a Ministry of Defence was ultimately to prepare for something that hopefully should not occur – a major war against foreign powers. In other words, the MoD often found itself having to argue for resources to train and equip troops that everyone hoped would not be used. Meanwhile, power ministries such as the MChS could maintain a high profile and send their men to help out in, for example, natural disasters.

The Kremlin jumpstarts reform: institutions and experts

To conduct a major military reform while bringing significant numbers of troops home from the former Warsaw Pact countries was in itself a gigantic undertaking. To do so with a drastically reduced budget, only part of which was actually disbursed, and with a political leadership that was not interested, was impossible. Although Grachev in announcing his reform plan clearly stated that the first few years would mainly involve the transfer of men and equipment back to Russia, neither he nor politicians could resist the temptation of talking of an ongoing military reform.[115] Indeed, at times they all expounded on the success of military reform. The war in Chechnya exposed this for what it was – wishful thinking at best. During Grachev's and later Rodionov's tenure as minister of defence, military reform did not take any drastic steps forward either in the field of military innovations (technology, organization and warfare) or in adapting to new international and domestic conditions. Grachev was dismissed in July 1996 and Igor Rodionov succeeded him. By this time, Grachev's reputation was damaged by corruption scandals, but ruined by the overall dismal state of the Armed Forces and their performance in Chechnya. He was never again appointed to a high post in government or within the Armed Forces.[116] Rodionov, on the other hand, had acquired the reputation of being an excellent commander and military officer within the Armed Forces, but he lacked support inside the Kremlin, and when Lebed was dismissed in October 1996, whatever possibilities Rodionov may have had of pursuing his own military reform agenda dwindled.[117] Rodionov was a stern critic of reductions during his short tenure as minister of defence. His views were not compatible with the kind of reform the Kremlin wished to implement and he never even got the opportunity to present his plans for reform to the Defence Council.[118]

Interestingly, while military reform remained at an almost complete standstill, defence decision making underwent changes, which made seminal decisions and plans for reform possible. There were two interconnected main reasons for this. First, the poor performance of the Russian military organization in Chechnya resulted in a shock that put forces in motion towards reform.[119] Military defeat was staring Russia in the face and the political humiliation was considerable. Second, and closely connected to the war in Chechnya, the presidential election in June 1996 and Yeltsin's low popularity ratings at the beginning of the year made the Kremlin highly sensitive to public opinion and susceptible to political pressure from interest groups such as the Committee of Soldiers' Mothers. Together with a growing realization of how bad the situation within the Armed Forces had become, these events put the political decision-making machinery into action. The necessary people were brought into the right decision-making structures.

The institutions and actors behind this push for reform were located within both the presidential and the government structures. However, it took some time for key actors to establish themselves at the critical junctions in this machinery. For a brief period it looked as if patriotic officers like Aleksandr Lebed and Igor Rodionov had gained the upper hand. Ironically, the involvement of the Security Council in Chechnya led the newpapers to describe it as crucial at a time when really it was losing influence at a rapid pace. Perhaps it was this inflated description of the Security Council's ability to wield power that made secretaryship of it an attractive prospect to Aleksandr Lebed, who claimed this post as his price for backing Yeltsin in the second round of the presidential election in 1996. He was set on finding a solution to the war in Chechnya, and the Security Council must have appeared a perfect vehicle. In June 1996 Lebed became its secretary. He combined this post with that of national security adviser to the president and took over the Commission on Higher Military Ranks from Yurii Baturin.[120]

While Lebed's star was still in the ascendant he managed to get his choice, Igor Rodionov, appointed minister of defence after Grachev was dismissed. The conservative Rodionov took over the Ministry of Defence on 17 July 1996 and was soon locked in bitter combat with Baturin, who was appointed secretary of the newly created Defence Council about a week later. Military reform was delayed while the conflict between Baturin and Rodionov was allowed to smoulder. Baturin advanced plans that were unacceptable to the MoD and Rodionov became increasingly intransigent in his dealings with the political level.[121] Rodionov proposed an expensive plan for rebuilding Russia's conventional forces, referring to the increasing threat from NATO.[122] He refused to present his own final plan for reform to anyone except to the president. The stand-off came to a head in May 1997 at a Defence Council meeting at which Yeltsin was present. The president placed the entire responsibility for the failure of reform on the shoulders of the generals, who 'grew fatter as soldiers grew thinner'. Rodionov was dismissed on the spot and replaced by Igor Sergeev. Also dismissed was the chief of the General Staff, Viktor Samsonov.[123] The humiliating way in which this was done damaged relations between the Kremlin and the military severely. In spite of his short tenure, Rodionov came to enjoy a very good reputation among Russian officers and they often name him as the best minister of defence and the one who came up with the best reform plan.[124]

The Security Council was faced with a rival structure for influencing defence policy making when Yeltsin issued a decree on the creation of the Defence Council in July 1996.[125] The reasons why the council came into being have been debated. At first sight, it would appear almost to duplicate the Security Council. The most common explanation is that Yeltsin was regarding the power ambitions of Aleksandr Lebed, then secretary of the Security Council, with increasing suspicion. However, another plausible explanation has been provided by Andrei Kokoshin, who claims that Yeltsin's poor health was a deciding factor. It had become impossible to move military reform forward with the Security Council as the main vehicle for political decision making.[126] Yeltsin's presence at its sessions, which was mandatory for it to make decisions, had become increasingly rare. The Defence Council, although similar to the Security Council in many ways, had a deputy chairman, the prime minister (see Table 5.2). According to the statutes of the Defence Council, the deputy chairman could fulfil the duties of the chairman in his absence.[127] The fact that Yeltsin was absent at the first

Table 5.2 Members of the Defence Council in July 1996

	Name	*Office*
Chairman	Boris Yeltsin	President of the Russian Federation
Deputy chairman	Viktor Chernomyrdin	Prime minister
Secretary	Yurii Baturin	
	Anatolii Chubais	Head of the Presidential Administration
	Nikolai Kovalev	Director of the FSB
	Andrei Kokoshin	State secretary and first deputy minister of defence
	Mikhail Kolesnikov	Chief of the General Staff and First deputy minister of defence
	Anatolii Kulikov	Minister of internal affairs
	Aleksandr Lebed	Secretary of the Security Council and presidential national security adviser
	Andrei Nikolaev	Director of the FPS
	Zinovii Pak	Minister of the defence industry
	Vladimir Petrov	First deputy minister of finance
	Yevgenii Primakov	Minister of foreign affairs
	Igor Rodionov	Minister of defence
	Sergei Stepashin	Head of the Administrative Department of the Government Apparatus
	Viacheslav Trubnikov	Director of the SVR
	Yevgenii Velikhov	Deputy president of Russia's Union of Industrialists and Entrepreneurs (RSPP)
	Yevgenii Yasin	Minister of economy

Source: *Rossiiskaia gazeta*, 27 July 1996, p. 4.

meeting of the Defence Council would seem to support Kokoshin's opinion as to why it was created. On the other hand, Aleksandr Lebed was not present either.[128] It would seem that the Defence Council performed both the functions outlined above.

A comparison with the membership of the Security Council at about this time (see Table 5.3) reinforces the impression that the Defence Council was something of a working commission on military reform. For example, Baturin was not a member of the Security Council, and nor were the first deputy ministers of defence, Kokoshin and Kolesnikov. Both the minister of the economy, Yevgenii Yasin, and the first deputy minister of finance, Vladimir Petrov, were included in the Defence Council. Even more significant was the membership of both the head of the Presidential Administration, Anatolii Chubais, and the head of the Administrative Department of the Government Apparatus, Sergei Stepashin in the Defence Council. Both Stepashin and Chubais were located at critical hubs in the Russian decision-making machinery at the time. In June 1997, the composition of the Defence Council changed somewhat when the deputy prime

Table 5.3 Members of the Security Council on 31 July 1996

	Name	Office
Chairman	Boris Yeltsin	President of the Russian Federation
Secretary	Aleksandr Lebed	
Permanent member	Viktor Chernomyrdin	Prime minister
Permanent member	Nikolai Kovalev	Director of the FSB
Permanent member	Yevgenii Primakov	Minister of foreign affairs
Permanent member	Igor Rodionov	Minister of defence
Member	Valentin Kovalev	Minister of justice
Member	Yurii Krapivin	Head of the FSO
Member	Anatolii Kulikov	Minister of internal affairs
Member	Viktor Mikhailov	Minister of atomic energy
Member	Andrei Nikolaev	Director of the FPS
Member	Zinovii Pak	Minister of defence industry
Member	Vladimir Panskov	First deputy minister of finance
Member	Viacheslav Trubnikov	Director of the SVR
Member	Sergei Shoigu	Minister of the MChS

Source: *Krasnaia zvezda*, 2 August 1996, p. 1.

minister and minister of economy, Yakov Urinson, and the new head of the Presidential Administration, Valentin Yumashev, were included.[129]

The Defence Council has often been somewhat derided – partly because it did not last long. Nevertheless, there is reason to assume that at a certain stage it did play a central role in formulating plans for an intensified military reform. According to Kokoshin, the plans that were discussed in the Defence Council were based on material provided by the Ministry of Defence under his own supervision, but in close cooperation with the heads of a number of directorates of the ministry (such as the Main Directorate of Operations, the Main Intelligence Directorate (GRU) and the Main Organizational-Mobilization Directorate).[130]

Kokoshin's account is probably coloured by the fact that he was appointed secretary of the Defence Council in August 1997. After Baturin was dismissed and the Defence Council disbanded, Kokoshin also became state military inspector.[131] True to his nature, Yeltsin created a control function of defence implementation, the State Military Inspectorate, within his own Presidential Administration rather than leaving such powers to the parliament. Formally, the State Military Inspectorate received considerable powers. It was to conduct checks of the activity of the Armed Forces and other units belonging to, for example, the FSB and had access to all buildings belonging to the military organization. It could demand necessary documents and recommend that the president dismiss personnel.[132] As usual, practical work proved more difficult. For a start, the majority of the personnel (80 out of a total 100) were recruited from the Armed Forces and other force structures – the very institutions the State Military Inspectorate was supposed to check on.[133]

In retrospect, it is obvious that important decisions were made on military reform at about this time. In June 1997, an agreement on military reform was reached at Sochi where the prime minister, Viktor Chernomyrdin, was on holiday. He was joined there by Kokoshin, Sergeev, the chief of the General Staff, Anatolii Kvashnin, and the head of the Government's Administrative Department, Sergei Stepashin. Together they prepared documents for the president to sign that were to form the cornerstone of the military reform project.[134] In July 1997 Yeltsin signed a decree on measures of military reform and in a radio speech in July 1997 he ended by proclaiming that: 'One thing is indisputable, reform has really begun. Each of its steps are calculated, settled, prepared and provided for. There will be no delays. The main thing is not to lose time.'[135]

The reform proposal did include ideas about how to introduce a system for civilian control of the Armed Forces. This would involve not simply naming a civilian minister of defence. The proposal was to create two commissions under the Defence Council. The first of these was to be responsible for military development (*stroitelstvo*) and headed by Chernomyrdin. It was tasked with developing proposals for military reform as well as concepts for military development up to 2001 and 2005. The second commission, headed by a first deputy minister, Anatolii Chubais, was to be in charge of finding the financial resources for the reform of the Armed Forces. On 25 July, the heads of the two commissions were to present their concepts for military development to the Defence Council. Yurii Baturin, as secretary of the Defence Council, would be in overall charge and the reform plans would have consequences for other ministries and authorities as well, such as the Border Troops and the Ministry of Internal Affairs.[136]

The Defence Council does appear to have been the main fulcrum for this activity even before Kokoshin took over as its secretary. The Security Council was nowhere near playing this role at the time. Lebed's successor, Ivan Rybkin, spent his time as secretary of the Security Council concentrating on the situation in Chechnya, while other defence matters were handled almost entirely by the Defence Council.[137] The businessman Boris Berezovskii was one of the deputy secretaries of the Security Council and one of his areas of responsibility was to suggest financial solutions that would contribute to a solution to the conflict in Chechnya.[138] His shady reputation and the council's close involvement with the Chechnya question contributed to a decline in the influence and authority of the Security Council during Rybkin's tenure.[139] In other words, the Security Council played at most a secondary role in military reform while the Defence Council existed.

On 3 March 1998, however, Andrei Kokoshin became secretary of the Security Council. At the same time the Defence Council and the State Military Inspectorate were merged with the Security Council. In a presidential decree, Yeltsin commissioned Kokoshin to present a new structure for the apparatus of the Security Council within a month. As mentioned above, a plan for 'military development and reform of the Armed Forces of the Russian Federation, other troops, military formations and organs' was to be presented within the same time frame.[140] The new structure of the apparatus of the Security Council was confirmed by decree on 28 March 1998. One of the new directorates was the Directorate for Military–Industrial Security.[141] Another indication that Kokoshin and the Security Council were to concentrate on planning military reform was that a 'special government organ' was created to handle the situation in the North Caucasus, to be headed by Deputy Prime Minister Viktor Khristenko.[142] In other words, the Security Council became one of the main engines of military reform at this time.

In the last years of Yeltsin's presidency, the office of the prime minister had a swing door. Until April 1998, Chernomyrdin remained in the Russian White House as head of government. The young Sergei Kirienko who replaced him only stayed in office for about four months. Meanwhile, the prime minister had a very limited staff for defence policy making. According to Kokoshin, the government and the prime minister gained the embryo of a secretariat for national defence (resembling that of the French government) when Colonel-General Valerii Mironov was appointed military adviser to the prime minister in 1995 and assigned a small staff of his own. (Mironov had recently been dismissed from his post as deputy minister of defence in January the same year, following his criticism of the war in Chechnya.[143]) However, this arrangement – instituted on the advice of Kokoshin – was dismantled.[144]

Kokoshin also claims that Chernomyrdin's Administrative Department played a crucial role when it was headed by Stepashin. As head of the Government's Administrative Department between November 1995 and July 1997, Stepashin was made a member of the Defence Council and created subdivisions of the Administrative Department that were responsible for defence financing and defence planning.[145] When he went on to become minister of justice, the Administrative Department lost much of its clout in military affairs. Aleksandr Piskunov probably took over some of the responsibility for military reform within the Apparatus of the Government when he became its deputy head. He left this post in January 2000 after being elected to the Duma in December 1999.[146]

A central part of the reform effort of 1997–98 was gaining control over defence spending. Starting in 1997, the Ministry of Finance intensified its efforts to control the way in which the defence budget was disbursed, something that hitherto had largely been handled by the Ministry of Defence.[147] Within the Ministry of Finance, the Department for Financing the Defence Complex and Law-Enforcement Organs was charged with this task. Liubov Kudelina headed this department between 1996 and 2001.

There was also an initiative to try and restructure the military–industrial complex in order to make it more viable and useful to the military organization. A special government commission was created in February 1998 and tasked with improving the financial conditions for the military industry and research agencies. First, it was to find funds and forms for liquidating the federal debts for the 1997 procurement and federal special-purpose programme for conversion of the military industry. Second, it was to find a way to transfer the debts of companies to the federal budget and restructure them. Finally, it was to decide the volume of arms and military technology as well as military research that was still in the process of being completed, and to decide the future fate of these.[148]

In August 1998, however, Russia's acute economic crisis dealt a fearful blow not only to military reform but also to the very people pushing it forward in the White House and the Security Council. The prime minister, Kirienko, was dismissed. After a battle in parliament, where Yeltsin sought to reappoint Chernomyrdin, a compromise was reached in appointing Yevgenii Primakov as prime minister. Primakov, in turn, managed to stay in office for less than ten months. Interestingly, during his tenure there were some signs that a new relationship was being considered between the executive and legislative branch, with more power accorded to the parliament.[149] Yeltsin's repeated changes of prime ministers and bouts of illness were becoming increasingly embarrassing and this opened the door for new ideas. Nevertheless, these plans were nipped in the bud when Yeltsin went on to dismiss Primakov and appoint Stepashin as prime minister in May 1999. There is no evidence of military reform playing a prominent role on Primakov's agenda. Stephashin stayed on as prime minister for an even shorter period than Kirienko, but his successor in August 1999, Vladimir Putin, appeared to be more attuned to the needs of the military.

All in all, the impression is that there was very little in the way of initiative on military reform by the government during the Yeltsin era. When military reform was high on the government agenda it was so by virtue of being prioritized within the Presidential Administration, with the Defence Council and then the Security Council as decision-making vehicles of reform. As the impetus for reform petered out in these two presidential institutions, the government's meddling in military reform was again reduced to efforts to curb expenditure and different reshufflings to manage the military–industrial complex.

The government organs in charge of the military–industrial complex and research and development (R&D) were subjected to constant changes. In 1992, there was a Ministry of Science and Technology Policy. Its minister, Boris Saltykov, was also awarded the rank of deputy prime minister. In March 1993, Saltykov was demoted from the rank of deputy prime minister, but remained as minister of science and technology policy until 1996, when the ministry was degraded to a state committee instead.[150] A Ministry of Defence Industry was created by presidential decree in May 1996. This ministry replaced an earlier arrangement whereby a State Committee on the Defence Branches of Industry had supervised these policy areas. The creation of a new ministry was accompanied by a decree on measures to improve conditions within the defence industry. Zinovii Pak became minister of defence industry and remained so for less than a year. His ministry was disbanded in March 1997 and the policy area transferred to the Ministry of the

Economy. The minister of the economy, Yakov Urinson was also awarded the rank of deputy prime minister.[151]

The Ministry of Science and Technology Policy was resurrected in March 1997 and Vladimir Fortov made its minister. At the same time, Deputy Prime Minister Vladimir Bulgak received overall responsibility for research policy. Bulgak was demoted in April 1998 and went on to replace Fortov as minister of science and technology policy.[152] In 1999, the defence industry underwent a structural reform again and was organized into five agencies – the Russian Aerospace Agency, the Russian Agency for Ammunition, the Russian Agency for Conventional Weapons, the Russian Agency for Control Systems and the Russian Agency for Shipbuilding. A total of over 1,600 companies were subordinated to this structure.[153]

The above description of the organizational changes that the MIC and R&D underwent during this period is far from exhaustive. Overall, the constant restructuring of the government machinery in charge of the defence industry and R&D creates the impression that this was a policy area that the political leadership was struggling with. Perhaps there was a real eagerness to restructure, but the government constantly found that it had failed to come up with the ultimate solution. However, it is even more probable that these questions were simply not given the priority they should have had if the MIC and military R&D were to be restructured. The sector remained largely unreformed. The average age of its personnel rose (especially within R&D) and production equipment grew obsolete. Meanwhile, the drop in defence production was in no way matched by a decrease in the number of companies of the MIC.[154]

The legislative branch continued to be marginalized in defence policy making. The Duma had little access to information about military spending. The main way in which the Duma could influence military matters was in the annual budget process.[155] However, its chances of exercising control and scrutiny over the defence budget or military policy as a whole were almost non-existent. Only a fraction of the different items of military spending were disclosed to the parliamentarians, with the exception of Duma deputies on the Committee on Defence.[156] Interestingly, the Duma deputies proved rather reluctant to become more familiar with military secrets. Since there are restrictions on travelling abroad the minute you become a bearer of state secrets, deputies preferred not to know about defence issues. The result was that only deputies who were former officers, and already had access to classified information, saw the defence budget details.[157]

On a more general level, the defence policy of the Duma was inconsistent during the Yeltsin period. The Duma, dominated by opponents of Yeltsin, made vociferous demands for more spending on the Armed Forces. Demands for more resources and respect for the Armed Forces was generally perceived as a vote-winner by politicians like Communist Party leader Gennadii Ziuganov and Vladimir Zhirinovskii on the nationalist wing. The Duma even started impeachment proceedings against Yeltsin, one of the accusations being that he had destroyed the army and thereby weakened Russia's ability to defend itself and its security.[158] The impeachment proceedings had little or no prospect of success. Like so many other activities of the Duma, it was to a large degree a public relations exercise for Duma deputies eager for media attention. At the same time, the Duma continued to approve budgets that left the Ministry of Defence with a very meagre budget.[159] This political track record of the Duma in defence affairs no doubt also explains why Yeltsin was loath to grant parliament powers of scrutiny like those accorded to the State Military Inspectorate.

When military officers gained seats in the Duma it sometimes appeared that the parliament would gain a role in military affairs. An example of this was Lev Rokhlin, who started his political career as chairman of the Defence Committee. He gained this position as a member of Chernomyrdin's political party Our Home Is Russia. However, as his frustration grew with the way the political leadership was handling the problems within the Armed Forces, he distanced himself increasingly from this party. In defiance, he founded his own political movement, the Movement in Support of the Army (Dvizhenie v podderzhku armii, DPA) on 20 September 1997.[160]

The central goals of Rokhlin's movement were, first, cooperation for a stronger army with a sounder financial basis and, second, improving the social conditions of military personnel and their families. His agenda was hardly innovative. It centred on restoring honour and budgetary means to the military, and Rodionov, who entertained similar views, soon joined ranks with Rokhlin.[161] However, Rokhlin also demanded the resignation of Yeltsin and Chernomyrdin and soon gravitated towards the Communist Party for political support.[162] In 1998, Rokhlin was murdered and his movement came under the leadership of of the communist politician, Viktor Iliukhin. It then rapidly lost influence.[163] Rokhlin's wife was charged with the murder, but rumours that Rokhlin had been disposed of because of his political opposition to the Kremlin were rife.

The former head of the FPS, Andrei Nikolaev, became a knowledgeable and leading voice in the debate on military reform after he became a member of parliament in April 1998. As chairman of the Committee on Defence, Nikolaev was more inclined towards recreating an 'old-fashioned draft army' than the smaller but leaner army that the Kremlin's reform plans envisaged.[164] His chances of influencing policy making were also hampered by the obstructive role that the Duma had come to play in Russian politics by this time. Military reform was one of the topics that a number of politicians were only too eager to use to score easy political points.

In 1998, the Committee on Defence made an attempt to strengthen its powers to scrutinize the Ministry of Defence. It presented a draft law, On Civil Control of the Military Organization. It is difficult to see why the law was drafted, since even the Committee on Defence seemed very pessimistic about it ever being enacted. In November 1998, the draft had been presented to the government, which the committee believed would be most reluctant to recommend it for legislation. One of the aims of the suggestion was to achieve greater transparency in the handling of the defence budget. On the one hand, the government would become obliged to actually disburse the money promised in the budget; on the other hand, the MoD would have to account 'for every rouble' it received.[165] The draft law continued to live on in different versions, and as late as February 2005 was still only a draft with very little prospect of passing into law.[166]

There were few groups outside the military who played any important role in military reform.[167] In the late 1990s, specialists in military affairs outside the Ministry of Defence did become more common, although many of them were retired officers.[168] The influence of the Council on Foreign and Defence Policy (SVOP) grew in the 1990s and it became established as one of the most important fulcrums of thinking on military affairs outside the General Staff. In 1997, SVOP presented its own suggestions for military reform or 'Theses on Defence Policy' in *Nezavisimoe voennoe obozrenie*.[169] Although its prescriptions were not adopted on any scale, it was clear that SVOP had gained a voice in defence policy making – partly thanks to the fact that many of its members were active or former members of the very decision-making machinery it sought to influence. Among NGOs, the Committee of Soldiers' Mothers constituted an exception in that it was able to influence policy making, at least during the war in Chechnya. Other organizations were less successful.[170] Rokhlin's DPA received considerable media attention in 1997–98, but there is no evidence of it having had a real effect on policy making.

Russia's military organization during Yeltsin's second term

Despite progress during Igor Sergeev's tenure as minister of defence, it is obvious that essential features of military reform were missing. There were structural reforms and reductions, but little in the way of reform of leadership, training and education; civilian control was not introduced, and so on. The military–industrial complex remained neglected and procurement plans suffered badly from the poor state of Russia's economy. Nor was there a serious attempt to solve the manning problem in a long-term perspective and there was little evidence of new military thinking and planning that was in line with the new security and military doctrines that were presented.

It is not entirely correct to talk of 'Sergeev's reform plan' (Box 5.2). Strictly speaking, the general thrust of the plans described below was elaborated before Sergeev became minister of defence. However, reform took several steps forward after his appointment. Sergeev was a man who was prepared to implement them. During his time as chief of the Stategic Missile Forces (Raketnye voiska strategicheskogo naznacheniia, RVSN), his troops were the ones that managed the difficult times that befell the Armed Forces the best. For example, the RVSN managed to keep hold of a higher proportion of its junior officers than any other service of the Armed Forces.[171] He was the first minister of defence ever to come from the RVSN. Another thing that set

Box 5.2 Defence Minister Sergeev's reform plans as presented in 1997

Phase 1 (1997–2000)

- In 1997, merger of the Strategic Missile Forces (RVSN), the Military Space Troops (VKS) and PKO forces to create a new service, the Strategic Missile Forces; reorganization of the Ground Forces Main Command.
- By 1 January 1998, presentation of draft statutes for the MoD and General Staff.
- During 1997–8, reduction of the number of military districts to six with the status of operative-strategic commands in strategic directions.
- By 1 January 1998 the Air Defence Forces (PVO) and the air force (VVS) were to be united into one service; the Armed Forces should be a four-service structure; optimization of the personnel of the VVS and PVO.
- By 1 January 1999 personnel reductions should have resulted in Armed Forces numbering 1.2 million.
- The government was to deliver suggestions on how to finance personnel reductions and social protection for servicemen and their families. Any funds that the Ministry of Defence received from privatization of military property or providing services were to provide benefits and housing for personnel who left the Armed Forces as a result of reductions.
- In 1998, the share of expenditure devoted to military training was to increase from 1% to 10%.

Phase 2 (2000–2005)

- A three-service structure of the Armed Forces according to their sphere of use: (1) ground, (2) air and space, and (3) sea. Prepare for a planned increase of the qualitative parameters for the forces by developing from 2005 the newest types of weaponry and military equipment, raising the level of operative and battle training, improving the command systems of the Armed Forces. Expenditure on weaponry and military equipment was to increase by three times by 2001 and by four times by 2005. Rearming of the Armed Forces would commence by 2005 and be concluded by 2025.

Sources: Excerpts from presidential decree no. 725s, 16 July 1997, in *Rossiiskaia gazeta*, 19 July 1997, p. 5; and article by Igor Sergeev in *Nezavisimoe voennoe obozrenie*, 1997, no. 35 (19–25 September), pp. 1, 3. See also *Kommersant daily*, 25 July 1997, p. 3.

Sergeev apart from earlier ministers of defence was the fact that he had studied economics.[172]

In June 1997, only one month after becoming minister of defence, Sergeev reported to the president that the Collegium of the Ministry of Defence had approved the plans to radically reorganize the army and navy. He claimed that the views of many senior commanders had changed radically. The 'reform proposals' had in fact been approved by all the deputy ministers of defence, as well as by the service chiefs – possibly in part out of fear of further purges following Rodionov's dismissal.[173] Sergeev went on to present his military reform proposal to the Defence Council's commission on military development, headed by the prime minister (see above), on 24 July 1997. Yeltsin was away on holiday and the Defence Council did not convene. After years of empty exhortations, discussions and general vacillation, plans were being proposed and adopted at an unprecedented speed, and Sergeev became widely criticized, not least by fellow officers, for the haste with which the reform proposal had been developed.[174] As mentioned above, the plans had probably existed before. Sergeev was to present and implement them. Consequently, the commission adopted the plans without much discussion.

Sergeev was also criticized for favouring the RVSN at the expense of (primarily) the Ground Forces. He brought with him to the Ministry of Defence a number of officers from the RVSN and placed them in key positions. This was, of course, not appreciated by officers from the Ground Forces who had traditionally occupied these posts.[175] It was not done merely to favour high-ranking officers from Sergeev's own service. The plan behind it was probably to curb the opposition to reform by placing less conservative officers in strategic positions within the ministry.[176] Likewise, the move to abolish the Ground Forces Command and divide its functions between a number of key directorates within the MoD, with the main responsibility being given to the newly instituted Main Directorate for the Ground Forces, could be interpreted as designed to overcome resistance to reform within the Ground Forces.[177]

The Armed Forces

The Ground Forces were subject to significant reductions both in personnel and in numbers of formations and units. The head of the newly established Main Directorate for the Ground Forces, Colonel-General Yurii Bukreev, stated in 1999 that the Ground Forces consisted of about 300,000 servicemen and that no further reductions were planned.[178] Compared to 1990 the number of formations (*soedineniia*) of the Ground Forces had been reduced from 212 to 24. Only seven formations, three divisions and four brigades, were in 'permanent readiness' (*v postoiannoi boevoi gotovnosti*), the new highest category for military formations and units, which meant that they were manned to 80 per cent and had received 100 per cent of the weapons and military equipment they were allotted. They should be ready for military operations within a few days. In the next category, 'formations and units with reduced personnel' (*soedineniia i chasti sokrashchennogo sostava*), there were 21 divisions and 10 brigades. These were only manned to 10–15 per cent but 100 per cent equipped and should be ready to deploy within thirty days. In addition, there was a third category – 'the strategic reserves' (*strategicheskie rezervy*) – with units (*chasti*) that were little more than mobilization stores equipped with weapons and military technology, but with no permanent personnel. These were intended for mobilization in the event of a large-scale aggression against Russia within three months. The peacekeeping formations (such as the 201st Motorized Rifle Division in Tajikistan) were fully manned, but were in administrative terms no longer part of the Ground Forces. All in all these formations numbered about 30,000 servicemen.[179]

Meanwhile, the star of the RVSN was in the ascendant with Igor Sergeev as minister of defence. Shortly after appointing Sergeev, Yeltsin signed a decree that merged the RVSN with the Military Space Troops (Voennye kosmicheskie voiska, VKS) and the Missile Space Defence Troops (Raketno-kosmicheskaia oborona, RKO). The idea had been maturing for some time and it 'united all the strike, information and early warning defence systems vital to the deterrence and retaliatory power of the state'.[180] Large savings were also anticipated as a result of increasing administrative effectiveness.[181] A significant share (perhaps as much as 80 per cent) of the R&D and procurement budget was to be devoted to RVSN-related projects (such the new generation of intercontinental ballistic missiles (ICBMs), the Topol-M (SS-27)).[182] This preferential treatment of the RVSN caused resentment among the other services of the Armed Forces and signified the opening of a battle of wills between Igor Sergeev and Anatolii Kvashnin. The latter defended the interests of the army while Sergeev represented a line of thinking that put emphasis on nuclear weapons to compensate for Russia's conventional military weaknesses. At first, it seemed that Sergeev's line would prevail. However, with time Kvashnin's influence grew and at a meeting of the Security Council in August 2000, the battle was settled in favour of Kvashnin.[183]

In 1992, Russia's Air Defence Forces (Protivo-vozdushnaia oborona, PVO) still constituted a service of the Armed Forces. Although there were suggestions early on that the PVO should be merged with the air force, these plans did not materialize while Grachev and Rodionov were ministers of defence. To the PVO, the fall of the Soviet Union signified the implosion of its structure with early-warning and space system installations scattered over a territory that was now mainly outside the borders of Russia – a structure that would take years to reconstruct even without severe budget cuts. The PVO, moreover, received little in the way of new weapons systems. One way of improving the situation somewhat was Russia's efforts to achieve air defence cooperation within the CIS. The CIS states had agreed to keep a common air defence system in July 1992, but this agreement was rapidly undermined by the individual states' wishes to create national armed forces. In February 1995, the defence ministers of CIS, with the exception of Moldova, Azerbaijan and Turkmenistan, joined forces to recreate a common air defence system.[184]

The Russian air force was hard hit by the dire economic situation. The number of its aircraft decreased drastically between 1992 and 1997 (from 10,000–20,000 to about 5,000) and procurement was low to non-existent. To further complicate matters, it inherited a number of different aircraft, many of which were old. This made maintenance a logistical nightmare. The older planes were disposed of (for example the MiG-27 and Su-17) and the air force concentrated on keeping its fourth-generation aircraft (such as the MiG-29, MiG-31 and Su-27). The infrastructure that the air force depended upon, such as airfields and maintenance, also deteriorated significantly during the same period and many facilities were disbanded. This infrastructure would take years to repair or replace. Even more serious was the lack of training that Russian pilots received. This was due partly to the fact that the number of pilots greatly exceeded the number of aircraft in good condition, and partly to the lack of fuel. Estimates of average flying time for air force pilots varied from 20 to 30 hours a year. Even taking into account the possibility that a prioritized group of pilots (or first-class pilots) received more training than others, the average lack of training was a serious problem. The prioritized group was bound to retire at some stage and there would not be a cadre of second- and third-class pilots to fill their place.[185]

The situation within the air force and the Air Defence Forces was difficult even in spite of the increased attention to these services that the Gulf War had prompted.[186] The military transport aviation, supposed to play one of the key roles in developing mobile forces, financed parts of its work by taking on commercial missions.[187] This also allowed its pilots to put in the necessary flying hours. Nevertheless, the air force did have an advantage in the fact that Russian aircraft manufacturers were among the military industries best positioned to keep up their know-how even as Russian procurement decreased. The production of military aircraft was able to compete on an international market and the development of fifth-generation aircraft (fourth-generation plus by Western standards) continued. The fourth-generation plus was produced mainly for export during the years 1992–97.[188]

Included in Yeltsin's decree on 16 July 1997 was the merging of the air defence component of the PVO with the air force.[189] (As mentioned above, the space defence component (the RKO) of the PVO was subordinated to the RVSN.) The objective was administrative savings and overall personnel reductions. The integration of the two services took place in two stages. By March 1998, the PVO and air force high commands had been merged. By 1 January 1999, the large formations of the VVS and PVO had been united. The intention was that the process should affect mainly the higher echelons of command and control while leaving the units to work as usual. However, this proved complicated, and one of the major hindrances was the lack of a unified command and control system. As a result, combat readiness dropped during the restructuring, despite Russian reassurances to the contrary,[190] and the rate of procurement remained low.[191]

The situation for the navy proved as difficult as it was for the other services of the Armed Forces. Although it did not have to bring home large numbers of men and equipment from Germany, the navy was left with an excess of ships that should have been decommissioned. The chief of the navy between 1956 and 1985, Admiral Sergei Gorshkov, had stubbornly resisted retiring ships. This was to prove a costly legacy, but it also makes any comparisons of Russia's present naval order of battle with that of the Soviet era precarious.[192] However, the Russian navy suffered severe reductions from 1992 and onwards. By 1997, it retained only about one third of its ships.[193] Its share of the defence budget fell from 23 per cent in 1993 to 9.2 per cent in 1998. The only high-profile naval procurement project was the completion of the missile cruiser *Petr Velikii* in 1996, which consumed enormous resources.[194] Perhaps more serious for the navy in the long term was the fact that most of its main functions of the Cold War era were no longer wanted. Only its role as one of the legs in the nuclear triad remained. This was obvious from the attention paid to nuclear submarines.[195] In other areas, the navy proved irrelevant. Yeltsin, of course, did not find it necessary to procure the support of the navy in his domestic political battle in 1993. Nor was the navy of much use in the war in Chechnya (apart from the Naval Infantry).[196]

When Sergeev took over as minister of defence, the navy had been subject to reductions with little trace of reform measures. Further reductions were imminent. As before, the naval component of the nuclear triad was preserved, but with gradual reductions planned.[197] Furthermore, a structural reform was set in train. In the Kaliningrad region and on the Kamchatka Peninsula, two joint commands were instituted with naval commanders at the helm (see below). This constituted an additional attack on the position of the Ground Forces since it was previously unheard of for units and formations of the Ground Forces to be subordinated to a naval commander.[198] Meanwhile, there was little evidence of adaptation to a new reduced role within the navy. For example, the navy's scientific committee suggested as late as November 2000 that the Northern and Pacific fleets ought to have two or three aircraft-carriers – each.[199] This was evidence of a lingering ambition throughout the 1990s to retain a blue-water navy that was in direct contradiction with economic realities and proclaimed strategic priorities.

In 1998, Yeltsin signed two decrees on the military districts of the Russian Federation.[200] After a revision within the Ministry of Defence it had become apparent that there were no normative documents or laws regulating the military districts. In addition to providing a legal framework, the decrees signified a revised territorial division into seven instead of eight military districts (Leningrad MD, Moscow MD, North Caucasus MD, Volga MD, Ural MD, Siberian MD and Far Eastern MD) and special military-administrative arrangements for the Baltic Sea exclave (the Kaliningrad Special Region) and for the Kamchatka and Chukotka peninsulas (a unified command for the Northeast).[201] Thus, parts of the Transbaikal MD had been transferred the Siberian and Far Eastern MD. Further reorganization of the military administrative division of Russia into six military districts was imminent. The Volga and Ural MDs were to be merged into one. The overall administrative goal was to facilitate coordination between the MoD and other power structures. Not only was this needed in the sphere of command and communications, but there were also potential gains to be made from making the logistical support for the different armed services and power structures in the districts more efficient.[202] As for operational authority, the aim was to make each military district responsible for a strategic direction. The military districts became the main structure for command and control of the military formations of the Armed Forces and other troops situated on their respective territories. Consequently, each military district administration thus became an operational-strategic command (*operativno-strategicheskoe komandovanie*).[203]

In practice, exercises continued to be few and far between during this phase. By 1996, only low-level exercises were conducted, hardly ever at regiment level, within the Ground Forces. There were some signs that military capability could improve somewhat by prioritizing individual units and formations, for example, one division in each military district.[204] The navy conducted a couple of major exercises during 1996 and 1997. Furthermore, a strategic exercise involving the RVSN, air force, navy and strategic command structures took place each October starting in 1993. During these exercises, intercontinental missiles were fired from land and sea as well as cruise missiles from the Long Range Aviation (LRA).[205] Although it is difficult to assess exactly how successful the strategic exercises were, there are indications that the RVSN was not as affected by the general state of decline as the other services of the Armed Forces at this time.[206] This is especially noteworthy, since they were subjected to severe budget decreases and had to tackle the problem of bringing significant amounts of weaponry and equipment from former Soviet republics back to Russia during the same period. Obviously, it was possible to maintain a reasonable level of battle readiness in spite of difficult conditions.

Nor was new military technology introduced into the Armed Forces to any significant extent. In 1999, Bukreev claimed that there were no plans to buy tanks or armoured personnel carriers for the Ground Forces during that year. In view of the financial situation there were no plans to replenish the weaponry of the Ground Forces until 2003. The main efforts were concentrated on R&D and modernization of the existing equipment.[207] The navy received hardly any new ships at all; the keels of those it received up to 2001 were all laid down in the Soviet era.[208]

One of the main problems in the sphere of military equipment was still the existence of a large number of different systems and the lack of standardization. This was the case not only for forces of different ministries, but at a much lower level as well. Bukreev provided an example of this when he claimed that within the motorized rifle regiments there were ninety-nine different weapons and specimens of military equipment. 'One of the main goals for developers is therefore to create standardized battle vehicles and weapons.'[209] Indeed, one of Kokoshin's main goals had been that procurement be organized in a manner that ensured that each new piece of weaponry fitted into military planning as a whole. Success in this area proved a distant prospect.[210]

Defence spending

The financial situation of the Ministry of Defence was untenable during most of the 1990s. For long periods, the ministry was not even able to pay its personnel, despite the lofty promises from the political leadership.[211] In November 1995, the Kremlin was eager to secure votes both in the forthcoming Duma elections, due to take place on 17 December, and in the pending presidential elections in June 1996. For the military organization this led to promises from Prime Minister Viktor Chernomyrdin to make sure the MoD regulated its debts.[212] The most pressing of these debts, in the view of military officers, was no doubt the wage arrears that had been accumulating. This notwithstanding, the defence budget for 1996 (adopted in December 1995) contained more reductions instead of the increases that officers had called for. In December 1995, the Duma approved a budget of 82,462 billion roubles for the defence of the nation. This represented a reduction of 30 trillion roubles for the Armed Forces as compared with the 1995 budget. It was a slight increase compared to the original proposal[213] but was still not enough to rectify the financial situation within the ministry. In the autumn of 1996, well after the election, servicemen and employees of the military–industrial complex together with their families picketed government buildings. They had still not been paid their wages.[214]

There was also a substantial gap in perceptions between the military and the political elite when it came to the question of whether military reform ought to be financed within the existing defence budget or separately by additional funding. Early on, Grachev expressed the view that the costs that reductions entailed ought not to be included in the defence budget.[215] Politicians, on the other hand, claimed that reductions should free additional resources within the framework of the defence budget. Yeltsin stated in November 1992 that the defence budget for 1993 would remain at the level of that of 1992 in comparable prices 'in spite of the reductions undertaken'.[216] Nor was there agreement on whether social costs (such as military pensions) should be included in the defence budget. In his first state of the nation address to the Duma in February 1994, Yeltsin underlined that defence expenditure did not equal war expenditure and exemplified that substantial parts of the budget went to science and the building of housing.[217] Military circles, of course, thought that the defence budget should not to be burdened by social costs. In 1998 this line prevailed and military pensions were moved from the defence budget to the social budget.[218]

Not only was the Ministry of Defence allotted what it regarded to be insufficient resources through the defence budget; a significant portion of it continued to be sequestered. According to Pavel Grachev, this had been the case since 1993. On 1 January 1994 only 6.5 of the 7.5 trillion roubles promised in the defence budget had been disbursed to the ministry. During 1994, 12.3 trillion roubles had been sequestred out of the original allotment of 37.7 trillion (the MoD had originally requested 83.0 trillion roubles). For 1995, the situation was equally sinister: on 1 November the MoD had received only 30.3 trillion roubles, while the original defence budget had been 45.6 trillion roubles. As a result, in November 1995 the debts of the MoD amounted to 16 trillion roubles.[219] It was obvious that Kokoshin's appeal to the Duma in December 1994 had resulted in no significant changes. Instead, the MoD had doubled its debts (according to Kokoshin they amounted to 8.7 trillion roubles in December 1994).[220] The situation in the defence industry was also critical. Procurement almost came to a halt in 1993. In spite of the meagre funding, the MoD continued to produce what was more or less a procurement wish list rather than one that was adapted to economic realities.[221] This probably added to the difficulties in finding a sound strategy for restructuring the defence industry.

As mentioned above, the parliament had only limited possibilities to scrutinize the defence budget. A member of the Committee on Defence, the liberal representative of the party Russia's Choice, Sergei Yushenkov, complained in 1994 that the Duma had access to only five specified expense lines in the defence budget.[222] All allegations of excessive secretiveness were, however, refuted by the Ministry of Defence. In 1994 the deputy head of the MoD's Main Directorate for the Defence Budget and Financing, Lieutenant-General Vasilii Kuznetsov, claimed that the defence budget was not secret, except for the secret weapons and research programmes. In his view, the defence budget was sufficiently scrutinized by the ministry itself and the Ministry of Finance.[223] This was a tacit acknowledgement that the Duma did not have the powers to scrutinize the budget. It only had the power to approve the proposed budget in its overall form, with five types of expenses specified: (a) the purchase and repair of military technology; (b) scientific R&D; (c) upkeep of the army and the navy; (d) major construction and repair works; and (e) providing pensions for servicemen in the reserve or in retirement.[224]

As stated above, approving or not approving the budget could have been a way of influencing defence policy for the Duma if it had had access to more information and analytical resources. However, between 1992 and 1997 the Russian national budgets were above all statements of intent.[225] Since the promised funds were not actually allocated to the Ministry of Defence, the budgets would have been poor instruments of scrutiny for the Duma.

In connection with the need to get military reform under way in 1996, there were also initiatives to gain control of the way in which the defence budget was spent. In September 1996, the government formed a Commission on Questions of Financing the National Defence, Law-Enforcement Activity and Ensuring State Security.[226] According to the commission's secretary, the deputy head of the Government's Administrative Department, now Aleksandr Piskunov, the gap between the demands of the power structures and the provisions in the budget had increased constantly during the past few years. A new practice had been established, according to Piskunov. The power ministries and agencies asked for what they knew was impossible sums of money. When they received only a fraction of what they asked for, they regarded it as wholly up to them to decide on how to spend it. The Ministry of Finance, in turn, regarded it the responsibility of, for example, the minister of defence to ensure that funds were used effectively. 'As a result, a very convenient system of collective irresponsibility has been established.'[227]

The Ministry of Defence and Ministry of Finance were thus responsible for scrutiny of the defence budget. A sign that this procedure was not working was the number of corruption scandals at the very highest level that were exposed later – and then through the efforts of the media rather than those of the MoD or Ministry of Finance. Piskunov stated in 1996 that the new head of the Main Directorate for the Defence Budget and Financing of the MoD, Major-General Georgii Oleinik, in contrast to his predecessor, admitted that the defence budget needed to be specified more in detail than the five expense lines mentioned above.[228] In other words, the civilian leadership was relatively optimistic about making progress in establishing control over defence spending at this time. However, the very same Oleinik was later convicted of corruption, having caused the state a loss of about 60 million US dollars or 344 million roubles.[229]

Even more damaging was the fact that there was no sign of the Kremlin gaining control over the defence spending of the entire military organization. While the Armed Forces were reduced and subject to decreasing budgets, the other power ministries appeared to be growing. In other words, there was reason to question whether the military burden on the economy had in fact been reduced. Russia had reached a situation where its spending on military and security was considerable and crippling much of its economy, while at the same time the army was in many ways impoverished and unable to fulfil some of its basic tasks.

The Ministry of Defence vs other power ministries

The initial reform plan in 1997 spoke of serious reductions in the troops of all the power ministries. There was a realization that the budgets and personnel of other power ministries had been allowed to grow partly at the expense of the Ministry of Defence. Consequently, there were plans for defence procurement and the rear services to be coordinated from the General Staff of the MoD in order for the defence sector to become more cost-effective.[230] In early 1998, there were also suggestions that the FPS should be subordinated to the FSB. According to newspapers at the time, Yeltsin had commissioned the government and the State-Legal Directorate of the Presidential Administration to prepare a presidential decree along these lines. This would have put an end to the far-reaching ambitions of the FPS, which had flourished during Andrei Nikolaev's time as its director. In the words of one newspaper, he had developed the Border Troops into a 'second army' with its own military schools, heavy equipment, intelligence and counter-intelligence.[231] In the event, the merger did not happen (until 2003). Possibly, allegations that the subordination of the FPS to the FSB was only the first measure to recreate the Soviet KGB played a role. It also seemed that the savings from the merger would not be as substantial as first imagined.[232]

Many of the structural changes of the military organization as a whole, which prioritized internal security at the expense of external military security, came about not as a result of an analysis of which security needs required which troop formations. Instead, the role and manpower of the Interior Troops and other paramilitary formations such as the Presidential Guards grew because Yeltsin felt these were more likely to buttress his own power. Accordingly, Yeltsin prioritized boosting the number of Interior Troops stationed inside and around Moscow by 50,000 men in 1994.[233] In addition, the Border Troops during this period started to demand funding not only for protecting (*okhrana*) but also for the *defence* (*oborona*) of Russia's frontiers.[234] The head of the FPS, Nikolaev, proved a very efficient lobbyist for the Border Troops, in contrast to the Ministry of Defence.[235] Nikolaev should be credited with having created a border troop service from what was in effect a shambles in the wake of the fall of the Soviet Union. However, it is equally true that the proliferation of power ministries with separate rear services, military schools and ambitious procurement plans was undermining any serious attempt at building a cost-effective and coordinated military organization at a national level. (This strengthened position of troops other than the Armed Forces is not entirely reflected in Table 5.1. For example, the Railway Troops, the troops of FAPSI and the FSO are not included.[236])

As mentioned above, there were initiatives in November 1996 to curb the influence of the power ministries and to reduce their manpower levels. Yeltsin's November decree 'On Measures to Ensure Defence Development in the Russian Federation' contained such intentions. The number of power structures to receive conscripts was limited to the Armed Forces, the Border Troops, the Interior Troops and the Railway Troops. Other ministries and agencies such as the MChS and FAPSI were thus to employ all their servicemen on a contract basis from 1 January 1997, according to Yeltsin's decree. It also stated that all troops other than the Armed Forces were to be reduced by 15 per cent during 1997. As so often before, these intentions were effectively countered by the different power structures concerned. The power structures outside the Armed Forces continued to rely on conscripts and their troops were by no means reduced by the stated 15 per cent.[237] That the power structures did not suffer reductions is also evident from the personnel figures for the late 1990s. Nor were the plans to centralize procurement and the rear services for all power ministries to the Ministry of Defence realized.

The rumours that the FPS would be subordinated to the FSB were, no doubt, regarded as a mixed blessing within the FSB. On the one hand, its powers would increase. On the other hand, the FPS had developed its own legal framework and routines during several years as an independent service. Incorporating the FPS into the FSB would thus be a significant task. There were also rumours at that time that the FSB would lose its Directorate of Investigation to either the Ministry of Justice or the General Procuracy and that FAPSI would be subordinated to the FSB.[238] Nothing came of this.

During this second phase, moreover, the plans to transfer military counter-intelligence from the FSB to the Ministry of Defence were shelved. This remained the responsibility of the third directorate of the FSB, the Directorate of Military Counter-intelligence, (Upravlenie voennoi kontrrazvedki, UVKR), which has its own units within the structure of the Armed Forces. Its personnel numbered about 6,000 in 1997 and were a mix of what should probably be termed military police and counter-intelligence personnel.[239] A new director of the FSB was appointed in July 1998 – Vladimir Putin, who succeeded Nikolai Kovalev. He would later, shortly upon becoming acting president, sign a decree approving new statutes on the FSB military counter-intelligence.[240] Clearly, the FSB was set to retain the responsibility for military counter-intelligence for the foreseeable future.

A partial reform of the MVD was conducted in 1998. At the time, this was mainly connected to the dismissal of Anatolii Kulikov in March 1998 and the appointment of Sergei Stepashin as minister of internal affairs.[241] This was also part of the overall attempt at reforming the military organization rather than just the Armed Forces of the Ministry of Defence. There were signs that the MVD had lost whatever favoured status it may have enjoyed as a result of its support for Yeltsin in October 1993. Stepashin announced in June 1998 that the Interior Troops were to be reduced from about 250,000 men to 120,000–140,000 over a two-year period (this is to a degree reflected in Table 5.4, but with a year's timelag). He also stated that Russia had no need for a parallel structure of armed forces duplicating that of the MoD.[242] However, the reductions Stepashin mentioned were not carried out in full and the Interior Troops increased somewhat in numbers in the following years again. One of the ideas behind the reform was to improve the quality of Russia's police force. This would become yet another example of half-measures since the MVD proved nowhere close to this goal in late 1999.

Again, the difficulties of calculating the manpower of Russia's military organization need to be stressed. This is demonstrated by the fact that only in 1998 did the Ministry of Defence conduct an inventory. The inventory revealed that the ministry employed approximately 300,000 more personnel than officially registered. Although this figure included mainly civilian personnel, it gives some indication of the degree of caution that is needed in interpreting official figures provided from the MoD.[243] Some of the changes in Table 5.4 are probably best explained by changes in the way the numbers

Table 5.4 Level of manpower within the military organization, 1997–2000

Year	MoD Armed Forces		MVD	FSB et al.	Paramil.	Total*
1996/7	Total	1,270,000	232,000	100,000**	352,000	1,622,000
1997/8	Total	1,089,000	329,000	220,000,(FPS)	583,000	1,672,000
	Ground	400,000		9,000 (FSB)		
	Air Def.	170,000		25,000 (FSO)		
	Navy	220,000				
	Air	130,000				
	RVSN	149,000				
1998/9	Total	959,000	237,000	200,000 (FPS)	543,000	1,502,000
	Ground	420 000		9,000 (FSB)		
	Air Def.	–		25,000 (FSO)		
	Navy	180,000		54,000 (FAPSI)		
	Air	210,000				
	RVSN	149,000				
1999/2000	Total	1,004,100	140,000	196,000 (FPS)	478,000	1,482,100
	Ground	348,000		4,000 (FSB)		
	Navy	171,500		25,000 (FSO)		
	Air	184,600		54,000 (FAPSI)		
	RVSN	149,000		59,000 (Railw.)		

Sources: *The Military Balance 1997{/}98, 1998/99, 1999/2000.*

Notes:
The totals of the services of the Armed Forces and the different paramilitary forces do not always add up. The totals presented are those given in *The Military Balance* except for the totals in the last column.
*   Total calculated from Armed Forces plus paramilitary forces total – not given in *The Military Balance.*
** The uncertainty in the numbers of paramilitary troops is demonstrated in the apparent jump back to 220,000 in the number of troops belonging to the FPS between *The Military Balance 1996{/}1997* and *1997/1998*.

were aggregated rather than a real increase.[244] Part of the increase in 1999–2000 described above could, for example, be explained by the inclusion of Railway Troops and similar units together with FAPSI's troops, which had not previously been included in the estimates in *The Military Balance*. The Interior Troops suffered reductions, but hardly any other paramilitary troops did. Furthermore, some of the apparent reductions of troop personnel could simply be an effect of draft evasion. In other words, the positions and units still existed, but sparsely manned or not manned at all.

In common with the efforts to carry out a thorough reform of the Armed Forces, the intention to reduce the power ministries faded with the dismissal of Kokoshin and the onset of the economic crisis in August 1998. The situation hardly improved when Putin became dependent on the power ministries for conducting a renewed war in Chechnya. The terrorist attacks against what the Russian public perceived as the Russian heartland, not least the bombings of apartment buildings in Moscow in 1999, meant that security policy was prioritized and authorities such as the FSB and the MVD came to the fore again. There was little evidence of reductions in the military troops and units of the power ministries other than the Ministry of Defence and the Interior Troops. By early 2001, the Armed Forces still constituted only about half of the military organization according to an estimate in *Nezavisimoe voennoe obozrenie.*[245] In other words, little had been done in the way of streamlining the military organization as a whole. Other signs of reform measures were also lacking. The power ministries continued to run parallel rear services and there was little evidence of improved cooperation between them or a system of joint procurement.

Manning the military organization – quantity and quality

Bringing troops home from, above all, East Germany was a formidable undertaking and left many servicemen stranded as they returned to Russia without accommodation prepared, while a number of highly placed officers profited substantially.[246] In the early 1990s there was widespread resentment within the Armed Forces. Trust in politicians was low – not least as a result of the break-up of the Soviet Union.[247] In addition to seeing the Armed Forces chopped up and their authority in society undermined, servicemen clenched their teeth as their political masters changed the emblems and banners that had once been a source of pride and tradition.[248]

To add insult to injury, the Ministry of Defence proved unable to pay its servicemen their wages. In 1992, Yeltsin had showed some interest in the social conditions of servicemen. A whole day was devoted to this subject in July 1992. Clearly, this problem appeared at the time to be soluble. *Krasnaia zvezda* started an article on the subject by stating that the days when servicemen and their families were expected to accept difficult living conditions were over. 'Today, thank God, there is another approach. Politicians have recognized that the state does not have the right to remain eternally in debt to the military, year after year just establishing the increasing figure of their chronic housing shortage.'[249]

Contrary to any expectations that *Krasnaia zvezda's* article may have produced, the situation was not to improve in the foreseeable future. In December 1993, Grachev listed this as a priority, but the problem remained. This left Russian officers to fend for their families as best they could, occasionally by selling uniforms and other items of military equipment in local markets.[250] The social conditions for servicemen deteriorated at a steady pace. Their wages lagged behind those of the rest of society, and were often not paid at all, and the benefits Russian officers had become used to were dwindling. For the servicemen of the Armed Forces yet another source of frustration was, no doubt, the fact that they were paid less than those working for other power agencies such as the Border Troops.[251]

The lack of structural changes of the Armed Forces had dire consequences for the personnel situation. The personnel structure that Russia inherited contained a high proportion of high-ranking officers.[252] Grachev claimed in July 1992 that the number of generals would be drastically reduced, especially within the central apparatus.[253] However, there is little evidence of this having happened in practice. The Russian Armed Forces continued to be over-whelmingly top-heavy. Many of these high-ranking officers were, of course, the same generals who were put in charge of reductions, which they were loath to implement. Meanwhile, Yeltsin probably avoided cutting back on the central military bureaucracy for fear of losing support that he might need in power battles with his opposition.[254]

The number of servicemen within the Armed Forces did diminish throughout much of the 1990s. However, Anatol Lieven makes the point that mere reductions of numbers were never a problem. Most units were not manned fully with soldiers (some were hardly manned at all) and there is even an argument to be made for the military organization having been smaller than officially stated. The resistance within the military against reductions focused on *units* rather than *personnel*, since fewer military units meant fewer commanding posts for officers.[255] For example, in late 1995, the Ground Forces underwent no substantial structural changes in spite of the personnel reductions that had taken place. Instead there was a multitude of 'empty units' and the waste of resources was considerable.[256]

For the development of the Armed Forces, this was highly detrimental. The lack of soldiers had serious consequences for the officer corps as a whole. At lower levels in the command chain, the lack of conscripts forced officers to perform menial tasks with the result that officers did not receive the training they needed for their future careers. This was further exacerbated by the fact that junior officers had started leaving the Armed Forces in 1994.[257] As a result of this and the increasing difficulties in recruiting conscripts, many units suffered from a serious lack not just of soldiers but of junior officers as well.[258] This led to unbearable conditions for the junior officers who were still employed, and by 1995 promising young officers were leaving the army in large numbers. In turn, this resulted in a serious deficit in company (*rota*) commanders.[259] In other words, a vicious circle had been created. The fact that the Ministry of Defence could not even pay its personnel for long periods of time fomented dissatisfaction and defeatism among officers. It also fuelled corruption within the ranks – sometimes for reasons of personal enrichment, but often as the only way of finding provisions and other necessities for the military units.

In 1992, one of the approaches to solving this problem was an ambitious plan for switching to contract-based employment and the partial abandonment of conscription. Soldiers (*soldaty*), sailors (*matrosy*), sergeants (*serzhanty*) and sergeant majors (*starshiny*) could be employed for contract service.[260] This was to take place in three stages: the first phase involved hiring 100,000 men on contract service during 1993–94; during the second phase, 1994–95, the target was to reach 30 per cent contract soldiers within the Armed Forces; and during phase three, by 2000, the target was 50 per cent.[261]

Although the programme seemed to start well, with the initial targets reached, the problems were soon obvious. Hiring contract soldiers was expensive and the programme was severely underfunded. Furthermore, the quality of the recruits was rarely up to standard.[262] Instead of bridging the gap between conscripts and officers by recruiting the equivalent of non-commissioned officers (NCOs) on a voluntary basis, the cohort that the Ministry of Defence managed to attract predominantly came to serve in the rear and administrative services.[263] Evidence suggests that the manner in which the programme of contract employment was implemented set targets in a Soviet manner which recruitment centres sought to fulfil in an equally Soviet manner. A considerable proportion of the contract-employed personnel were women and there were reports of 'family operation' – commanders manning their units with wives, children and friends.[264] In other words, the programme did little to solve what was a long-term problem for the Armed Forces – creating a cadre that could, on the one hand, provide continuity and experience at lower levels in the command chain, and, on the other hand, constitute a future basis for promoting promising talent to senior command positions. The Armed Forces continued to lack officers to command battalions and units below.

To solve the problem, officers in the reserve were called up. These officers had received their military training at civilian institutions of higher education. However, the head of the Ministry of Defence's Main Directorate for Cadres and Military Education, Colonel-General Ilia Panin, was not satisfied with the quality of the military training at civilian institutions. In August 1998 he did have certain hopes for the experiment that had been initiated with the establishment of officers' schools in the military districts in order to bring the junior officers corps up to strength.[265] However, after the first batch of graduates from these graduated in 1999, the head of the Main Directorate for the Ground Forces, Colonel-General Bukreev, did not consider the experiment a success. The graduates were simply not up to standard.[266] Apart from the failed attempt to institute schools in the respective MDs, the main effort seemed to involve trying to get those who had done a course of a few months to sign on as *kontraktniki*.[267] In other words, there were few signs of a concerted effort to create a new cadre of junior officers.

In spite of these difficulties, large parts of the military establishment were reluctant to make changes in the system for manning Russia's military organization. Abandoning conscription met with opposition. Armed forces manned on contract bases would inevitably mean smaller armed forces. For officers who were unwilling to accept that NATO was no longer the main enemy, rejecting the option of a mass army implied rejecting NATO as the overarching threat. Fewer soldiers also meant fewer units and, thus, fewer career opportunities for the professional officer. In addition, there was a notion that military service was a unique opportunity to make young men into better, patriotic citizens. Finally, certain officers had purely pecuniary reasons for wanting to retain conscription. Conscripts represented not only cheap labour for the Ministry of Defence but also a potential milch cow for the entrepreneurial officer willing to hire his conscripts out as farm workers, builders and so on.[268] The fact that contract soldiers were considerably more expensive than conscripts also made it a less than attractive option to the MoD, which was struggling even to pay its officers their wages on time. Indeed, the plans were unrealistic when it came to force levels and financing these from the very start.

A part of the reform programme agreed upon in 1997 concerned the need to reorganize the system of military training. The main emphasis seemed to be on savings by closing down smaller institutions in order to create large complexes where 1,500 or more could be offered military training. In August 1998, the plan was that by 2000 the Ministry of Defence was to have fifty-seven institutions of higher education (eight military academies, ten military universities and thirty-nine military institutes and colleges). This signified a reduction by almost 50 per cent of the number of institutes for military training. In connection with these changes, a slightly modified hierarchical structure for military training would be introduced (see Table 5.5). The structural reform of the system was more or less implemented by 2003.[269]

There were also ambitions to change the military training curriculum. According to Panin, it was essential to 'organize and conduct training in a manner that put emphasis on developing the students' independent thinking and their creative abilities with extensive use of computer technology in the training process'. He was critical of the level of foreign language training provided by the system; most of the officers only acquired the ability to 'read and understand with the aid of a dictionary'.[270] This would hardly be adequate if Russia were serious in its ambitions to cooperate internationally on a wider basis. However, it is difficult to find evidence of changes in the curriculum of the different military academies. Sarah Mendelson found while doing interviews in Moscow that military and civilian experts were eager to cooperate with the United States in order to gain experience of how the curriculum had changed there after the war in Vietnam. Apparently, the teaching staff at the Russian academies had not incorporated the experiences that the Soviet Union and Russia had gained in Afghanistan and Chechnya.[271]

Initially, Yeltsin demonstrated a certain interest in the new way in which the personnel and conscripts should be trained, and especially in the need to reform the section of the military organization that had been in charge of the political education of servicemen. In a speech to the Collegium of the Ministry of Defence in November 1992, Yeltsin outlined a new role for the personnel

Table 5.5 Hierarchy of institutions of military education according to the 1997 proposal

The Military Academy of the General Staff
1 Military academies of the services of the Armed Forces and the rear services
2 Military universities of the different arms of the Armed Forces
3 Military institutes, military colleges and military faculties at civilian
4 Institutions of higher education

who in the Soviet era had been charged with the political education of the Armed Forces. The infrastructure, previously belonging to Glavpur, would be used 'to educate and inform in order to achieve a spirit of service to the Russian state, respect for the constitution, the laws of Russia and its traditions'.[272] It is worth noting that at this time the constitution and legal framework of Russia were still a patchwork based on the Soviet constitution and laws. There was also much confusion as to what exactly the traditions of Russia as opposed to those of the Soviet Union were and what constituted 'Russian patriotism and military ethic'[273] in the new Russian state. The guidelines for 'educational work' within the military organization changed throughout much of the 1990s. The directorate in charge of educational work was usually given the unrewarding task of combating hazing and corruption by instilling patriotic values.

This was little more than an empty gesture, since the roots of such problems as hazing were considerably more complex. Most importantly, the military organization was in dire need of a trained corps of junior officers or NCOs that did not need to rely upon the *dedy*, the conscripts who had already served most of their term, to instil discipline in the units. The difficulty of finding junior officers coupled with the absence of a corps of NCOs thus compounded the discipline problems that the Armed Forces were suffering from.[274] In addition, more effort was needed in punishing the offenders and the officers who failed to ensure the physical safety of their conscripts. Little progress was made in either of these fields.

It was then hardly surprising that young men with the support of their families proved increasingly unwilling to devote years of their lives to military service. In 1993, the chief of the General Staff, Colonel-General Kolesnikov, was still optimistic that the ability of the Armed Forces to attract conscripts and volunteers would improve substantially:

> If the plan to call up on a voluntary basis, on contract, if the reasons for deferment from army service are revised and the military commissariats fulfil their functions well, then as early as in next year the strength of the Armed Forces could be brought up to 95 per cent.[275]

Earlier the same year Kokoshin had emphasized the need to build 'a new relationship between citizens and the army'.[276]

This optimism was to wane. The military became increasingly worried by the difficulties it encountered in enlisting suitable candidates for military service. In December 1995, the Ministry of Defence, the Ministry of Internal Affairs and the General Procuracy joined forces to combat the increasing level of draft evasion. The goal was to bring more draft evaders to justice.[277] This approach proved less than satisfactory. Enlisting the help of the General Procuracy focused on the problem of draft evasion rather than the reasons behind it.

There were at least four pressing reasons for why the military proved unable to fill its units with conscripts. First, there were a number of perfectly legal provisions that a young man could invoke for not being drafted, such as university studies or medical reasons (and a black market in medical certificates for this purpose soon arose). Second, a number of conscripts proved highly unsuitable for service for medical reasons or because of a social history of alcohol and drug abuse. Five per cent of the draftees in the autumn of 1996 had been convicted of crimes.[278] Russia was faced with a growing demographic problem that had direct consequences for its ability to man its military organization. Third, and perhaps more seriously as a threat to conscription in the long term, the horrific conditions of military service had become well known in society. Not even the military could deny that hazing existed within the Armed Forces. The question of hazing was a concern for the political leadership and, to a certain degree, it cooperated with organizations such as the Committee of Soldiers' Mothers.[279]

Finally, malnourishment and overall difficult living conditions made military service an anything but tempting prospect, not to mention the prospect of being sent to Chechnya. In 1993 the little-known island of Russkii in the Pacific Ocean became a symbol of the dire conditions and lack of discipline that some conscripts were forced to serve under. Four conscripts died from conditions connected with starvation since they were denied their rations by their *dedy*, in other words by the conscripts who had served the longest and forced new recruits to live in unbearable conditions. The scandal was too great for the Ministry of Defence to try and brush it aside and the military and the procuracy conducted an investigation into the incident.[280] Finally, by 1996 the war in Chechnya was probably the last straw for anyone even considering doing military service out of a sense of national duty.

The problems of corruption, crime and hazing in the Armed Forces had not abated by 1998. On the contrary, Igor Sergeev spoke of an increase to the Collegium of the Ministry of Defence in February 1998. He deplored the lack of discipline in the Armed Forces. Among the crimes committed he singled out hazing as one reason why the standing of the Armed Forces had eroded and young men sought to avoid military service.[281] Yet again, however, the measures to rectify the situation were half-measures. Instead of finding ways of guaranteeing the physical and mental safety of conscripts, the MoD devoted considerable effort to achieving legislative changes that would allow it to draft students. It also fought bitterly to block the possibilities for conscientious objection, in spite of the fact that this right was guaranteed in the 1993 constitution.

The other power ministries struggled with similar difficulties as the Armed Forces, but not on the same scale. In the new reform plans and the discussions leading up to these, considerable attention had been been devoted to the need to extend military reform to other ministries as well as the Ministry of Defence.[282] Indeed, one of the solutions to the problems of manning the military organization had been to prioritize the MoD at the expense of the other power ministries. Resistance to this was, of course, strong within the power structures concerned, which had become used to a relatively favoured position. The power ministries were loath to abandon conscription. For example, the interior minister, Anatolii Kulikov, made it clear that he did not consider it possible to abolish conscription. In his view, a ratio of 70:30 of conscripts to contract-employed was a possible recipe in the future. He also rejected the view that the risk of a major global war was minimal.[283] The unwillingness to comply with the new directives was equally strong within other power structures. In the end, the power ministries continued to receive conscripts and very little was done to abolish parallel structures, which could have resulted in savings.

Threat perceptions in the Kremlin and at the Arbat

The military doctrine of 1993 was only intended as a provisional document. The preamble even stated as much. Work on a new military doctrine started in earnest in August 1996.[284] However, a new doctrine would not appear until 2000. Meanwhile, the Russian military was more or less left to formulate its own ideas of threats within the Ministry of Defence on Arbat Street close to the Kremlin and, as a result, the force posture of the military organization remained dimensioned for a major war with the West. It is fortunate that there was little risk of such a war, considering that many of the military units poised to meet NATO aggression lacked personnel and morale was at an all-time low.

Work was also in progress on a new national security concept, which should provide guidelines for the military doctrine that was being developed. The honeymoon with the USA and NATO was definately over by this time and the Defence Council declared that Russia faced new geopolitical conditions. It pointed, for example, to attempts to supplant Russia in regions such as Asia and the Caucasus and to NATO enlargement as new international developments to take into consideration. However, there was also emphasis on local and regional conflicts in Russia or its neighbouring states.[285] In December 1997, the national security concept was adopted by presidential decree and published.[286] The Kremlin appeared to retreat to 'Cold War Lite phraseology'.[287] In effect, the concept was already a thing of the past before it was adopted. The final wording had been hammered out in the Security Council during Rybkin's secretaryship without any real endorsement from Yeltsin.[288] Instead, there circulated a security policy memorandum authored by Yeltsin's adviser Yurii Baturin that in practice overrode the concept.[289]

However, the national security concept raised Russian generals' hopes that money would be forthcoming – which proved a mistaken conclusion. The Kremlin continued to regard the precarious economic situation as one of the main threats to Russia. There was no intention of increasing the defence budget.[290] In less than two years, a new national security concept appeared. In November 1999, a draft concept was published, later to be adopted by Putin in January 2000.[291] The concept of 2000 carried considerably more weight than that of 1997, not least due to the fact that the president, in his former capacity as secretary of the Security Council, had been party to its development. In addition, it appeared before the military doctrine and foreign policy concept and thus, for the first time, it seemed as if doctrinal development was on track in Russia.[292]

The national security concept discussed threats on a general level and failed to provide the clear guidelines that the military organization had been calling for in identifying future enemies. Consequently, military planning did not mirror the foreign policy goals decided in the Kremlin.[293] This was evident not least when the formal doctrines and concepts that circulated were compared to, for example, military planning for the Ground Forces. Clearly, the Cold War obsession with NATO as the main enemy lived on within the army.[294] This was intensified when NATO's campaign in Kosovo started in 1999. Anti-Western criticism in general and anti-NATO views in particular intensified over almost the entire political spectrum. The NATO campaign in Kosovo also appeared to reveal the hollowness of Sergeev's assertion that nuclear weapons could compensate for conventional weakness. It was obvious that this was true only for nuclear deterrence, whereas Russia's possibilities of influencing NATO decision making in Kosovo, short of threatening nuclear war, were almost non-existent without the capability to project conventional force on any kind of scale.[295] The rhetoric of great power ambitions and the real state of Russia's military organization proved a mismatch for everyone to see.

Any lingering doubts as to where the General Staff considered the main threat to lie were dispersed when it staged the first strategic exercise since the fall of the Soviet Union. The Zapad-99 exercise, conducted in the summer of 1999 after NATO's operation in Kosovo, involved a scenario with a hostile attack against Kaliningrad and Belarus. The main elements of the scenario were probably formulated in the General Staff well before NATO's bombing of Serbia, but there were nevertheless too many coincidences for observers not to assume that events in Kosovo had played a part in the way Zapad-99 developed and the way it was portrayed in the media. For example, the number of attacking aircraft corresponded to that used by NATO in Kosovo (although a claim could also be made that the number corresponded roughly to what Russian and Belarusan air defences could reasonably be expected to assemble). As if to emphasize that NATO and the USA was the attacking side, the exercise ended with a demonstrative Russian nuclear response against the American West Coast and continental Europe.[296]

Civil–military relations

Civil–military relations developed unevenly and reform was limited to certain areas and short periods of time. After years of virtual inattention to defence policy making and of letting the different power ministries formulate their own policy goals, the Kremlin suddenly turned its attention to military reform between late 1996 and 1998. There was a concerted effort on the part of the political leadership during this period to wrest control over defence policy making from the military establishment, and results were evident in the coming years, mainly within the Armed Forces. Decision making became coordinated first in the Defence Council and later in the Security Council. However, even during this active period of defence policy making, fundamental elements were missing. The main weakness was that success in reforming the military organization was dependent upon the determination of a few critically positioned decision makers (such as Baturin and Kokoshin), rather than on an institutional framework that could provide long-term stability and fixity of purpose. Perhaps if this had been achieved or crucial actors had remained in their positions, military reform would have embraced the whole of the military organization and the MIC, rather than being concentrated on the Armed Forces.

The legislative and judicial branch remained impotent when it came to scrutinizing the defence decisions of the executive and the extent of their implementation within the military organization. In other words, institutional mechanisms for ensuring that military reform stayed on track were weak outside the Kremlin. Society grew somewhat stronger in its ability to scrutinize and exercise influence on defence policy during the 1990s as think tanks appeared, as well as an independent press that wrote on military affairs. The Committee of Soldiers' Mothers also played a certain role. However, this could never be a substitute for parliamentary and judicial control, and it would later become obvious that this development was reversible.

The Ministry of Defence remained largely unreformed and was nowhere nearer to becoming an integrated ministry where military and civilian personnel worked alongside each other. During Andrei Kokoshin's tenure as first minister of defence, there were efforts to improve cooperation between the two first deputy ministers of defence, Kokoshin and the chief of the General Staff, Mikhail Kolesnikov. Two councils were created within the MoD. Kokoshin headed the Council on Military Technological Policy, for which the chief of the General Staff was deputy chairman. Similarly, Kokoshin was deputy chairman for the Council for Military Strategic Questions, which was headed by the chief of the General Staff.[297] In 1996, Kokoshin was also appointed state secretary by presidential decree.[298] This, at first glance, would appear to have strengthened his position within the MoD. However, there were no other civilians in high posts within the ministry and Kokoshin's own staff remained very small. Furthermore, the post of state secretary involved responsibility for contacts with parliament. Any hopes the military officers within the MoD might have had that Kokoshin would prove an efficient lobbyist there were dashed, thus undermining his position within the ministry.

No civilian minister of defence was appointed under Yeltsin's presidency. Igor Sergeev was the first ever to have been picked from the Strategic Missile Forces and favourable towards reform, but he was certainly not a civilian. When Kokoshin left the ministry the role of civilians in central positions diminished even further. His successor in the Ministry of Defence, Nikolai Mikhailov, proved even less successful in influencing defence policy in spite of his background within the military industry.[299] In other words, although questions related to the military–industrial complex certainly had received a powerful advocate in the Security Council as Kokoshin became its secretary, its position within the MoD had weakened.

Typically, a civilian was not picked for the delicate task of coming to grips with budget spending in January 1997. The role of the Main Directorate for the Military Budget and Financing was intended to increase within the Ministry of Defence as part of an overall aim to improve financial control over the defence sector.[300] The new head of the Main Directorate of Military Budget and Financing, Major-General Oleinik, signalled changes in this area in 1998.[301] These hopes did not materialize and, as it turned out, Oleinik was part of the problem rather than the solution. Nor did the newly proclaimed efforts to make defence budgeting more detailed promise much in the way of progress.

Starting in 1998, the minister of defence was given the right to decide the areas of responsibility of his deputy ministers. This had previously been done by the president.[302] Initially, it thus seemed as if the powers of the minister of defence were on the increase. Certainly, the suggestions of Sergeev appeared to be favoured by the Kremlin at this stage, but these were mainly based on plans emanating from the Defence Council and the Security Council. Sergeev's position vis-à-vis the Armed Forces was far from ideal. As the role of the Strategic Missile Forces grew substantially relative to those of the Ground Forces, so did resentment within the ministry, not least within the General Staff headed by Anatolii Kvashnin and among the chiefs of the other armed services.[303] As mentioned above, the fact that Sergeev also brought with him his own selected deputy ministers also caused tensions within the ministry.

Sergeev was initially effective in pushing through many of Baturin's and Kokoshin's reform plans, but his position within his own ministry was gradually weakened when the political leadership tended to side with his subordinate, Kvashnin, in the battle of wills between the two men. Nor was anything done to curb the influence of the General Staff – rather the opposite. According to a decision of the Defence Council, the role of the General Staff was significantly increased in that it was given responsibility for coordinating all the power structures. The intention was to make not least procurement more cost-effective and to curb the other power ministries' tendency to prescribe new duties and enlarged roles for themselves.[304] In effect, it constituted an admission that the power ministries' lobbying in the Kremlin had been effective up until then and, also, destructive as the political leadership had proven unable to control and coordinate its ministries and agencies.

After the NATO operation in Kosovo, the scales had tilted in favour of the General Staff and Kvashnin and against Sergeev. Not only did Sergeev find it difficult to manage his own ministry and the General Staff, which was supposed to be a part of his ministry, but there were instances of open insubordination from high-ranking officers that further undermined his position and called the whole idea of unified command (*edinonachalie*) into question.[305] Coupled with Russia's economic difficulties, this could not but have dire consequences for the future of military reform.

Military reform in the twilight of the Yeltsin era

In 1997–98, the defence decision-making machinery was alive with energy. As late as February 1998, Yeltsin in connection with a meeting with the minister of defence stated that he kept a very close eye on the progress (and setbacks) of the military reform.[306] An important driving force behind this new impetus for military reform was undoubtedly Andrei Kokoshin and his central position as secretary of the Defence Council and the later Security Council, into which the State Military Inspectorate was integrated. However, when Kokoshin was dismissed as a result of siding with Moscow mayor Yurii Luzhkov, the impetus faded. In the words of Aleksandr Golts: 'In Russia, even the most sensible plans live only as long as their authors occupy important posts.'[307] However, as will be evident in the following chapter, many of the seminal decisions from these years came to fruition under Putin.

Overall, though, it is the lethargic approach to military reform that is the most striking feature of Yeltsin's defence policy-making machinery. That a few people like Baturin and Kokoshin for a short time managed to occupy the right positions in order to push reform forward appears first and foremost to have been a fortuitous consequence of the power struggles that dominated Yeltsin's second term. It is interesting, however, to note that even this brief activity in decision making produced tangible results that were obvious a few years later: the overall performance of the Armed Forces did improve, albeit from a low level, and the forces subordinated to the Ministry of Defence underwent a series of structural reforms. However, there was never an attempt to institutionalize a decision-making structure with independent levers of power that would have provided the necessary checks and balances to keep up momentum in the reform process when political will at the centre flagged. Instead, reform was yet again allowed to become bogged down in the bureaucratic struggles between the power ministries, which were never really affected by the reform process initiated in 1997. When Yeltsin was given the choice between reforms in order to improve Russia's military security on the one hand, and securing his own personal position of power on the other, he consistently favoured the latter.

6 Enter Putin

The obsession with the power vertical

Before the end of Putin's first year as president, he achieved what Yeltsin had failed to do during his entire tenure – legislation on Russia's national symbols. Ever since 1992, Yeltsin's decrees had dictated that these were the tricolour, the double-headed eagle and a national anthem by Glinka without words to it, but the Duma had stubbornly blocked legislation. Putin suggested a compromise, retaining the tricolour and double-headed eagle while reintroducing the Soviet national anthem, albeit with a new text.[1] At the same time, legislation was adopted on the red banner of the Armed Forces and a navy banner from the tsarist era with a blue cross on a white background, the Saint Andrew Cross.[2] The conciliatory gesture of restoring many of the Soviet symbols, emblems and banners to the Armed Forces in 2000 constituted a signal to the military officers that their authority in society might be about to change. Their entire legacy was no longer in question.[3]

Even as prime minister in 1999, Putin often appeared before the media in military uniform during exercises and other military occasions. As president and supreme commander he even flew a strategic bomber during a conventionally armed cruise missile launch in 2005. This projected an image of Putin as a leader and a man of action, while at the same time making sure that the Armed Forces came firmly into the limelight. This, together with his granting the military leadership more or less a free hand to handle the Second Chechen War, bridged the gap that Yeltsin had opened wide between the political and military spheres. The military must certainly have experienced Putin as a positive change compared to the previous administration.[4]

The legislation on state symbols was also indicative of the fact that Putin had established considerable influence over the legislative assembly. He was, moreover, determined to concentrate more power in the Kremlin at the expense of the legislative and judicial branches as well as of the constituent parts of the Russian Federation. The independence of societal organizations and the media was also curtailed. The catchphrase for this process was that of 'establishing a power vertical'. Some of the reforms Putin undertook were set in motion only weeks and months after the presidential election in March 2000. Most importantly, he moved quickly to curb the independence of Russia's regions by creating seven federal districts which he superimposed upon the eighty-nine constituent parts of the federation.

Putin won the presidential election partly thanks to the early military successes in Chechnya. An impressive share of the military personnel voted for him – 80 per cent as compared with the just over 50 per cent of the overall vote in favour of Putin.[5] Clearly, it was worth treading carefully in order not to lose this power base. The question of military reform had been brewing in the Security Council while Putin was its secretary. With his trusted former colleague from the KGB and its successor services, Sergei Ivanov, as secretary of the Security Council, Putin went ahead to push through new plans and commissions on military reform, even transferring Ivanov to the Ministry of Defence in order to increase Kremlin control over the process.

The Second Chechen War

There is little doubt that the second war in Chechnya played a deciding role in Putin's increased popularity after he became prime minister in August 1999. The most important difference between the two wars lay in the terror bombings of Russian blocks of flats in 1999. Although responsibility for these acts was yet to be established, the Russian leadership unequivocally connected the bombings to the conflict in Chechnya. As a result, the war in 1999 was not criticized the way the war of 1994–96 was. The attacks on residential areas in Moscow constituted a strike against the Russian heartland. The Chechen enemy was portrayed as bandits and terrorists and continually connected to the bombings of residential blocks in Russia, especially those in Moscow.[6] Chechen incursions into the neighbouring republic of Dagestan also enabled the Kremlin to point to the risk of the conflict spreading to and destabilizing all of the North Caucasus. Suddenly, the war in Chechnya had become an existential threat to Russians rather than an ethnic conflict on the periphery of Russia. The impression of military success that was given through the reports of military advances in Chechnya reinforced the favourable public opinion of the war in 1999.

On the international scene, Russia emphasized that it was not engaged in a civil war, but combating international terrorism. This strategy had been used in the First Chechen War as well, but after the terrorist attack on the World Trade Center in New York in September 2001, Russia received tacit support for this view. Overall, the second war in Chechnya was less criticized internationally than the first war.[7] Moscow was able to control most media reporting from the area and few independent observers were allowed to go there. Nor did the international community appear very keen to examine the situation in Chechnya.[8] The result was that the second war in Chechnya was less of a political burden for the Kremlin than the first war had been. The Kremlin could even legitimize its measures to tighten control and repress dissent in Russia as a whole by connecting them to the war in Chechnya and to that waged against terrorism.[9]

For Russia's military organization the Second Chechen War was an opportunity to revenge itself for the humiliation it had suffered in 1994–96. It was also important to the new president to be able to deliver something that could plausibly be described as military victories. A kind of symbiosis was thus established between Putin and the military organization, and military reform started to move up the political agenda early in Putin's first term.

Different power ministries were given overall responsibility for the war in Chechnya at different times. The MVD and the FSB were originally tasked with repelling the Chechen separatists who had entered Dagestan. They did so, albeit with obvious difficulties. For the military operation against Chechnya, a Unified Grouping of Federal Forces was created. The Ministry of Defence was in command until January 2001, when responsibility was transferred to the FSB in an attempt to claim that the operation had gone from being a military one to an anti-terrorist operation. In July 2003, the MVD took charge of the operation in Chechnya.[10] Although far from perfect, cooperation between the different power ministries active in Chechnya appears to have improved compared to the first war.[11] Nevertheless, the MVD continued to suffer criticism, not least from the General Staff, for its poor performance in Chechnya and it is obvious that, for example, the MoD more or less considers itself in charge of its activity in the mountainous regions rather than subordinated to the MVD.[12]

Certainly, the Russian military performance had improved compared to the dismal record in the First Chechen War. Cooperation between different services of the Armed Forces and with troops of other power ministries worked better than before, as did command and control. On the tactical level, a number of improvements were evident.[13] Nevertheless, problems continued to haunt the Russian troops there. Cooperation between the different ministries still broke down at times of stress and poor discipline and low morale persisted among the soldiers. The increased use of *kontraktniki* did not solve this problem. On the tactical level, Russian units continued to be vulnerable to ambushes and snipers (something that further undermined morale) as well as to Chechen mines and improvised explosive devices. In addition, the Chechen side proved successful in shooting down Russia's helicopters and aircraft.[14] The setting up of two special mountain brigades to secure Russia's southern border in the North Caucasus proved considerably more time-consuming and complicated than originally envisaged.[15] On the other hand, this project appears to have been a priority within the MoD.[16] New input on counter-insurgency warfare could gradually be integrated into the Armed Forces' thinking on the basis of the experience of these two brigades once they were fully operational.

With time, terrorist attacks undermined the image of the war in Chechnya as an unqualified success. This was reflected in opinion polls: the Russian public increasingly demanded peace negotiations and proved overwhelmingly sceptical about a continuation of the military operation in Chechnya.[17] The most spectacular terrorist attacks with clear connections to the conflict in

Chechnya were those on the Dubrovka Theatre in Moscow in October 2002 and against a school in the small town of Beslan in September 2004. At first sight, these attacks provided further ammunition for the Kremlin's rhetoric on anti-terrorism. However, it was also obvious that the Russian state was unable to prevent terrorist attacks. In the case of Beslan, moreover, it was impossible to disguise the lack of professionalism of the Russian security forces.[18] Consequently, opinion polls clearly indicated that the Russian public did not think that the state was able to protect it against acts of terrorism.[19]

Gradually, the risk of instability spreading throughout the North Caucasus came to feature prominently on the Kremlin agenda. Dmitrii Kozak was appointed Putin's presidential envoy in the Southern Federal District (one of the seven federal districts introduced in 2000) following the tragedy in Beslan.[20] The military presence in the area increased and perhaps as many as every third male under forty in the reserve was called up for military service in a short period of time.[21] Far from providing a military solution to the conflict in Chechnya, the Kremlin's strategy in the area had created a tin-derbox of new conflicts waiting to erupt in republics such as Dagestan and Kabardino-Balkaria.[22]

The *Kursk* is lost

Soon after assuming the presidency, Putin was prompted to turn his attention to the question of military reform. One event that probably changed Putin's view on, among other things, the state of the Armed Forces was the *Kursk* disaster in August 2000. Putin had been sworn in as president for little over three months when the accident happened. In the early morning of 12 August 2000 a torpedo exploded on board the submarine *Kursk* during a major Northern Fleet exercise. A larger explosion occurred only about two minutes later. It was recorded by Norwegian seismologists as reaching 3.5 on the Richter scale. In other words, it is highly unlikely that the commander of the Northern Fleet, Admiral Viacheslav Popov, who was supervising the exercise from the missile cruiser *Petr Velikii* only a few miles away from the *Kursk*, did not realize that something serious had happened. However, the command of the Northern Fleet decided from the earliest hours of the disaster to try and cover it up and put the blame on NATO under the pretext that one of the Alliance's submarines had collided with the *Kursk* or fired a torpedo at it.

Putin was not informed of what had happened until 7 a.m. on the fol-lowing day. Reassured by his minister of defence, Igor Sergeev (who in turn relied on information from the commander of the navy and Popov), that everything was under control, Putin decided not to cancel his holiday on the Black Sea – a decision he was to regret when he later came under heavy criticism for how the whole affair was handled.[23] A year later, after a com-mission had investigated the event, Putin dismissed a number of high-rank-ing navy officers and probably lost much of any faith he might have had in the military leadership's ability to handle similar events. True to his habit of letting dismissed officials make a soft landing, the discharged naval officers were all provided with new positions. The commander of the Northern Fleet, Popov, became a representative for the Murmansk oblast Duma in the upper house of parliament from January 2002, where he became deputy chairman of the Committee on Defence and Security of the Federal Council.[24]

It is hardly unique for an accident to happen, although in the Russian case the dismal funding of the navy may have increased the likelihood and consequences of such accidents. The torpedo that first exploded was probably from 1976 and loaded with a highly explosive fuel – a type of construction that was abandoned in the West in the 1950s due to the risks it entailed. However, there were at least three additional factors that made the *Kursk* accident unique. First, the search and rescue service had not been a priority within the Russian navy for many years; nor could the escape hatch on board the *Kursk* be opened from the inside and the crew members had never received training in free ascent. In fact, there was very little Popov could have done to rescue the surviving crew members on board the submarine even had he reacted immediately after the first explosion. Second, the Northern Fleet displayed a staggering disregard for the families of the crew and to the dead crewmen in, for example, not disclosing a complete list of crew members on board, not providing the relatives with other information and not responding directly to the emergency. Third, the Northern Fleet and other members of the Russian military leadership disseminated false rumours of SOS signals being heard from the sunken submarine, of the explosion being caused by a collision with a Western submarine, and so on. Clearly, the military system did not hesitate to obfuscate facts and still regarded NATO as its main enemy.[25]

The *Kursk* incident provided evidence of how far the decline had gone within the Armed Forces, and the navy in particular. It was not just a question of underfunding. A number of safety measures had been ignored and there was evidence of this having become routine. The poor information provided both to the public and to the political leadership was reminiscent of how things were done in the Soviet era. The international community, which offered assistance early on, was baffled by the lack of response. In the event, the incident stimulated closer cooperation with NATO. In February 2003, a framework agreement was signed on submarine crew escape and rescue, and in August 2005, British search and rescue teams were able to provide assistance when a small Russian submarine was trapped outside the Kamchatka Peninsula.[26] To Putin, who probably did not feel entirely secure in his new position at the time, the *Kursk* accident gave rise to two main concerns. First, he could not trust the military to report to him accurately. Second, the media could change public opinion overnight on the basis of mismanagement of similar events. True to what would later turn out to be Putin's backbone reflex, his remedy was to strengthen direct presidential control over the military and to curb the independence of the media.[27]

Putin's power vertical unfolds

Both the war in Chechnya and the *Kursk* incident provided ample reasons for concentrating on military reform. However, Putin's first priority remained domestic political control and the most important expression of this was building a 'power vertical'. The concept was in no way new or invented by the Putin administration. The Yeltsin administration had wished to build such a vertical but never succeeded. Putin, however, entered the Kremlin with new resolve. Originally, the expression was primarily intended to describe a new relationship between Russia's regions and the federal centre. Within the Kremlin there was frustration at the way federal laws and even the constitution were flouted in the regions. The first measures in building a power vertical were thus aimed at solving this problem. With time, the power vertical affected other fields where the Kremlin wished to wield more or less complete control as well. For example, the independence of the parliamentary branch was even further undermined and independent media were curtailed. What originally seemed an efficient means of coming to grips with corruption and intransigence in the regions and in the state bureaucracy developed into a sort of Kremlin panacea for all problems whatever their nature and complexity.

As was the case in the Yeltsin years, power is very much personlized and it is the person rather than the formal position that is important in order to understand where the centre of gravity in decision making is located. This complicates analysis of the decision-making system since it means that it is imperative to be aware of how close a specific person is to Putin. To avoid depending on newspaper rumours of the influence of this or that official, it is possible to substantiate claims of influence by looking at who meets with important foreign guests and so on. Over time, moreover, person and position have a tendency to coincide. In other words, the éminence grise tends to get his formal position confirmed sooner or later.

When it comes to defence decision making, the most important person to keep track of has been Sergei Ivanov. In his case, it is easy to establish his close relationship with the president since Ivanov was described by Putin early on as someone with whom he had a feeling of comradeship or *chuvstvo loktia*.[28] Ivanov was secretary to the Security Council (2000–1), minister of defence (2001–5), minister of defence and deputy prime minister with responsibility for defence industry-related questions (2005–7) and, finally, first deputy prime minister with responsibility for the military–industrial complex and related questions from February 2007. To a considerable extent, activity on military reform questions followed his lead with a special focus on whatever issues he prioritized. Although the picture was always more complicated than suggested above, decision making on military reform under Putin is impossible to understand without first establishing the important role of Sergei Ivanov. In a system where ever more power was concentrated to the Kremlin, Putin became dependent on his closest advisers and Ivanov was certainly one of these.

The introduction of federal districts

While he was working in the Presidential Administration under Yeltsin, one of Putin's responsibilities had been to come up with ways of increasing the level of control that the Kremlin had over the regions. Putin's introduction in May 2000 of seven federal districts under the supervision of presidential envoys was a surprise to many and the speed with which it was implemented nothing short of breathtaking after the Yeltsin era. Although there were also purely economic motivations behind the reform, the areas of competence of the power ministries were also involved. This was reflected not least in the fact that five of the original seven presidential envoys had made their career within the power ministries.[29] All the presidential envoys became members of the Security Council.

The reform was also intended to have an impact on Russia's military organization.[30] For example, it was intended to facilitate coordination of the rear services and other support functions for the troops of different power ministries. The federal districts were designed on the basis of the MVD districts and corresponded closely with the military districts and those of, for example, the MChS. In addition, many agencies and ministries gradually adapted their organization in the regions to mirror that of the federal districts.[31] Gradually, this opened a new career opportunity for people within the power ministries. The presidential envoys in the districts were largely left to their own devices when it came to appointing their entourage. Consequently, many chose their deputies from the power ministries; three quarters of the chief federal inspectors in the regions came from them.[32] The introduction of this new administrative level thus became a vehicle for career advancement for officers and other employees of the power ministries as new positions were created, and staff turnover approached that seen in wartime.[33]

The Southern Federal District, which more or less coincided with the North Caucasus MD, became a key area. After the terrorist attack on the school in Beslan, Dmitrii Kozak became presidential envoy there with considerable powers. A special coordinating commission, chaired by Kozak, was created to coordinate efforts to calm the region. Another consequence of Beslan was that the federal districts were given central roles in combating terrorism. Anti-terrorist commissions were to be created in all the federal districts and these would in turn lead and coordinate similar commissions in all of the federal regions. A deputy head of these subcommissions, an MVD officer, was to play a key role in organizing day-to-day work.[34] In 2006, the overall responsibility for combating terrorism was transferred to the FSB, when the National Anti-Terrorist Committee (Natsionalnyi antiterroristicheskii komitet, NAK) was founded and the head of the FSB made its chairman.[35]

In spite of all the above, the success of the federal districts is still very much in doubt. Their introduction did not appear to force the power ministries to comply with directives to create an integrated rear service. Nor have there been reports on, for example, success in combating corruption and terrorism or reduced adminstrative costs. Although the Kremlin managed to force the regions to adapt their legislation to that on the federal level, it is not entirely certain that this is an effect primarily of the introduction of the federal districts. The overall climate has become considerably less favourable to regional self-determination under Putin, and Russia is even less of a federation today than it was before.

The Presidential Administration

A number of officials within the Presidential Administration are involved in defence policy making. In March 2004, Putin relieved two of his military advisers, Yevgenii Shaposhnikov and Igor Sergeev, of their duties.[36] As a consequence, there remained only one military adviser within the Presidential Administration – Lieutenant-General Aleksandr Burutin, who was appointed presidential adviser on military-technological policy and the development of the military–industrial complex in April 2003. An officer from the Ground Forces, Burutin graduated from the General Staff Academy in 1997. He then served as deputy head of the Main Directorate of Operations of the General Staff.[37] In other words, his career rise had been very swift indeed. Burutin took on more of a real role in defence policy making within the Presidential Administration than Shaposhnikov or Sergeev had been allowed to do. Their appointments were probably mainly a way of providing nice offices for two former ministers of defence. Burutin was certainly not an adviser on military affairs from outside the military establishment, someone who would provide an alternative view to that provided by the Ministry of Defence. In 2007, Burutin was rumoured to be on the way back to a top position within the General Staff, where there is reason to suspect that he would be regarded as the Kremlin's man, not least because of the meteoric career he has had since Putin took notice of him.

There was another military man inside the Presidential Administration. Colonel-General Gennadii Troshev was appointed presidential adviser on the question of the Cossacks and, more particularly, on the possible use of Cossack units in Russia's military organization (not least in the North Caucasus) in February 2003.[38] However, Troshev's appointment was again more a way of providing a position for an officer who fell from grace than an attempt to instil new sources of advice into the Presidential Administration. Troshev's clout within the Administration was negligible, as was his influence on military reform.

For most of Putin's presidency, Sergei Prikhodko was presidential aide on foreign policy, although he lost his rank as deputy head of the Presidential Administration as a result of the administrative reform conducted in 2004. Prikhodko probably influenced foreign policy, but there was also evidence of a former FSB official, Viktor Ivanov, taking over some of that role (not least where questions such as energy exports were concerned) within the Presidential Administration.[39] Viktor Ivanov, in his capacity as presidential aide, became formally responsible for cadre questions, the award of decorations and reforming the state service. Since power over appointments is an important source of influence, there is every reason to expect that Ivanov's ability to play a role within the Presidential Administration was considerable.

The Security Council and its apparatus played a significant role in military reform in the first year of Putin's presidency. Under the secretaryship of Sergei Ivanov, the Security Council reached its apex of influence, not least over defence policy making. Military reform plans that had been put to one side were again brought forward.[40] In 2000, in his capacity as secretary of the Security Council, Ivanov made a series of inspection tours of all Russia's military districts and navies.[41] In addition, there was a Security Council expert commission on personnel reductions and military reform, chaired by Deputy Prime Minister Ilia Klebanov.[42] A new plan for reform was adopted and Ivanov moved on to become minister of defence. With the appointment of Sergei Rushailo as the new secretary of the Security Council in March 2001, the council yet again received responsibility for the situation in Chechnya – never a promising sign for an institution. Consequently, the Security Council's influence on military reform waned.

This situation did not change significantly when the former minister of foreign affairs, Igor Ivanov, was secretary of the Security Council in 2004–7. The Security Council had nowhere near the kind of influence it had had under Sergei Ivanov.[43] Nevertheless, the inner circle of permanent members of the Security Council meets each week and probably provides an important forum for discussions and decision making on security policy. It is difficult to determine whether the apparatus of the Security Council plays a role in planning military affairs. Certainly, its interdepartmental commissions could play an important role in drafting documents and forging agreements on them between different ministries and agencies.[44] Certain directorates of the Security Council are probably used for preparing new plans and programme documents simply because it is one of the few coordinating institutions with a sizeable analytical staff.

There was also a Presidential Commission on Questions of Military-Technological Cooperation with Foreign States. This commission was dominated by people from the power ministries, which is hardly surprising. In addition to the heads of the power ministries, the general director of the state arms export corporation, Rosoboronexport, Sergei Chemezov, who allegedly started his career within the First Main Directorate of the KGB (later to become the SVR),[45] and the head of the Federal Service for Military-Technological Cooperation Mikhail Dmitriev, who had worked for the KGB and later for the SVR,[46] were on the commission.[47]

While people from the Yeltsin administration, such as the head of the Presidential Administration, Aleksandr Voloshin, were left in place during most of Putin's first term, his second term was characterized by a clear trend towards the increasing influence of former KGB/FSB officials. The pattern is more complicated than that, though, and energy companies and other sectors yielding considerable profits (such as arms export) are equally well represented. However, there is also a tendency for ex-power ministry officials to fill posts in these companies. In addition, a past career in St Petersburg and a connection to the administration of Anatolii Sobchak there has proved an asset for anyone wishing to make a career within the Presidential Administration. The same is true for personnel policy concerning influential sections of the government. Overall, Putin has appointed people he trusts because he has worked with them earlier in his career (as a student, in the KGB, during his stationing in Germany, and from his time in the St Petersburg mayor's office). This is an example of how much depends on persons rather than formal institutions in Putin's power vertical.

Putin's government

During his first term as president, Putin, contrary to the expectations of many commentators, held on to his prime minister, Mikhail Kasianov. Military reform was high on Putin's agenda and, therefore, also on the government's. However, Kasianov never stood out as an ardent implementer of military reform. He belonged to the 'economic wing' of the political elite that had established itself in power under Yeltsin, and later Putin, rather than the 'security wing'. Only with his pending re-election did Putin dismiss Kasianov to appoint Mikhail Fradkov, who had been first deputy secretary of the Security Council under Sergei Ivanov and headed the Federal Service of the Tax Police between 2001 and 2003. Fradkov had more of a security policy profile than Kasianov, but nevertheless kept a relatively low profile on defence-related matters. In September 2007, he was replaced by Viktor Zubkov, formerly head of the Federal Service for Financial Monitoring. Zubkov would have ample opportunity to discuss defence matters at his dining table at home, since the minister of defence since February 2007 was his son-in-law, Anatolii Serdiukov.

In the Government Apparatus, there is a Department for Military Industry and Advanced Technology. The head of this department, Igor Borovkov, went on to become head of the apparatus of the Military–Industrial Commission in May 2006 under Sergei Ivanov. The responsibilities of the department were also under the purview of one of the deputy heads of the Government Apparatus, Dmitrii Ryzhkov. He was previously director of the Administrative Department of the Government (mentioned by Kokoshin as one of the organs within the Government Apparatus that sometimes could play an important role in defence policy making), and started his career within the security organs. His successor as head of the Administrative Department, Mikhail Lychagin, had a past career that suggests that he took over Ryzhkov's earlier role in the government's defence policy making.[48]

Fradkov also had his own aide on military-technological policy and military-technological cooperation. Andrei Nikolaev was appointed to this post after losing his seat in the Duma election in December 2003. He was also to assist the prime minister in the Maritime Collegium, of which the prime minister was chairman at the time. On the whole, however, there was little reason to expect that Nikolaev would have any decisive influence on defence policy making. Probably, the appointment was a way of yet again providing a soft landing for someone the Putin administration had decided to drop. By then, Nikolaev had lost his seat in the Duma to a candidate from the Putin-loyal party, United Russia.[49] Vladimir Shamanov, another general in the reserve, was appointed military aide to the prime minister in 2004. His areas of responsibility would include questions of the social protection for servicemen and relations with veterans' organizations. In common with Nikolaev, Shamanov received this post mainly as compensation for the Kremlin not supporting his bid to be re-elected as governor in the Ulianovsk region.[50]

Although Stepashin achieved a record in holding on to the premiership for only three months, one of his deputy prime ministers, Ilia Klebanov, stayed on. He was appointed in May 1999 and received responsibility for the military–industrial complex and other policy areas connected to scientific and technological-industrial questions. In June 1999, the government Commission on Military–Industrial Questions was created. Its chair was the prime minister (Stepashin until September 1999, then Putin succeeded by Kasianov in June 2000). Klebanov became the deputy chairman of this commission.[51]

New statutes for the government commission on military–industrial policy were issued in June 2000, but in essence its structure remained the same. The commission was chaired by the prime minister. Interestingly, Fradkov had been a member of the commission at its very inception in June 1999 in his capacity as minister of trade. Sergei Ivanov as minister of defence now received a more prominent role than he had had before, as a deputy chair of the commission.[52]

When Sergei Ivanov was appointed deputy prime minister in November 2005, he took over a number of responsibilities from the prime minister. Most importantly, the Commission on Military–Industrial Questions, which the prime minister had chaired, was abolished. A new, similar commission was created, the Military–Industrial Governmental Commission, and Ivanov was made its chair. The new commission was also given slightly different areas of responsibility and there was greater representation of the defence industry among its members. Its first deputy chair, Vladislav Putilin, received the rank of minister in spite of not having a portfolio. In addition there were two deputy chairs – the minister of defence, Anatolii Serdiukov, and the chair of the scientific-technical council of the commission, Vladimir Dmitriev. In other words, the commission was not simply created to coordinate policy among ministers. It received a more independent position and a substantial apparatus.

In addition, Ivanov took over as chair of the Maritime Collegium, of which the prime minister was no longer even a member. The Maritime Collegium had been created in September 2001 under the aegis of the government. Originally an idea from the chief of the navy at the time, Admiral Vladimir Kuroedov, in his doctoral dissertation, there were probably hopes within the navy that the Maritime Collegium would become something of a naval ministry. Any such hopes were, however, dashed when the statutes on the collegium were published. The prime minister, Mikhail Kasianov, became its chairman and the deputy prime minister, Ilia Klebanov, its first deputy chairman. The chief of the navy was only one of four deputy chairmen of the collegium, all of whom outranked him. The remit of the Maritime Collegium was broad; it was to coordinate the field of naval activity of the Russian Federation. Consequently, representatives of authorities such as the State Fishing Agency and the Ministry of Transport were included on the Collegium as well.[53] By 2004, the Maritime Collegium had expanded considerably and its military component been weakened even further in that the chief of the navy was no longer one of its deputy chairmen and the list of members with non-military missions had grown.[54] In the aftermath of an incident involving a Russian trawler intercepted by Norwegian fishing inspectors in the Barents Sea, in November 2005 the Maritime Collegium discussed a larger role for the navy in protecting Russian economic interests at sea.[55] This was also an institution that Ivanov took over from the prime minister when he became deputy prime minister. All in all, the role of the prime minister in defence politics diminished after Ivanov moved to the White House.

The MIC policy area continued to be subject to constant reshuffles of the chains of decision making. The whole structure for policy making on the military industry and R&D had changed suddenly in May 2000 when a Ministry for Industry, Science and Technology (*Minpromnauka*) was created anew and Klebanov appointed its minister (by this time he had lost the rank of deputy prime minister).[56] The five different MIC agencies were subordinated to the Ministry of Industry, Science and Technology Policy. Then in 2004 Putin carried out another government reshuffle and as a result Minpromnauka was disbanded and the five agencies were subordinated to a newly formed agency, the Federal Agency on Industry.[57] Boris Aleshin was appointed to head this agency. Aleshin was previously (from April 2003) deputy prime minister responsible for industrial policy. He had previously resigned his post as deputy minister of industry, science and technology in protest against Klebanov. The new structure made Klebanov his subordinate.[58] The Federal Agency on Industry, in turn, was subordinated to the Ministry of Industry and Energy, which was also created in 2004 and headed by Viktor Khristenko.

The Ministry of Atomic Energy had previously been characterized by stability. It was not reorganized the way the ministries concerned with the MIC were and changes of minister were rare. However, one of the ministers of atomic energy, Yevgenii Adamov, was accused in the USA of having misappropriated funds that were intended for improving the security of nuclear facilities during his tenure (1998–2001).[59] The ministry was transformed into the Federal Agency of Atomic Energy (Rosatom) in 2004. It still retained some responsibilities for defence-related affairs, although most of these questions were moved to the Ministry of Defence.[60] Rosatom became subordinated to the Ministry of Industry and Energy.

Since 1991, the management of the MIC and R&D questions has been characterized by reshuffles and ever-changing lines of subordination – something that was hardly conducive to reform of these sectors. Figure 6.1 gives an overview of the twists and turns of decision making on the MIC and R&D since 1992. Although hardly exhaustive, it gives an idea of the unstable structure of the decision-making machinery. In 2004, moreover, certain R&D questions were probably moved to the purview of the Ministry of Education and Science and to the Federal Agency on Science and Innovations, which became subordinated to the Ministry of Education. It was hardly suprising that the defence industry remained unreformed and in a state of decline. It may have been due to a growing frustration with the

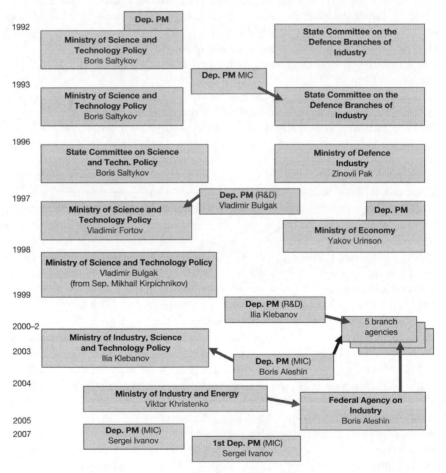

Figure 6.1 Overview of the MIC and R&D decision-making structure, 1992–2007

difficulties encountered when trying to coordinate procurement and reform the MIC that Sergei Ivanov was appointed deputy prime minister with responsibility for MIC-related questions in November 2005 and then promoted to become first deputy prime minister in 2007. It remains to be seen whether Ivanov manages to move reform of the MIC forward from his new position. The conditions are not auspicious for the MIC as a whole, but he may at least be able to achieve a more coherent process for establishing the defence order.

The development of the framework for defence decision making within the government suggests that financial control of military reform and a greater focus on the MIC became central questions during Putin's second term in office. The institutional changes made to strengthen such mechanisms as well as the persons in charge of central functions suggest as much. A number of efforts aimed to increase the scrutiny of how defence money was spent. Liubov Kudelina moved from the Ministry of Finance to the Ministry of Defence in 2001 and Vera Chistova filled her post at the Department of the Defence Complex and Law Enforcement Organs there. In May 2004, this department changed its name to Department of Budget Policy in the Sphere of State Military, Law-Enforcement Service and the State Defence Order.[61] In the Ministry of Economic Development and Trade, Vladislav Putilin became head of the Department of Economy of Defence and Security Programmes in 2004.[62] Putilin went on to become first deputy chair of the Military–Industrial Governmental Commission in 2006.

Reshuffling of the power ministries and administrative reform

In 2003–4 there were two major changes in the decision-making structure that affected security and defence policy. First of all, Putin reshuffled his power ministries in March 2003. In the event, the number of power ministries was reduced and the position of the FSB substantially strengthened. In 2004, moreover, the Kremlin launched an administrative reform that aimed to make the government machinery more efficient. The architect of this reform was Dmitrii Kozak, who started his career in St Petersburg and went on to become head of the Government Apparatus in 1999, and deputy head and then first deputy head of the Presidential Administration in 2000 and 2003, respectively. Within the Presidential Administration, Kozak had been a key official in a number of reform projects such as working out a new relationship between the centre and the regions, and judicial reform. The administrative reform started at the top level of the bureaucracy, but was planned to continue at lower levels and in the regions.

In March 2003, FAPSI and the FPS were dissolved as independent institutions. FAPSI was split up with parts of its areas of responsibility being merged into the structures of the FSB, the FSO and the SVR. Meanwhile the Border Troops were subordinated to the FSB, giving the latter a structure very reminiscent of that of the KGB. Only the SVR, the Main Directorate for Special Programmes, GUSP, and the FSO were still outside the FSB structures after the reform.[63] In the process, the power and influence of the FSB increased considerably – at a stroke its budget was doubled and its staff tripled.

The reasons for the changes were many, but foremost was a wish to streamline the system for internal and external security for both budgetary and other efficiency gains. In the case of FAPSI, the fact that the agency had been surrounded by rumours of corruption also played a role.[64] FAPSI had experienced a time of prosperity under Yeltsin. With its areas of responsibility ranging from signals intelligence to control of government communications, it proved an invaluable source of information on both foreign and internal friends and foes. During this period, FAPSI was one of the few agencies and ministries not to experience drastic cuts in its budget or personnel reductions. In addition, FAPSI entered the commercial market and, as it turned out, its top leadership were provided with ample opportunities to enrich themselves.[65]

The FPS becoming part of the FSB also signified a victory for both the FSB and the Ministry of Defence. It put an end to the intra-bureaucratic feud over who should be responsible for the defence (*oborona*) of Russia's borders and was settled to the MoD's advantage; the Border Troops were left with the mission of guarding (*okhrana*) the borders. The degradation of the FPS from an independent service with ministerial status to a service within the FSB meant that its head and first deputy director of the FSB, Colonel-General Vladimir Pronichev, did not become a member of the Security Council as his predecessor, Konstantin Totskii, had been.[66] The structure of the MVD also underwent significant change. The Federal Service of the Tax Police was abolished and subordinated to the MVD in the shape of a new department, the Federal Service for Economic and Tax Crimes. It would be headed by a deputy minister of internal affairs – a newly created post within the MVD. At the same time, the State Committee for Combating Illegal Trade in Narcotic Substances, formerly under the MVD, became an independent agency.[67]

The administrative reform that Dmitrii Kozak masterminded for the entire Russian bureaucracy and launched in 2004 had consequences for the power ministries as well. It reduced the numbers of deputies each minister or director could have. Nevertheless, many ministries found a way round these regulations and let key officials enjoy the 'authority' of deputy ministers. For example, the MChS minister was limited to having three deputy ministers (one of them a first deputy minister). However, in addition there was a head military expert and a head state inspector for fire supervision – both enjoying the authority of deputy ministers.[68] A year later, the Duma complained that its legislative work was being hampered by the absence of state secretaries within the ministries since these are responsible for handling contacts with parliament. In September 2005, the Ministry of Defence thus received a state secretary again when Nikolai Pankov was appointed.[69] Similar developments took place in other ministries, not least the power ministries.

In an effort to streamline the bureaucracy, there would only be three top levels – ministries, federal services and federal agencies. This meant that, for example, the FSB lost its 'ministerial rank' and was reduced to merely being a federal service. In practice, of course, this meant very little since the FSB's influence increased rather than the opposite. The reform also aimed to reduce the number of managerial levels inside ministries, services and agencies as well as to reduce the number of deputy ministers and directors.[70] This had consequences for the power ministries as well since the total number of agencies and services was reduced when a number of them were subordinated to ministries rather than directly to the president.

Three services and agencies previously under the direct control of the president were subordinated to the Ministry of Defence. The State Committee on the Defence Order, which had existed for only one year, was subordinated to the MoD. Earlier, these functions had been performed by the Ministry of Economic Development and Trade, where Colonel-General Vladislav Putilin, as deputy minister of economic development and trade, had managed the defence order. The Federal Service for Military-Technological Cooperation (formerly the Committee on Military-Technological Cooperation with Foreign States) and the Federal Service for Technological and Export Control (formerly the Presidential State Technological Commission) were no longer directly subordinated to the president. All in all, the MoD had four services and agencies under its purview after March 2004:

- The *Federal Service for Military-Technological Cooperation* (formerly the Presidential Committee on Military-Technological Cooperation with Foreign States directly subordinated to the president);
- The *Federal Service for Technological and Export Control* (formerly the Presidential State Technologial Commission directly subordinated to the president);
- The *Federal Service for the Defence Order* (formerly the State Committee on the Defence Order directly subordinated to the president); and
- The *Federal Agency for Special Construction* (formerly the Federal Service for Special Construction).

In 2003 and 2004, it was evident that the Kremlin was making a concerted effort to strengthen the impression that the internal and external security of Russia was a priority area for the government – no doubt the hostage taking and the inability of the power ministries to handle the situation in Beslan in 2004 made it necessary for the Kremlin to show initiative in this area.[71] For example, the minister of finance, Aleksei Kudrin, claimed that the FSB budget had tripled since 2000. Although there may have been a real increase in the budgets of some of the power ministries, the sensational manifold increases that Kudrin mentioned are no doubt explained by the fact that they took over personnel and tasks from disbanded agencies. This was the case not only for the FSB, but also for the MVD, whose budget Kudrin stated had increased by 250 per cent. The Federal Service of the Tax Police which was included in the MVD probably had a significantly larger budget than the State Committee for Combating Illegal Trade in Narcotic Substances, which became independent from the MVD in March 2003.[72] In addition, more money probably was allocated to the security forces during this period as well.

All in all, the administrative reform did not realize the intended goals. The Russian bureaucracy showed few signs of deceasing in size or of simplifying its procedures. Corruption had grown rather than abated, according to Transparency International.[73] The power ministries and the military were no exception. Increased budgets appear only to open new possibilities to siphon off money illegally and neither the political nor the military leadership showed any serious intention of coming to grips with the problem.[74] A few years after the administrative reform was launched, the number of deputy prime ministers was more or less the same as before the reform and one of the few tangible results left was the subordination of a number of services and agencies to ministries. Russia's bureaucracy, and not least the power ministries, had yet again demonstrated its resilience in the face of attempts at reform.

Putin's control over parliamentary and judicial scrutiny

In contrast to Yeltsin, Putin never needed to struggle with a recalcitrant Federal Assembly. The parliament, especially the Duma, became dominated by party factions loyal to Putin after the elections in 1999. As a result of the success of the Unity party, the Communist Party of the Russian Federation (KPRF) lost its strong position in the Duma. Unity went on to claim some of the most influential posts and, as it became increasingly clear that membership in this faction was an important new career vehicle in political life, Duma deputies elected on other party lists or as independents rushed to join forces with it.[75] In order to further consolidate its position, Unity amalgamated its main competitor in the 1999 elections, the electoral faction Fatherland–All Russia (Otechestvo–Vsia Rossiia), into its own organization in April 2001, changing its name to United Russia (Edinaia Rossiia). In the next election, in 2003, United Russia secured 38 per cent of the party list votes (compared to 13 per cent for the KPRF). After a considerable bandwagon effect in the Duma it was clear that an impressive 68 per cent of the deputies had joined the United Russia faction. As a result of this, United Russia, which never hid the fact that its main loyalty was to Putin, was able to secure all the chairs of the Duma committees as well as the post of speaker.[76]

In the autumn of 2002, parts of the defence budget were declassified on the repeated demands of the State Duma. The bulk of the budget was still secret, but there were promises that in the following year the declassifying process would go further and only about 10 per cent of the expenses – such as secret projects and the financing of the GRU – would be kept secret.[77]

This was a necessary prerequisite for the Duma ever to be able to exercise any measure of control over military spending. However, the extent to which this constituted a breakthrough should not be exaggerated. As the then chairman of the Duma Committee of Defence, Andrei Nikolaev, noted, 'the extent of the information is approximately the same as that which Russia each year reports to the United Nations'.[78] In the view of Aleksei Arbatov and Petr Romashkin, colonel in the reserve, the lack of transparency was convenient for the Ministry of Defence and the Ministry of Finance. Although the power ministries did not receive the funding they needed, they were free to dispose of the money they did get as they saw fit. Meanwhile, the political leadership could escape much of its responsibility for the decisions taken by pointing to the military.[79]

In 2003, parts of the formerly secret defence budget became public. For the first time, the Duma was able to vote on a defence budget with some rudimentary knowledge of how the resources would be used. However, Alexei Arbatov remained unimpressed and stated that the sections made public were of little relevance to the overall discussion on central issues such as force postures and modernization. Instead, the Duma was provided information on 'the money spent on kindergartens and schools for the children of military personnel, transportation costs for military members on vacation, funding for electricity and communal housing services, the cost of storing special fuels and lubricants and so on'.[80] In the budget for 2007, the number of secret lines was again increased.[81] In other words, there was nothing approaching a trend towards greater transparency – rather the reverse. In addition, the size of total spending on defence and security was unclear to most of the people involved (if not all). The lack of information provided to the deputies coupled with the control exercised by the Kremlin over the Duma through United Russia rendered the Duma even less able to exercise any kind of serious oversight over defence policy. As under Yeltsin, the few independent initiatives taken by Duma deputies usually concerned rather harmless demands for better social protection for servicemen and military veterans.[82]

Under Putin, the Audit Chamber started to look more closely into how the military spent its money. For example, in June 2003 the Audit Chamber published a critical review of how the General Staff had spent its budget.[83] In the following year, it was clear that the Audit Chamber was not satisfied with the way in which the rear service of the Armed Forces had managed its procurement of equipment. The Central Clothing Directorate and the Main Military-Medicine Directorate of the Ministry of Defence were especially singled out for criticism. In some instances, the reason was to be found in general inefficiency and poor routines, but in other cases there were suspicions of criminal activity. Soon, the Military Procuracy started an investigation of the activities of the Central Clothing Directorate.[84] During 2004, criminal proceedings were instituted against almost twenty commanders of military units and forty-three officials in the food supply, clothing and financial services. Of these thirty-five were convicted by November the same year. The officials and commanders of the MoD were far from alone in attracting this attention. A number of officers of the Aircraft Directorate of the MChS were also being investigated.[85] All in all, however, this was most probably only the tip of an iceberg.

In December 2004 Putin strengthened his control when the law on the Audit Chamber was amended. Now, although formally the Duma still decided who should be its chairman by vote, it was up to the president to suggest a candidate. Duma factions, committees or one fifth of the Duma deputies were only able to suggest candidates to the president, and the law did not state that the president must choose his candidate from among those suggested by the Duma. If the Duma voted against the president's suggestion, he was required to make a new suggestion within two weeks. However, the president was free to put forward the same candidate again.

The same changes applied to the way the deputy chairman of the Audit Chamber was confirmed by the Federal Council.[86] The auditors, six appointed by the Duma and six by the Federation Council, were not formally appointed by the president. In spite of this, the Duma dismissed its six auditors in February 2005. There was little doubt among commentators that this move was dictated by the Kremlin.[87] This increased influence of the president over what was originally a parliamentary institution of oversight was part of the overall trend towards greater presidential power over just about all institutions. Nowhere was this more evident than in the defence and security sector. All in all, the amendment of the law on the Audit Chamber deprived the political system of yet another possibility of independent scrutiny.[88]

Earlier, the Audit Chamber and Military Procuracy had taken measures to improve their ability to scrutinize how the defence budget was implemented. In May and July 1999, the first steps were taken to formalize cooperation between the two bodies. In June 2000 a joint collegium of the General Procuracy and the Audit Chamber discussed cooperation in order to scrutinize and control how federal budget resources and state property were used. In practical terms, this meant that the Military Procuracy was to react more promptly when the Audit Chamber discovered violations of the law.[89] However, it is worth emphasizing that the cases all concerned petty corruption rather than a penetrating analysis of whether the military organization was able to perform its tasks, and did so according to the intentions spelled out by the political leadership.

There were signs that the military courts had become a way for servicemen to defend their rights. As proof of this, one analyst brought forward statistics according to which about 43,000 servicemen brought suits to the military courts in 1998. Of these about 80 per cent won their case. In addition, about 100 orders or directives emanating from the Russian Ministry of Defence were determined to be illegal by military courts.[90] However, on the whole the judicial system continued to exercise only weak scrutiny over the military organization. As the number of acts of cruelty committed in Chechnya mounted and few, if any, were brought to justice, this became ever more apparent. Again, rather trivial pecuniary cases dominated over more principled questions of human rights violations suffered by, for example, conscripts or the population in Chechnya.

According to an interview with a high-ranking official within the military courts system, in 2004 these were no longer dependent on the Ministry of Defence. The legal foundations for their activity guaranteed this and, according to a law issued in 1999, the military courts were no longer financed through the military budget but through the federal budget of the Courts Department of the Supreme Court. As further evidence of this independence, the official mentioned that during the first nine months of 2004, 375 senior officers had been sentenced for various crimes in military courts. The majority of these were commanding officers.[91] According to the same source, the military courts had increasingly become an institution for the protection of rights rather than the severe institution for issuing punishment that they used to be regarded as. Moreover, efforts to prevent crime had come to the forefront. As part of this effort, some of the court cases were conducted at the units in the presence of fellow servicemen. Another aspect of crime prevention was more active work with the media to publicize military court cases as examples to inform and warn. A number of military courts had therefore set up press service departments and regularly called press conferences.[92] However, other signs of a strengthened position of the judicial branch were lacking. For example, when the Military Procurator publicly criticized the MoD for its laxity when it came to preventing crime and corruption within its ranks, he was promptly rebuffed by Sergei Ivanov and little more happened.[93]

In general, neither the parliament nor the judicial branch improved its ability to exercise independent scrutiny of defence policy making and of the implementation of policy within the military establishment. This was indicated not least by the number of Russian cases that ended up in the European Court of Human Rights in Strasbourg. Rather, Putin created a system where all reins of power were gathered in the hands of the Presidential Administration. Although it would seem that the Duma and the Audit Chamber were now better able to check up on defence policy implementation (not least the finances of the Ministry of Defence), Putin made sure that the very same organs that were to exercise independent scrutiny were heavily dependent upon the president by taking control of appointments to the Audit Chamber and the Federation Council. In the case of the Duma, Putin managed to control it through the party United Russia, whose deputies after the 2003 election occupied all the truly influential posts.

In April 2005, new legislation appeared on a new institution in Russian politics. The Public Chamber was to become a consultative institution, created to 'stimulate the development of civil society'.[94] Putin had created the Public Chamber to control civil society rather than allowing it to develop independently of state intervention. Indeed, the Public Chamber presented 'itself as the only legitimate forum for civil society'.[95] In 2006, the president decided to use this new institution as a vehicle for instituting at least a semblance of independent scrutiny of the power ministries. According to a presidential decree, public councils were to be attached to all ministries, services and agencies directly subordinated to the president.[96] In the case of the Ministry of Defence, it organized its public council shortly after the presidential decree appeared.

Just as the Public Chamber was heralded as a triumph of Russian democracy, the Ministry of Defence quickly embraced its Public Council as a vehicle for demonstrating its commitment to transparency and 'civilian control'.[97] At its first session, the chairman of the Public Council, the charismatic film director Nikita Mikhalkov, underlined that it was to act independently. However, the Public Council was dependent on the MoD.[98] For example, it did not have its own budget and its only powers consisted in issuing recommendations to the MoD. It was reliant on the MoD to allot it financial assistance and to allow it, for example, to attend meetings of the MoD Collegium or travel to units in the regions.[99] However, overall the MoD proved forthcoming when it came to allowing the different commissions of the Public Council to visit units and ask questions of the soldiers and officers. One of Mikhalkov's first statements in his new role was that it was imperative that 'the people must love its army'. In his opinion 'the army for Russia should be not simply a means of offence and defence, it should be a model for life'.[100] Obviously, one important task of the Public Council was to influence society, instil patriotic ideals and attract young potential draftees rather than exercising control over the Ministry of Defence. Overall, the public councils were instruments for the executive rather than examples of independent oversight.

Curtailed freedom of the press and independent organizations

Starting with the war in Chechnya, the Kremlin demonstrated that it had realized the importance of information management and imposed strict control over reporting from the area. This complicated the work of human rights organizations and journalists wishing to cover events in Chechnya. As mentioned above, Putin's experiences of negative press coverage as a result of the *Kursk* disaster further increased the Kremlin's determination to control the dissemination of information. Shortly thereafter, the privately owned television channels, such as NTV, found themselves brought firmly under state control.[101]

There were also clear signs that the Ministry of Defence was determined to manage information on defence affairs. In 2005, the ministry announced the creation of a new television channel, *Zvezda*.[102] It had also produced its own glossy journal, *Rossiiskoe voennoe obozrenie* (*Russian Military Review*) since 2004. The creation of an information office as one of three directorates of the minister's apparatus (headed by Sergei Ivanov's right-hand man, Andrei Chobotov) was a clear sign that the ministry intended to control what was reported on military affairs. The head of the new information office, Sergei Rybakov, was – in common with Chobotov – a product of the

FSB. He attained the rank of general-major in early 2006 and did his best to expand the empire of his information office inside the ministry.[103] His rapid climb to the rank of general together with his far-reaching ambitions no doubt caused considerable resentment among the military officers.

The overall climate of debate in Russia deteriorated during Putin's tenure as president and this had a negative impact on the defence debate as well.[104] The Ministry of Defence was far from alone in trying to manage the dissemination of information to society. Other power ministries did the same.[105] Meanwhile, journalists and researchers were charged and convicted of disclosing defence secrets after having compiled and analysed open sources.[106] Independent organizations found it difficult to promote their message and in the case of, for example, the Committee of Soldiers' Mothers, representatives of the military establishment tried to discredit its activities. The different measures introduced by Putin to curtail political competition from non-desirable opposition parties made it difficult for dissenting parties and organizations to achieve registration and promote their cause. The introduction of a Public Chamber was merely yet another example of the way the Kremlin sought to control every field of political activity.

However, a degree of independent reporting on military affairs was still evident. In 2005, *Nezavisimoe voennoe obozrenie* celebrated its 10th anniversary. It had an impressive track record.[107] In a few years it had become the leading forum for defence debate. While *Krasnaia zvezda* tended to reproduce the official line, *Nezavisimoe voennoe obozrenie* provided the reader with different viewpoints. In 2006, however, *Nezavisimaia gazeta*, and thus *Nezavisimoe voennoe obozrenie* as well, had been taken over by business interests close to the Kremlin.[108] Nevertheless, this newspaper remained a forum for military debate. The journalist Aleksandr Golts published a monograph highly critical of Russian military reform in 2004 and other journalists, such as Anna Politkovskaia, continued to report from Chechnya in spite of the displeasure the articles aroused among both political and military decision makers. In other words, the Kremlin appeared to tolerate a degree of criticism as long as it did not reach national broadcast channels. However, in 2006, Politkovskaia was murdered and the defence columnist Ivan Safronov died in early 2007 in what was officially described as a suicide. However, the circumstances were curious to say the least and his colleagues dismissed the idea that Safronov was in any way suicidal.[109]

The Ministry of Defence – under the thumb of the FSB

The Kremlin proudly announced that Sergei Ivanov was the first civilian minister of defence of the Russian Federation, since he had previously relinquished the rank of lieutenant-general that he had held within the SVR.[110] A civilian minister of defence had apparently become a somewhat more acceptable option by the time Ivanov entered the ministry.[111] However, the idea of civilian control was far from being internalized within the General

Staff. When discussing the appointment of a Russian civilian minister of defence, it is important to keep in mind that the overall tradition in Russian public administration is that the head of a ministry is appointed from within the ministry. The practice has not been for the prime minister or president to pick someone from a ruling political party as minister, but rather a career bureaucrat. In other words, the appointment of Sergei Ivanov as head of the Ministry of Defence was not as much a step towards civilian control as a radical step away from a bureaucratic culture that had long prevailed and a strengthening of Kremlin control. It is also interesting to note that one of the other ministries that received an 'outsider' as minister was the Ministry of Internal Affairs. As in the case of the MoD, the minister, Colonel-General Rashid Nurgaliev, had made his career within the KGB (and later the FSB). This trend hardly escaped attention of the military officers within the MoD.

Sergei Ivanov's appointment as minister of defence also signalled that Putin was taking military reform seriously and that the Ministry of Defence would become an important wheel in the decision-making machinery.[112] He took with him something of a new team when he moved from the Security Council to the MoD (see Table 6.1). Of the new appointees, Liubov Kudelina attracted much attention. She came from the Ministry of Finance where she had been responsible for defence spending. In other words, she was familiar with the field and was expected to be able to come to grips with the misuse of funds that had been rife under her predecessor, Colonel-General Georgii Oleinik. However, her staff were dominated by the same military officials who had been there for years. She also proved a stern opponent of increased transparency of the military budget.[113] It would be easy to assume this was a result of Kudelina 'going native' inside the MoD, but evidence suggests that this was actually an attitude that she brought along from the Ministry of Finance. During this period, Kudelina probably started receiving support from her former employer, the Ministry of Finance, where all defence contracts were checked before companies received payment – payment that was channelled through the Ministry of Finance rather than directly from the MoD.[114] Nevertheless, it is doubtful whether control over defence spending was achieved on any scale. For example, the expenses generated by the war in Chechnya were not channelled through Kudelina's service. The fact that the next minister of defence, Anatolii Serdiukov, came from a position as head of the Federal Tax Service rather than from the military or security sphere and came to the MoD with a clear mission to monitor money flows, suggests that the Kremlin did not feel it had achieved control over how its increasing defence budgets were actually spent.

What received relatively less attention at the time of Ivanov's appointment was his team, which consisted of a not insignificant number of people from the security services and people who had worked with him in the Security Council. In essence, Ivanov's appointment very much reflects Putin's view of how best to achieve control. If one of the lessons he drew from the *Kursk* disaster was that he needed to curb the independence of the media, the other

Table 6.1 Defence Minister Sergei Ivanov's 'team' in the Ministry of Defence in 2001

Name	Rank	Background	Position within the Ministry of Defence
Andrei Chobotov	Lt-gen.	FSB	Assistant to the minister and head of the MoD apparatus
Nikolai Kormiltsev	Col-gen.	Mil., com. of the Siberian MD	Dep. minister of defence and commander of the ground forces
Liubov Kudelina	Civ.	Dep. Min. of finance	Dep. minister of defence and head of the Financial Economical Directorate
Anatolii Mazurkevich	Lt-gen.	Ministry of Defence (GRU)	Head of the Main Directorate for International Military Cooperation
Aleksei Moskovskii	Col gen.	Mil. and 1st dep. secr. of the Security Council	Head of procurement for the Armed Forces
Nikolai Pankov	Lt-gen.	KGB, FPS, FSB and head of the Security Council apparatus	Head of the Main Directorate for Cadres and Military Education
Igor Puzanov	Col-gen.	Mil., com. of Moscow MD	Dep. minister of defence and state secretary

Source: *Nezavisimoe voennoe obozrenie*, 2002, no. 44 (20–26 December), p. 3. See also *Nezavisimoe voennoe obozrenie*, 2001, no. 26 (20–27 July), p. 3.

was the need to control the military, and the best way he knew of doing this was to appoint people he trusted, usually from the security sphere, to influential posts. Achieving control through independent scrutiny and transparency was obviously never really an option that Putin seriously considered.

Although Ivanov undoubtedly enjoyed the advantage of having close access to the president – outlined in Chapter 3 as an essential condition for the military corps to accept him as an asset to the ministry – the rapid advancement of FSB officers inside the ministry created resentment and divisions (an exception to this appears to be Nikolai Pankov, who managed not to rub up the military officers the wrong way). In other words, the ministry did not seem to be advancing towards becoming an integrated ministry of defence with civilian and military experts working jointly along the lines described in Chapter 3.

Certain other changes within the Ministry of Defence are also of interest. In July 2001, the influential Leonid Ivashov was replaced by Anatolii Mazurkevich as head of the Main Directorate for International Military Cooperation (GUMVS). Ivashov had headed the GUMVS since 1996 and under his leadership the directorate had become an influential part of the MoD.[115] Ivashov's fierce statements and actions during the negotiations on NATO enlargement as well as his well publicized anti-Western statements during the Kosovo crisis were indications of his high profile within the ministry.[116] With his departure, such brash statements from the MoD became rarer and its representatives appeared to speak more in unison.

In spite of his bringing with him a team of loyal officials, there were many misgivings about Sergei Ivanov's prospects within the Ministry of Defence. Nor did it take long before military analysts in the Russian and Western media claimed that Ivanov had failed miserably in his reform efforts. Certainly, he faced daunting opposition, especially from the General Staff, but also from other high-ranking officers, many of them with experience of Chechnya. In 2002 it became increasingly common for generals and admirals to oppose decisions publicly. General Georgii Shpak, commander of the airborne forces (VDV) held a press conference to voice his resentment when it became clear that the MoD might oppose his continued service after age sixty. General Gennadii Troshev, commander of the North Caucasus MD, refused transfer to the 'rear district', the Siberian MD.[117] The commander of the Black Sea Fleet, Admiral Vladimir Komoedov also publicly opposed a cadre decision. This, together with frequent incidents of conscripts defecting from military units, suggested to journalists on military affairs at *Nezavisimoe voennoe obozrenie*, Vadim Solovev and Mikhail Khodarenok, that Sergei Ivanov had lost control of the Armed Forces.[118]

> One gets the impression that the Russian military department has turned into a peculiar debating society: orders are more often debated than obeyed. Who knows – offended 'Chechen' generals as well could unite with other bypassed military commanders in opposing the centre. At all events, one or two steps remain to a situation reminiscent of the appearance of the Decembrists in 1825. Furthermore, December is outside now.[119]

In 2003, after Ivanov had bestowed the rank of general on a number of people, this was taken as a proof that he had become the hostage of the military. One newspaper made a comparison with 'the Brezhnev era, when the lack of progress was compensated for through state decorations' and concluded that the fact that Ivanov had made a number of subordinates to Kvashnin army generals led one to expect that Kvashnin would become a marshal in the next round of promotions.[120] In the event, it turned out quite the reverse. Sergei Ivanov had found himself in contention with the chief of the General Staff, Anatolii Kvashnin, just as his predecessor, Igor Sergeev, had.[121] The trench warfare between Sergeev and Kvashnin had culminated in 2000. However, the antagonism between the minister of defence and the General Staff hardly decreased when Ivanov succeeded Sergeev. Quickly rumours spread of widespread disagreements between Kvashnin and the 'civilian' team of Ivanov within the ministry.

This situation, if allowed to continue, would have undermined the position of Ivanov and made it impossible for him to push through reforms. In a speech in January 2004, Sergei Ivanov finally announced his intention to get the better of the General Staff. Although in superficially veiled language, Ivanov's speech made it clear that the General Staff, if he was left to decide the matter, was to be 'relieved of superfluous administrative functions' and concentrate on strategic planning. The General Staff was to become the 'brain of the army' (a term coined by the Second World War hero Marshal Boris Shaposhnikov). Furthermore, Ivanov made it clear that he thought the training of staff officers must be significantly improved. 'There are those who say that command experience from real combat situations is more worth than years of working in staff appointments and studying in academies. This is a dangerous illusion. [...] Command experience, valuable though it may be, cannot replace staff culture.'[122] This was a clear dig at the present General Staff – largely made up of officers with combat experience from the wars in Chechnya.

In the spring and summer of 2004, the untenable situation within the Ministry of Defence was finally resolved in Ivanov's favour. New regulations for the MoD and, thus, the General Staff were issued, the Law on Defence was amended and Kvashnin was dismissed in July.[123] As always, Putin made sure that Kvashnin did not leave empty-handed and appointed him presidential envoy in the Siberian Federal District. This position allowed Kvashnin to retain an influential position, albeit entirely at the discretion of the president. Kvashnin also retained his membership of the Security Council, but in a new capacity. Yurii Baluevskii became the new chief of the General Staff. His name had circulated in speculation as to who would succeed Kvashnin, but always with the caveat that he lacked necessary combat experience since he had pursued what could be termed a staff career. In July 2004, this was apparently no longer a drawback. He had earlier been involved in negotiations on the Treaty on Strategic Offensive Reductions (SORT) and Anti-ballistic Missiles (ABM) treaties with the USA and had probably gained a reputation as a loyal and able candidate for the post of chief of the General Staff.[124]

The way in which the Law on Defence was amended is significant. The changes were prepared in the Duma Defence Committee, allegedly without the chief of the General Staff receiving any information about this.[125] It was then voted upon in parliament and passed in what almost amounts to record time. Among the significant alterations in the law and in the new regulations was the fact that the uncertainty as to who really headed the Armed Forces was dispelled. The minister of defence headed all the ministry's forces although operational command was left to the General Staff. In addition, the chief of the General Staff was deprived of his right to report to the president without informing the minister of defence. Unity of command had been formally established.[126]

The minister of defence, moreover, received his own apparatus, the head of which, Andrei Chobotov, became his trusted associate. This strengthened Ivanov's leverage within the ministry. Very little information was available about the exact functioning of this apparatus, although Rybakov's Directorate for Information and Contacts with Society alone comprised 350 people.[127]

The changes introduced in 2004 could, of course, have been merely cosmetic. That central tasks were moved from the General Staff to other sections in the ministry does not automatically mean that Ivanov's ministry became more pliant to him. If the very same officers coming from the General Staff occupied the new posts, only outside the General Staff, the changes signified little change. However, the anger with which the reforms were met by high-ranking generals indicated that the measures did imply a real change in the power relationships within the ministry.[128]

However, three main directorates responsible for some of the most important tasks inside the MoD were still subordinated to the General Staff:

* The *Main Directorate of Operations* of the General Staff
* The *Main Organisational-Mobilization Directorate* of the General Staff
* The *Main Intelligence Directorate* of the General Staff, GRU.[129]

Sergei Ivanov made it clear in a speech in November 2004 that further changes were on the way. He spoke in particular of two 'negative elements' that were still present – one of which was the number of officers seconded to various state institutions. All in all, this concerned only about 3,500 officers (1 per cent of the officer corps), but they were mainly colonels and generals. 'In our view, the arrangements and conditions for their secondment need correcting with the introduction of necessary changes into the current legislation.'[130] First of all, the number of military personnel in expert positions outside the MoD ought to be reduced and in the structures where military expertise was necessary it was, in Ivanov's view, preferable for these officers to leave active duty.[131] In other words, the military establishment was faced with the prospect of potentially losing even more of its influence. Figure 6.2 shows the MoD structure after November 2004.

Not only was Ivanov's position within the ministry strengthened during this period. The Ministry of Defence also received additional powers and gained influence at the expense of some of the other power ministries in 2003–4. As part of Putin's administrative reform in 2004, the MoD took over the State Railway Troops and part of the disbanded Ministry of Atomic Energy. These were integrated into the ministry. As mentioned above, three federal services and one federal agency were subordinated to the MoD. In addition, the MoD was to manage the rear service and coordinate procurement for the troops of other power ministries. As a result, the personnel of the MoD increased significantly – according to *Nezavisimoe voennoe obozrenie*, by about 10 per cent.[132]

With his appointment as deputy prime minister, Ivanov's position became even stronger. In fact, no previous Soviet or Russian minister of defence had enjoyed the kind of position Ivanov obtained in 2005. His areas of responsibility as deputy prime minister were the policy programmes connected to the defence order, procurement programmes, R&D concerning military technology and military–industrial questions generally. It was especially notable

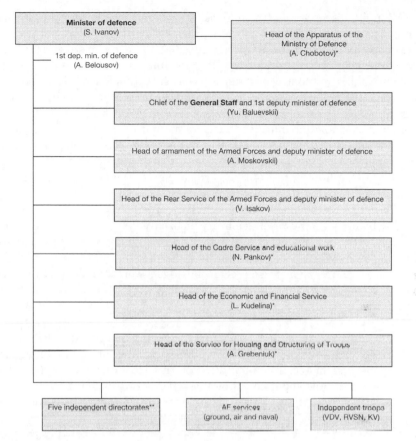

Figure 6.2 Structure of the Ministry of Defence after November 2004
Source: *Nezavisimoe voennoe obozrenie*, 2004, no. 44 (19–26 November), p. 3.

Notes:
*   With the rights belonging to a deputy minister of defence.
**   The independent directorates are the Military Inspection, the Military Scientific
     Directorate, the Main Directorate for International Military Cooperation, the
     Directorate of External Relations and the 12th Main Directorate of the Ministry
     of Defence (responsible for transportation and the handling of nuclear weapons
     and related safety concerns). (On the 12th Main Directorate, see J. Leijonhielm et
     al., *Rysk militär förmåga i ett tioårsperspektiv: en förnyad bedömning 2002*,
     Stockholm: FOI, February 2003, User Report, FOI-R–0811–SE, p. 119; and
     Golts, *Armiia Rossii: 11 poteriannykh let*, Moscow: Zakharov, 2004, p. 72.)

that his responsibility included not only the Ministry of Defence but also
'other troops, military units and organs'. In other words, at a stroke his
influence over the other power ministries had become considerably stronger.
Ivanov's appointment was also testimony to the fact that earlier plans for
coordinating procurement for all the power ministries through the MoD had
probably failed yet again.

All in all, the position of both Sergei Ivanov and his ministry was strengthened considerably in 2003–4. However, there was little in the way of efforts to create an integrated Ministry of Defence. The placing of former FSB and SVR officials in central positions within the ministry may have strengthened Ivanov's ability to control his ministry and subordinated services and agencies, but it did not infuse the necessary know-how on non-military matters that an integrated ministry would have provided. Nor did the reforms within the ministry allow the minister to ensure himself of more alternative advice and information from non-military officials. Even more potentially damaging, the high profile of the FSB within the MoD involved a risk of antagonizing the officer corps of the Armed Forces and of serious tensions building up between the power ministries.

This situation changed only marginally when Anatolii Serdiukov succeeded Ivanov as minister of defence in February 2007. As mentioned above, there is every reason to suspect that his appointment was connected to a growing discomfort in the Kremlin over the fact that it still had very little control over how the increasing defence budgets were actually spent. In fact, Putin's comments in connection with Serdiukov's appointment bear testimony to this fact.

> I would like for the ministry, in any case, the sections that will occupy themselves with development, to devote serious attention to the economic and financial component. For this reason, I will sign a decree today about the appointment of a new minister of defence, a civilian, but nevertheless a person who is able to carry out these tasks thanks to his knowledge in the economic and financial sphere.[133]

The prospects of Serdiukov succeeding in bringing order in defence spending did not appear promising. Although, as Putin pointed out, he brought with him considerable experience from the economic and financial sphere, he did not have a sizeable staff of his own at his disposal in order to make his own analyses of, for example, procurement needs or maintenance costs. He would, like his predecessors, have to rely to a considerable extent on the advice and analysis of military officers not infrequently from the General Staff (which, incidentally, received signals from Putin that its influence was to increase again).[134] Nor were there independent think tanks that could perform this function for Serdiukov.[135] Again, Putin's instinct to appoint his own *controlleur* rather than allowing mechanisms of transparency or independent functions of scrutiny to develop made him hostage to his own power vertical.

Military reform becomes 'modernization'

There was probably a growing realization within the Ministry of Defence that the term 'military reform' had become compromised by the failure of earlier attempts – not least under Grachev. In October 2003, the Ministry of Defence published a document, *Priority Tasks of the Development of the Armed Forces,* which declared the military reform to have been accomplished.[136] The document, often referred to as the 'Ivanov doctrine', declared that a new phase had begun where the focus was to be on developing the Armed Forces through 'modernization'. The term signalled that all efforts would now go into consolidating the Armed Forces by concentrating on training and procurement. In actuality, this was more of a play on words than an actual end to military reform. Many considered it premature to declare the military reform process over.[137] As the previous chapters have concluded, the problems that the military organization, including the Armed Forces, faced demanded a comprehensive reform that could not be limited to measures taken by the MoD.

The military–industrial complex needed reforming and, yet again, the question of how much resources should be devoted to defence and security needed to be settled. Military service had to become an attractive prospect again and this required coming to grips with all the problems, from the wages and social benefits provided to ensuring that soldiers' human rights were not violated while they were serving in the military organization. None of these questions could be solved solely from within the Ministry of Defence. Instead, relations between the state and the military, society and the military, and state and society needed to be transformed in order to reach a new social contract.[138] Certainly, draft evasion coupled with the fact that the Russian public did not believe that the state was able to protect it against terrorism pointed in this direction. Very few people were ready to become soldiers and officers and there was nothing approaching consensus between the military and society on how much public spending to devote to defence relative to other needs. It was furthermore highly doubtful whether the military organization was dimensioned to meet the most urgent threats that Russia was facing. The Kremlin would have to prioritize how resources were to be distributed between the MoD and the other power ministries, and to define which threats Russia was facing and what military force posture was required.

Important initiatives did come to light in the sphere of military reform. Not least the early efforts to reform the entire military organization, in other words the other power structures as well as the Armed Forces, gave grounds for optimism when it came to moving military reform forwards. However, many of these initiatives met stiff resistance from the power ministries. Nor did the military–industrial complex show signs of being susceptible to attempts at reform. However, there were tangible improvements within the Armed Forces and the Ministry of Defence was able to stage major complex exercises such as Mobilnost 2004. The military districts were reorganized, as was the structure of the Armed Forces. Indeed, there was evidence of reform of the Armed Forces, while military reform as such made only modest progress.

The Armed Forces vs other power ministries

As mentioned above, Sergei Ivanov had started working on a renewed reform plan while he was secretary of the Security Council and two documents with the main guidelines were adopted in January 2000, a few months before Ivanov became minister of defence.[139] In fact, Ivanov's plans for reform (Box 6.1) were continuously developed in a number of documents concerning different aspects of military reform, such as the transition to contract-based armed forces, measures to improve military-scientific work and procurement, and so on. Only a few of these were published. The content of Ivanov's plans for reform became clear from interviews, statements and the programme declarations that appeared on the websites of the Ministry of Defence and the Presidential Administration. Evidently, many of the measures implemented under Ivanov were in fact a product of the plans made for military reform in 1996–97, but there were new initiatives as well.

In contrast to the measures and reform results that were a continuation of the process started in 1997, changing the overall ratio between the resources spent on upkeep and procurement was a new political goal. The plans were, however, subject to revisions and often postponed. In November 2004, the new chief of the General Staff, Colonel-General Yurii Baluevskii, announced the priorities for further development of the Armed Forces up to 2010. The revised plan of the General Staff included:

- further development of the command system for the Armed Forces;
- completing the transition to joint (*mezhvedomstvennye*) and unified systems for the rear service of the Armed Forces, other forces, military units and organs; their infrastructure for storage, transport, medical service, repairs and others would thus be unified according to the territorial principle and administered by the military district;
- formation and realization of a unified technology policy for the Armed Forces and the state military organization as a whole;
- beginning the planned re-equipment of troops and forces with new weapon models, military and special technology; and
- intensified military training.[140]

The plan thus intensified and prioritized certain reform activity within the Armed Forces. However, the measures that demanded coordination with other power ministries were again postponed, while the sections of the plan that concerned the Armed Forces were more likely to be implemented.

The position of the Ground Forces strengthened after Kvashnin had got the upper hand in his battle with Sergeev. In 2001, the post of commander of the Ground Forces was reintroduced and his command of the military districts restored. Hitherto, this task had been the responsibility of the General Staff. The commander of the Ground Forces was also accorded the rank of deputy minister of defence.[141] This was justified by the fact that the commander

Box 6.1 Ivanov's reform plan

Phase 1 (2001–2005)

- Structural developments continued. The RVSN to be downgraded from a service (*vid*) of the Armed Forces to an arm (*rod*). It would lose the Missile Space Defence Troops and the Military Space Command. The latter would form a new arm of troops, the Space Troops (*Kosmicheskie Voiska*, KV). The RVSN was, however, to retain the nuclear triad. As a result, by 2002 there would be only three services of the Armed Forces – the ground forces, the navy and the air force. Within the ground forces, permanent readiness formations and units were prioritized and the Main Command of the Ground Forces resurrected.
- The military organization to be reduced by 365,000 servicemen and 100,000 civilian personnel.
- The Volga MD and the Ural MD to be merged into the Volga-Ural MD, responsible for the Central Asian strategic direction.
- The units in the North Caucasus to be developed further.
- Central command and control structures to be optimized.
- A central and coordinated process for procurement for the entire military organization. Unified and developed rear services and the system for military education and training.

Phase 2 (2001–10)

- Enhanced social protection for servicemen.
- An experiment initiated in Pskov aiming to recruit soldiers and specialists on contract basis. On the experiences in Pskov: a programme for transferring more units from conscripts to employed *kontraktniki* (contract employees).

Phase 3 (2006–)

- The RVSN incorporated in the air force.
- Procurement share of the defence budget to be increased from 30% to 40%.

Phase 4 (2011–)

- Procurement share of the defence budget to be increased to 50%.

Sources: *Krasnaia zvezda*, 25 April 2001, pp. 1, 2; and Ministry of Defence of the Russian Federation, *Voennaia reforma*, 2002. Online. Available HTTP: www.mil.ru/index.php?menu_id = 60 (accessed 3 October 2002).

of the Ground Forces was tasked with creating joint commands in the military districts. At the same time, the Directorate for the Head of the Engineering Troops and Troops for Chemical Protection was transferred from the General Staff to the commander of the Ground Forces. The other (navy and air force) service chiefs did not become deputy ministers.[142]

This constituted nothing short of a resurrection of the central role of the Ground Forces within the Armed Forces. In fact, its position was strengthened in that the commander of the Ground Forces was given increased command power over the military districts. The new commander of the Ground Forces, Colonel-General Nikolai Kormiltsev, was probably best described as a 'tactical conservative'. He tended to assert that local conflicts and counter-insurgency were indeed what should be the focus, while the exercises planned during his time as commander were of a more traditional or conservative nature with scenarios resembling those of the Cold War.[143]

The Airborne Troops, the VDV, were given priority, especially in terms of combat readiness, and remained directly subordinated to the General Staff. Although destined to be used for combat behind enemy lines, the VDV were increasingly used as elite units in local wars. This high profile generated a substantial amount of animosity from other sections of the Armed Forces, not least the Ground Forces.[144] However, even the formations of the VDV struggled to achieve the combat-readiness goals prescribed by the reform plans – especially at division level.[145] By Sergei Ivanov's own admission, much work was still needed in January 2003 in order for Russia to have at its disposal 'well-trained and equipped forces constantly prepared for action'.[146]

The RVSN was reduced from a service to an arm of the Armed Forces as early as April 2001. That the RVSN no longer retained the favoured position it had had during Sergeev's first years as minister of defence was also obvious from the fact that the plans for production of the Topol-M (SS-27) ICBM were cut back. Instead of the twenty missiles per year previously envisaged, only five to six would be produced. The last two rail-mobile divisions were removed from combat duty during 2005. The plan was for the RVSN to be merged with the Air Force around 2006 and for the number of strategic missile divisions to be reduced from 15 to 10 by 2010.[147] However, in 2007 the RVSN was still an independent arm of the Armed Forces. To a certain degree, the RVSN had in common with the navy that its main use for the Kremlin was that of a political tool on a global level, but it was of less practical use in the local conflicts that had entered the agenda after the end of the Cold War.

It is probably against this background that Putin's much publicized pronouncements on the development of new nuclear missile systems and so on should be assessed.[148] Nevertheless, when it became clear that the USA would place missile defence installations in Poland and the Czech Republic, nuclear deterrence entered the Kremlin agenda and rhetoric very prominently. On a number of occasions, Putin claimed that Russia was developing secret missiles or 'new strategic systems' that would be able to penetrate any existing missile defence system.[149] At the European Union (EU)–Russia summit in

Mafra in October 2007, Putin even compared the situation 'technically' with that which led to the Cuban Missile Crisis of 1962.[150]

The air force received only modest additions to its aircraft fleet. The number of aircraft increased partly as a result of the transfer of Ground Forces aviation to the air force by January 2003, partly because a number of Tu-95s and Tu-160s had been transferred from Ukraine to Russia between 1998 and 2001.[151] Work was under way to introduce a fifth-generation aircraft into the Russian Air Force. Sukhoi was awarded the contract to develop this aircraft.[152] However, the next generation of Russian aircraft would not be able to compete with the American Joint Strike Fighter (F-35) and the Eurofighter, and was usually described as a four-plus generation air craft (or on occasion four-plus-plus).[153] As one Russian commentator lamented, you would not receive a fifth-generation aircraft no matter how many pluses you put after four.[154] Meanwhile, pilots were gradually receiving more training (albeit from the very low level of 2000–2001) as a direct result of the increased defence budgets. The average flying time varied considerably between different air force units and attempts were made to concentrate on training a new generation of pilots. Nevertheless, the overall average flying time in 2007, 40 hours per year, was still very low compared to what Western pilots enjoyed.[155]

Although Putin initially seemed to show some concern about the situation in the navy, few investments were made in this service. Its ships were neglected and run-down and there were few signs that the navy had carried through the necessary restructuring to adjust to new financial realities. Lingering dreams of a blue-water navy proved resilient to both political and financial pressure. The threat the navy wished to prepare for before all others was that from NATO and the USA. Consequently, with only modest new funding forthcoming and no inherent wish to restructure itself according to new geopolitical realities, it would be difficult for the navy to recover.[156] Its tasks within the nuclear triad were prioritized. The construction of Borei Class submarines went ahead, as did the testing of the new submarine-launched ballistic missile (SLBM), the Bulava, which was designed for the new submarines. However, a number of tests of the Bulava failed and, although the Ministry of Defence described this as normal during trials, there was deep scepticism among Russian commentators as to how successful the new missile had proved.[157]

In the military districts (now six, after restructuring), there were eight army commands and two corps commands in 2002. However, this did not mean that formations of these sizes did in fact exist. Rather, the formations were intended to be able to grow into such a force structure if a major war threatened. The largest formations that were manned and had a permanent structure were those at the division level.[158] For obvious reasons, the importance of the Moscow and North Caucasus MDs had increased.[159]

In early 2006, the General Staff indicated that further structural reforms of the Armed Forces were under way.[160] In particular, there were plans to try a new command system based on three strategic directions or 'joint commands'

(West, South and East) instead of the six military districts, which would be demoted to serving administrative functions.[161] From 2006, there would be experiments to evaluate how efficient such a new command system would be and the results would be evaluated in 2008–10.[162] The new command system appeared to be inspired by the American system, building on strategic commands, although the Russian equivalent did not encompass the entire globe. The experiment was very much associated with Baluevskii, who was in charge of its introduction. Undoubtedly, to a degree it became entangled in power struggles inside the Ministry of Defence. There were early rumours that the experiment was proving extremely unsuccessful. As *Nezavisimoe voennoe obozrenie* observed, 'Baluevskii's reform is a response to modern challenges, but does not correspond to the level of development of the national MIC and military theory'.[163] Indeed, many of the difficulties experienced were closely connected to the difficulties in achieving a greater degree of interoperability. This also put new demands on the military training system.

In 2005, there was another major overhaul of the military training system. In particular, the training of officers at military faculties at civilian institutions of higher education was targeted. It was clear that these often maintained a low standard and that a surplus of reservist officers were being trained each year. In future, thirty-three institutions of higher education would organize military education centres on the basis of the former military faculties. To enrol, the student would have to sign up for military service for at least three years. In an additional thirty-five institutions of higher education, military faculties would be preserved. Students who received their education at these institutions would not serve in the Armed Forces, and beginning in 2008 there would be no reservist officers. In the future Armed Forces, where the majority would be employed on a contract basis, 'the reservist officer would become an anachronism'.[164] You could hardly expect a reservist officer with only rudimentary military knowledge and training to command contract soldiers with considerably more experience, not infrequently from combat zones. The reform was not only intended to improve the quality of training. The students that underwent education at the military faculties were exempt from regular military service and only about 10 per cent of them were actually called upon to serve at all. In other words, the Ministry of Defence probably hoped to be able to enrol a larger number of young men as a result of the reform as well.

Structural reform of the Armed Forces was thus well under way. Efforts were made to improve command and control structures. According the head of the Main Directorate of Operations, Colonel-General Aleksandr Rukshin, the time when the services and arms of the Armed Forces conducted independent operations was over. 'Joint operations have moved to the forefront, [operations] in which groups of different troops and forces take part, acting under a joint command with a joint purpose and plan'.[165] An integrated command and control system was introduced in order to make it possible for not only different services and arms of the Armed Forces, but also different power ministries and agencies whose troops formed part of the military organization, to communicate with each other.

This was a costly and difficult process, which was coordinated by the General Staff. New computer-based command and control technology was used in troops active in the North Caucasus region, where mechanisms for cooperation with the regional authorities were developed as well. Although the technology was there, significant problems remained in getting the troops to cooperate in the way intended. The military training the officers had received proved inadequate for commanding joint task forces, and they were incapable of processing the information flow that the new command and control systems generated. In addition, the cultural differences between the different services and arms of the Armed Forces – not to mention between different power ministries – proved an often insurmountable obstacle.[166]

Nevertheless, the reforms undertaken resulted in better performance in military exercises, which became larger and more complex than had been the case during most of the 1990s. Frequently, different services of the Armed Forces and forces belonging to other power ministries participated in joint exercises. This was in line with the priorities in Ivanov's plans for reform. In addition, the large-scale Mobilnost 2004 exercise aimed to test mobilization as well as transportation capacity. In the exercise, performed like so many others under the banner of 'anti-terrorism', units were airlifted from western to eastern Russia. Although the terminology was far from unequivocal, it was clear that the exercises carried less of an anti-Western imprint than, for example, Zapad-99 had.[167]

Not only the Armed Forces were called upon to start reforms. Both the MVD and the FSB were required to reorganize in order to better mirror the increased emphasis on anti-terrorist measures. By 2001, the time had become ripe for another major reorganization of the MVD. In an article in *Voennaia mysl*, the commander-in-chief of the Interior Troops outlined the main plans for reform.[168] In 2002, plans were announced to make the Interior Troops into a National Guard by 2005 (later the year 2006 was mentioned). In line with military reform of the Armed Forces, the National Guard was to be manned by volunteers rather than conscripts. In addition, the *spetsnaz* forces were to be made into rapid deployment forces. The regional organization of the Interior Troops was to be divided into five regional commands and two regional directorates in order to correspond to the federal districts.[169] In 2004, the Interior Troops faced demands similar to those placed upon the Armed Forces when it came to manning on a contract basis, and by 2007, 12,500 Interior Troops were intended to be hired on a contract basis. The first unit to undergo this change was the 46th Special-Purpose Brigade stationed in Chechnya.[170] However, it appeared that the Interior Troops in the North Caucasus were to remain military units rather than moving towards becoming a National Guard. Instead of the brigade–battalion structure, the Interior Troops would revert to the division–regimental one and in line with this the Interior Troop battalions deployed in the North Caucasus would become regiments.[171] The military nature of the battle against terrorism in the North Caucasus reinforced the impression that the Interior Troops were not moving towards becoming a National Guard.

On 11 July 2004, Putin issued a decree ordering the FSB to reorganize in order to better meet the new threats to national security. Later the same year, the main changes were announced. In line with the administrative reform, the number of deputy directors of the FSB was reduced from eleven to four. Earlier, the FSB had had a number of directorates and departments. Now, it was to consist of eight services (*sluzhby*) with subordinated departments. However, much suggested that the FSB Investigative Directorate would retain its independent position.[172] The Service for Protection of the Constitutional Order and Combating Terrorism had undergone the greatest changes. Under this service, a new department had been created, the Directorate for Combating International Terrorism.[173] In addition, the regional organization of the Border Troops underwent change in order to fit with the federal districts of the Russian Federation. Thus, in November 2004, the North Caucasian Regional Border Directorate became the FSB Regional Border Directorate of the Southern Federal District.[174] In 2006, the FSB received overall responsibility for combating terrorism when the National Anti-Terrorist Committee (NAK) was created in February 2006. The director of the FSB became head of the NAK, which replaced the earlier anti-terrorist organization, in which the MVD had played the central role.[175]

In other words, there were attempts to reform other power ministries as well, not least in order to intensify the anti-terrorist part of their activities. Nevertheless, there was little evidence of a cohesive effort at military reform. Many of the changes described above were dictated by the administrative reform or by power struggles between the different ministries and agencies involved. Even in Chechnya in the midst of a major military operation there were reports of breakdowns in coordination and command due to rivalry between the different power ministries. The efforts to create an integrated rear service for all of Russia's military organization and to coordinate the procurement process under the aegis of the Ministry of Defence were both resisted by the other power ministries.[176]

Nor did any of the measures improve interoperability or Russia's ability to take part in international operations together with, for example, NATO. The only operation Russia took part in was Operation Active Endeavour in the Mediterranean, and even this limited engagement with NATO was fraught with considerable frustrations on both sides. Russia remained unimpressed with the European Union as a military actor on the international scene and showed little or no interest in participating in international operations under EU command.[177] In 2006, Russia declined participating in a UN mission to Lebanon despite its professed preference for UN operations.[178] In the end, Russia opted for sending its own mission on a bilateral basis to help in reconstruction.[179] Overall, Russia did conduct joint exercises with, for example, NATO and the Shanghai Cooperation Organization, but prioritized cooperation within its 'own' regional security organization, the Collective

Security Treaty Organization (CSTO), which it sought to have recognized as a regional security organization according to chapter VIII of the UN Charter.[180]

The unreformed military–industrial complex

In many ways, the Russian military–industrial complex represents a problem in its own right and would deserve a separate study. However, it would be impossible to carry out a military reform while leaving the MIC unreformed.[181] Again, this brings out the conclusion that military reform must be coordinated and forced through at the very apex of defence decision making, since the Ministry of Defence would never be able to dictate the development of vital components of the military system such as the MIC. Only the political leadership can make such priorities and set an agenda for military reform as a whole.

As demonstrated above, the decision-making structures and lines of authority for the MIC and R&D were in disarray and the subject of constant reshuffling from 1992 onwards. This had a paralysing effect on the policy making on the MIC and as a result it remained largely unreformed. The decision-making muddle also suggests that for most of the time this was not a priority policy area. In 2003 and 2004, the number of companies officially registered as part of the Russian defence industry was 1,600–1,700, with about 2 million employees. These numbers were more or less identical to those in 1992.[182]

The overwhelming majority of the problems that MIC faced under Yeltsin remained under Putin, in spite of the reform programme for the MIC 2002–6, decreed in October 2001. The MIC reform programme aimed to reduce the number of companies to about 530. Even before it was launched, however, there were serious doubts as to whether sufficient financial resources were available, and there was an uneasy contradiction between the aim of streamlining the MIC and cutting away the dead wood, on the one hand, and that of keeping a substantial mobilization potential, on the other.[183]

According to defence industry analyst Vitalii Shlykov, the defence industry faced two main challenges in 2004. First, it needed to acquire new foreign technology and equipment. Second, it lacked a new generation of scientists and workers in these factories.[184] Russia was nowhere near solving either of these problems in a satisfactory manner. Instead, the conditioned reflex of the Kremlin was to pursue a policy leading to a 'patchwork structural military reactivization along Soviet lines'.[185] To restructure the defence industry according to market conditions would inevitably involve the Kremlin losing some of its control. In addition, it would gradually lose the ability to mobilize on a massive scale and militarize the country again. Neither of these prospects seemed to appeal to the Kremlin.

The strategy Russia adopted combined limited procurement (in order to maintain production facilities) with investments in R&D (to keep up with the rapid military-technological development). The lion's share of the investment was obviously supposed to be borne by the industry (financed through arms exports), as the government funding for R&D did not increase in line with the intentions stated. The plan was for Russia to skip stages and only develop experimental versions while waiting for conditions that would allow it to start serial production of modern weapons systems of the latest generation.

A number of risks were inherent in this strategy. First, it was unclear how long the state would be able to carry the economic weight that this would entail. Nor was it clear whether or when Russia would be able to devote the resources needed to start serial production of modern weapons on any scale without resorting to a policy of remilitarization. Second, it was a survival strategy rather than a strategy of development. There was little in the way of measures to restructure the MIC to the needs of the military organization. Nor were there signs that the MIC was attracting new, young researchers, programmers and engineers that would secure the next generation of R&D. Third, the military organization would have to procure a limited range of the defence industry's products on a regular basis. This demanded a high degree of coordination and discipline in the military planning – something that has not been a prominent feature in military–industrial policy making. Finally, the military organization would not be able to conduct large exercises with new weaponry and equipment and thus develop its performance according to the demands that new generations of technology would put upon it.[186]

As mentioned above, Sergei Ivanov left the Ministry of Defence in early 2007 to concentrate on his new task of heading the Military–Industrial Commission and reforming the military–industrial complex as well as the mechanisms for compiling and implementing the defence order. To many commentators, this constituted a clear sign that the Kremlin was finally determined to reform the MIC. However, the tasks ahead were daunting to say the least. In early 2007, Putin decreed a new agency into existence – the Federal Agency for Supply of Arms, Military and Special Technology and Equipment.[187] It was emphasized that this would be a purely civilian agency, which would coordinate procurement.[188] However, according to the presidential decree that appeared in June 2007, the personnel, a total of 1,100, for the new agency would come entirely from the power ministries concerned, of which 871 were from the Armed Forces.[189] It is impossible to determine how many of those transferred to the new agency were military officers and how many were civilian personnel, but there is reason to suspect that military personnel dominated the new agency in spite of its civilian status.

When it came to reforming the military industry, the focus was very much on centralization of control inside the executive and on gigantism. The plan was to create giant holding companies and reduce the number of producing companies to about 500. Meanwhile, the export of weapons was centralized under Rosoboroneksport and Sergei Chemezov, who was made its head. Although the results of this centralization would be visible only years later, there was much doubt among analysts as to how effective the measures would prove. Indeed, centralization only appeared yet again to confirm the Kremlin's obsession with control and its lack of confidence in transparency and independent scrutiny as a means of improving the system. Chemezov claimed in 2006 that centralizing exports would ensure the fulfilment of contracts as well as the quality of weapons delivered. 'The idea that the market or contract law enforced by courts might ensure this fulfilment apparently seems to have escaped Chemezov and his masters.'[190] Something that probably did not escape Chemezov and his associates was the fact that arms exports generate profits. One of the motives for centralizing it was, no doubt, the desire to control this money flow.

All in all, it remained to be seen whether Ivanov would be able to deliver a reformed MIC that delivered the weapons and equipment that Russian national security demanded. And the question of how to stimulate R&D in the long term and decrease the average age of the personnel involved in R&D appeared unresolved.

Manning the military organization

Finding the right conscripts and in sufficient numbers continued to prove a challenge to the Ministry of Defence and the other power ministries. Demographic trends were anything but auspicious and health among the young men available for military service gave increasing cause for concern. According to a health census made among children aged 0–17 in 2002, overall poor health among 15–17-year-olds was 'a strategic concern'. The problems ranged from tuberculosis, psychological disorders and alcoholism to chronic disabilities. In Russia, moreover, people carrying the HIV/AIDS virus are considerably younger than in other European countries (80 per cent are between 18 and 27 years old). Birth rates dropped dramatically at about the time of the fall of the Soviet Union. This will lead to a drastic decrease in the number of young men available for military service in 2009 (from about 1 million in 2008 to 900,000 in 2009, 800,000 in 2010 and 700,000 in 2011; and if birth rates do not increase significantly in the coming years the number will hover at about 600,000–700,000 in 2025 as well).[191] In other words, urgent measures were called for and it was probably partly with these statistics as a dramatic backdrop that the Kremlin and the MoD started searching for new ways of manning the military organization.

From inside the Ministry of Defence, in an interview in January 2003, Sergei Ivanov stated that much had been achieved during 2002. The MoD, together with the relevant federal executive authorities, had developed a draft document with the cumbersome name, 'Concept for a federal goal programme for switching to manning military posts mainly with servicemen fulfilling military service on contract'. Ivanov also gave details of the experiment in Pskov with contract-employed servicemen. It had started on

1 September 2002 and was planned to go on until October 2003. After manning one airborne regiment completely with contract-employed service-men, the staff would undergo individual training during the first six months and become divided into sections (*otdeleniia*), platoons (*vzvoda*), companies (*roty*) and battalions (*bataliony*). In the following six months it would be verified that the regiment was ready to fulfil active duty in so-called 'hot spots'; in the case of the airborne regiment of contractees in Pskov this would mean Chechnya. During 2003, the MoD would prepare to transfer mainly units of constant readiness to contract service.[192]

The Pskov experiment is significant in that not only the Kremlin and the Ministry of Defence were involved in preparing it. Liberal politicians such as Boris Nemtsov played a significant part in influencing Putin in the direction of forcing the army to consider the abandonment of conscription. A pro-gramme for switching to manning on a contract basis had been developed by Yegor Gaidar's Institute for the Economy in Transition together with the right-wing Soiuz Pravykh Sil (Union of Right Forces) and, to a certain degree, the liberal party Yabloko.[193] In order to thwart such reforms at an early stage or at least secure substantial funding for future *kontraktniki*, the General Staff made every effort to convince Putin and the minister of defence that the costs of abandoning conscription would be astronomical. The Pskov experiment proved a perfect opportunity for the military to drive this point home. Salaries for the contractees were fixed at an unusually high level for Russian conditions. In addition, the contract-employed soldiers would be provided with housing of a high standard.[194]

The 76th Airborne Divison in Pskov consists of two airborne regiments – the 234th in Pskov and the 104th in Cherekha (Pskov). Of these, the latter was to start the experiment. The 234th would follow, as would the operations and supply directorates of the 76th division. The experiment got off to a good start with a manning level of 77 per cent in the 104th regiment after only three months. Soon, however, problems arose both with manning the 234th regiment and with the quality of contractees. It was also clear that the contract-employed soldiers were inclined to leave service as soon as possible after having enjoyed the pay and benefits associated with service in Pskov and were reluctant to sign a second contact. In other words, the experiment did not solve the problem of keeping soldiering experience within the Armed Forces.[195]

Nevertheless, it became increasingly clear that the Kremlin was deter-mined to push through contract service on a wider basis than before. In Putin's state of the nation address in 2003, the national economy was the main priority, but military reform was also in focus. According to Putin, there were plans for rearming and moving towards a military employed on a contract basis. Putin argued in favour of contract service within not only the Armed Forces but also the Interior and Border Troops. Between the lines, Putin was saying that he did not intend to send ill prepared conscripts to places like Groznyi as had been done in Afghanistan during the Soviet era and Chechnya in 1994. 'In simple and understandable words ... this means the following: only trained and professional units will take part in hot spots and local conflicts if Russia, God forbid, has to face such challenges'.[196]

In a press conference on 20 June 2003, Putin made a similar remark when asked about the progress of military reform. He started by saying that the decision to use contract servicemen increasingly was dictated by the demographic situation as well as by the fact that the weaponry of the Armed Forces was becoming more and more sophisticated. He promised that only contract personnel would be used in 'hot spots'.

> Only professionals should, of course, serve in 'hot spots'. Conscripts, young boys of 18–19 years should not be there. Professional people, who chose this as their profession consciously and consciously take the risk, should be there. We plan that by the end of 2007, more than 100,000 in the Russian army should serve on contract basis. And in 2008 we will reduce the number who serve as conscripts and reduce their service to one year.[197]

Clearly, there was a political realization that society was unwilling to send its conscripted sons to Chechnya. Nevertheless, there was little evidence of Russia's population becoming more inclined to accept the hardships and risks that military service entailed. According to opinion polls conducted in 2005, there was a clear dichotomy in that there were sentiments in favour of a strong Russian military organization, while the population was dubious about military service. In other words, Russians did not mind a strong army as long as they themselves or their children were not required to serve in it. 'This should be the task of some kind of faceless contract employees, who nobody feels sorry for.'[198] In addition, there was little evidence of hazing disappearing from the military units. Although the numbers of non-combat deaths were disputed, even the Ministry of Defence was finding it difficult to ignore the problem or claim that it had been solved.[199] This was especially true since gruesome cases of hazing continued to make the headlines.

The officer corps appeared set on retaining something that could, at least, potentially become a mass army. Officers like the commander of the Ground Forces, Colonel-General Nikolai Kormiltsev, remained ambivalent on the question of contract employment. Although he professed to be in favour of contract service, he favoured introducing this over a period of 11–15 years. He considered it necessary to keep conscription in order to preserve the possibility of mobilizing large sections of the male population. The need to maintain a mass army was obviously an important component part of Russian strategic thinking.[200] Consequently, generals continued to determine the terms on which young men could refuse military service on ideological or religious grounds. This right had been inscribed in the constitution since 1993 (article 59:3), but legislation on the topic proved difficult to achieve.

Only in 2004 did a law on alternative civic service appear, but the alternatives that the Ministry of Defence offered for conscientious objectors often proved longer and harsher than regular conscription might have been.[201] There were also attempts to make it more difficult to escape conscription through bribing. In 2007, the number of drafting offices, *voennye kommissariaty* or *voenkomaty*, was reduced. This was combined with new rules to combat corruption – not least the habit of selling deferments. Most importantly, the *voenkomat* personnel would have to rotate.[202]

In exchange for complying with the Kremlin's determination to force through contract service, the military also demanded measures to increase the conscription level. The number of young men eligible for conscription had continued to decline, and the Ministry of Defence expressed disappointment with the conscript soldiers' health and social background. When it was decided that from 2008 military service would be reduced to one year, the ministry's demands for a larger recruitment base (and thus fewer grounds for deferral) increased in strength and the Kremlin complied.[203]

The year 2008 would be the last year when a number of power ministries (the MChS and the Border Troops) could rely on conscripts to fill their ranks. Nevertheless, all these measures together would go only a little way towards solving the Armed Forces' manning problems. Overall population decline and the poor health situation could not but have dire consequences for the military organization.[204] The political leadership seemed aware that the solution to manning problems did not lie in allowing the military to draft students again; this would only produce poorly motivated reserve officers with little if any will to continue active service. In other words, they would prove a poor substitute for a corps of NCOs.[205]

In 2002, work continued with converting benefits for servicemen into monetary allowances. Wages within the military sectors were in the process of being adjusted to the levels within other state service sectors. Work also continued on finding housing for servicemen in service and those dismissed from the Armed Forces.[206] An ambitious mortgage programme for providing housing for servicemen was launched. In spite of the assurances that this time nothing could go wrong, even this housing programme soon displayed weaknesses.[207] Thus in 2006 in his speech at the annual evaluation of the year inside the Ministry of Defence, Putin 'expressed the *hope* that the accumulative mortgage mechanism to ensure housing for new servicemen would be implemented efficiently', rather than the determination.[208] In addition, any increments in wages Russia's military servicemen received tended to be eaten up by inflation and by the fact that they simultaneously lost a number of benefits. The situation was even more precarious for military veterans and pensioners.

Clearly the problems with filling the ranks were destined to continue. There were a number of policy measures that needed to be implemented in order for Russia ever to be able to fill its military ranks with the kind of soldiers and officers it wanted. First, military service would have to be made safe. Human rights had to be safeguarded and the overall living conditions of the conscripts and contract soldiers improved. Second, both the remuneration and the prestige enjoyed by military servicemen had to be raised considerably. The officer corps tended to concentrate on this second set of much-needed measures. Nevertheless, neither remuneration nor prestige would be forthcoming if Russia's military organization were not brought into line with the country's security needs and its ability to pay for it. Finally, therefore, the size of Russia's military organization needed further adaptation. This would be difficult to achieve without a clear picture of how large the military actually was and the extent of the resources it was already consuming – figures that were constantly obfuscated and clouded in a veil of secrecy.

During 2002, the Ministry of Defence claimed to have reduced the number of posts for servicemen by 100,000 men. This was done to bring the organization and staffing structure of the Armed Forces into accord with plans.[209] However, as Table 6.2 shows, the number quickly surged to 1.2 million men again. This probably reflected the inclusion of the Railway Troops and Construction Troops, but that only accounts for part of the increase. Possibly, the fact that the Ministry of Defence was to be in charge of the rear service led to an increase of personnel. However, the numbers still create confusion. Such arithmetic would signify that none of the transfers of troops and services to the MoD led to personnel reductions or rationalizations.

However, the question should not be reduced to the overall number employed by the Ministry of Defence. In connection with the process of coordinating the rear services of the power ministries in September 2005, new figures on how many would be affected by this reform appeared. The head of the Main Military-Medical Directorate of the Ministry of Defence, Lieutenant-General Igor Bykov, stated that the merged system would provide medical care for 7.5 million people.[210] Although this figure must have included civilian personnel as well as troops, it gives an idea of how confusing manpower figures tend to be when it comes to the power ministries and their personnel.[211] It also suggests that spending on defence must be considered in conjunction with spending on domestic security. If Russia is spending considerable amounts on personnel primarily responsible for domestic security, and the various troops under the control of different power ministries are allowed to grow, then this will have consequences for the amount of resources that can be devoted to military defence.

To conclude, the number of servicemen active as defined here within Russia's military organization is probably somewhere between 1.5 and 2 million men. Ultimately, the definition of 'armed forces', of course, determines what the overall level is, but this range should be a reasonable approximation. The numbers given in *The Military Balance* do not include, for example, certain special forces within the Ministry of Internal Affairs which reasonably should be added to the list.[212] Civilian personnel should not, however, be included, nor should all persons in uniform (such as procurators

Table 6.2 Level of manpower within the military organization, 2000–2007

Year	MoD Armed Forces		MVD	FSB and other	Paramil.	Total*
2000/1	Total	1,004,100	140,000	140,000 (FPS)	423,000	1,427,100
	Ground	348,000		4,000 (FSB)		
	Navy	171,600		35,000 (FSO)***		
	Air	184,600		54,000 (FAPSI)		
	RVSN	149,000		50,000 (Railw.)		
2001/2	Total	977,100	151,100	140,000 (FPS)	409,100	1,386,200
	Ground	321,000		10–30,000 (FSO)		
	Navy	171,500		4,000 (FSB)		
	Air	184,600		54,000 (FAPSI)		
	RVSN	149,000		50,000 (Railw.)		
2002/3	Total	988,100	151,100	140,000 (FPS)	409,100	1,397,200
2003/4	Total	960,600	151,100	140,000 (FPS)***	409,100	1,369,700
	Ground	321,000		10–30,000 (FSO)		
	Navy	155,000		4,000 (FSB)		
	Air	184,600		54,000 (FAPSI)***		
	RVSN	149,000		50,000 (Railw.)		
2004/5	Total**	1,212,700	151,100	140,000 (FPS)***	359,100	1,571,800
	Ground	360,000		10–30,000 (FSO)		
	Navy	155,000		4,000 (FSB)		
	Air	184,600		54,000 (FAPSI)***		
	RVSN	149,000				
2005/6	Total**	1,037,000	170,000	160,000 (FPS)***	418,000	1,455,000
	Ground	395,000		10–30,000(FSO)		
	Navy	142,000		4,000 (FSB)		
	Air	170,000		54,000 (FAPSI)***		
	RVSN	129,000				
2006	Total**	1,027,000	170,000	160,000 (FPS)***	418,000	1,445,000
	Ground	395,000		10–30,000 (FSO)		
	Navy	142,000		4,000 (FSB)		
	Air	160,000		54,000 (FAPSI)***		
	RVSN	129,000				
2007	Total**	27,000	170,000	160,000 (FPS)***	418,000	1,445,000
	Ground	395,000		10–30,000 (FSO)		
	Navy	142,000		4,000 (FSB)		
	Air	160,000		54,000 (FAPSI)***		
	RVSN	80,000				

Sources: *The Military Balance 2000/2001, 2001/2002, 2002/2003, 2003/2004, 2004/2005, 2005/2006, 2006, 2007.*

Notes: The totals of the services of the Armed Forces and the different paramilitary forces do not always add up. The totals presented are those given in *The Military Balance* except for the totals in the last column.

* Total calculated from Armed Forces plus paramilitary forces total – not given in *The Military Balance.*
** The Railway Troops and Construction Troops were incorporated in the MoD during 2004. They are listed under paramilitary forces in *The Military Balance*, but not incorporated in its total of paramilitary forces. Later editions estimate

and customs inspectors); this is why numbers of 3 million and above appear exorbitant if the object is to determine the number of servicemen available to ensure Russia's military security. Nevertheless, the fact that the power ministries taken together have millions of employees at their disposal cannot but have consequences for Russia's spending on national security and military security.

Defence and security spending

During Ivanov's tenure as minister of defence, the defence budget started to increase significantly for the first time since the fall of the Soviet Union. The Ministry of Defence received additional resources earmarked for military reform. Social costs connected with defence, such as military pensions, were also excluded from the defence budget. (This is not the practice in, for example, NATO countries.[213]) There was also an effort finally to achieve progress in the task of providing housing for officers, not least for those leaving active service, since according to all regulations these had to be prioritized. The increase in defence spending was facilitated by the improved finances of the Russian state, mainly the result of high energy prices, in particular oil.[214]

The strategy involved several risks. Relatively few efforts were made to reduce costs (the expected savings from, for example, centralizing the rear services and defence procurement would undoubtedly be slow to materialize). The Ministry of Defence seemed determined to keep at least 1 million men under arms within the Armed Forces – something that exceeds what most outside experts consider the Russian state could finance. Taking into account the mobilization capacity that the General Staff seems set to retain, somewhere in the excess of 10 million men, even the increased budgets of Putin's second term in office could prove insufficient. The required size of the Armed Forces, moreover, seems to have been calculated on the basis of Russia's geographical size rather than its ability to pay, equip and recruit soldiers for its military organization and on which threats are most imminent.[215] Estimates of how many people in active service Russia is able to carry as a financial burden differ, but usually range somewhere between

---

that they employ about 100,000 men together. Of these, 50,000 are Railway Troops, which have been part of the Armed Forces since 2003, and 50,000 are Construction Troops employed by the Federal Agency for Special Construction, which have been subordinated to the MoD since 2003.

*** In *The Military Balance 2000/2001*, 'Forces for the Protection of the Russian Federation' included 25,000 men and the 'Federal Protection Service' 10,000. Both of these have been interpreted as FSO forces. In *The Military Balance 2003/ 2004* and *2004/2005* and subsequent editions, the forces of FAPSI and the FPS are still accounted for separately, although these were incorporated in the FSB, FSO and SVR in 2003.

500,000 and 750,000.[216] The requirement to provide housing for all the retired and active officers continued to place an enormous, indeed, untenable financial burden on the state. It will, inevitably, drain resources from much-needed procurement and training and, in effect, make any savings that might have resulted from reductions impossible because of the costs involved in retiring officers from active service.

In addition to the defence budget, there were attempts to find extra-budgetary resources to devote to defence. An example of how pressure on the defence budget was relieved somewhat was the All-Russian National Military Fund, which Putin established in 1999. Its director was the former FSB head of military counter-intelligence, Aleksei Moliakov. Its purpose was to fund social programmes for acting and former servicemen of the Armed Forces and other military units. The fund was successful in raising money, not least from large Russian companies such as Alfa-Bank, and enjoys the patronage of the president.[217] In November 2005, there was even a suggestion that commercial companies should pay for the construction of new vessels for the navy, and they were also encouraged to help finance the National Anti-Terror Committee.[218]

The actual size of the Russian defence budget continued to be a topic of considerable disagreement. Although some of the secrecy surrounding it was shed, a number of questions remained unanswered. For example, it was unclear how much the military operation in Chechnya was costing. Compounding this question was of course the fact that a number of expenses were covered by other ministries. In this, Chechnya was not a unique case. As already stated, military pensions were moved to other sections of the state budget. In addition, Russian official statistics are inherently unreliable. The figures on gross national product (GNP) built to a considerable degree on approximations of, for example, the size of the shadow economy. In other words, the official figures that show defence spending amounting to about 3 per cent of Russia's GNP should be treated with caution. Most analysts would put it at about 5 per cent or more.[219] When the costs that the Russian state devotes to internal security are added, the burden this places on Russian society becomes difficult to maintain – estimates of the share of GNP vary between 10 and 30 per cent.[220]

The increases in defence spending initially encountered considerable opposition from some sections of the government, most notably the Ministry of Finance. Inflation also ate into the budget and the ratio spent on maintenance and personnel compared to procurement and development continued to be unfavourable.[221] Although this ratio improved considerably in 2006–7, there were doubts as to how effective this was in improving defence capacity. In the words of Stephen Blank, 'the real issue remains not the amount of spending, but rather its efficiency or effectiveness in providing Russia with the weapons it needs'.[222]

The former minister of defence, Igor Rodionov, continued to enjoy high esteem in military circles and many of his views probably mirrored the sentiments in the officer corps rather well. In an interview in 2003, Rodionov, who was standing to become a Duma deputy for the KPRF, blamed Yurii Baturin, Boris Nemtsov, Anatolii Chubais and Andrei Kokoshin for their role in undermining the Armed Forces.[223] Asked how he would like to see military reform implemented, Rodionov provided the following description:

> Military reform of the country is first of all reform of the economy in the interest of the defence in new conditions, and the readiness of the economy to go over for a limited time to producing the weapons and equipment necessary for reserve formations in order to help the army in peace. Military reform of the country is creating and educating human reserves, it is gathering strategic reserves of weapons, technology and stock. Military reform of the state is developing the infrastructure in the regions and the country in the interests of the defence, it is educating the rising generation and it is maintenance of a healthy defence consciousness among the population and many other things.[224]

These proposals, if implemented, would signify a considerable remilitarization of Russian society. Especially when bringing into the equation the wish to retain a mass army, the ambition to build a blue-water navy and demands to equip the Armed Forces with new weaponry and equipment that would be able to compete with NATO. Even the larger defence budgets of the late Putin era will thus not satisfy military demands and there is, moreover, every reason to ask how long such spending on defence and security can go on. Since Russia's economic recovery under Putin relied on high energy prices on the international market, defence spending will by implication also be dependent on high oil prices. A 'petro-bust' would quickly 'deflate Kremlin's national security ambitions' and thus current military reform ambitions.[225]

Russia's military security: 'keeping the powder dry for global tasks'

Work on a new military doctrine had been initiated already in 1996–97. It was developed by a group headed by the first deputy chief of the General Staff, Colonel-General Valerii Manilov. In practice, the military dominated the drafting of the new military doctrine.[226] A draft of the new military doctrine was published in September 1999 and a final somewhat revised version signed by Putin on 21 April 2000. This 2000 version put even more emphasis on local conflicts – such as that in Chechnya. In line with this, irregular warfare and the need for improved cooperation between different force structures came to the fore in the new document. There was also a clear anti-Western pitch in this military doctrine.[227] Under Putin, the national security concept was adopted before the military doctrine in 2000. Although this may not have reflected the whole truth of how the documents were drafted, it at least gave the impression that the military doctrine, in fact, proceeded from the guidelines provided in the national security concept.

The emphasis the national security concept put on the war against terrorism was vindicated by the events of 11 September 2001. Both the national security concept and the military doctrine underlined the need for reform – albeit in very general terms. There were no specific goals or time frames.[228]

Although the new national security concept and military doctrine prepared and launched under Putin were more in line with each other than earlier documents, it was soon clear that they would have to be revised again. The terror attack on the Dubrovka Theatre in Moscow in October 2002 underlined the need for new guidelines.[229]

In January 2003, Sergei Ivanov summarized the events of 2002 and outlined the priorities for the Armed Forces during the coming year. He acknowledged that the increased danger of terrorism might come to influence the wording in the national security concept and possibly also lead to alterations in the laws on state of emergency and on state of war. All in all, however, Ivanov concluded that provisions for using the Armed Forces to combat illegal armed groups on the territory of the Russian Federation already existed.[230] The document produced by the Ministry of Defence in October 2003 clearly was a step along the way of developing a new national security framework.[231] In the aftermath of the terrorist act in Beslan in September 2004, the Security Council was commissioned to develop a new national security concept[232] and work on a new military doctrine was also under way.[233]

After curbing the ever-growing influence of the General Staff in 2004, it seemed that the Kremlin had managed to make the top officials of the Ministry of Defence adhere to the official security policy line at least in public. Discontent with the writing-off of NATO as the main threat probably still prevailed within the ranks of the Armed Forces, but the top generals started to refrain from contradicting Kremlin policy openly. Thus, after Baluevskii had replaced Kvashnin as chief of the General Staff, there was less evidence of open contradiction of the official national security policy within the upper echelons of the military establishment. Other hardliners such as Leonid Ivashov had left the MoD even before then.

However, there was also evidence of many of the old sentiments living on within military circles. Much attention was devoted to the war on terrorism, but it was clear that NATO had not disappeared from the threat agenda. At the annual session of the Russian Academy of Military Science, the AVN, in January 2003 the overwhelming majority of the speakers were mainly preoccupied with the threat they perceived as coming from NATO and the USA. The chief of the Navy Staff, Admiral Viktor Kravchenko, dwelled on the need to prepare for battles on the high seas.[234] The first deputy chief of the General Staff and head of the Main Directorate of Operations, Colonel-General Aleksandr Rukshin, expanded on the need to secure command posts from high-precision weapons. These concerns hardly reflected the official policy of concentrating on local wars and combating terrorism.[235] In the debate on a new military doctrine in early 2007, singling out the USA, NATO and the West as the most pressing threat to Russia's national security, was apparently again encouraged by the Kremlin. In Chief of Staff Yurii Baluevskii's enumeration of threats, the first three came from the West.[236]

Leaving the rhetoric aside, the very force posture of Russia's military organization and the exercises that it staged suggested that adaptation to new threats was still in the future. As mentioned above, many of the exercises carried out under the banner of 'anti-terrorism' contained elements that were difficult to connect with counter-insurgency operations. Often the sheer size of the exercise, the number of units involved and the weapons and technology employed made it an unlikely claim.[237] Meanwhile, the unwillingness of the military establishment to reduce the number of units of the military organization and the obsession with keeping a mobilization potential suggested that NATO was still very much a threat that loomed large in the minds of military decision makers.

Although the Kremlin expressed a clear aim to direct resources into procuring high-precision weapons, there was also a lingering conservative perception that Russia would be able to meet modern military technology with its traditional resources. The debate that followed the war in Iraq in 2003 was in many ways illustrative of some of the different positions that existed in the Russian debate on military reform. Whereas many reformers argued for new investments in technology, education and training in order to match the new demands of warfare, a considerable contingent argued in favour of the old Soviet system. One issue that came to the fore was the issue of morale. Conservatives argued that the Russian army would remain invincible through its morale and fighting spirit once it forced its opponents into close combat (*kontaktnaia voina*)[238] This view was not representative of the military officer corps as a whole but nevertheless provides an example of how divergent the views on where military reform ought to lead still were.

On a political level, Russia's concern with NATO should probably be viewed in context other than that of sheer threat evaluation. Not only does a mass army serve the career advancement of officers; it also allows the Kremlin to portray Russia as a great power, something that is an important basis of legitimacy for the country's leadership. Russia's resistance to NATO enlargement and the indignation it expressed in the UN Security Council at the US war against Iraq were evidence of a nation's problems with coming 'to terms with both a more benign external environment and its own much reduced status'.[239]

In late June 2005, the Security Council met to discuss the development of Russia's military organization. Putin called for an exact analysis of the threats to the country's security. He started by listing threats such as 'terrorism, the narcotics trade, emergency situations stemming from technical failures, social and ethnic conflicts in regions neighbouring to Russia'. The latter threat was present also in Russia. However, Putin did not entirely dismiss major wars as a possibility. In his view, in Russia, 'we must keep our powder dry in order to solve other tasks of a global nature, we will never forget this'.[240]

In other words, the political leadership was nowhere near ready to write off Russia's role as a major power in international affairs. Indeed, in February 2007, at a conference in Munich, Putin's speech indicated that the Kremlin had approached the position of the General Staff rather than the other way round, when he focused on the dangers of a unilateral world with the USA as sole leader. He also identified NATO enlargement as detrimental to Russia's national security:

> I think it is obvious: the NATO enlargement process has nothing to do with the modernization of the alliance itself or to ensuring security in Europe. On the contrary, it is a seriously provoking factor, which decreases the level of mutual trust.[241]

There is every reason to ask why Russia would need to rewrite its military doctrine if this were the direction strategic thinking was to take. There was no evidence of the military officers in charge of the process being prepared to discuss the introduction of new concepts of warfare or radically rethink strategic designs. Instead the guidelines proposed by Gareev, who appeared destined to have a considerable role in the drafting process, promised to revisit the lessons learnt in the Second World War – hardly what the Russian Armed Forces needed in 2007.

Conclusion
Presidential will, know-how and perseverance

Celebrating his 55th birthday on 7 October 2007, Putin entertained a large number of military officers. No secret was made of this. Instead, it was publicized and Putin's welcoming words were available on the presidential website. His rationale for inviting them was that he wanted to spend his birthday 'with people that I respect deeply' and who had done much 'for the rebirth of the Army, for Russia'. Needless to say, this was a public display of Putin's good relations with the Armed Forces in the pre-election season, but it was also indicative of the fact that Putin was convinced that the Russian army had in fact been reborn. Although he admitted that additional measures were needed in the sphere of procurement, training and social protection of servicemen, his main message, designed to soothe the military, was that the time of great upheavals and reforms was over. However, to an outside observer much remained to be done before Putin could join the ranks of Peter the Great, Dmitrii Miliutin and Mikhail Frunze as a military reformer. In fact, many of the improvements Putin took credit for were the results of decisions taken in the late 1990s, when he was nowhere near the inner workings of the defence decision-making machinery.

It would be far too easy only to conclude that the record of military reform ever since the early 1990s has been dismal. Even countries with a healthier economy and without the legacy of a militarized society have found military reform a challenge. Indeed, contrary to the oft-received wisdom, many of the plans for the Russian Armed Forces that were formulated during the 1990s were in the main fulfilled. Even the basic points in Grachev's plan, however modest their goals and prospects, were accomplished to some extent. The plan presented by Grachev was realistic in that it concentrated the initial efforts upon bringing home troops and equipment from the former Warsaw Pact countries and Soviet Union to Russia proper and on substantial reductions in manpower. Perhaps the greatest mistake was to fall for the temptation to describe these measures as 'military reform'.

There is a tendency to underestimate the considerable time it takes before results are visible in the form of improved performance, new weaponry and equipment and so on. Although Putin is often credited with bringing about military reform, the reforms of the Armed Forces that have been evident since the Zapad-99 exercise were the result of decisions taken in the late 1990s. The next years saw further reductions in the numbers of units and men under arms, as well as structural reforms: the number of services of the Armed Forces went from five to three and the military districts were reduced in number and reorganized. Much work was also devoted to achieving a greater degree of interoperability between different power ministries and services. Most importantly, there was clear evidence of improved performance in military exercises and in Chechnya compared to the mid-1990s. The main conclusion must be that it was not the ability of the military organization to carry out the reform plans that was lacking; most of the time the Kremlin displayed insufficient political will, know-how and perseverance in carrying through its programmes. The Armed Forces did undergo considerable changes when the Kremlin was determined to break the bureaucratic resistance to reforms.

Nevertheless, military reform as defined in the Russian military encyclopaedias did not materialize. As evidenced above, the military–industrial complex remained unreformed and the necessary coordination between power ministries and other sections of the government in order to solve such fundamental problems as manning and procurement ran into bureaucratic resistance.

In other words the military organization as a whole was not targeted seriously and coordination was fundamentally lacking. The definition of military reform in Chapter 4, moreover, draws attention to the presence of three challenges that need to be addressed: first, new political tasks and threats; second, new military technology; and, third, the new economic realities.

The indecision and ambivalence of approach remained as to whether the Russian military organization should be optimized for local wars and counter-insurgency operations or keep the option of a mass mobilization army for the eventuality of total war. While there were signs that the General Staff gradually adapted its official position to that of the political leadership, in Putin's second term NATO again appeared to come to the fore as a military threat to prepare for. The future of the treaties on Conventional Forces in Europe (CFE) and on Intermediate-range Nuclear Forces (INF) were in doubt in 2007 as Russia imposed a moratorium on the CFE Treaty and threatened to abrogate the INF Treaty unilaterally. Washington, of course, had already cancelled the 1972 Anti-Ballistic Missile (ABM) Treaty and overall the web of international treaties that had tied the USA and Russia together began to unravel. On a more practical level, the moratorium on the CFE Treaty signified a halt to mutual inspections and, thereby, to the exchange of experiences that it had involved. Although this did not signify that each of the two parties regarded the other as its main enemy, relations were certainly not improved by these measures.

There was little evidence of new concepts of warfare being introduced into the education and training of Russia's military organization. The time when Russian soldiers and junior officers would be trained in mission-based tactics still appeared remote. Counter-insurgency warfare continued to play a subordinate role in the debate on a new military doctrine in 2007 and overall the dearth of innovation was striking. As the agent of reform, the Kremlin ought to have given the military clear guidelines as to which threats to prepare for (and, consequently, which to downgrade) as well as how to do this. It should then have enforced these in military planning documents within the Ministry of Defence. However, the political leadership was sadly lacking in methods of verifying that its instructions were being heeded within the military organization and that the force posture and training were being changed accordingly.

Nor has Russia arrived at a new determination of the balance between the resources to be devoted to the military and to society. A military reform also ought to have established a new social contract of sorts between society and the military organization. The first concern here was that of finding a balance between the resources the military considered necessary in order to fulfil its tasks, on the one hand, and the amount of resources society could afford to spend on defence without jeopardizing long-term economic development, on the other. This proved a difficult task not least because there was considerable confusion over what the country's defence budget actually was and because of the legacy of militarization. When Yeltsin was president, the budget for the Armed Forces was reduced while other parts of the military organization, mainly the power ministries, expanded. There was a dearth of interest and know-how on these questions within the political sphere, especially when it came to financial decision making; the defence budget was reduced, but few questions were asked about how the money was spent. The lack of military expertise and of efficient mechanisms for scrutinizing defence spending outside the military sphere was seriously detrimental. Under Putin, the defence budget as well as the resources devoted to other power ministries increased. In the absence of control mechanisms and independent oversight it is impossible to judge how efficiently these resources were employed. Previous experiences suggest that there was considerable room for improvement.

The second major concern, and closely connected to that of an accord between the Russian military and society, was that of finding a tenable manning policy for the military organization. Indeed, military service is 'the most onerous form of taxation a government can impose on its citizens'.[1] The chronic shortage of soldiers and junior officers stands out as all the more noteworthy given the stated intention to make the battalion the basic unit of the Armed Forces. The lack of able commanders and supporting officers at this level and below seriously undermines any such ambitions. Nor do the measures taken so far promise a solution to the problem within a reasonable time. Contract service is struggling with a number of problems. The pervasive hazing, disregard for soldiers' human rights and low morale, coupled with the prospect of being sent to conflicts such as the one in Chechnya, are discouraging young men from choosing the military profession. The living conditions and career prospects for a junior officer hardly attract the kind of cadre that the military organization desperately needs.

The question remains whether Russia needs such a wide array of power ministries with military units under their command. It would be far more economical and give a greater clarity of structure if the number of agencies and ministries with military missions were significantly reduced or, indeed, limited to the MoD.[2] Even if Russia achieves better coordination and prioritization between the different power ministries, the country is facing a formidable demographic challenge and the fact remains that only the political leadership can prioritize and coordinate the manning policy and strike the difficult balance between societal and military needs for a labour force and soldiers.

Again, we come upon the crucial role of the leadership in enforcing reform. Many reforms suffered a fate similar to that of military reform during Yeltsin's time in the Kremlin. There is a multitude of examples of failed reforms that were launched with a big bang and ended with a whimper in Russia during this period. In view of this, it is hardly surprising that military reform proved yet another example of a much-heralded reform that stumbled at the very first obstacles it met, only for Yeltsin to lose interest and disappear from the scene for a while or turn his attention elsewhere. Although it would seem that the prospects were more auspicious for Putin, he found himself halted at many of the very same hurdles as Yeltsin. Both presidents, moreover, tended to show more concern for their own position of power than for Russia's military security. They were careful not to antagonize the very power ministries that controlled important assets in the domestic political power struggle, such as intelligence and internal troops. The political will to force through measures that were unpopular with the military often wavered, and national security in the minds of the two presidents was intimately connected to regime survival – if not identical.

Very much in line with the findings of Barry S. Posen, for much of the period under investigation Russian military reform was successfully mired by the bureaucracy tasked with carrying it out. This is exactly what the theories discussed in Chapter 3 would lead us to expect from a bureaucracy that wishes to protect its own interests. Russia's political leadership at times did make an effort to put Russia's military organization in order and regain control over its headstrong General Staff and the power ministries. For a short time, the corridors of the Kremlin bustled with energy as the political leadership made every effort to enforce its will upon the military organization. Decrees were signed, commissions formed and long-term plans developed. During this period, the generals retreated somewhat, but only to consolidate their positions; they knew from experience that the intense activity was bound to peter out. Sure enough, the Kremlin soon retreated into inertia and the plans for military reform were left half-implemented or shelved. This is the very nature of the way bureaucracies work, and should have come as no surprise. The task for the political leadership was to find ways of overcoming this deeply entrenched resistance.

In other words, the main problem was the fact that the political leadership lacked the will, the ability and the means (know-how) to construct meaningful reform plans for the military to fulfil, as well as the mechanisms to scrutinize and evaluate implementation (perseverance). The institutional legacy of the Soviet era compounded these problems. The lack of political control over the military sector was manifest not least in the difficulties in even deciding the military sector's share of GNP and the true size of the defence budget. Military know-how outside the General Staff was sadly lacking, as was transparency and, thus, accountability. There was a need for civilian expertise both inside the government structures and outside in the form of think tanks and in academia. One of the main problems within the Ministry of Defence still remained to be solved – the lack of civilian officials with military knowledge and clout. The civilians who worked in the ministry found themselves dependent on military officials for their career prospects.[3] Putin's idea of increasing control was to infuse the MoD with ex-FSB officials who report to the Kremlin. This did not rectify the problem and appointing a civilian as minister of defence was only a symbolic first step that did not go far towards creating the kind of integrated ministry of defence that was discussed in Chapter 3.

Although the presence of political will and, preferably, know-how are important conditions for reform, they are not sufficient. There is also a need for perseverance, and this can only be guaranteed by the presence of institutions and mechanisms for scrutiny and critical oversight, which results in information on the progress (or lack thereof) being fed back into the machinery. It is worth spelling out at this point that calling for strong political interest and interference in military matters does not amount to calling for a 'strong hand' or a dictatorship. Quite the contrary: achieving military reform involves keen political interest on the part of the politicians at the helm as well as scrutiny from other parts of the political machinery and from society at large. Throughout the period under investigation in this book, Russia lacked an autonomous political core that would provide incisive scrutiny of the military and suggest corrections of policy.[4] Such a political mechanism would supply additional fuel to the process when the Kremlin directs its attention to other pressing policy areas.

A misguided reliance on centralization and on the concentration of control in the executive predominated in the Kremlin. As a consequence, both defence decision making and scrutiny of its implementation have been centralized in the president and his government. Neither the judicial nor the parliamentary branches of the Russian state exercise any effective scrutiny of the military organization. There is, in other words, every reason to suspect that the decision-making and control system created by Putin over the military organization forms a vicious circle where the same people as are responsible for making decisions influence the possibilities for oversight of the implementation of those decisions. Even more worrying, however, is the tendency of the Kremlin under both Yeltsin and Putin to ensure the support of the military in political power struggles rather than focusing on what Russia's national security really requires. Putin's birthday speech indicated that this practice is bound to continue.

Putin's urge to control everything, combined with his deeply ingrained suspicion of transparency and independent institutions, put him in a position where he was able to control nothing. In the end, he received very little in the way of reliable information on how military reform was progressing. He and his minister of defence as well as other ministers and directors of the power structures will be dependent for information and basic data on the very bureaucracies they wish to control. There is, in practice, little or no independent parliamentary or judicial control. Nor do societal organizations have any meaningful leverage over concrete policy. Even more devastating is the dearth of alternative sources of information – a problem that could be leading the Kremlin into a blind alley. The power vertical that Putin created is at best an efficient rhetorical device, at worst a chimera that hides the real dangers and threats to Russia from its political leadership. The appointment of Serdiukov as minister of defence in 2007 suggested that the Kremlin was suspicious about how the MoD spent its increased budget. A future deterioration in the economic situation (as a result, for example, of a dramatic fall in energy prices on the world market) would make this question even more pertinent. To be sure, the demographic realities that the future holds in store for Russia and the security situation in the Caucasus are bound to force the Kremlin to think hard soon about the reform record so far and about how to ensure Russia's military security in the future.

Notes

Preface

1 J. Leijonhielm, *Russian Military Capability in a Ten-Year-Perspective*, Stockholm: FOA, April 1999, Strategiskt forum, no. 5; J. Leijonhielm, *Russian Military Capability in a Ten-Year-Perspective*, Stockholm: FOI, September 2003, Strategiskt forum, no. 11; J. Leijonhielm, *Russian Military Capability in a Ten-Year-Perspective: Problems and Trends in 2005*, Stockholm: FOI, June 2005, FOI Memo 1396; and *Nezavisimoe voennoe obozrenie*, 1999, no. 28 (23–29 July), p. 4.
2 The abbreviation 'VPK' is not used for the MIC since it also designated the Military–Industrial Commission (*Voennaia promyshlennaia kommissiia*), which in the Soviet era coordinated the military–industrial complex.
3 NATO, *Slovar sovremennykh voenno-politicheskikh i voennykh terminov Rossiia–NATO*, 21 June 2002. Online. Available HTTP: www.nato.int/docu/glossary/rus/index.htm (accessed 26 September 2005).
4 M. Wheeler and B. Unbegaun (eds), *The Oxford Russian Dictionary*, Oxford: Oxford University Press, 1995, p 519
5 See, for example, H. Fast Scott and W. F. Scott, *Soviet Military Doctrine: continuity, formulation, and dissemination*, Boulder, Col.: Westview Press, 1988, pp. 169–70; and W. Odom, *The Collapse of the Soviet Military*, New Haven, Conn.: Yale University Press, 1998, pp. 23–25.
6 N. Ogarkov (ed.), *Voennyi entsiklopedicheskii slovar*, Moscow: Voennoe izdatelstvo, 1983. See also the translation in NATO, *Slovar sovremennykh ...* where *voennoe stroitelstvo* is translated as 'development of military capability'.
7 S. Huntington, *The Soldier and the State: the theory and politics of civil–military relations*, London: Belknap Press of Harvard University Press, 1957, pp. 7–18.

1 The Kremlin and military reform

1 C. Donnelly, 'Civil–military relations in the new democracies', in D. Betz and J. Löwenhardt (eds), *Army and State in Postcommunist Europe*, London: Frank Cass, 2001, pp. 7–10. Huntington pointed out that this was the 'problem in a modern state' in the late 1950s. S. Huntington, *The Soldier and the State: the theory and politics of civil–military relations*, London: Belknap Press of Harvard University Press, 1998, p. 20. See also D. Bland, 'Managing the "expert problem" in civil–military relations', *European Security*, 1999, vol. 8, no. 3, p. 25.
2 There is D. Herspring, *The Kremlin and the High Command: presidential impact on the Russian military from Gorbachev to Putin*, Lawrence, Kans.: Kansas University Press, 2006. His focus is mainly on presidential will and perseverance and he does not examine the overall institutional framework for defence decision

making in detail. Also of great interest is Z. Barany, *Democratic Breakdown and the Decline of the Russian Military,* Princeton, N.J.: Princeton University Press, 2007.

2 The debate on Russian military reform

1 J. Moran, 'Back to the future? Tolstoy and post-communist Russian military politics', *Journal of Slavic Military Studies,* 1999, vol. 12, no. 4, pp. 54–77. See also C. Locksley, 'Concept, algorithm, indecision: why military reform has failed in Russia since 1992', *Journal of Slavic Military Studies,* 2001, vol. 14, no. 1. Locksley considers that 'the Mongol conquest, Tsarist autocracy and Bolshevism' have 'conspired to isolate Russia from the most important and original Western currents' (p. 20). 'This is why all Russians reforms since 1992 are doomed to fail' (p. 21). For a sophisticated political-cultural explanation of the dismal reform record which singles out Russian Imperial and Soviet 'defence-mindedness' or a 'hierarcy of social values rooted in militarism', see A. Golts and T. Putnam, 'State militarism and its legacies: why military reform has failed in Russia', *International Security,* 2004, vol. 29, no. 2, pp. 123–24.

2 D. Herspring, 'Russia's crumbling military', *Current History,* 1998, vol. 97, no. 621, p. 328.

3 J. Leijonhielm et al., *Rysk militär förmåga i ett tioårsperspektiv,* Stockholm: FOA, May 1999, User Report, FOA-R–99-01151-170–SE; and J. Kipp, *Russian Military Reform: status and prospects (views of a Western historian),* Foreign Military Studies Office. Online. Available HTTP: http://call.army.mil/fmso/fmso-pubs/issues/rusrform.htm (accessed 8 July 2002).

4 The head of the Main Directorate of Operations of the General Staff, Colonel-General Viktor Barynkin, claimed in 1996 that 'with the present financing, it is impossible to create a base for radical changes within the army and the fleet. In such a situation, it is first of all necessary to preserve the existing potential of the Armed Forces'. V. Barynkin, 'Problemy stroitelstva Vooruzhennykh Sil Rossiiskoi Federatsii na sovremennom etape', *Voennaia mysl,* 1996, no. 1, p. 2.

5 See, for example, Dmitrii Volkogonov, *Krasnaia zvezda,* 5 January 1994, p. 2; and Makhmut Gareev's article in *Nezavisimoe voennoe obozrenie,* 2002, no. 23 (12–18 July), p. 4.

6 S. Foye, 'The Soviet High Command and the politics of military reform', *Report on the USSR,* 1991, vol. 3, no. 27, p. 12.

7 A. Nikolaev, 'Voennuiu reformu kavalereiskim naskokom ne provesti', *Rossiiskaia Federatsiia segodnia,* 1999, no. 4, p. 20.

8 A. Nikolaev, 'Russia's stalled military reform', *International Affairs,* 2001, vol. 47, no. 3, p. 99.

9 S. Rosefielde, 'Back to the future? Prospects for Russia's military industrial revival', *Orbis,* 2002, vol. 46, no. 3, p. 504. See also F. Daucé, 'L'armée dans l'histoire de l'État russe contemporain', *Hérodote,* 2002, no. 104, p. 127.

10 Leijonhielm et al., *Rysk militär förmåga,* 1999, p. 129.

11 W. Unge, *The Russian Military–Industrial Complex in the 1990s: conversion and privatisation in a structurally militarised economy,* Stockholm: FOA, December 2000, FOA-R–00-01702-170–SE, p. 69. See also V. Lopatin, 'Armiia i ekonomika', *Voprosy ekonomiki,* 1990, no. 10, pp. 4–12; and V. Shlykov, 'The economics of defense in Russia and the legacy of structural militarization', in S. E. Miller and D. Trenin (eds), *The Russian Military: power and policy,* Cambridge, Mass.: MIT Press, 2004, pp. 157–66.

12 A. Arbatov, 'Military reform in Russia: dilemmas, obstacles, and prospects', *International Security,* 1998, vol. 22, no. 4, pp. 118–19.

13 *Nezavisimoe voennoe obozrenie,* 2002, no. 18 (7–13 June), p. 3. See also Locksley, 'Concept, algorithm, indecision', pp. 16–17. Jan Knoph lists as a prerequisite for

civilian control that the military is fully financed through the state budget. J. Knoph, *Civilian Control of the Russian State Forces: a challenge in theory and practice*, Stockholm: FOI, February 2004, User Report, FOI-R–1175–SE, p. 94.

14 Daucé, 'L'armée dans l'histoire de l'État russe', p. 130. See also B. Lambeth, 'Russia's wounded military', *Foreign Affairs*, 1995, vol. 74, no. 2, pp. 92–93.

15 The war in Chechnya has also been advanced as an explanation why military reform has been difficult or even impossible. However, there is an equally good argument to be made to the effect that the Chechen wars were incentives for reform. A. Golts, *Armiia Rossii: 11 poteriannykh let*, Moscow: Zakharov, 2004, p. 165.

16 Moreover, the same conflict was present, for example, in late ninteenth-century Russia. The Imperial Ministry of Finance pursued an agenda that the military leadership considered as leading to severe underfunding of the military. W. Fuller, *Civi–Military Conflict in Imperial Russia, 1881–1914*, Princeton, N.J.: Princeton University Press, 1985.

17 M. O'Hanlon, 'Rumsfeld's defence vision', *Survival*, 2002, vol. 44, no. 2, p. 112.

18 W. Odom, *The Collapse of the Soviet Military* (New Haven, Conn.: Yale University Press, 1998), pp. 375–87.

19 A. Konovalov, 'The changing role of military factors', in V. Baranovsky (ed.), *Russia and Europe: the emerging security agenda*, Oxford: Oxford University Press for the Stockholm International Peace Research Institute (SIPRI), 1997, p. 207.

20 P. Baev, *The Russian Army in a Time of Troubles*, London: Sage, 1996, pp. 3–4, 25.

21 A. Nikolaev, 'Military aspects of Russia's security', *International Affairs*, 1993, no. 10, p. 7.

22 *Nezavisimoe voennoe obozrenie*, no. 1 (17–23 January), 2003, p. 1.

23 For a definition of local, regional and total (*krupnomasshtabnaia*) war, see Ministry of Defence of the Russian Federation, *Aktualnye zadachy razvitiia vooruzhennykh sil Rossiiskoi Federatsii*, Moscow: Voenintorm, 2003, p. 39. It should be noted that 'regional war' in this definition is limited to a region but involves 'national or coalition forces of two or more states (groups of states)' and could include the use of nuclear weapons. It also presupposes the complete deployment of the armed forces and the mobilization of the economy. Meanwhile, local wars are also defined as wars between 'two or more states', but only involving the deployment of a contingent of the armed forces. Interestingly, the prospect of Russia's armed forces becoming involved in low-intensity or sub-state conflict is not really covered by these definitions. See also D. Herspring, *The Kremlin and the High Command: presidential impact on the Russian military from Gorbachev to Putin*, Lawrence, Kans.: Kansas University Press, 2006, pp. 90–91, on how this aspect was overlooked in the 1990s.

24 D. Lynch, 'Maneouvring with the military', *The World Today*, 1997, vol. 53, no. 11, p. 275; and Rosefielde, 'Back to the future?', p. 504. See also Odom, *The Collapse of the Soviet Military*, p. 2; and Unge, *The Russian Military–Industrial Complex*, p. 69.

25 I. Facon, 'La réforme de l'armée russe: Enjeux et obstacles', *Courrier des pays de l'Est*, 2002, no. 1022 (February), pp. 22–23.

26 A. Rutskoi, 'Voennaia politika Rossii: soderzhanie i napravlennost', *Voennaia mysl*, 1993, no. 1, p. 9.

27 F. Umbach, 'Zwang zur Militärreform: Die Krise der russischen Streitkräfte', *Internationale Politik*, 1996, vol. 51, no. 9, pp. 58–60. See also Foye, 'The Soviet High Command', p. 14; and D. Herspring, 'Putin and military reform: some first hesitant steps', *Russia and Eurasia Review* (Jamestown Foundation), 2002, vol. 1, issue 7 (10 September). Online. Available HTTP: http://russia.jamestown.org/pubs/view/rer_001_007_001.htm (accessed 16 October 2002).

28 Arbatov, 'Military reform in Russia', p. 107. See also S. Blank, 'Valuing the human factor: the reform of Russian military manpower', *Journal of Slavic Military Studies*, 1999, vol. 12, no. 1, p. 66; I. Facon, 'La réforme de l'armée russe', pp. 22–23; J. Godzimirski, *Russian National Security Concepts 1997–2000: a comparative analysis*, Security Policy Library, no. 8–2000, Oslo: Norwegian Atlantic Committee, 2000. Online. Available HTTP: www.atlanterhavskomiteen.no/publikasjoner/sp/2000/8-2000_utskrift.htm (accessed 25 June 2001); the interview with former minister of defence Igor Rodionov, in *Nezavisimoe voennoe obozrenie*, 2003, no. 1 (17–23 January), p. 1; and the article by Lieutenant-General Valerii A. Dementev and Anton V. Surikov in *Nezavisomoe voennoe obozrenie*, no. 7, pp. 1, 4, available as supplement in *Nezavisimaia gazeta*, 11 April 1996. In 2007, the debate on the new military doctrine made it obvious that the USA and NATO still feature prominently on the list of military threats that Russia should prepare itself for. See, for example, M. Gareev, 'Struktura i osnovnoe soderzhanie novoi voennoi doktriny Rossii', *Voennaia mysl*, 2007, no. 3, pp. 6–7; and Yu. Baluevskii, 'Teoreticheskie i metodologicheskie osnovy formirovaniia voennoi doktriny Rossiiskoi Federatsii', *Voennaia mysl*, 2007, no. 3, p. 16.
29 Arbatov, 'Military reform in Russia', p. 84; and S. Kortunov and S. Vikulov, 'Military reform and foreign policy', *International Affairs*, 1997, vol. 43, no. 6, p. 167.
30 Barynkin, 'Problemy stroitelstva Vooruzhennykh Sil', p. 6.
31 M. Kramer, *Civil–Military Relations in Russia and the Chechnya Conflict*, Center for Strategic and International Studies, PONARS, Policy Memo 99, December 1999. Online. Available HTTP: www.csis.org/ruseura/ponars/policymemos/pm_0099.pdf (accessed 3 February 2003); and J. Kipp, 'War scare in the Caucasus: redefining the threat and the war on terrorism', in A. C. Aldis and R. McDermott (eds), *Russian Military Reform 1992–2002*, London: Frank Cass, 2003, p. 248.
32 S. Talbott, *The Russia Hand: a memoir of presidential diplomacy*, New York: Random House, 2002, pp. 353–54.
33 However, according to David Betz, Arbatov was one of many Duma deputies who deliberately did not wish to know the details of the defence budget since becoming a 'bearer of state secrets' would hinder him from travelling abroad. D. Betz, 'No place for a civilian? Russian defense management from Yeltsin to Putin', *Armed Forces and Society*, 2002, vol. 28, no. 3, p. 498.
34 *Moscow News*, no. 37 (25 September–1 October), 2002, p. 2.
35 See, for example, Locksley, 'Concept, algorithm, indecision', p. 19; and Leijonhielm et al., *Rysk militär förmåga*, 1999, p. 217.
36 Foye, 'The Soviet High Command', p. 9.
37 Baev, *The Russian Army*, p. 27; and P. Baev, 'Reforming the Russian military: history and trajectory', in Yu. Fedorov and B. Nygren (eds), *Russian Military Reform and Russia's New Security Environment*, Stockholm: Swedish National Defence College, May 2003, ACTA B28, p. 41. See also Arbatov, 'Military reform in Russia', pp. 112–13; Kipp, *Russian Military Reform*; and Nikolaev, 'Russia's stalled military reform', p. 99.
38 Daucé, 'L'armée dans l'histoire de l'État russe', pp. 125, 127.
39 I. Yerokhin, 'O razrabotke kontseptsii voennoi reformy', *Voennaia mysl*, 1991, nos 11–12, p. 43.
40 Umbach, 'Zwang zur Militärreform', p. 59.
41 Locksley, 'Concept, algorithm, indecision', p. 18. See also K. Sorokin, 'Vozrozhdenie rossiiskoi armii: blizhaishie perspektivy', *Mirovaia ekonomika i mezhdunarodnye otnosheniia*, 1993, no. 1, p. 12, who talks of the risk that reform 'could provoke opposition from the Armed Forces and in certain groups in society serve as a detonator for social unrest'.

42 B. Taylor, 'Russian civil–military relations after the October uprising', *Survival*, 1994, vol. 36, no. 1, p. 20. See also the interview with Army General Vladimir Lobov in *Krasnaia zvezda*, 7 September 1991, p. 2.

43 Lynch, 'Maneouvring with the military', p. 277; and Betz, 'No place for a civilian?', p. 485.

44 Arbatov, 'Military reform in Russia', p. 113; Daucé, 'L'armée dans l'histoire de l'État russe', p. 125; and Taylor, 'Russian civil–military relations', p. 20.

45 M. Galeotti, 'Russia's military reforms?', *Jane's Intelligence Review*, 2000, vol. 12, no. 9, pp. 8–9.

46 See, for example, the excellent paper by Mark Kramer where he dismisses the rumours of a military 'silent coup' in 1999. He concludes that civilian control of the military was not in danger. However, his focus is entirely on the risk of a military coup and he acknowledges that there was every possibility that the military could increase its influence over defence affairs. Kramer, *Civil–Military Relations in Russia.*

47 D. Betz, J. Löwenhardt and H. Strachan, 'Conclusion', in D. Betz and J. Löwenhardt (eds), *Army and State in Postcommunist Europe,* London: Frank Cass, 2001, pp. 151–52.

3 Defence decision making

1 For an account of Yeltsin's initial high popularity ratings within the Armed Forces and his subsequent fall from grace, see V. Baranets, *Eltsin i ego generaly: zapiski polkovnika genshtaba,* Moscow: Sovershenno sekretno, 1998, pp. 27–31, 62–64. See also A. Kokoshin, *Strategicheskoe upravlenie: teoriia, istoricheskii opyt, sravnitelnyi analiz, zadachi dlia Rossii,* Moscow: MGIMO, ROSSPEN, 2003, pp. 329–30 on how the Belovezha Accords, which codified the fall of the Soviet Union, affected politicians' standing within the Armed Forces.

2 This point was emphasised by Vladimir Lopatin in 1990 as he called for military reform. V. Lopatin, 'Armiia i ekonomika', *Voprosy ekonomiki*, 1990, no. 10, p. 5.

3 B. Posen, *The Sources of Military Doctrine: France, Britain, and Germany between the world wars,* Ithaca, N.Y.: Cornell University Press, 1984, p. 60.

4 G. Allison and P. Zelikow, *Essence of Decision: explaining the Cuban missile crisis,* 2nd edn, New York: Longman, 1999, p. 24.

5 Posen, *The Sources of Military Doctrine*, p. 60. R. V. Jones offers a similar analysis based upon his practical experience during the Second World War. His insistence on developing more effective countermeasures against German bombings won the day over the complacent arguments of the Air Staff because 'war is different from peace: in the latter fallacies can be covered up more or less indefinitely and criticism suppressed, but with the swift action of war the truth comes fairly quickly to the light'. R. W. Jones, *Most Secret War: British scientific intelligence 1939–1945,* London: Hodder & Stoughton, 1979, p. 191.

6 Posen, *The Sources of Military Doctrine*, p. 59.

7 Allison and Zelikow, *Essence of Decision,* pp. 143–85, 255–313.

8 This was noted by Aleksandr Svechin in the 1920s. A. Svechin, *Strategy,* Minneapolis, Minn.: East View Publications, 1997, pp. 100–1.

9 Posen, *The Sources of Military Doctrine*, p. 52–53; V. Hudson, *Foreign Policy Analysis: classic and contemporary theory,* Lanham, Md.: Rowman & Littlefield, 2007, p. 80; and M. Halperin and P. Clapp, *Bureaucratic Politics and Foreign Policy,* 2nd edn, Washington, D.C.: Brookings Institution Press, 2006, pp. 51–54.

10 M. Weber, *From Max Weber: essays in sociology,* eds H. H. Gerth and C. W. Mills, London: Routledge, 1991, pp. 232–33.

11 Posen, *The Sources of Military Doctrine*, p. 57.

12 Ibid., p. 45.

13 Ibid., p. 57; and Hudson, *Foreign Policy Analysis*, pp. 78–80.
14 Former General Staff Colonel Viktor Baranets claims that Grachev reported to the Kremlin every morning about the 'high level of battle readiness' of the Armed Forces firmly under his 'safe control'. Baranets, *Eltsin i ego generaly*, p. 33.
15 Not only must the military withdraw from politics, but 'civilians must step into leadership roles and equip themselves with the knowledge and expertise necessary to oversee and monitor the military establishment'. D. Betz, *Civil–Military Relations in Russia and Eastern Europe*, London: RoutledgeCurzon, 2004, p. 12.
16 E. Huskey, *Presidential Power in Russia*, Armonk, N.Y.: M. E. Sharpe, 1999, pp. 103–7.
17 Similarly, the heads of other power ministries such as the FSB and the MVD also made their careers within their respective ministries or agencies. When Igor Rodionov was appointed minister of defence in 1996, he retired from the army. However, he was still very much a military officer at heart and can hardly be described as a 'civilian minister of defence'. See also D. Herspring, *The Kremlin and the High Command: presidential impact on the Russian military from Gorbachev to Putin*, Lawrence, Kans.: Kansas University Press, 2006, p. 122.
18 D. Bland, 'Managing the "expert problem"' in civil–military relations', *European Security*, 1999, vol. 8, no. 3, p. 31.
19 Betz, *Civil–Military Relations in Russia and Eastern Europe*, pp. 13–18. See also Svechin, *Strategy*, p. 101; and Bland, 'Managing the "expert problem"', p. 38.
20 Bland, 'Managing the "expert problem"', p. 31. On the separation of Russian militaries from general political (especially financial) considerations, see also Kokoshin, *Strategicheskoe upravlenie*, p. 327.
21 D. Bland, 'A unified theory of civil–military relations', *Armed Forces and Society*, 1999, vol. 26, no. 1, p. 15.
22 Bland, 'Managing the "expert problem"', p. 34.
23 Ibid., p. 32.
24 Kokoshin, *Strategicheskoe upravlenie*, pp. 295–96.
25 Bland, 'Managing the "expert problem"', p. 34.
26 Kokoshin, *Strategicheskoe upravlenie*, pp. 335, 339–40.
27 Bland, 'Managing the "expert problem"', p. 32.
28 The Audit Chamber, which until 2004 was primarily subordinated to the Federal Assembly, should ideally work along the same pattern as, for example, the US Government Accountability Office, GAO (formerly the General Accounting Office). In practice, the Audit Chamber has proved more open for political pressure – not least from the Kremlin. Putin, moreover, strenghthened his control over the Audit Chamber in 2004.
29 V. Shlykov, 'The economics of defense in Russia and the legacy of structural militarization', in S. E. Miller and D. Trenin (eds), *The Russian Military: power and policy*, Cambridge, Mass.: MIT Press, 2004, pp. 165–66.
30 D. Herspring, *Russian Civil–Military Relations*, Bloomington: Indiana University Press, 1996, p. xix.
31 D. Herspring, 'Putin and the Armed Forces', in D. Herspring (ed.), *Putin's Russia: past imperfect, future uncertain*, Lanham, Md.: Rowman & Littlefield, 2003, p. 157.
32 H. Fast Scott and W. F. Scott, *Soviet Military Doctrine: Continuity, Formulation, and Dissemination*, Boulder, Col.: Westview Press, 1988, pp. 165–99. See also T. Colton, *Commissars, Commanders, and Civilian Authority: the structure of Soviet military politics*, Cambridge, Mass.: Harvard University Press, 1979, pp. 10–20.
33 W. Odom, *The Collapse of the Soviet Military* (New Haven, Conn.: Yale University Press, 1998), p. 18.
34 Ibid., p. 36.
35 Baranets, *Eltsin i ego generaly*, pp. 28–29.

36 Odom, *The Collapse of the Soviet Military*, p. 21. See also 'Gosudarstvennyi komitet oborony (GKO)' in N. Ogarkov, *Voennyi entsiklopedicheskii slovar*, Moscow: Voennoe izdatelstvo, 1983, p. 206; and P. Grachev (ed.), *Voennaia entsiklopediia, tom 2*, Moscow: Voennoe izdatelstvo, 1994, pp. 467–68.
37 Fast Scott and Scott, *Soviet Military Doctrine*, p. 190.
38 Odom, *The Collapse of the Soviet Military*, p. 21.
39 C. Rice, 'The Party, the military, and decision authority in the Soviet Union', *World Politics*, 1987, vol. 40, no. 1, pp. 65–67.
40 Odom, *The Collapse of the Soviet Military*, p. 21.
41 H. Gelman, *The Rise and Fall of National Security Decisionmaking in the Former USSR: implications for Russia and the Commonwealth*, Santa Monica, Calif.: RAND, 1992, R-4200-A, pp. 14–15.
42 Odom, *The Collapse of the Soviet Military*, pp. 19–20.
43 J. Leijonhielm et al., *Den ryska militärtekniska resursbasen: Rysk forskning, kritiska teknologier och vapensystem*, Stockholm: Swedish Defence Research Agency (FOI), October 2002, User Report, FOI-R–0618–SE, p. 41.
44 O. Grinevsky, 'Disarmament: the road to conversion', in V. Genin (ed.), *The Anatomy of Russian Defense Conversion*, Walnut Creek, Calif.: Vega Press, 2001, p. 160. See also Gelman, *The Rise and Fall of National Security Decisionmaking*, pp. 22–23.
45 Odom, *The Collapse of the Soviet Military*, p. 25.
46 Kokoshin, *Strategicheskoe upravlenie*, p. 245. See also Rice, 'The Party ... ', pp. 61–64 on how expert knowledge on warfare was concentrated within the General Staff.
47 M. Kalashnikova, '"Ostavalos dat signal i vse by rinulos"', *Kommersant Vlast*, 2005, no. 12 (28 March), p. 37. Jan Leijonhielm cites additional evidence of this state of affairs in J. Leijonhielm, 'Ryssland och hotbilden – i går, i dag och i morgon', *Kungliga Krigsvetenskapsakademins Handlingar och Tidskrift*, 2005, vol. 209, no. 3, pp. 3–19.
48 Odom, *The Collapse of the Soviet Military*, pp. 18–19
49 Presidential decree no. 867, 20 May 2000, 'On the Structure of the Federal Organs of Executive Power', published in *Rossiiskaia gazeta*, 20 May 2000, pp. 1, 2.
50 For an account of how the Presidential Administration developed after the fall of the Soviet Union, see Huskey, *Presidential Power*, pp. 43–82.
51 *Krasnaia zvezda*, 18 August 1993, p. 2.
52 C. Vendil, 'The Russian Security Council', *European Security*, 2001, vol. 10, no. 2, p. 69.
53 D. Betz, 'No place for a civilian? Russian defense management from Yeltsin to Putin', *Armed Forces and Society*, 2002, vol. 28, no. 3, p. 494.
54 Huskey, *Presidential Power*, pp. 69–70.
55 Betz, 'No place for a civilian?', p. 494; and Huskey, *Presidential Power*, pp. 62–63, 122.
56 Vendil, 'The Russian Security Council', p. 82.
57 Kokoshin, *Strategicheskoe upravlenie*, p. 302. See also Baranets, *Eltsin i ego generaly*, pp. 48–55, on how Yeltsin's poor health affected defence decision making.
58 *Krasnaia zvezda*, 5 November 1996, p. 1.
59 Presidential decree no. 946, 28 August 1997, published in *Rossiiskaia gazeta*, 3 September 1997, p. 4.
60 Statutes of the State Military Inspectorate, *Rossiiskaia gazeta*, 3 September 1997, p. 4. See also Kokoshin's account of the functioning of the State Military Inspectorate in Kokoshin, *Strategicheskoe upravlenie*, p. 303, and footnote 15, pp. 474–76.
61 Presidential decree no. 946, 28 August 1997, published in *Rossiiskaia gazeta*, 3 September 1997, p. 4.

62 As deputy prime minister Klebanov was also responsible for five government agencies for the arms industry. Klebanov then went on to head the Ministry of Industry, Science and Technology. The five government agencies also became coordinated by the ministry. W. Unge, *The Russian Military–Industrial Complex in the 1990s: conversion and privatisation in a structurally militarised economy*, Stockholm: FOA, December 2000, FOA-R–00-01702-170–SE, p. 14; and the website of the Ministry of Industry, Science and Technology, www.mpnt.gov.ru

63 The name of this department has varied over time. In 2005, its name was the Department for Defence Industry and Advanced Technologies.

64 Kokoshin, *Strategicheskoe upravlenia*, p. 307.

65 Ibid., pp. 304–6.

66 Ibid., p. 304.

67 A choice not unique to the Russian defence bureaucracy. See Halperin and Clapp, *Bureaucratic Politics and Foreign Policy*, pp. 51–54.

68 J. Leijonhielm et al., *Rysk militär förmåga i ett tioårsperspektiv*, Stockholm: FOA, May 1999, User Report, FOA-R–99-01151-170–SE, pp. 262–63.

69 *Krasnaia zvezda*, 12 May 1996, p. 1.

70 Leijonhielm et al., *Rysk militär förmåga*, 1999, pp. 266–67.

71 Unge, *The Russian Military–Industrial Complex*, pp. 14–15.

72 Presidential decree no. 867, 17 May 2000, 'On the Structure of the Federal Organs of Executive Power'. See also Government Statute no. 515, 12 July 2000, 'Questions concerning the Ministry for Industry, Science and Technology of the Russian Federation'; and J. Leijonhielm et al., *Rysk militär förmåga i ett tioårsperspektiv – en förnyad bedömning 2002*, Stockholm: FOI, February 2003, User Report, FOI-R–0811–SE, pp. 174–75.

73 Kokoshin, *Strategicheskoe upravlenie*, p. 327.

74 This was not unique to the MoD. To an overwhelming extent, the old bureaucracy lived on in post-Soviet Russia. K. Ryavec, *Russian Bureaucracy: power and pathology*, Lanham, Md.: Rowman & Littlefield, 2005, pp. 12–14.

75 Kokoshin, *Strategicheskoe upravlenie*, p. 325.

76 An attempt was made during 1994–95 to reintroduce the Soviet system, but the MoD abandoned this idea. According to Kokoshin, this made the demarcation of duties between the chiefs of the services and the ministry clearer. Ibid., p. 328.

77 Odom, *The Collapse of the Soviet Military*, p. 27.

78 However, there is still a Centre for Foreign Military Information and Communication, which is subordinated to the General Staff. *Rossiiskoe voennoe obozrenie*, 2006, no. 1 (January), pp. 78–79.

79 See, for example, the speech by the then head of the Presidential Administration, Anatolii Chubais, at the annual evaluation session of the Armed Forces. *Krasnaia zvezda*, 13 November 1996, p. 1. See also A. Golts, *Armiia Rossii: 11 poteriannykh let*, Moscow: Zakharov, 2004, p. 44.

80 Betz, *Civil–Military Relations in Russia and Eastern Europe*, pp. 108–9.

81 With this appointment Grachev had made a remarkably swift rise in his career. For a biographical sketch of Grachev, see Golts, *Armiia Rossii*, pp. 18–24.

82 Kokoshin, *Strategicheskoe upravlenie*, p. 299. During the August Coup, Grachev as commander of the Airborne Troops did obey the orders of the State of Emergency Committee to command his men to Moscow on 19 August 1991. He also kept in close contact with the leadership of the RSFSR. On 20 August he, together with among others Yevgenii Shaposhnikov, refused to storm the White House (the official premises of the Supreme Soviet). See also, Herspring, *The Kremlin and the High Command*, pp. 68–69.

83 Betz, *Civil–Military Relations in Russia and Eastern Europe*, p. 95.

84 Grachev quoted in Betz, 'No place for a civilian?', p. 485. See also Betz, *Civil–Military Relations in Russia and Eastern Europe*, p. 95.

85 Betz, 'No place for a civilian?', p. 490. By a twist of fate, however, Kokoshin found himself equipped with a direct connection to the president. This was a leftover from the early arrangement when Yeltsin was minister of defence and needed direct access to his then first deputy minister, Grachev. Kokoshin, *Strategicheskoe upravlenie*, p. 305.
86 For a detailed study of this centre, see S. Main, *The 'Brain' of the Russian Army: the Centre for Military Strategic Research, General Staff 1985–2000*, Conflict Studies Research Centre, C101, March 2000. Online. Available HTTP: www.csrc. ac.uk/pdfs/c101-sjm.pdf (accessed 16 October 2002).
87 Personal communication with officers from the Centre for Military Strategic Research.
88 See also C. Vendil Pallin, 'The Russian power ministries: tool and insurance of power', *Journal of Slavic Military Studies*, 2007, vol. 20, no. 1, pp. 1–25.
89 Presidential decrees no. 867, 17 May 2000, published in *Rossiiskaia gazeta* on 20 May 2000, and no. 314, 9 March 2004, in *Rossiiskaia gazeta*, 12 March 2004.
90 For example, the internal security budget tended to be met in full, in contrast to the defence budget. M. Galeotti, 'Russia's internal security forces: does more mean better?', *Jane's Intelligence Review*, 1994, vol. 6, no. 6, p. 271.
91 B. Taylor, *Putin and the Military: how long will the honeymoon last?*, Center for Strategic and International Studies, PONARS, Policy Memo 116, April 2000. Online. Available HTTP: www.csis.org/ruseura/ponars/policymemos/pm_0116.pdf (accessed 3 February 2003).
92 Baranets, *Eltsin i ego generaly*, p. 50.
93 B. Lo, *Vladimir Putin and the Evolution of Russian Foreign Policy*, London: Royal Institute of International Affairs, 2003, pp. 33–34.
94 T. Thomas, 'EMERCOM: Russia's Emergency Response Team', *Low Intensity Conflict and Law Enforcement*, 1995, vol. 4, no. 2, p. 233.
95 M. Galeotti, 'Emergency presence', *Jane's Intelligence Review*, 2002, vol. 14, no. 1, p. 50.
96 *Nezavisimaia gazeta*, 24 September 2003, p. 10. See also presidential decree no. 1115, 23 September 2003.
97 Galeotti, 'Emergency presence', p. 50.
98 Ministry of Civil Defence, Emergency Situations and Liquidating the Consequences of Natural Disasters of the Russian Federation, *Voiska GO*. Online. Available HTTP: www.mchs.gov.ru/ministry.php?fid=1054730499538967&cid= (accessed 22 November 2004).
99 Galeotti, 'Emergency presence', p. 51.
100 Ministry of Civil Defence Matters, Emergency Situations and Liquidating the Consequences of Natural Disasters of the Russian Federation, *Regionalnye tsentry*. Online. Available HTTP: www.mchs.gov.ru/ministry.php?fid=1054731434674752 (accessed 22 November 2004).
101 The Interior Troops were part of the MoD until 1989. The rationale for transferring them to the MVD was that it would keep the Armed Forces from becoming involved in internal conflicts that were on the rise in the multi-ethnic Soviet Union at the time. G. Bennett, *The Ministry of Internal Affairs of the Russian Federation*, Conflict Studies Research Centre, C106, October 2000. Online. Available HTTP: www.csrc.ac.uk/pdfs/C106-GB.pdf (accessed 16 October 2002), p. 3.
102 T. Thomas, 'Restructuring and reform in Russia's MVD: good idea, bad timing?', *Low Intensity Conflict and Law Enforcement*, 1998, vol. 7, no. 2, p. 97.
103 The statement sometimes quoted that the Interior Troops grew to encompass 2,000,000 men during Yeltsin's period in office is most likely a misunderstanding based on the number of the overall personnel subordinated to the MVD (including, for example, the police).

104 A. Dadonov, 'The Russian Interior Ministry's special Internal Troop units for combating terrorism: organization, training system and the conduct of special operations', *Low Intensity Conflict and Law Enforcement*, 1997, vol. 6, no. 2, p. 125.
105 Bennett, *The Ministry of Internal Affairs*, p. 14.
106 There have been reports in Russian media that the SVR has a special unit, the Zaslon, at its disposal, but the evidence is inclonclusive. According to the SVR, it took a strategic decision not to have special units in the early 1990s. Vendil Pallin, 'The Russian power ministries', p. 15.
107 G. Bennett, *The Federal Border Guard Service*, Conflict Studies Research Centre, C107, March 2002. Online. Available HTTP: www.csrc.ac.uk/pdfs/c107-gb.pdf (accessed 13 May 2002), p. 5.
108 Ibid., p. 12.
109 Kokoshin, *Strategicheskoe upravlenie*, p. 310.
110 Its activity was regulated in part by the law 'On Federal Organs of Government Communication and Information', no. 4524-I, 1 February 1993.
111 Article 3, FSO statutes, established by presidential decree no. 1013, 7 August 2004.
112 The regulations were enacted with presidential decree no. 1146, on 7 September 2004.
113 Kokoshin, *Strategicheskoe upravlenie*, p. 330.
114 T. Troxel, *Parliamentary Power in Russia, 1994–2001: president vs parliament*, New York: Palgrave Macmillan, 2003, pp. 68–69.
115 Betz, *Civil–Military Relations in Russia and Eastern Europe*, p. 135.
116 Ibid., p. 136.
117 Ibid., p. 139.
118 P. Baev, *Putin's Court: how the military fits in*, Center for Strategic and International Studies, PONARS, Policy Memo 153, November 2000. Online. Available HTTP: www.csis.org/ruseura/ponars/policymemos/pm_0153.pdf (accessed 3 February 2003).
119 Of these, only Vorobev was re-elected to the Duma in 1999.
120 B. Taylor, *The Duma and Military Reform*, Center for Strategic and International Studies, PONARS, Policy Memo 154, October 2000. Online. Available HTTP: www.csis.org/ruseura/ponars/policymemos/pm_0154.pdf (accessed 3 February 2003).
121 Audit Chamber of the Russian Federation, Federalnyi zakon 'O Schetnom Palate Rossiiskoi Federatsii', No 4-F3, 11 ianvaria 1995 goda, 11 January 1995. Online. Available HTTP: www.ach.gov.ru/zakon/fedzakon/zakon.php (accessed 25 January 2005).
122 Audit Chamber of the Russian Federation, *Schetnaia palata Rossiiskoi Federatsii kak vyshchii organ gosudarstvennogo kontrolia*. Online. Available HTTP: www.ach.gov.ru/about/history/sprf.php (accessed 25 January 2005).
123 Kokoshin, *Strategicheskoe upravlenie*, p. 314.
124 Odom, *The Collapse of the Soviet Military*, p. 366.
125 For a description of the Procuracy, see A. Jonsson, 'Judicial review and individual legal activism: the case of Russia in theoretical perspective', doctoral thesis, Uppsala: Uppsala University, Faculty of Law and Department of East European Studies, 2005, pp. 96–98.
126 A. Savenkov, 'Na zashchite federalnoi sobstvennosti', *Finansovyi kontrol*, 2004, no. 11, pp. 42–46.
127 Federal constitutional law no. 1-FKZ, 'On the Military Courts of the Russian Federation', 23 June 1999: see State Duma of the Russian Federation, Information Channel, *O voennykh sudakh Rossiiskoi Federatsii*, 23 June 1999. Online. Available HTTP: www.akdi.ru/gd/proekt/079698GD.SHTM (accessed 26 April 2005).
128 Federal constitutional law no. 1-FKZ, 31 December 1996: see Supreme Court of the Russian Federation, *O sudebnoi sisteme Rossiiskoi Federatsii*, 31 December

1996. Online. Available HTTP: www.supcourt.ru/law1.html (accessed 22 March 2005).

129 Department for Information about Court Practice of the Military Collegium of the Supreme Court of the Russian Federation, *Voennye sudy v Rossiiskoi Federatsii*. Online. Available HTTP: www.supcourt.ru (accessed 22 March 2005).

130 See, for example, Human Rights Watch, *Backgrounder on the Case of Kheda Kungaeva: trial of Yuri Budanov set for February 28*, 26 February 2001. Online. Available HTTP: www.hrw.org/backgrounder/eca/chech-bck0226.htm#N_4_ (accessed 3 November 2004).

131 For an account of how the Budanov case followed the political agenda of the Kremlin, see P. Baker and S. Glasser, *Kremlin Rising: Vladimir Putin's Russia and the end of revolution*, New York: Scribner, 2005, pp. 99–120.

132 For example, Army General Konstantin Kobets, deputy minister of defence and state military inspector, managed to avoid prosecution up until 1997 – this in spite of newpaper articles exposing him as corrupt. He was dismissed by presidential decree on 18 May 1997. *Kommersant daily*, 21 May 1997, p. 3.

133 It was possibly in response to this that the Ministry of Defence started its own journal in 2003/4, *Rossiiskoe voennoe obozrenie*.

134 Examples of prominent journalists on military affairs are Pavel Felgenhauer and Aleksandr Golts – both known to express views discordant with the view of the military establishment. Another example, though not restricted to strictly military journalism, is Anna Politkovskaia's critcal reporting from the war in Chechnya. She was murdered in 2006. Defence correspondent Ivan Safronov also died tragically in 2006 (see also Chapter 6).

135 *Nezavisimoe voennoe obozrenie*, no. 25 (12–18 March), 1997, pp. 1, 4–7.

136 See, for example, Council on Foreign and Defence Policy, *Kratkii variant doklada SVOP: Voennoe stroitelstvo i modernizatsiia vooruzhennykh sil Rossii*, 30 March 2004. Online. Available HTTP: www.svop.ru/live/materials.asp?m_id=8481&r_id=8482 (accessed 21 April 2004).

137 V. Shlykov, 'Nuzhen li Rossii Generalnyi shtab? Rossiiskaia sistema vyshego voennogo upravleniia v mezhdunarodnom kontekste', *Voennyi vestnik MFII*, 2000, no. 7 (October).

138 *Nezavisimoe voennoe oboezrenie*, no. 6 (13–19 February), 1998, p. 3.

139 Many of these focus on issues that concern individual branches or troops of the Armed Forces. Others were formed to enhance the social protection of servicemen, such as Shchit: see J. Mathers, 'Outside politics? Civil–military relations during a period of reform', in A. C. Aldis and R. McDermott (eds), *Russian Military Reform 1992–2002*, London: Frank Cass, 2003, p. 32.

140 There was actually a number of similar organizations of soldiers' mothers; the Committee of Soldiers' Mothers was the most well-known. See F. Daucé, 'Les mouvements de mères de soldats à la recherche d'une place dans la société russe', *Revue d'études comparatives Est–Ouest*, 1997, vol. 28, no. 2, pp. 124–28, for a presentation of the organizations existing in 1997.

141 For example, Gorbachev issued a decree as early as 1990 creating a special commission for investigating the deaths of conscripts in peacetime conditions. There is a specific reference to the Committee of Soldiers' Mothers in the text of decree no. 1037, *Vedomosti Sezda narodnykh deputatov SSSR*, no. 47, 1990, pp. 1270–271.

142 *Krasnaia zvezda*, 9 September 1990, p. 1.

143 See, for example, Fond 'Pravo materi', *Sto is 15 tysiach: Kniga pamiati*, Moscow: Izvestiia, 1992.

144 Golts, *Armiia Rossii*, p. 9.

145 O. Timofeeva, *Prokuratura proverit Soldatskikh materei*, Izvestiia.ru, 21 October 2004. Online. Available HTTP: www.izvestia.ru/community/554982_printv (accessed 3 November 2004).

146 Terekhov was retired from the Armed Forces. R. Allison, 'The Russian Armed Forces: structures, roles and policies', in V. Baranovsky (ed.), *Russia and Europe: the emerging security agenda*, Oxford: Oxford University Press for the Stockholm International Peace Research Institute (SIPRI), 1997, p. 168.

147 L. Belin, *Competition Intensifies for the 'Patriotic' Vote*, Radio Free Europe/Radio Liberty (RFE/RL), 12 November 1999. Online. Available HTTP: www.rferl.org/specials/russianelection/archives/02-121199.asp (accessed 3 November 2004).

4 Russian military reform: definitions and goals

1 An example of this was the presentation at a conference (arranged for the Russian MoD) by Colonel (ret.) Aleksandr Paderin, senior research fellow of the Institute of Military History of the Russian Ministry of Defence. A. Paderin, 'Uroki otechestvennykh voennykh reform i prichiny tormozheniia voennogo reformirovaniia v kontse XX veka', International Scientific-Practical Conference on The Military Science, Art and Practice of Russia and Its Neighbours: Past, Present, Future, St Petersburg, 29–31 March 2005 (not published).

2 N. Ogarkov, *Voennyi entsiklopedicheskii slovar*, Moscow: Voennoe izdatelstvo, 1983, p. 634.

3 See, for example, the definition provided by the Council on Foreign and Defence Policy in *Nezavisimoe voennoe obozrenie*, 1997, no. 25 (12–18 July), p. 1. See also S. Kortunov and S. Vikulov, 'Military reform and foreign policy', *International Affairs*, 1997, vol. 43, no. 6, pp. 168–69. The chairman of the Duma Committee on Defence, Andrei Nikolaev, who had a long career within the military system, defined military reform in a similar manner (A. Nikolaev, 'Voennuiu reformu kavalereiskim naskokom ne provesti', *Rossiiskaia Federatsiia segodnia*, 1999, no. 4, pp. 20–21), as did Alexei Arbatov, member of the same committee. A. Arbatov, 'Military reform in Russia: dilemmas, obstacles, and prospects', *International Security*, 1998, vol. 22, no. 4, p. 85. After becoming minister of defence, Igor Rodionov also defined military reform in this way when he outlined his plans for the Armed Forces. D. Herspring, *The Kremlin and the High Command: presidential impact on the Russian military from Gorbachev to Putin*, Lawrence, Kans.: Kansas University Press, 2006, pp. 122–23.

4 Presidential Administration, *Voennaia reforma: Zadachi i resheniia*. Online. Available HTTP: www.president.kremlin.ru/withflash/varPriorityPTemplPriorId5747.shtml (accessed 7 October 2002); and Ministry of Defence of the Russian Federation, *Voennaia reforma*. Online. Available HTTP: www.mil.ru/index.php?menu_id=6 (accessed 3 October 2002). See also the way in which Igor Sergeev described the reasons for military reform in 1997: 'Military reform is always the answer to the demands of the times, to radical changes of the geo-strategic situation, the state structure and to developments of means and methods of armed battle.' *Nezavisimoe voennoe obozrenie*, 1997, no. 35 (19–25 September), p. 1.

5 S. Ivanov (ed.), *Voennaia entsiklopediia, tom 7*, Moscow: Voennoe izdatelstvo, 2003, p. 222. Italics in the original, since these terms are also entries in the encyclopaedia.

6 Ibid., p. 222.

7 Ibid.

8 Accordingly, the 2003 military encyclopaedia states that military reform in the Russian Federation began in 'the second half of the 1990s'. Ibid., p. 223.

9 W. Parchomenko, 'The Russian military in the wake of the *Kursk* tragedy', *Journal of Slavic Military Studies*, 2001, vol. 14, no. 4, p. 37. See also M. Galeotti, 'Russia's phantom cuts', *Jane's Intelligence Review*, 2000, vol. 12, no. 11, p. 9; and J. Kipp, *Russian Military Reform: status and prospects (views of a Western historian)*, Foreign Military Studies Office, 1998. Online. Available HTTP: http://call.army.mil/fmso/fmsopubs/issues/rusrform.htm (accessed 8 July 2002).

10 Ogarkov (ed.), *Voennyi entsiklopedicheskii slovar*, p. 634; and Ivanov (ed.), *Voennaia entsiklopediia*, p. 222.
11 Articles 5 and 6 of the Russian Law on Defence, published in *Rossiiskaia gazeta*, 6 June 1996, p. 5.
12 Arbatov, 'Military reform in Russia', p. 85; and Kipp, *Russian Military Reform*. See also Boris Gromov's emphasis on what a military reform ought to include: *Nezavisimoe voennoe obozrenie*, no. 9, p. 1 (supplement in *Nezavisimaia gazeta*, 16 May 1996); and the interview with former Minister of Defence Igor Rodionov in *Nezavisimoe voennoe obozrenie*, 2003, no. 1 (17–23 January), p. 1.
13 *Krasnaia zvezda*, 23 October 1991, p. 1. In the 1970s, it was probably mainly the technological development that inspired Lobov. See, for example, Marshal Andrei Grechko's views on the new relationship between 'a scientific technological revolution' and the armed forces in the mid-1970s: A. Grechko, *Vooruzhennye sily sovetskogo gosudarstva*, Moscow: Voenizdat, 1974, pp. 170–81. For example, Grechko concluded that conventional weapons, because of their newly acquired ability to strike with more precision and greater firepower, in certain instances could replace nuclear weapons. Ibid., p. 173.
14 Ogarkov, *Voennyi entsiklopedicheskii slovar*, p. 634; and Ivanov, *Voennaia entsiklopediia*, p. 222.
15 Nikolaev, 'Military aspects of Russia's security', *International Affairs*, 1993, no. 10, p. 8. When writing the article, Nikolaev had recently been appointed commander of the Border Troops. He was later appinted director of the Federal Border Service, FPS, and awarded the highest military rank, army general.
16 I. Yerokhin, 'O razrabotke kontseptsii voennoi reformy', *Voennaia mysl*, 1991, nos 11–12, p. 45.
17 M. de Haas, 'The development of Russia's security policy, 1992–2002', in A. C. Aldis and R. McDermott (eds), *Russian Military Reform 1992–2002*, London: Frank Cass, 2003, p. 13.
18 Interview with Kokoshin in *Nezavisimaia gazeta*, 3 June 1993, p. 5.
19 M. J. Orr, 'Reform and the Russian Ground Forces, 1992–2002', in Aldis and McDermott (eds), *Russian Military Reform*, p. 126.
20 V. Lobov, 'Voennaia reforma: istoricheskie predposylki i osnovnye napravleniia', *Voenno-istoricheskii zhurnal*, 1991, no. 11, p. 2.
21 See, for example, T. Thomas, '"The War in Iraq": an assessment of the lessons learned by Russian military specialists through 31 July 2003', *Journal of Slavic Military Studies*, 2004, vol. 17, no. 1, pp. 153–80; and C. Vendil Pallin, 'Iraq war prompts debate over Russian military reform', *Jane's Intelligence Review*, 2004, vol. 16, no. 8, pp. 54–55.
22 Interview with Kokoshin in *Nezavisimaia gazeta*, 3 June 1993, p. 5.
23 W. Odom, *The Collapse of the Soviet Military* (New Haven, Conn.: Yale University Press, 1998), p. 247.
24 A. Arbatov, 'The transformation of Russia's military doctrine in the aftermath of Kosovo and Chechnya', in G. Gorodetsky (ed.), *Russia Between East and West: Russian foreign policy on the threshold of the twenty-first century*, London: Frank Cass, 2003, pp. 28–32.
25 Vendil Pallin, 'Iraq war prompts debate', pp. 54–55.
26 Glonass became active, but major problems remained when it came to practical use of the system. Apart from Glonass there are two military position systems, Paurus and Tsikada. However, these should be compared to the US Transit system, which was shut down in 1996, rather than to Navstar. Neither Paurus nor Tsikada are presumably of much use for guiding high-precision weapons. See E. Engnér, *Satellituppskjutningar 2000–2002*, Stockholm: Swedish Defence Research Agency (FOI), February 2005, Internal Report, FOI-D–0208–SE, p. 24; and D. Baker (ed.), *Jane's Space Directory 2003–2004*, Coulsdon: Jane's, 2003, pp. 602–7.

27 *Nezavisimoe voennoe obozrenie*, 2004, no. 13 (9–15 April), p. 6.
28 Ogarkov, *Voennyi entsiklopedicheskii slovar*, p. 634; and Ivanov, *Voennaia entsiklopediia*, p. 222.
29 The Baltic states were, of course, not members since they had not even joined the CIS. By the time of the 10th anniversary of the Collective Security Treaty in May 2002, six states were members: Russia, Belarus, Armenia, Kyrgyzstan, Kazakhstan and Tajikistan. Uzbekistan joined in 2006.
30 A. Golts, *Armiia Rossii: 11 poteriannykh let*, Moscow: Zakharov, 2004, pp. 116–24.
31 *Krasnaia zvezda*, 23 October 1991, p. 1.
32 S. Mendelson, *Current Russian Views on US–Russian Security Relations and Military Reform*, Center for Strategic and International Studies, PONARS, Policy Memo 25, January 1998. Online. Available HTTP: www.csis.org/ruseura/ponars/policymemos/pm_0025.pdf (accessed 3 February 2003).
33 Ogarkov, *Voennyi entsiklopedicheskii slovar*, p. 634; and Ivanov, *Voennaia entsiklopediia*, p. 222.
34 Odom, *The Collapse of the Soviet Military*, p. 43.
35 P. Baev, 'The Russian Armed Forces: failed reform attempts and creeping regionalization', in D. Betz and J. Löwenhardt (eds), *Army and State in Postcommunist Europe*, London: Frank Cass, 2001, p. 36.
36 T. Gerber and S. Mendelson, *Strong Public Support for Military Reform in Russia*, Center for Strategic and International Studies, PONARS, Policy Memo 288, May 2003. Online. Available HTTP: www.csis.org/ruseura/ponars/policymemos/pm_0288.pdf (accessed 3 February 2003).
37 *Nezavisimoe voennoe obozrenie*, 2002, no. 40 (15–21 November), p. 4.
38 M. Kramer, 'The perils of counterinsurgency: Russia's war in Chechnya', *International Security*, 2004/2005, vol. 29, no. 3, pp. 16–18.
39 Golts, *Armiia Rossii*, p. 106.
40 For a brief description of the 'hazing' hierarchy in the Russian Armed Forces – *dedovshchina* – see J. van Bladel, 'Russian soldiers in the barracks: a portrait of a subculture', in Aldis and McDermott (eds), *Russian Military Reform*, pp. 60–72.
41 F. Daucé, 'L'armée dans l'histoire de l'État russe contemporain', *Hérodote*, 2002, no. 104, pp. 130–31.
42 S. Foye, 'Rebuilding the Russian military: some problems and prospects', *RFE/RL Research Report*, 1992, vol. 1, no. 44, pp. 52–53.
43 Malnutrition was an additional problem even before the fall of the Soviet Union. In an account of the process of withdrawing troops from East Germany, the former commander, Colonel-General Matvei Burlakov, stated in an interview that when he asked for 1,000 men more than 185 cm tall, many of those that turned up weighed about 50 kg. Even allowing for a degree of exaggeration, these soldiers were clearly underweight. M. Kalashnikova, 'Ostavalos dat signal i vse by rinulos', *Kommersant vlast*, 2005, no. 12 (28 March), p. 38.
44 *Nezavisimoe voennoe obozrenie*, 2002, no. 44 (20–26 December), p. 2.
45 S. Blank, 'The general crisis in the Russian military', *Journal of Slavic Military Studies*, 2003, vol. 16, no. 2, p. 4.
46 ORTV International, *Novosti*, 12 November 2003, 18.00 Moscow time. See also 'V armii i na flote', *Rossiiskoe voennoe obozrenie*, 2004, no. 6 (June), p. 50.
47 Ivanov, *Voennaia entsiklopediia*, p. 222.
48 P. Baev, *Putin's Military Reform: two trajectories for the first presidency*, Oslo: Norwegian Atlantic Committee, 2001, Security Policy Library no. 6–2001, pp. 4–5.
49 S. Huntington, *The Common Defense: strategic programs in national politics*, New York: Columbia University Press, 1961, pp. 7–8.
50 Kipp, *Russian Military Reform*.

5 The Yeltsin era: virtual reform

1 V. Baranets, *Eltsin i ego generaly: zapiski polkovnika genshtaba*, Moscow: Sovershenno sekretno, 1998, p. 24.

2 For example, an article in 1991 mentions that 'The practice of the first years of reform has demonstrated its complexity'. V. Slipchenko and E. Shevelev, 'Metodologiia reformy Vooruzhennykh Sil', *Voennaia mysl*, 1991, nos 11–12, p. 30.

3 See, for example, P. Cronin, 'Perestroika and Soviet military personnel', in W. C. Green and T. Karasik (eds), *Gorbachev and His Generals: the reform of Soviet military doctrine*, Boulder, Col.: Westview Press, 1990, pp. 125–45.

4 C. Rice, 'The Party, the military, and decision authority in the Soviet Union', *World Politics*, 1987, vol. 40, no. 1, pp. 75–76.

5 On the tense relations between Gorbachev and the military, see D. Herspring, *The Kremlin and the High Command: presidential impact on the Russian military from Gorbachev to Putin*, Lawrence, Kans.: Kansas University Press, 2006, pp. 29–32.

6 D. Herspring, *Russian Civil–Military Relations*, Bloomington, Ind.: Indiana University Press, 1996, pp. 76–77.

7 S. Foye, 'The Soviet High Command and the politics of military reform', *Report on the USSR*, 1991, vol. 3, no. 27, pp. 10–12. The two drafts were both published in *Pravitelstvennyi vestnik*, 1990, no. 48, pp. 5–12.

8 The speech was published in *Krasnaia zvezda*, 19 August 1990, pp. 1–2.

9 V. Lopatin, 'Armiia i ekonomika', *Voprosy ekonomiki*, 1990, no. 10, p. 4.

10 Foye, 'The Soviet High Command', pp. 9–14.

11 The Soviet General Staff had started evaluating the impact of new technologies on warfare much earlier. See, for example, J. Kipp, 'War scare in the Caucasus: redefining the threat and the war on terrorism', in A. C. Aldis and and R. McDermott (eds), *Russian Military Reform 1992–2002*, London: Frank Cass, 2003, p. 240.

12 M. Webber, *The International Politics of Russia and the Successor States*, Manchester: Manchester University Press, 1996, p. 68.

13 C. Vendil, *The Belovezha Accords and Beyond: delineating the Russian state*, Stockholm: FOA, May 2000, Scientific Report, FOA-R–00-01504-170-SE, pp. 25–37.

14 W. Odom, *The Collapse of the Soviet Military* (New Haven, Conn.: Yale University Press, 1998), p. 377. See also R. Allison, 'The Russian Armed Forces: structures, roles and policies', in V. Baranovsky (ed.), *Russia and Europe: the emerging security agenda*, Oxford: Oxford University Press for the Stockholm International Peace Research Institute (SIPRI), 1997, p. 185.

15 Vladimir Lobov's vision of military reform, published in *Krasnaia zvezda*, 23 October 1991, pp. 1, 2. See also Herspring, *The Kremlin and the High Command*, p. 46 on how Lobov decided to 'break ranks' in the late 1980s.

16 This was most probably the concern uppermost in Lobov's mind during the turbulent autumn of 1991. Ibid. See also V. Lobov, 'Voennoe stroitelstvo: na novom fundamente', *Voennaia mysl*, 1991, no. 10, pp. 2 10.

17 D. Clarke, 'Soviet military reform: a moving target', *Report on the USSR*, 1991, vol. 3, no. 47, p. 16.

18 S. McMichael, 'Military reform plan begins to take shape', *Report on the USSR*, 1991, vol. 3, no. 43, p. 8.

19 See, for example, the interviews with Aleksandr Piskunov, Duma deputy and former general, in *Segodnia*, 10 March 2000, p. 4, and with Minister of Defence Sergei Ivanov in Ye. Zherebenkov, 'Pravo na silu', *Itogi*, 2002, no. 37 (17 September), p. 20.

20 On the scale of this task, see Allison, 'The Russian Armed Forces', p. 175.

21 Odom, *The Collapse of the Soviet Military*, p. 369.

22 *Nezavisimaia gazeta*, 9 April 1992, p. 1. The deputy heads of the commission all received key positions in security policy making and implementation. Grachev became minister of defence; both Kokoshin and Kobets became deputy ministers of defence; and Skokov was appointed secretary of the Russian Security Council.

23 BBC, *Summary of World Broadcasts*, SU/1351 (9 April 1992), C1/7.

24 *Nezavisimaia gazeta*, 9 April 1992, p. 1.

25 A. Kokoshin, *Strategicheskoe upravlenie: teoriia, istoricheskii opyt, sravnitelnyi analiz, zadachi dlia Rossii*, Moscow: MGIMO, ROSSPEN, 2003, p. 332.

26 C. Vendil, 'The Russian Security Council', *European Security*, 2001, vol. 10, no. 2, pp. 79–80.

27 A. Golts, *Armiia Rossii: 11 poteriannykh let*, Moscow: Zakharov, 2004, p. 39.

28 Viktor Barannikov subsequently wrote an open letter to Yeltsin in which he claimed to be the victim of 'palace intrigues' in the Kremlin and laid the blame for the tragic incident on the Afghan–Tajik border squarely at the door of the MoD. The letter was published in *Nezavisimaia gazeta*, 1 September 1993, pp. 1, 3. During the October Events in 1993, Barannikov was nominated minister of security again by the vice-president, Aleksandr Rutskoi, who had sided with the parliament against Yeltsin.

29 G. Bennett, *The Ministry of Internal Affairs of the Russian Federation*, Conflict Studies Research Centre, C106, October 2000. Online. Available HTTP: www. csrc.ac.uk/pdfs/C106-GB.pdf (accessed 16 October 2002), p. 4. In fact all the heads of the central power ministries, Grachev, Yerin, Golushko, Mikhail Barsukov (head of the GUO) and Vasilii Kursakov (commander of the Presidential Security Service belonging to the GUO), received awards after the October Events. Barannikov, on the other hand, had been made an army general earlier than that, before his loyalty to the Kremlin became open to question. V. Yasmann, 'The role of the security agencies in the October uprising', *RFE/RL Research Report*, 1993, vol. 2, no. 44, pp. 14, 18.

30 A. Golts and T. Putnam, 'State militarism and its legacies: why military reform has failed in Russia', *International Security*, 2004, vol. 29, no. 2, p. 131; and Baranets, *Eltsin i ego generaly*, pp. 26–27. However, Yeltsin was probably grateful to the Armed Forces as well after the October Events of 1993. According to Dmitrii Volkogonov, Yeltsin was pleased with the work of the Ministry of Defence. 'The army played an important role in avoiding civil war.' Interview with Dmitrii Volkogonov in *Krasnaia zvezda*, 5 January 1994, p. 2. See also Pavel Grachev's emphasis on the role of the military in avoiding civil war when he summed up the work of the Armed Forces in 1993 at a press conference on 29 December 1993: BBC, *Summary of World Broadcasts*, SU/1884, 1994, 1 January, S1/1.

31 Yasmann, 'The role of the security agencies', pp. 16–18.

32 Odom, *The Collapse of the Soviet Military*, pp. 385–86. See also Herspring's account of the choice between Shaposhnikov and Grachev in Herspring, *The Kremlin and the High Command*, pp. 68–69.

33 Kokoshin, *Strategicheskoe upravlenie*, p. 328. Both Gromov and Kondratev were dismissed in 1995 as a result of their opposition to the war in Chechnya.

34 Interview with Dmitrii Volkogonov in *Krasnaia zvezda*, 5 January 1994, p. 2.

35 *Nezavisimaia gazeta*, 7 May 1993, p. 1.

36 Kokoshin, *Strategicheskoe upravlenie*, p. 331.

37 Kokoshin's speech at the annual evaluation at the Ministry of Defence in 1993. *Krasnaia zvezda*, 9 December 1993, p. 1.

38 *Krasnaia zvezda*, 21 July 1992, p. 2.

39 Ibid., p. 2.

40 Ibid., 25 November 1992, p. 1.
41 For example, the army units in the highest state of readiness were mainly located outside Russian territory. M. Orr, 'Reform and the Russian Ground Forces, 1992–2002', in Aldis and McDermott (eds), *Russian Military Reform*, p. 125; and Herspring, *The Kremlin and the High Command*, p. 79.
42 *Krasnaia zvezda*, 21 July 1992, p. 1.
43 Ibid.
44 Address to the Collegium of the Ministry of Defence, *Krasnaia zvezda*, 25 November 1992, p. 1.
45 A. Konovalov, 'The changing role of military factors', in Baranovsky (ed.), *Russia and Europe*, p. 205.
46 *Krasnaia zvezda*, 18 December 1992, p. 2. See also J. Leijonhielm et al., *Rysk militär förmåga i ett tioårsperspektiv*, Stockholm: FOA, May 1999, User Report, FOA-R–99-01151-170-SE, pp. 151–52.
47 *Nezavisimaia gazeta*, 7 May 1993, p. 1.
48 *Krasnaia zvezda*, 18 December 1992, p. 2.
49 *Nezavisimaia gazeta*, 7 May 1993, p. 1.
50 *Krasnaia zvezda*, 9 December 1993, p. 3. See also Allison, 'The Russian Armed Forces', pp. 181–82.
51 Orr, 'Reform and the Russian Ground Forces', p. 129.
52 P. Baev, 'Reforming the Russian military: history and trajectory', in Yu. Fedorov and B. Nygren (eds), *Russian Military Reform and Russia's New Security Environment*, Stockholm: Swedish National Defence College, May 2003, ACTA B28, p. 47.
53 Allison, 'The Russian Armed Forces', p. 185.
54 Ibid., pp. 188–90.
55 R. Allison, 'Russia, regional conflict, and the use of military power', in S. E. Miller and D. Trenin (eds), *The Russian Military: power and policy*, Cambridge, Mass.: MIT Press, 2004, p. 124.
56 C. Dick, 'The military doctrine of the Russian Federation', *Journal of Slavic Military Studies*, 1994, vol. 7, no. 3, pp. 494–95. See also the singling out of the USA as a 'main military threat' in an early draft for a new military doctrine published in 1990 in a supplement presenting concepts for military reform and military doctrine in *Voennaia mysl*.
57 P. Baev, *The Russian Army in a Time of Troubles*, London: Sage, 1996, p. 37.
58 Vendil, 'The Russian Security Council', pp. 77–79.
59 *Nezavisimaia gazeta*, 29 April 1993, pp. 1, 3.
60 *Krasnaia zvezda*, 25 November 1992, p. 1.
61 *Nezavisimaia gazeta*, 3 June 1993, p. 5.
62 Ibid., p. 5. In May 1993, Grachev also regarded the risk of nuclear war as very low and pointed to local conflicts as the most 'serious destabilizing factor' facing Russia. *Nezavisimaia gazeta*, 7 May 1993, p. 1.
63 *Krasnaia zvezda*, 7 October 1993, p. 1.
64 Ibid., 19 November 1993, pp. 3–4.
65 Ibid., p. 3. See also Baev, *The Russian Army*, pp. 24, 33.
66 M. de Haas, 'The development of Russia's security policy, 1992–2002', in Aldis and McDermott (eds), *Russian Military Reform*, p. 5.
67 *Krasnaia zvezda*, 4 November 1993, p. 1. See also ibid., 19 November, p. 3; and Dick, 'The military doctrine', pp. 495–96.
68 In spite of the emphasis put on the nuclear component of Russia's defence, the situation in the Strategic Missile Forces was problematic. Moreover, it would later become obvious (not least during the Kosovo conflict) that the nuclear component constituted a blunt political instrument without strong conventional forces to back it up.

69 Dick, 'The military doctrine', p. 494. See also the views expressed at a conference organized by the Military Academy of the General Staff in May 1992. Orr, 'Reform and the Russian Ground Forces', pp. 126–27.

70 Allison, 'The Russian Armed Forces', p. 179.

71 According to Grachev, there were plans to create mini-ministries of defence in the Far East, Transbaikal and Volga districts, to be headed by deputy ministers of defence – a step towards introducing 'territorial command of the forces': *Nezavisimaia gazeta*, 7 May 1993, p. 1. See also M. Galeotti, *The Kremlin's Agenda: the new Russia and its Armed Forces*, Coulsdon: Jane's Intelligence Review, 1995, pp. 126–28.

72 *Krasnaia zvezda*, 17 November 1995, p. 1.

73 Kokoshin, *Strategicheskoe upravlenie*, p. 302.

74 Presidential decree no. 1373, 28 June 1994.

75 Presidential decree no. 2251, 30 December 1994.

76 Kokoshin, *Strategicheskoe upravlenie*, p. 302. Korzhakov was dismissed in June 1996 and elected to the Duma in 1999 where he became deputy chairman of the Committee on Defence.

77 *Nezavisimaia gazeta*, 8 October 1994, pp. 1, 2. By 1996, the number of generals had been reduced to 2,865 from 3,159 in 1992. Kokoshin, *Strategicheskoe upravlenie*, p. 301.

78 Ibid., p. 301.

79 On the controversy and different versions of how this decision was made, see Vendil, 'The Russian Security Council', pp. 84–85.

80 *Krasnaia zvezda*, 30 December 1994, p. 1.

81 Kokoshin, *Strategicheskoe upravlenie*, pp. 300–1.

82 *Krasnaia zvezda*, 15 November 1994, p. 1. See also Yeltsin's statement of June 1994: 'Today the Armed Forces of the Russian Federation as a whole meet the contemporary requirements for ensuring the country's security.' *Segodnia*, 29 June 1994, p. 2. These figures probably included personnel other than troops as well (compare Table 5.1).

83 M. J. Orr, *Manpower Problems of the Russian Armed Forces*, Conflict Studies Research Centre, D62, February 2002. Online. Available HTTP: www.csrc.ac.uk/frames/frames_page.htm (accessed 23 February 2005), p. 2; and A. Lieven, *Chechnya: tombstone of Russian power*, New Haven, Conn.: Yale University Press, 1998, p. 105.

84 *Segodnia*, 13 January 1995, p. 2; and *Moscow News*, 1995, no. 3 (20–26 January), pp. 1, 2.

85 *Rossiiskie vesti*, 1 August 1995, p. 1.

86 Baranets, *Eltsin i ego generaly*, p. 40.

87 Golts, *Armiia Rossii*, pp. 61–63. Initially, the operation was under the command of Grachev with the aid of Yerin and Stepashin. The first deputy commander of the Ground Forces, Eduard Vorobev, refused to take command of the operation, stating that the preparations made were totally inadequate. As a consequence, he was dismissed from the Armed Forces. Lieven, *Chechnya*, pp. 106, 281.

88 *Moscow News*, 1995, no. 2 (13–19 January), p. 1.

89 Allison, 'Russia, regional conflict and ... ', p. 127.

90 On the successes and failures of the Committee of Soldiers' Mothers in influencing military policy in Chechnya and in general, see A. Caiazza, *Mothers and Soldiers: gender, citizenship, and civil society in contemporary Russia*, New York: Routledge, 2002, pp. 123–43.

91 In 1995, Russian newspapers described the hazing hierarchy and its role in the overall command structures at the lower levels of the Armed Forces in great detail. *Nezavisimoe voennoe obozrenie*, 1995, no. 1, p. 8 (supplement to *Nezavisimaia gazeta*, 11 February 1995).

92 D. Betz, *Civil–Military Relations in Russia and Eastern Europe*, London: RoutledgeCurzon, 2004, p. 56. See also Allison, 'The Russian Armed Forces', p. 175; and D. Betz and V. Volkov, 'A new day for the Russian army? Reforming the Armed Forces under Yeltsin and Putin', in Aldis and McDermott (eds), *Russian Military Reform*, p. 45.
93 See, for example, Leijonhielm et al., *Rysk militär förmåga*, 1999, p. 136.
94 S. E. Miller, 'Moscow's military power: Russia's search for security in an age of transition', in Miller and Trenin (eds), *The Russian Military*, p. 23.
95 For interesting examples of how representatives of the military organization present entirely inconsistent personnel numbers according to the policy effect desired at a specific time, see Golts, *Armiia Rossii*, pp. 170–71.
96 BBC, *Summary of World Broadcasts*, SU/1351, 1992, 9 April, C1/7; and *Nezavisimaia gazeta*, 9 April 1992, p. 1.
97 Press conference given by Pavel Grachev on 29 December 1993. BBC, *Summary of World Broadcasts*, SU/1884, 1994, 1 January, S1/1–2.
98 B. Lambeth, 'Russia's wounded military', *Foreign Affairs*, 1995, vol. 74, no. 2, p. 89. See also the evaluation of 1994 made by the military council of the Ground Forces, *Krasnaia zvezda*, 18 November 1994, p. 1. Not one tactical exercise on divisional level had been conducted since 1992 and in certain army and corps exercises were planned only at company (*rota*) level and below.
99 *Nezavisimaia gazeta*, 7 May 1993, p. 1.
100 See, for example, the command and staff exercise conducted in November 1993. *Krasnaia zvezda*, 9 November 1993, p. 1.
101 *Krasnaia zvezda*, 9 December 1993, p. 1.
102 Lambeth, 'Russia's wounded military', p. 88. Another example was provided by Igor Sergeev in 1993, who claimed that only 60 per cent of the defence enterprises for the RVSN remained within Russia, quoted in S. J. Main, 'The Strategic Rocket Forces, 1991–2002', in Aldis and McDermott (eds), *Russian Military Reform*, p. 107.
103 Kokoshin's speech at the annual evaluation session, *Krasnaia zvezda*, 9 December 1993, p. 1.
104 *Nezavisimoe voennoe obozrenie*, 1995, no. 3, p. 3 (supplement to *Nezavisimaia gazeta*, 18 November 1995).
105 *Krasnaia zvezda*, 17 November 1995, p. 3.
106 Ibid., p. 1.
107 S. Blank, *Russia's Armed Forces on the Brink of Reform*, Royal Military Academy Sandhurst, Conflict Studies Research Centre, C97, October 1997, p. 3.
108 See, for example, A. Dadonov, 'The Russian Interior Ministry's special Internal Troop units for combating terrorism: organization, training system and the conduct of special operations', *Low Intensity Conflict and Law Enforcement*, 1997, vol. 6, no. 2, p. 125.
109 J. Mathers, 'Outside politics? Civil–military relations during a period of reform', in Aldis and McDermott (eds), *Russian Military Reform*, pp. 29–30.
110 Bennett, *The Ministry of Internal Affairs*, p. 15. See also Lieven, *Chechnya*, p. 287.
111 G. Bennett, *The Federal Security Service of the Russian Federation*, Conflict Studies Research Centre, C102, March 2000. Online. Available HTTP: www.csrc. ac.uk/pdfs/c102.pdf (accessed 16 October 2002), pp. 12–13.
112 Furthermore, regulations that had facilitated the work of the Border Troops, such as tight control of the movement of Soviet citizens and severely limited opportunities for foreigners to visit the Soviet Union, disappeared almost overnight. G. Bennett, *The Federal Border Guard Service,* Conflict Studies Research Centre, C107, March 2002. Online. Available HTTP: www.csrc.ac.uk/pdfs/c107-gb.pdf (accessed 13 May 2002), pp. 3–4.
113 Ibid., pp. 13–14.

114 Lieven, *Chechnya*, p. 287.
115 For example, in his speech at the Collegium of the Ministry of Defence in November 1992, Grachev refuted allegations that military reform was not moving ahead. *Krasnaia zvezda*, 25 November 1992, p. 3.
116 Golts, *Armiia Rossii*, p. 19.
117 Betz and Volkov, 'A new day for the Russian army?', pp. 45–46.
118 *Kommersant daily*, 25 July 1997, p. 3.
119 P. Baev, 'The Russian army and Chechnya: victory instead of reform?', in S. J. Cimbala (ed.), *The Russian Military into the Twenty-first Century*, London: Frank Cass, 2001, p. 81.
120 Kokoshin, *Strategicheskoe upravlenie*, p. 301; and *Rossiiskaia gazeta*, 6 August 1996, p. 1.
121 Golts, *Armiia Rossii*, pp. 40–48. See also Kokoshin, *Strategicheskoe upravlenie*, p. 303.
122 Baev, 'Reforming the Russian military', pp. 42–43. There were, of course, many more facets to the conflict between Rodionov and Baturin. See Golts, *Armiia Rossii*, pp. 40–48; and P.-O. Nilsson, 'Om den ryska militärreformen', *Kungliga Krigsvetenskapsakademins Handlingar och Tidskrift*, 1997, no. 1, pp. 77–136.
123 *Nezavisimaia gazeta*, 23 May 1997, p. 1. See also Golts, *Armiia Rossii*, pp. 46–47. Rodionov's ignominy was increased by the fact that Yeltsin dismissed him 'in full glare of the TV cameras'. Main, 'The Strategic Rocket Forces', p. 109.
124 Personal communication with Russian officers. See also Herspring, *The Kremlin and the High Command*, p. 120.
125 Presidential decree no. 1102, 25 July 1996, published in *Rossiiskaia gazeta*, 27 July 1996, p. 1.
126 Kokoshin, *Strategicheskoe upravlenie*, p. 302.
127 The statutes of the Defence Council were established by presidential decree no. 1102 and published in *Rossiiskaia gazeta*, 27 July 1996, p. 4.
128 *Rossiiskaia gazeta*, 5 October 1996, p. 1.
129 *Nezavisimaia gazeta*, 10 June 1997, p. 1.
130 Kokoshin, *Strategicheskoe upravlenie*, pp. 302–3.
131 Presidential decree no. 946, 28 August 1997, published in *Rossiiskaia gazeta*, 3 September 1997, p. 4.
132 Statutes of the State Military Inspectorate, *Rossiiskaia gazeta*, 3 September 1997, p. 4. See also Kokoshin's account of the functioning of the State Military Inspectorate: Kokoshin, *Strategicheskoe upravlenie*, p. 303, and footnote 15, pp. 474–76.
133 Presidential decree no. 946, 28 August 1997, published in *Rossiiskaia gazeta*, 3 September 1997, p. 4.
134 Kokoshin, *Strategicheskoe upravlenie*, p. 307.
135 *Krasnaia zvezda*, 26 July 1997, p. 1; and presidential decree no. 725s, 16 July 1997, excerpts of which were published in *Rossiiskaia gazeta*, 19 July 1997, p. 5.
136 *Nezavisimaia gazeta*, 10 June 1997, p. 1.
137 Kokoshin, *Strategicheskoe upravlenie*, p. 309; and I. Rybkin, *Consent in Chechnya, Consent in Russia*, London: Lytten Trading & Investment Ltd, 1998, p. 47. During Rybkin's time as secretary of the Security Council, the council was sometimes referred to disrespectfully as the 'Ministry of Chechen Affairs'. See *Segodnia*, 27 December 1997, p. 3.
138 *Nezavisimaia gazeta*, 21 January 1997, p. 2.
139 Vendil, 'The Russian Security Council', p. 86.
140 Presidential decree no. 220, 'On Some Measures to Develop State Direction in the Sphere of Defence and Security', 2 March 1998, published in *Rossiiskaia gazeta*, 4 March 1998, p. 3. See also Kokoshin, *Strategicheskoe upravlenie*, p. 303.
141 Presidential decree no. 294, 28 March 1998, confirming the statutes of the Security Council apparatus, published in *Vedomosti Federalnogo sobraniia Rossiiskoi Federatsii*, 1998, no. 14, pp. 2984–89.

142 *Rossiiskaia gazeta*, 26 May 1998, p. 1.
143 *Segodnia*, 20 January 1995, p. 1.
144 Kokoshin does not state exactly when this took place. Possibly, it was when Mironov left his office in November 1998 during Primakov's tenure as prime minister. Kokoshin, *Strategicheskoe upravlenie*, p. 307.
145 Interview with Sergei Stepashin in *Krasnaia zvezda*, 11 January 1997, p. 1.
146 Piskunov went on to become one of twelve auditors of the Audit Chamber in 2001 with responsibility for the budget for the national defence.
147 P. J. Sutcliffe and C. Hill, 'An economic analysis of Russian military reform proposals: ambition and reality', in Aldis and McDermott (eds), *Russian Military Reform*, p. 288.
148 *Krasnaia zvezda*, 20 February 1998, p. 1.
149 Indeed, the very fact that Yeltsin was forced into a compromise in selecting a prime minister when the Duma refused to accept his candidate, Chernomyrdin, is telling. According to Aleksandr Golts, Yeltsin contemplated using armed force in order to subdue the Duma, but was dissuaded by a paper prepared by the then secretary of the Security Council, Kokoshin. Kokoshin stated in this paper, based on data from the military counter-intelligence, that the prevailing sentiment in the army and Interior Troops made it unlikely that they would support Yeltsin in such a scenario. Golts, *Armiia Rossii*, pp. 154, 180.
150 Leijonhielm et al., *Rysk militär förmåga*, 1999, pp. 262–63.
151 Ibid., pp. 266–67.
152 Ibid.
153 W Unge, *The Russian Military–Industrial Complex in the 1990s: conversion and privatisation in a structurally militarised economy*, Stockholm: FOA, December 2000, FOA-R–00-01702-170–SE, pp. 14–15.
154 Ibid., pp. 70–72.
155 Petr Romashkin, staffer for the Duma Defence Committee, displayed a keen interest in literature on civilian control of the military and the relationship between the US Congress and the Pentagon, when Sarah Mendelson interviewed him in 1997. See S. Mendelson, *Current Russian Views on US–Russian Security Relations and Military Reform*, Center for Strategic and International Studies, PONARS, Policy Memo 25, January 1998. Online. Available HTTP :www.csis. org/ruseura/ponars/policymemos/pm_0025.pdf (accessed 3 February 2003).
156 *Moskovskii komsomolets*, 24 October 2002, p. 2. Nor did the USSR parliament have access to details of the military budget: see Lopatin, 'Armiia i ekonomika', pp. 7–9.
157 D. Betz, 'No place for a civilian? Russian defense management from Yeltsin to Putin', *Armed Forces and Society*, 2002, vol. 28, no. 3, p. 498.
158 These accusations were repudiated by Yeltsin's presidential representative in the Duma at the time, Aleksandr Kotenkov. State Duma of the Russian Federation, *Stennogramma plenarnogo zasedaniia Gosudarstvennoi Dumy RF: 13 maia 1999, dnevnoe zasedanie*, AKDI Ekonomika i zhizn. Online. Available HTTP: www. akdi.ru/gd/PLEN_Z/1999/s13-05_d.htm (accessed 14 November 2001).
159 B. Taylor, *The Duma and Military Reform*, Center for Strategic and International Studies, PONARS, Policy Memo 154, October 2000. Online. Available HTTP: www.csis.org/ruseura/ponars/policymemos/pm_0154.pdf (accessed 3 February 2003).
160 *Nezavisimaia gazeta*, 23 September 1997, p. 1.
161 *Sovetskaia Rossiia*, 27 September 1997, p. 5; and Mendelson, *Current Russian Views*.
162 *Kommersant daily*, 20 September 1997, p. 3.
163 *Sovetskaia Rossiia*, 23 July 1998, p. 1. See also Mathers, 'Outside politics?', pp. 31–34.
164 P. Baev, *Putin's Court: how the military fits in*, Center for Strategic and International Studies, PONARS, Policy Memo 153, November 2000. Online. Available HTTP: www.csis.org/ruseura/ponars/policymemos/pm_0153.pdf (accessed 3 February 2003). See also Taylor, *The Duma and Military Reform*.

165 *Segodnia*, 16 November 1998, p. 1.
166 For a desciption of the draft, see Yu. Ivanov, 'Legal, political and budgetary aspects of civilian control of the military in Russia', in D. Betz and J. Löwenhardt (eds), *Army and State in Postcommunist Europe*, London: Frank Cass, 2001, pp. 11–22. The draft (no. 97801758–2) was still on the Duma's database on its website, www. duma.gov.ru, on 3 February 2005.
167 Blank, *Russia's Armed Forces*, p. 11; and Mendelson, *Current Russian Views*.
168 For example, the Center for Policy Studies in Russia (PIR) was founded in 1994 and in November the same year started to issue its own journal, *Yadernyi kontrol (Nuclear Control)*. One of the researchers, Major-General (ret.) Vladimir Dvorkin, came to the institute with forty years of experience from working within the defence establishment.
169 *Nezavisimoe voennoe obozrenie*, 1997, no. 25 (12–18 July), pp. 1, 4–7.
170 See, for example, the experiences of the Antimilitarist Radical Association described in Caiazza, *Mothers and Soldiers*, pp. 147–54.
171 *Krasnaia zvezda*, 10 June 1994, p. 1.
172 Golts, *Armiia Rossii*, p. 51.
173 *Nezavisimaia gazeta*, 10 June 1997, p. 1; and ibid., p. 74.
174 *Kommersant daily*, 25 July 1997, p. 3. For a description of the generals in charge of the services in the ministry when Sergeev arrived, see *Moscow News*, 1997, no. 28 (24–30 July), pp. 1, 5.
175 Orr, 'Reform and the Russian Ground Forces', p. 131.
176 According to Aleksandr Golts, the officers of the Strategic Missile Forces were the generals most apt to realize the new demands put on modern warfare, since they did not live in 'the mythological "experience" of the Great Patriotic War' that put all the emphasis on numbers. Golts, *Armii Rossii*, p. 80. See also Leijonhielm et al., *Rysk militär förmåga*, 1999, p. 149.
177 Michael Orr dismisses the abolition of the Ground Forces Command as 'military nonsense' and as a product of internal politics within the ministry: Orr, 'Reform and the Russian Ground Forces', p. 131.
178 This is about 100,000 less than given in *The Military Balance*: see Table 5.4.
179 Interview with Bukreev in *Nezavisimoe voennoe obozrenie*, 1999, no. 9 (12–18 March), p. 3; and ibid., 1999, no. 10 (19–25 March), p. 1. See also Orr, 'Reform and the Russian Ground Forces', p. 132; and L. Ulfving, *Rysk krigs-konst*, Stockholm: Swedish National Defence College, 2005, pp. 106–7. Bukreev claimed that seven formations were in the first category whereas *Nezavisimoe voennoe obozrenie*, 1999, no. 9, states that there were three divisions in this category plus four brigades. This is an indication that the brigades in question were rather more substantial than usual or were intended to transform into divisions if needed. For a discussion of the transfer from an army-division structure to a corps-brigades structure and the possibility of reverting to an army-division structure, see Leijonhielm et al., *Rysk militär förmåga*, 1999, p. 150. It could also mirror the turf wars within defence decision making between the proponents of a reformed structure for the Ground Forces and the conservatives' wish to maintain the mass army option.
180 Main, 'The Strategic Rocket Forces', p. 111.
181 Leijonhielm et al., *Rysk militär förmåga*, 1999, pp. 200–1.
182 Main, 'The Strategic Rocket Forces', p. 111; and Golts, *Armiia Rossii*, p. 73. In addition, a new submarine missile was to be developed. This was, no doubt, the Bulava (SS-N-27) to be fitted to the Borei Class submarine. For a description see, for example, M. Galeotti, 'Putin puts confidence in new generation of missiles', *Jane's Intelligence Review*, 2005, vol. 17, no. 2, p. 54.
183 Main, 'The Strategic Rocket Forces', pp. 114–15. For a description of the stand-off between Sergeev and Kvashnin, see Golts, *Armiia Rossii*, pp. 71–82.

184 E. Hagström, *Integration eller sönderfall? En studie av utvecklingen av samarbetet inom OSS 1991–1997*, Stockholm: FOA, February 1998, User Report, FOA-R–97-00728-180–SE, p. 11.
185 Leijonhielm et al., *Rysk militär förmåga*, 1999, pp. 155–59; and S. Lefebvre, 'The reform of the Russian air force', in Aldis and McDermott (eds), *Russian Military Reform*, pp. 142–43.
186 Lefebvre, 'The reform of the Russian air force', pp. 144–45.
187 Leijonhielm et al., *Rysk militär förmåga*, 1999, p. 161.
188 Ibid., pp. 157–58.
189 Presidential decree no. 725s, 16 July 1997, excerpts in *Rossiiskaia gazeta*, 19 July 1997, p. 5.
190 Leijonhielm et al., *Rysk militär förmåga*, 1999, pp. 159–60; J. Leijonhielm et al., *Rysk militär förmåga i ett tioårsperspektiv: en förnyad bedömning*, Stockholm: FOA, November 2000, User Report, FOA-R–00-01758-170–SE, pp. 88–89; and Lefebvre, 'The reform of the Russian air force', pp. 146–49.
191 Lefebvre, 'The reform of the Russian air force', pp. 153–54.
192 M. Tsypkin, 'Rudderless in the storm: the Russian navy, 1992–2002', in Aldis and McDermott (eds), *Russian Military Reform*, p. 163.
193 Ibid., pp. 162–63; and Leijonhielm et al., *Rysk militär förmåga*, 1999, pp. 170–72.
194 Kokoshin devoted considerable attention to the completion of the *Petr Velikii* as part of the overall strategy to concentrate R&D and production resources on key projects. Kokoshin, *Strategicheskoe upravlenie*, footnote 7, pp. 498–99. In spite of of the priority accorded to the project, there were indications that the government and the navy were far from happy with the *Petr Velikii*. By early 1997, there had already been three incidents of breakdowns (*avarii*) aboard the ship – leading the then head of the government's Administrative Department, Sergei Stepashin, to note the paradox that the worse defence companies performed, the more work, and thus the more money, they received. *Krasnaia zvezda*, 11 January 1997, p. 1.
195 Tsypkin, 'Rudderless in the storm', p. 168; and Leijonhielm et al., *Rysk militär förmåga*, 1999, p. 172.
196 Tsypkin, 'Rudderless in the storm', p. 168.
197 Ibid., pp. 170, 180.
198 Ibid., pp. 170–71; and Leijonhielm et al., *Rysk militär förmåga*, 1999, pp. 177–78.
199 Leijonhielm et al., *Rysk militär förmåga*, 2000, p. 101.
200 Presidential decree no. 900, 27 July 1998, 'On the Military-Administrative Division of the Russian Federation'; and no. 901, 27 July 1998, 'On Confirming the Statutes for the Military District of the Armed Forces of the Russian Federation'.
201 Yu. Baluevskii, 'Novaia rol voennogo okruga', *Voennaia mysl*, 1999, no. 3, p. 5. On the arrangements for Kamchatka and Chukotka, see *Krasnaia zvezda*, 21 March 1998, p. 1.
202 Baluevskii, 'Novaia rol voennogo okruga', p. 3. See also interview with Baluevskii in *Krasnaia zvezda*, 18 August 1998, pp. 1, 2.
203 *Krasnaia zvezda*, 18 August 1998, p. 2. See also Orr, 'Reform and the Russian Ground Forces', pp. 131–32.
204 Leijonhielm et al., *Rysk militär förmåga*, 1999, p. 141.
205 Ibid., p. 142.
206 Main, 'The Strategic Rocket Forces', pp. 107–9. See also Golts, *Armiia Rossii*, pp. 52–53.
207 *Nezavisimoe voennoe obozrenie*, 1999, no. 9 (12–18 March), p. 3.
208 Tsypkin, 'Rudderless in the storm', p. 180; and J. Leijonhielm et al., *Rysk militär förmåga i ett tioårsperspektiv: en förnyad bedömning 2002*, Stockholm: FOI, February 2003, User Report FOI-R–0811–SE, pp. 102–3.
209 *Nezavisimoe voennoe obozrenie*, 1999, no. 9 (12–18 March), p. 3.

210 'I am tired of these conversations on yet another superweapon – unique in the world', Kokoshin complained to Golts in an interview. Golts, *Armiia Rossii*, pp. 58–59.

211 As early as 1992, Yeltsin promised in his address to the Collegium of the Ministry of Defence that improving the social conditions for servicemen would become a priority. Indeed, the weight of the 'social sphere' in the defence budget was to increase substantially, according to Yeltsin. *Krasnaia zvezda*, 25 November 1992, pp. 1, 3.

212 See, for example, *Krasnaia zvezda*, 21 November 1995, p. 1.

213 Ibid., 9 December 1995, p. 5.

214 See, for example, *Krasnaia zvezda*, 20 September 1996, p. 1.

215 Speech at the Collegium of the Ministry of Defence, *Krasnaia zvezda*, 25 November 1992, p. 3.

216 Ibid., p. 1.

217 *Rossiiskie vesti*, 25 February 1994, p. 2.

218 S. Rosefielde, *Russia in the 21st Century: the prodigal superpower*, New York: Cambridge University Press, 2005, p. 97.

219 Press conference after the annual evaluation session, *Krasnaia zvezda*, 17 November 1995, p. 3.

220 *Krasnaia zvezda*, 22 December 1994, p. 1. The inflation rate at the time meant, of course, that in real terms the increase was less significant. Nevertheless, the trend was clearly downhill rather than towards improvement of the state of Russia's defence finances.

221 Allison, 'The Russian Armed Forces', pp. 170–71.

222 *Krasnaia zvezda*, 2 December 1994, p. 1.

223 Ibid.

224 Ibid.

225 Betz, *Civil–Military Relations*, p. 149.

226 Governmental statute no. 1144, 26 November 1996.

227 Interview in *Krasnaia zvezda*, 19 November 1996, p. 1. See also Yeltsin's decree on measures to finance military development, presidential decree no. 1592, 25 November 1996, *Rossiiskaia gazeta*, 5 December 1996, p. 3.

228 *Krasnaia zvezda*, 19 November 1996, p. 2.

229 Savenkov, 'Na zashchite federalnoi sobstvennosti', *Finansovyi kontrol*, 2004, no. 11, p. 44.

230 Interview with Sergei Stepashin in *Krasnaia zvezda*, 11 January 1997, p. 1.

231 *Segodnia*, 27 January 1998, p. 1. See also *Nezavisimaia gazeta*, 24 January 1998, p. 1; and 28 January 1998, pp. 1, 2.

232 Golts, *Armiia Rossii*, p. 144.

233 Baev, *The Russian Army*, p. 24. See also M. Galeotti, 'Russia's internal security forces: does more mean better?', *Jane's Intelligence Review*, 1994, vol. 6, no. 6, pp. 271–72.

234 Kokoshin, *Strategicheskoe upravlenie*, p. 310.

235 Interview with Aleksandr Piskunov in *Krasnaia zvezda*, 19 November 1996, p. 2.

236 The deputy head of the Government's Administrative Department, Aleksandr Piskunov, stated that because of the personnel increases in troops other than the Armed Forces, the overall force level remained at the Soviet level. Ibid., p. 1. This would have signified that the overall size of Russia's military organization was about 4 million men. However, it seems likely that civilian personnel and, for example, the police are included in this figure.

237 Presidential decree no. 1592, 25 November 1996, published in *Rossiiskaia gazeta*, 5 December 1996, p. 3. A summary based on information supplied by the Presidential Press Service was available in *Krasnaia zvezda*, 27 November 1996, p. 1. See also the interview with Piskunov in *Krasnaia zvezda*, 19 November 1996, p. 1; and Golts, *Armiia Rossii*, pp. 30–31.

238 *Nezavisimaia gazeta*, 28 January 1998, p. 1. The Directorate of Investigation is controversial, not least since it runs one of the most famous prisons in Russia, the Lefortovo (or 'isolator') in Moscow.

239 Interview with the head of the FSB Directorate of Military Counter-intelligence, Colonel-General Aleksei Moliakov, in *Nezavisimaia gazeta*, 19 July 1997, pp. 1, 2. Moliakov went on to receive a leading position in the State Military Inspectorate in January 1998. He was succeeded by FSB Lieutenant-General Vladimir Petrishchev as head of military counter-intelligence. See Bennett, *The Federal Security Service*, p. 30.

240 Presidential decree, no. 318, 7 February 2000, published in *Rossiiskaia gazeta*, 12 February 2000, p. 6.

241 T. Thomas, 'Restructuring and reform in Russia's MVD: good idea, bad timing?', *Low Intensity Conflict and Law Enforcement*, 1998, vol. 7, no. 2, pp. 96–97.

242 Radio Free Europe/Radio Liberty, 'Interior Troops face sharp cuts', *RFE/RL Newsline*, 16 June 1998. Online. Available HTTP: www.rferl.org/newsline/1998/06/1-rus/rus-160698.asp (accessed 9 March 2005).

243 Interview with Andrei Kokoshin in *Literaturnaia gazeta*, O. Moroz, 'Chto budet s nashei armiei?', *Literaturnaia gazeta*, 30 August 2000. Online. Available HTTP: www.lgz.ru/archives/html_arch/lg34-352000/polit/art2.htm (accessed 13 May 2002).

244 For example, Anatol Lieven gives the number of 40,000 men belonging to the Presidential Guard 'at least on paper' in 1996. Lieven, *Chechnya*, p. 287. This figure appears rather high and probably includes GUO troops as well as vacant positions.

245 *Nezavisimoe voennoe obozrenie*, 2001, no. 2 (19–25 January), p. 1. Again, it should be emphasized that these figures are riddled with inconsistencies and it is not clear which troops the numbers include. The statement in *Nezavisimoe voennoe obozrenie* probably included personnel other than strictly military units in its estimate.

246 See, for example, former General Staff Colonel Viktor Baranets' account of how generals enriched themselves in the process and how the Military Procuracy was prevented from prosecuting the guilty: Baranets, *Eltsin i ego generaly*, pp. 15–18. See also Allison, 'The Russian Armed Forces', pp. 166–67; and the allegations against Colonel-General Matvei Burlakov, who commanded the Soviet Group of Forces in Germany and was in charge of dismantling them. Herspring, *The Kremlin and the High Command*, p. 82.

247 Kokoshin, *Strategicheskoe upravlenie*, pp. 329–30. On 17 January 1992, Yeltsin was confronted with the hostility of the All-Army Officers Meeting. *Nezavisimaia gazeta*, 18 January 1992. See also Baranets, *Eltsin i ego generaly*, pp. 103–6; and Golts, *Armiia Rossii*, pp. 17–18.

248 Kokoshin, *Strategicheskoe upravlenie*, p. 330.

249 *Krasnaia zvezda*, 23 July 1992, p. 1.

250 Ibid., 9 December 1993, p. 3. See also Baranets, *Eltsin i ego generaly*, pp. 6–8.

251 Betz, *Civil–Military Relations*, p. 54.

252 Odom, *The Collapse of the Soviet Military*, pp. 39–40.

253 *Krasnaia zvezda*, 21 July 1992, p. 2.

254 Baev, 'Reforming the Russian military', pp. 41–42.

255 Lieven, *Chechnya*, pp. 279–80.

256 Orr, 'Reform and the Russian Ground Forces', p. 129.

257 *Krasnaia zvezda*, 10 June 1994, p. 1. See also Lambeth, 'Russia's wounded military', pp. 90–92; Allison, 'The Russian Armed Forces', p. 166; Betz, *Civil–Military Relations*, pp. 54–55; and Orr, *Manpower Problems*, pp. 1–2.

258 *Nezavisimoe voennoe obozrenie*, 1995, no. 3, p. 3 (supplement in *Nezavisimaia gazeta*, 18 November 1995)

259 Ibid. See also Golts, *Armiia Rossii*, pp. 10–11; and Herspring, *The Kremlin and the High Command*, pp. 79–80.

260 Government statute no. 918, 30 November 1992, published in *Krasnaia zvezda*, 3 December 1992, p. 1.
261 Allison, 'The Russian Armed Forces', p. 174; and Orr, *Manpower Problems*, p. 2.
262 S. Foye, 'Manning the Russian army: is contract service a success?', *RFE/RL Research Report*, 1994, vol. 3, no. 13, p. 36; and Allison, 'The Russian Armed Forces', pp. 174–75.
263 *Krasnaia zvezda*, 18 August 1993, p. 2.
264 Foye, 'Manning the Russian army', p. 44.
265 *Krasnaia zvezda*, 4 August 1998, pp. 1, 2. In addition, it would seem that the number of officers in the reserve that were in fact called up was not overly impressive. In 2005, the MoD stated that, out of the 60,000 officers in the reserve educated at military departments of civilian educational establishments, only 6,000 were called up. See Ministry of Defence of the Russian Federation, *Vstupitelnoe slovo Nachalnika Sluzhby kadrovoi i vospitatelnoi raboty Ministerstva oborony RF, generala armii N. A. Pankova na zasedanii Press-kluba voennykh obozrevatelei rossiiskikh SMI pri Upravlenii informatsii i obshchestvennykh sviazei MO RF*, 1 July 2005. Online. Available HTTP: www.mil.ru/articles/article10951.shtml (accessed 4 October 2005).
266 *Nezavisimoe voennoe obozrenie*, 1999, no. 9 (12–18 March), p. 3.
267 Golts, *Armiia Rossii*, p. 102.
268 R. Thornton, 'Military organizations and change: the "professionalization" of the 76th Airborne Division', *Journal of Slavic Military Studies*, 2004, vol. 17, no. 3, pp. 453–54. See also Foye, 'Manning the Russian army', p. 38.
269 In 2003, there were ten military academies, nine military universities and thirty-eight military institutes according to Ministry of Defence of the Russian Federation, *Aktualnye zadachy razvitiia Vooruzhennykh Sil Rossiiskoi Federatsii*, 2003. Online. Available HTTP: www.mil.ru/index.php?menu_id=886 (accessed 22 October 2003), p. 55. The Academy of the General Staff was probably included in the ten military academies in the document in 2003.
270 *Krasnaia zvezda*, 4 August 1998, p. 2.
271 Mendelson, *Current Russian Views*.
272 *Krasnaia zvezda*, 25 November 1992, p. 1.
273 Ibid.
274 The problem of the lack of NCOs had already been pointed out in the Soviet era. The introduction in the early 1970s of warrant officers (*praporshchiki* in the army and *michmany* in the navy) was an attempt to address this problem: E. Jones, *Red Army and Society: a sociology of the Soviet military*, London: Allen & Unwin, 1985, pp. 95–98. During Miliutin's reforms in the 1860s, the need for more independent commanders was difficult to satisfy because of the lack of well trained junior officers: G. Persson, 'The Russian army and foreign wars 1859–1871', doctoral thesis, Government Department, London School of Economics and Political Science, 1999, p. 99.
275 Kolesnikov's speech at the annual evaluation session of the Armed Forces in December 1993. *Krasnaia zvezda*, 9 December 1993, p. 1.
276 *Nezavisimaia gazeta*, 3 June 1993, p. 5.
277 *Krasnaia zvezda*, 20 December 1995, p. 1. The same situation was described by Deputy Commander of the Ground Forces Colonel-General Anton Terentev, in an interview in *Nezavisimoe voennoe obozrenie*, 1995, no. 3, p. 3 (supplement in *Nezavisimaia gazeta*, 18 November 1995).
278 *Kommersant daily*, 15 February 1997, p. 3.
279 Human Rights Watch, 'To serve without health: inadequate nutrition and health care in the Russian Armed Forces', *Human Rights Watch*, vol. 15, no. 9 (D), November 2003. Online. Available HTTP: www.hrw.org/reports/2003/russia1103/russia1103.pdf (accessed 21 January 2005), p. 13; and *Krasnaia zvezda*, 23 July 1992, p. 2.

280 See, for example, *Krasnaia zvezda*, 19 November 1996, p. 2.
281 *Krasnaia zvezda*, 11 March 1998, p. 1. See also M. Galeotti, 'Russia's criminal army', *Jane's Intelligence Review*, 1999, vol. 11, no. 6, pp. 8–10; and *Nezavisimoe voennoe obozrenie*, 1998, no. 21 (5–18 June), pp. 1, 3.
282 See, for example, Igor Sergeev's presentation of the military reform when visiting the Motorized Rifle Division in Taman outside Moscow. *Krasnaia zvezda*, 26 September 1997, p. 1. See also *Nezavisimaia gazeta*, 10 June 1997, p. 1.
283 *Nezavisimoe voennoe obozrenie*, 1998, no. 8 (13–19 February), p. 3. See also the interview with the head of the Centre for Military Strategic Research of the General Staff, Lieutenant-General Vladimir Potemkin, *Krasnaia zvezda*, 10 September 1998, p. 2.
284 *Krasnaia zvezda*, 10 September 1998, p. 2.
285 Ibid., 6 November 1996, p. 1.
286 Presidential decree no. 1300, 17 December 1997. The decree and the text of the national security concept were published in *Krasnaia zvezda*, 27 December 1997, pp. 1, 3–4.
287 Tsypkin, 'Rudderless in the storm', p. 168.
288 In fact, the national security concept had been longer in the making mainly because of infighting between the different power ministries and agencies concerned. de Haas, 'The development of Russia's security policy', pp. 6–7.
289 The first news that such a document was being developed trickled out in 1996. In *Nezavisimoe voennoe obozrenie*, 1996, no. 8 (supplement to *Nezavisimaia gazeta*, 25 April 1996), pp. 1, 3, an article claimed that a group headed by the national security adviser, Iurii Baturin, was writing a 'national security policy of Russia' and that it would form an important part of the president's annual state of the nation address.
290 Tsypkin, 'Rudderless in the storm', p. 168.
291 *Nezavisimoe voennoe obozrenie*, 1999, no. 46 (26 November–3 December), pp. 1, 4 5.
292 An information security doctrine was developed under the aegis of the Security Council and published the same year, and a naval doctrine came into force by presidential decree in June 2001.
293 This was not a unique situation. It occurred in the Soviet Union as well. Rice, 'The Party, the military, and decision authority', pp. 70–71.
294 Orr, 'Reform and the Russian Ground Forces', p. 132.
295 Tsypkin, 'Rudderless in the storm', p. 171–72. See also Golts, *Armiia Rossii*, pp. 74–75.
296 *Segodnia*, 2 July 1999. Actually, the final stage of the exercise, the nuclear response, was mainly symbolic and demonstrative. For example, the Tu-95 Bears delivering the missiles were intercepted by US F-15s outside Iceland. Lacking fighter support, they would not have been able to carry out the attack in real life. Tsypkin, 'Rudderless in the storm', p. 172. See also Aleksandr Golts' scathing criticism of the planning and ideas behind Zapad-99 in Golts, *Armiia Rossii*, pp, 127–30; and B. Ljung (ed.), *Aspects of the Kosovo Operation March–June 1999*, Stockholm: FOI, May 2001, User Report, FOI-R-0070-SE, p. 54.
297 Kokoshin, *Strategicheskoe upravlenie*, p. 332.
298 Betz, 'No place for a civilian?', p. 491.
299 Ibid.
300 Interview with Sergei Stepashin in *Krasnaia zvezda*, 11 January 1997, p. 1.
301 Interview with Oleinik in *Nezavisimoe voennoe obozrenie*, 1998, no. 17 (8–14 May), pp. 1, 3.
302 Koksoshin, *Strategicheskoe upravlenie*, p. 325.
303 *Moscow News*, 1997, no. 28 (24–30 July), pp. 1, 5.
304 Interview with the head of the Administrative Department of the Government Apparatus, Sergei Stepashin, *Krasnaia zvezda*, 11 January 1997, p. 1.

305 Leijonhielm et al., *Rysk militär förmåga*, 2000, pp. 64–66.
306 *Krasnaia zvezda*, 11 February 1998, p. 1.
307 Golts, *Armiia Rossii*, p. 71.

6 Enter Putin

1 C. Vendil, 'The Russian legitimation formula, 1991–2000', doctoral thesis, Government Department, London School of Economics and Political Science, 2002, pp. 156–67.
2 Federal Law no. 162-F3, 29 December 2000, published in *Krasnaia zvezda*, 5 January 2001, p. 1.
3 Kokoshin early on argued in favour of retaining the use of the old Soviet symbols, but years would pass before there was formal legislation on the issue. A. Kokoshin, *Strategicheskoe upravlenie: teoriia, istoricheskii opyt, sravnitelnyi analiz, zadachi dlia Rossii*, Moscow: MGIMO, ROSSPEN, 2003, p. 497.
4 D. Herspring, *The Kremlin and the High Command: presidential impact on the Russian military from Gorbachev to Putin*, Lawrence, Kans.: Kansas University Press, 2006, pp. 200–1.
5 *Nezavisimoe voennoe obozrenie*, 2000, no. 11 (31 March–6 April), p. 1.
6 BBC, *Summary of World Broadcasts*, SU/3651 (28 September 1999), B/1. See also *Novosti, Vechernii vypusk, Informatsionnaia programma*, ORT (Russian TV), 27 October 1999, 1800 hrs (Moscow time).
7 The international reactions to human rights violations during the first war in Chechnya were neither coordinated nor forceful. Strategic considerations more often than not overrode human rights concerns. S. Cornell, 'International reactions to massive human rights violations: the case of Chechnya', *Europe–Asia Studies*, 1999, vol. 51, no. 1, pp. 85–100; and M. Evangelista, *The Chechen Wars: will Russia go the way of the Soviet Union?*, Washington, D.C.: Brookings Institution Press, 2002, pp. 144–48. World leaders turned up in Moscow to celebrate the 50th anniversary of victory in the Second World War in 1995, in spite of the ongoing war in Chechnya and without seizing the opportunity to criticize the Russian manner of waging the war: Vendil, *The Russian Legitimation Formula*, pp. 175–76.
8 See, for example, Interfax, *PACE Will Not Monitor Elections in Chechnya – Davis*, 9 October 2005. Online. Available HTTP: www.interfax.com/17/96160/Interview.aspx (accessed 28 October 2005).
9 P. Baev, *Putin's War in Chechnya: who steers the course?*, Center for Strategic and International Studies, PONARS, Policy Memo 345, November 2004. Online. Available HTTP: www.csis.org/ruseura/ponars/policymemos/pm_0345.pdf (accessed 4 March 2005), p. 6.
10 M. Kramer, 'The perils of counterinsurgency: Russia's war in Chechnya', *International Security*, 2004/2005, vol. 29, no. 3, p. 12.
11 P. Baev, 'The Russian army and Chechnya: victory instead of reform?', in S. J. Cimbala (ed.), *The Russian Military into the Twenty-first Century*, London: Frank Cass, 2001, p. 77.
12 G. Bennett, *The Ministry of Internal Affairs of the Russian Federation*, Conflict Studies Research Centre, C106, October 2000, pp. 15–16. Online. Available HTTP: www.csrc.ac.uk/pdfs/C106-GB.pdf (accessed 16 October 2002); and Kramer, 'The perils of counterinsurgency', pp. 13–14.
13 For analyses of the Russian military performance in Chechnya see, for example, R. Allison, 'Russia, regional conflict and the use of military power', in S. E. Miller and D. Trenin (eds), *The Russian Military: power and policy*, Cambridge, Mass.: MIT Press, 2004, p. 130; Baev, 'The Russian army and Chechnya', pp. 76–78; Kramer, 'The perils of counterinsurgency', p. 61; and S. Lefebvre, 'The

reform of the Russian air force', in A. C. Aldis and R. McDermott (eds), *Russian Military Reform 1992–2002*, London: Frank Cass, 2003, pp. 153–54.

14 Kramer, 'The perils of counterinsurgency', pp. 17ff.

15 *Nezavisimoe voennoe obozrenie*, 2005, no. 27 (22–28 July), pp. 1, 3. See also ibid., 2005, no. 29 (5–11 August), p. 2; *Nezavisimaia gazeta*, 15 January 2007, p. 14; and C. W. Blandy, *North Caucasus: on the brink of far-reaching destabilisation*, Conflict Studies Research Centre, Caucasus Series, 05/36, August 2005. Online. Available HTTP: www.da.mod.uk/CSRC/documents/Caucasus/05%2836%29-CWB. pdf (accessed 6 October 2005).

16 *Nezavisimoe voennoe obozrenie*, 2007, no. 36 (19–25 October), p. 1.

17 For example, in September 2005, only 20 per cent were in favour of a continued military operation in Chechnya, while 68 per cent wanted peace negotiations to be initiated. Levada Tsentr, *Sotsialno politicheskaia situatsiia v Rossii v sentiabre 2005 goda*, 5 October 2005. Online. Available HTTP: www.levada.ru/press/ 2005100506.html (accessed 7 October 2005).

18 See, for example, J. Eyal, 'The tragedy of Russia: lessons unlearnt', *RUSI Newsbrief*, 2004, vol. 24, no. 9, pp. 97–98; B. Lo, 'A people's trauma', *The World Today*, 2004, vol. 60, no. 10, pp. 5–6; and H. Plater-Zyberk, *Beslan: lessons learned?*, Conflict Studies Research Centre, Russian Series, 04/34, November 2004. Online. Available HTTP: www.da.mod.uk/CSRC/documents/Russian/04% 2834%29-HPZ.pdf (accessed 29 November 2004). In the case of the Dubrovka, the Kremlin appears to have approved of the performance of the units involved since the people in charge of the operation to free the hostages were decorated and later promoted. Argumenty i fakty, *Nagrazhdenie chinovnikov ordenami za operatsiiu na Dubrovke vyzvalo protest boitsov, shturmovavshikh 'Nord-Ost'*, Press-Tsentr, 4 March 2003. Online. Available HTTP: http://news.aif.ru/news.php? id=10659 (accessed 18 April 2006).

19 Levada Tsentr, *Sotsialno-politicheskaia situatsiia v Rossii*.

20 Kozak left this post on 24 September 2007, when he was appointed minister of regional development.

21 *Nezavisimaia gazeta*, 29 September 2005, p. 3; and Blandy, *North Caucasus*. See also *Nezavisimaia gazeta*, 15 January 2007, pp. 13–14.

22 C. W. Blandy, *Chechnya: continued violence*, Conflict Studies Research Centre, Caucasus Series, 06/54, December 2006. Online. Available HTTP: www.defac.ac. uk/colleges/csrc/document-listings/caucasus/ (accessed 3 October 2007).

23 P. Truscott, *Kursk*, London: Pocket Books, 2002, pp. 5–43; and Z. Barany, *Democratic Breakdown and the Decline of the Russian Military*, Princeton, N.J.: Princeton University Press, 2007, pp. 19–43.

24 M. Tsypkin, 'Rudderless in the storm: the Russian navy, 1992–2002', in Aldis and McDermott (eds), *Russian Military Reform*, p. 177; and A. Golts, 'The social and political condition of the Russian military', in Miller and Trenin (eds), *The Russian Military*, p. 90.

25 For a description of how political and naval authorities handled the *Kursk* incident in the media, see G. Simons, *Russian Crisis Management Communications and Media Management Under Putin*, Uppsala, Sweden: Department of East European Studies, Uppsala University, January 2005, Working Papers no. 85, pp. 6–9.

26 However, certain aspects of the way the Russian navy handled this incident have been criticized as well: see Barany, *Democratic Breakdown*, pp. 41–42.

27 According to Zoltan Barany, Putin's main lesson from the *Kursk* accident was that he must control the media. Barany, *Democratic Breakdown*, p. 39.

28 C. Vendil, 'The Russian Security Council', *European Security*, 2001, vol. 10, no. 2, p. 86.

29 N. Petrov, 'Seven faces of Putin's Russia: federal districts as the new level of state-territorial composition', *Security Dialogue*, 2002, vol. 33, no. 1, pp. 82–84.

30 P. Baev, 'Reforming the Russian military: history and trajectory', in Yu. Fedorov and B. Nygren (eds), *Russian Military Reform and Russia's New Security Environment*, Stockholm: Swedish National Defence College, May 2003, ACTA B28, pp. 48–49.

31 J. Leijonhielm et al., *Rysk militär förmåga i ett tioårsperspektiv: en förnyad bedömning 2002*, Stockholm: Swedish Defence Research Agency (FOI), February 2003, User Report, FOI-R–0811–SE, pp. 33–36; and Petrov, 'Seven faces of Putin's Russia', pp. 73–81.

32 Petrov, 'Seven faces of Putin's Russia', pp. 82–84.

33 N. Petrov, 'Siloviki in Russian regions: new dogs, old tricks', *Journal of Power Institutions in Post-Soviet Societies*, 2005, no. 2. Online. Available HTTP: www.pipss.org/document331.html (accessed 10 May 2005).

34 J. Leijonhielm et al., *Rysk militär förmåga i ett tioårsperspektiv: problem och trender 2005*, Stockholm: FOI, June 2005, User Report, FOI-R–1662–SE, pp. 51–52.

35 C. Vendil Pallin, 'The Russian power ministries: tool and insurance of power', *Journal of Slavic Military Studies*, 2007, vol. 20, no. 1, pp. 13–14.

36 Presidential Administration, *Soobshchenie Press-sluzhby Prezidenta Rossii*, 30 March 2004. Online. Available HTTP: www.kremlin.ru/text/news/2004/03/62552.shtml (accessed 1 March 2005).

37 Presidential Administration, *Burutin Aleksandr Germanovich*. Online. Available HTTP: www.president.kremlin.ru/state_subj/43499.shtml (accessed 1 March 2005).

38 Presidential Administration, *Troshev Gennadii Nikolaevich*. Online. Available HTTP: www.president.kremlin.ru/state_subj/27784.shtml (accessed 14 October 2005).

39 *Nezavisimaia gazeta*, 18 April 2005, p. 1. Viktor Ivanov rose to become deputy director of the FSB before moving to the Presidential Administration in 2004.

40 Kokoshin, *Strategicheskoe upravlenie*, p. 303.

41 Vendil, 'The Russian Security Council', pp. 86–87.

42 *Nezavisimoe voennoe obozrenie*, 2000, no. 45 (1–7 December), pp. 1, 4.

43 For example, it was Sergei Ivanov rather than Igor Ivanov who discussed disarmament and energy policy with George W. Bush in Washington in preparation for the summit meeting in Bratislava between Bush and Putin. *Nezavisimaia gazeta*, 13 January 2005, p. 5.

44 In October 2005, the number of interdepartmental commissions was reduced and their areas of responsibility were altered by presidential decree. The new Interdepartmental Commission on Strategic Planning seems to have been tasked with determining the main threats facing Russia and the resources that should be allotted to meeting them. The secretary of the Security Council became chairman of this commission. The regulations and membership of the commissions accompanied presidential decree no. 1244, 28 October 2005.

45 Novaia Gazeta, *Agenty vliianiia*, NovaiaGazeta.ru. Online. Available HTTP: http://2004.novayagazeta.ru/nomer/2004/63n/n63n-s45.shtml (accessed 13 October 2005). On Chemezov's close contacts with Putin, see also A. Vandenko, 'Chelovek vo vseoruzhii', *Itogi*, 2005, no. 44 (31 October), pp. 22–26.

46 Government of the Russian Federation, *Dmitriev Mikhail Arkadevich*. Online. Available HTTP: www.government.gov.ru/institutions/ministries/management.html?he_id=918 (accessed 14 October 2005).

47 On the membership of the commission, see presidential decrees no. 1003, 2 August 2004, and no. 362, 17 March 2007.

48 Government of the Russian Federation, *Lychagin Mikhail Ivanovich*. Online. Available HTTP: www.government.gov.ru/government/minister/index.html?he_id=1053 (accessed 1 March 2005).

49 K. Lantratov and I. Safronov, *Premer vzial v pomoshchniki generala*, Kommersant Daily. Online. Available HTTP: www.kommersant.ru/doc.html?DocID=469616& IssueId=18270 (accessed 13 October 2005).
50 Shamanov was elected governor in the Ulianovsk region in 2000. Before that, he had occupied central command positions in both the wars in Chechnya. *Krasnaia zvezda*, 18 October 2004, pp. 1, 2; and D. Guseva and N. Gorelov, *Karera generala*, Vremia novostei. Online. Available HTTP: www.vremya.ru/2004/209/4/ 112395.html (accessed 26 October 2005).
51 Government Statute no. 665, 22 June 1999, 'On the Government Commission of the Russian Federation on Military-Industrial Questions'. See also Leijonhielm et al., *Rysk militär förmåga i ett tioårsperspektiv: en förnyad bedömning*, Stockholm: Swedish National Defence Research Establishment (FOA), November 2000, User Report, FOA R 00-01758-170-SE, p. 159.
52 For the membership and regulations of the commission, see Government of the Russian Federation, *Sostav Kommissii Pravitelstva Rossiiskoi Federatsii po voenno-promyshlennym voprosam*. Online. Available HTTP: www.government.gov.ru/data/ static_text.html?st_id=7776&he_id=755 (accessed 25 February 2005); and Government of the Russian Federation, *Polozhenie o Kommissii Pravitelstva Rossiiskoi Federatsii po voenno-promyshlennym voprosam*. Online. Available HTTP: www.government.gov.ru/data/static_text.html?st_id=7791&he_id=755 (accessed 25 February 2005).
53 Statutes, no. 662, 1 September 2001, Government of the Russian Federation, *Soobshchenie dlia pechati No. 1241, Postanovlenie ot 1 septiabria 2001, No. 662 O Morskoi kollegii pri Pravitelstve Rossiiskoi Federatsii*. Online. Available HTTP: www.government.gov.ru/data/news text.html?he_id=103&news_id=3213 (accessed 18 February 2005). See also *Nezavisimoe voennoe obozrenie*, 2001, no. 28 (3– 9 August), p. 1; and Tsypkin, 'Rudderless in the storm', pp. 178–79.
54 Government instruction no. 1405-r, 4 November 2004, Government of the Russian Federation, *Sostav Morskoi kollegii pri Pravitelstve Rossiiskoi Federatsii*. Online. Available HTTP: www.government.gov.ru/data/static_text.html?st id=7747 &he_id=755 (accessed 18 February 2005).
55 *Nezavisimaia gazeta*, 3 November 2005, p. 1.
56 Presidential decree no. 867, 17 May 2000, 'On the Structure of the Federal Organs of Executive Power'. See also government statute no. 515, 12 July 2000, 'Questions concerning the Ministry for Industry, Science and Technology of the Russian Federation'; and Leijonhielm et al., *Rysk militär förmåga*, 2002, pp. 174–75.
57 Leijonhielm et al., *Rysk militär förmåga*, 2005, p. 225.
58 V. Shlykov, 'The economics of defense in Russia and the legacy of structural militarization', in Miller and Trenin (eds), *The Russian Military*, p. 171.
59 *Nezavisimaia gazeta*, 5 October 2005, pp. 1, 2; and Presidential decree no. 1244, 28 October 2005.
60 Government of the Russian Federation, *Federalnoe agenstvo po atomnoi energii*. Online. Available HTTP: www.government.gov.ru/institutions/ministries/details. html?he_id=988 (accessed 21 September 2005).
61 Ministry of Finance of the Russian Federation, *Chistova Vera Yergeshevna*. Online. Available HTTP: www.minfin.ru/org_str/chistova.htm (accessed 3 March 2005).
62 Putilin, formerly head of the General Staff's Main Organizational-Mobilization Directorate, was initially deputy minister of economic development and trade, but lost this rank as a result of the administrative reform. Ministry of Economic Development and Trade of the Russian Federation, *Struktura Ministerstva*. Online. Available HTTP: www.economy.gov.ru/wps (accessed 3 March 2005).
63 *Nezavisimoe voennoe obozrenie*, 2003, no. 9 (14–20 March), p. 1.
64 Leijonhielm et al., *Rysk militär förmåga*, 2005, p. 48.

65 G. Bennett, *The Federal Agency of Government Communications & Information*, Conflict Studies Research Centre, C105, August 2000. Online. Available HTTP: www.csrc.ac.uk/pdfs/C105.pdf (accessed 16 October 2002).
66 For Putin's decree on the membership of the Security Council as of April 2004, see presidential decree no. 561, 24 April 2004.
67 Presidential decrees no. 307, 11 March 2003, and no. 306, 11 March 2003.
68 Presidential decree no. 868, 11 July 2004.
69 *Nezavisimoe voennoe obozrenie*, 2005, no. 36 (23–30 September), pp. 1, 3.
70 Leijonhielm et al., *Rysk militär förmåga*, 2005, pp. 42–45.
71 On the bungling of Russia's security services in Beslan, see Eyal, 'The tragedy of Russia', pp. 97–98; M. Galeotti, 'Beslan shows growing Islamist influence in Chechen war', *Jane's Intelligence Review*, 2004, vol. 16, no. 10, pp. 12–17; Lo, 'A people's trauma', pp. 5–6; and Plater-Zyberk, *Beslan: lessons learned?*.
72 Kudrin's statement was much noticed at the time and was quoted, for example, in D. Lynch, *'The Enemy Is at the Gate': Russia after Beslan*, Note for the PSC, IESUE/COPS(04)10, Paris: Institute for Security Studies, 2004, p. 8.
73 In 2007, Russia shared 143th position out of 180 countries on the Corruption Perception Index (CPI) with Gambia, Indonesia and Togo. In 2004, it had ranked 90th. The annual ratings are available on Transparency International's website, www.transparency.org
74 T. Bukkvoll, 'Their hands in the till: scale and causes of Russian military corruption', *Armed Forces and Society*, 2007, vol. 34. no. 2. See also *Nezavisimoe voennoe obozrenie*, 2006, no. 16 (19–25 May), p. 1.
75 For an analysis of the changed power balance in the Duma after December 1999, see Leijonhielm et al., *Rysk militär förmåga*, 2000, pp. 34–36.
76 Leijonhielm et al., *Rysk militär förmåga*, 2005, pp. 40–41.
77 *Moskovskii komsomolets*, 24 October 2002, p. 2.
78 Ibid.
79 *Nezavisimoe voennoe obozrenie*, 2003, no. 1 (17–23 January), p. 1.
80 A. Arbatov, 'Military reform: from crisis to stagnation', in Miller and Trenin (eds), *The Russian Military*, pp. 98–99. Indeed, when Sergei Ivanov appeared in the Duma on 7 February 2007, he claimed that he could not disclose even an approximate number of tanks in the Armed Forces since it was an open session. However, Russia reports such numbers to a number of international institutions on a voluntary basis and the foreign intelligence services that Ivanov feared probably had a very good estimate already. 'Minutes of State Duma of the Federal Assembly', no. 209, 7 February 2007. Online. Available HTTP: www.cir. ru/docs/duma/302/1099390?QueryID'984852&HighlightQuery=984852 (accessed 19 September 2007).
81 *Nezavisimoe voennoe obozrenie*, 2006, no. 23 (7–13 July), pp. 1, 3.
82 See, for example, *Nezavisimaia gazeta*, 19 October 2005, pp. 1, 4.
83 *Nezavisimoe voennoe obozrenie*, 2003, no. 20 (20–26 June), p. 1.
84 Ibid., 2004, no. 19 (28 May–3 June), pp. 1, 2.
85 Savenkov, 'Na zashchite federalnoi sobstvennosti', *Finansovyi kontrol*, 2004, no. 11, p. 44.
86 Audit Chamber of the Russian Federation, Federalnyi zakon ot 1 dekabria 2004 goda No 145-FZ 'O vnesenii izmenenii v federalnyi zakon "O Schetnom palate Rossiiskoi Federatsii"'. Online. Available HTTP: www.ach.gov.ru/zakon/fedzakon/chapter5.php (accessed 25 January 2005).
87 I. Granik, *Gosduma svodit schety so Schetnoi palatoi*, Kommersant Daily. Online. Available HTTP: www.kommersant.ru/doc.html?docId=549135 (accessed 21 February 2005).
88 For an excellent overview of the lack of transparency of Russia's defence budget, see J. Cooper, 'Society–military relations in Russia: the economic dimension', in

S. Webber and S. Mathers (eds), *Military and Society in Post-Soviet Russia*, Manchester: Manchester University Press, 2006, pp. 131–56.

89 Article by the deputy general procurator and main military procurator of the Russian Federation, Judicial Colonel-General Aleksandr Savenkov, 'Na zashchite federalnoi sobstvennosti', pp. 43–44.

90 Yu. Ivanov, 'Legal, political and budgetary aspects of civilian control of the military in Russia', in D. Betz and J. Löwenhardt (eds), *Army and State in Postcommunist Europe*, London: Frank Cass, 2001, p. 16.

91 *Nezavisimoe voennoe obozrenie*, 2004, no. 46 (3–9 December), pp. 1, 3.

92 Ibid., p. 3.

93 *Nezavisimoe voennoe obozrenie*, 2005, no. 19 (27 May–2 June), pp. 1, 2; ibid., 2005, no. 21 (10–16 June), pp. 1, 3; and ibid., 2005, no. 38 (7–13 October), pp. 1, 2. See also the interview with Main Military Procurator A. Savenkov in 'Kradut!', *Itogi*, 2004, no. 43 (26 October), pp. 22–24.

94 President of Russia, *Stenograficheskii otchet o pervom plenarnom zasedanii Obshchestvennoi palaty Rossiiskoi Federatsii*, 22 January 2006. Online. Available HTTP: www.kremlin.ru/text/appears/2006/01/100457.shtml# (accessed 4 October 2007). See also *Nezavisimaia gazeta*, 13 October 2005, p. 1.

95 N. Petrov and D. Slider, 'Putin and the regions', in D. R. Herspring (ed.), *Putin's Russia: past imperfect, future uncertain*, 3rd edn, Lanham, Md. and Boulder, Col.: Rowman & Littlefield, 2007, p. 95.

96 Presidential decree no. 842, 4 August 2006. See also R. Sakwa, *Putin: Russia's choice*, 2nd edn, London: Routledge, 2007, pp. 169–73.

97 See the interview with Deputy Minister of Defence and State Secretary Nikolai Pankov, 'Kurs – na grazhdanskii kontrol', *Rossiiskoe voennoe obozrenie*, 2007, no. 4, p. 6. In fact, the MoD was the first of the ministries and services concerned to create a public council, perhaps partly because it found itself having to tackle another hazing scandal which hit the headlines at about this time. *Nezavisimaia gazeta*, 17 January 2007, p. 3.

98 *Krasnaia zvezda*, 13 February 2007, p. 1.

99 Presidential decree no. 842, 4 August 2006, and the supplement to Order of the Ministry of Defence, no. 490, 16 November 2006. At a round table on discipline and crime within the Armed Forces organized by the Military Procuracy in September 2007, not a word was said about the impact of the Public Council. See *Nezavisimoe voennoe obozrenie*, 2007, no. 33 (28 September–4 October).

100 '"Sovet dobrykh del" nachinaet rabotu', *Rossiiskoe voennoe obozrenie*, 2007, no. 3, p. 35.

101 Z. Barany, 'The tragedy of the *Kursk*: crisis management in Putin's Russia', *Government and Opposition*, 2004, vol. 39, no. 3, p. 501.

102 J. Bransten, 'Patriotic TV channel launches, but is anyone watching?', *RFE/RL Media Matters*, 2005, vol. 5, no. 5 (24 February). Online. Available HTTP: www.rferl.org/reports/mm/2005/02/5-240205.asp (accessed 28 September 2005).

103 *Nezavisimoe voennoe obozrenie*, 2004, no. 44 (19–25 November), p. 3. See also ibid., 2005, no. 35 (16–22 September), p. 1; and 2006, no. 34 (22–28 September), p. 1.

104 See, for example, B. Renz, 'Media–military relations in post-Soviet Russia: who is the watchdog?', in Webber and Mathers (eds), *Military and Society in Post-Soviet Russia*, pp. 61–79.

105 I. Safranchuk, *Contemporary Russian Military Journalism: achievements, problems, perspectives*, Center for Defense Information. Online. Available HTTP: www.cdi.org/program/issue/index.cfm?ProgramID=29&issueid=154 (accessed 4 April 2005).

106 Arbatov, 'Military reform: from crisis to stagnation', p. 98.

107 See the compilation of highlights in *Nezavisimoe voennoe obozrenie*, 2005, no. 5 (10–16 February), p. 1.

108 C. Walker and R. Orttung, 'No news is bad news', *Wall Street Journal Europe*, 7 September 2006, on Freedom House's website. Online. Available HTTP: www. freedomhouse.org/template.cfm?page=72&release=411 (accessed 6 November 2007).

109 V. Litovkin, *Pamiati Ivana Safronova*, RIA Novosti, 6 March 2007. Online. Available HTTP: www.rian.ru/analytics/20070306/61641899.html (accessed 25 October 2007).

110 The fact that Yeltsin had hailed Igor Rodionov as the first 'civilian' minister of defence when he was appointed in 1996 was mercifully forgotten. Rodionov had reached the age of mandatory retirement (sixty) by the time he became minister of defence and thus, technically, retired from the Armed Forces. D. Betz, *Civil–Military Relations in Russia and Eastern Europe*, London: RoutledgeCurzon, 2004, p. 96.

111 B. Taylor, *The Duma and Military Reform*, Center for Strategic and International Studies, PONARS, Policy Memo 154, October 2000. Online. Available HTTP: www. csis.org/ruseura/ponars/policymemos/pm_0154.pdf (accessed 3 February 2003).

112 D. Betz, 'No place for a civilian? Russian defense management from Yeltsin to Putin', *Armed Forces and Society*, 2002, vol. 28, no. 3, p. 489.

113 Ibid., p. 492.

114 P. J. Sutcliffe and C. Hill, 'An economic analysis of Russian military reform proposals: ambition and reality', in Aldis and McDermott (eds), *Russian Military Reform*, p. 288.

115 *Nezavisimoe voennoe obozrenie*, 2001, no. 26 (20–27 July), p. 3.

116 Ibid.; and S. Talbott, *The Russia Hand: a memoir of presidential diplomacy*, New York: Random House, 2002, pp. 353–54. For Ivashov's views, see, for example, his article in *Nezavisimoe voennoe obozrenie*, 1999, no. 45 (19–25 November), p. 3, in which he accused Washington of conducting an 'anti-Russian campaign'. Ivashov continued to propound his own military foreign policy even after having left the MoD from a position as vice-president of the Academy of Geopolitical Problems.

117 Gennadii Troshev later denied that he had refused to obey orders. According to Troshev the minister of defence, Sergei Ivanov, had only proposed a transfer over the telephone, and he had declined it. In his view, the media and certain politicians had inflated the matter into a political affair or 'generals' plot': G. Troshev, *Chechenskii retsediv: Zapiski komanduiushchego*, Moscow: Vagrius, 2003, pp. 6–8. In February 2003, moreover, Troshev was appointed presidential adviser (see above, p.). On the insubordination of Russian generals to the Kremlin, see also Golts, 'The social and political condition of the Russian military', pp. 88–90.

118 *Nezavisimoe voennoe obozrenie*, 2002, no. 44 (20–26 December), pp. 1, 8.

119 Ibid., p. 8. In December 1825, a number of tsarist officers revolted against the absolute monarchy in Russia in what became known as the Decembrist uprising.

120 Ibid., 2003, no. 21 (27 June–3 July), p. 1.

121 On the battle between Ivanov and Kvashnin, see, for example, *Nezavisimoe voennoe obozrenie*, 2002, no. 44 (20–26 December), p. 3.

122 Ministry of Defence of the Russian Federation, *Vystuplenie ministra oborony Rossiiskoi Federatsii S. B. Ivanova na zasedanii Akademii voennykh nauk*, 24 January 2004. Online. Available HTTP: www.mil.ru/print/releases/2004/01/241203_4779. shtml (accessed 20 April 2004). Compare also A. Kokoshin, 'Defence leadership in Russia: the General Staff and strategic management in a comparative perspective', Conference proceedings from *BCSIA Discussion Paper 2002–15*, Kennedy School of Government, Harvard University, November 2002.

123 The new regulations for the Ministry of Defence were adopted through presidential decree no. 1082, on 1 August 2004.

124 See also M. Galeotti, 'Russia's emerging security doctrine', *Jane's Intelligence Review*, 2004, vol. 16, no. 11, p. 47.

125 *Nezavisimoe voennoe obozrenie*, 2004, no. 18 (21–27 May), p. 1.
126 In effect, the lack of unity of command had been another main point in Sergei Ivanov's speech in January 2004. He made a comparison with the situation in the Russian Empire in 1905–8 to demonstrate his point. S. Main, *Couch for the MoD or the CGS? Defence and the General Staff 2001–2004*, Conflict Studies Research Centre, Russian Series 04/09}, April 2004. Online. Available HTTP: www.da.mod.uk/CSRC/documents/Russian/04%2809%29-SJM.pdf (accessed 26 October 2004).
127 *Nezavisimoe voennoe obozrenie*, 2004, no. 44 (19–26 November), p. 3.
128 Ibid., 2004, no. 42 (5–11 November), pp. 1, 2. See also, for example, the heavy-handed personnel shifts within the Directorate of Head of Command and Control (*Nachalnik Sviazi*) of the General Staff and the anger they incurred: ibid., 2005, no. 29 (5–11 August), p. 3.
129 Ibid., 2004, no. 44 (19–26 November), p. 3.
130 Ministry of Defence of the Russian Federation, *Vystuplenie Ministra oborony RF, S. B. Ivanova na soveshchanii rukovodiashchego sostava Vooruzhennykh Sil Rossiiskoi Federatsii*, 17 November 2004. Online. Available HTTP: www.mil.ru/releases/2004/11/171230_8578.shtml (accessed 17 November 2004).
131 Ibid.
132 *Nezavisimoe voennoe obozrenie*, 2004, no. 9 (12–18 March), p. 1.
133 RIA Novosti, *Putin obeshchaet usilit znachenie Genshtaba VS Rossii*, 15 February 2007. Online. Available HTTP: www.rian.ru/defense_safety/army_navy/20070215/60808273.html (accessed 26 October 2007).
134 Ibid.
135 V. Shlykov, 'Odin v pole ne voin', *Russia in Global Affairs*, 2007, no. 3. Online. Available HTTP: www.globalaffairs.ru/numbers/26/7704.html (accessed 26 October 2007).
136 Ministry of Defence of the Russian Federation, *Aktualnye zadachi* … (online version).
137 See, for example, the interview with Colonel-General (ret.) Eduard Vorobev in *Nezavisimoe voennoe obozrenie*, 2005, no. 25 (8–14 July), pp. 1, 3.
138 I. Kobrinskaya, 'The military reform as a social contract', in Fedorov and Nygren (eds), *Russian Military Reform*, pp. 85–98.
139 The titles of the two documents were 'Plan for the development of the Armed Forces 2001–5' and 'State program for weapons, military and special technology 2001–10'. *Nezavisimoe voennoe obozrenie*, 2001, no. 3 (26 January–1 February), p. 1.
140 *Krasnaia zvezda*, 6 November 2004, p. 1.
141 This arrangement probably lasted until the administrative reform in mid-2004, when the overall number of deputy ministers was reduced.
142 Kokoshin, *Strategicheskoe upravlenie*, p. 329.
143 M. J. Orr, 'Reform and the Russian Ground Forces, 1992–2002', in Aldis and McDermott (eds), *Russian Military Reform*, p. 133.
144 R. Thornton, 'Military organizations and change: the "professionalization" of the 76th Airborne Division', *Journal of Slavic Military Studies*, 2004, vol. 17, no. 3, pp. 458–59.
145 Leijonhielm et al., *Rysk militär förmåga*, 2002, p. 106.
146 Speech at the AVN's annual session, *Nezavisimoe voennoe obozrenie*, 2003, no. 2 (24–30 January), p. 1.
147 S. Main, 'The Strategic Rocket Forces, 1991–2002', in Aldis and McDermott (eds), *Russian Military Reform*, pp. 116–21; Leijonhielm et al., *Rysk militär förmåga*, 2002, pp. 116–17; and Leijonhielm et al., *Rysk militär förmåga*, 2005, p. 125. See also the interview with the commander of the Strategic Missile Forces, Colonel-General Nikolai Solovtsov, Interfax, *Russia's Strategic Missiles*

Guarantee Deterrence – Commander, Interfax's interview, 3 August 2005. Online. Available HTTP: www.interfax.com/17/80995/Interview.aspx (accessed 28 October 2005).

148 See, for example, the statement by Putin made at the annual evaluation session in November 2004: President of Russia, *Zakliuchitelnoe slovo na soveshchanii rukovodiashchego sostava Vooruzhennykh Sil Rossii*, 17 November 2004. Online. Available HTTP: www.president.kremlin.ru/appears/2004/11/17/1845_type63378_79565.shtml (accessed 21 February 2005).

149 See, for example, Putin's annual question-and-answer session with the Russian public: President of Russia, *Stennogramma priamogo tele-i radioefira ('Priamaia linia s prezidentom Rossii')*, 18 October 2007. Online. Available HTTP: www.president.kremlin.ru/appears/2007/10/18/1259_type63381type82634type146434_148 629.shtml (accessed 27 October 2007). Often, the secret technology that Putin referred to was that of equiping existing missiles with multiple independently targetable re-entry vehicle (MIRV) warhead technology.

150 President of Russia, *Zaiavlenie dlia pressy i otvety na voprosy po itogam XX sammita Rossiia-Evrosoiuz*, 26 October 2007. Online. Available HTTP: www.president.kremlin.ru/appears/2007/10/26/2205_type63377type63380_149679.shtml (accessed 27 October 2007).

151 Leijonhielm et al., *Rysk militär förmåga*, 2002, pp. 100, 107–8.

152 Lefebvre, 'The reform of the Russian air force', p. 156.

153 Leijonhielm et al., *Rysk militär förmåga*, 2005, pp. 231–32.

154 *Nezavisimoe voennoe obozrenie*, 2007, no. 32 (21–27 September), p. 3.

155 V. Tsimbal and V. Zatsepin, 'Reforma armii', *Kommersant Vlast*, 2007, no. 42 (29 October).

156 Tsypkin, 'Rudderless in the storm', pp. 178–82; Leijonhielm et al., *Rysk militär förmåga*, 2002, pp. 105, 107; and Leijonhielm et al., *Rysk militär förmåga*, 2005, p. 126. See also the speech by the chief of the Navy General Staff, Admiral Viktor Kravchenko, at the AVN's annual session, *Nezavisimoe voennoe obozrenie*, 2003, no. 3 (31 January–6 February), p. 4.

157 'Bratstvo "Boreev"', *Rossiiskoe voennoe obozrenie*, 2007, no. 5, pp. 26–27; *Krasnaia zvezda*, 27 October 2006, p. 1; and *Nezavisimoe voennoe obozrenie*, 2007, no. 32 (21–27 September), pp. 1, 3.

158 Leijonhielm et al., *Rysk militär förmåga*, 2002, pp. 109–10.

159 Ibid., pp. 110–11; and Leijonhielm et al., *Rysk militär förmåga*, 2005, pp. 122–25.

160 See Baluevskii's article in *Krasnaia zvezda*, 25 January 2006, pp. 1–2.

161 *Nezavisimoe voennoe obozrenie*, 2006, no. 8 (17–23 March), pp. 1, 6. See also Sergei Ivanov's speech at the annual evaluation session in November 2006: *Krasnaia zvezda*, 17 November 2006, p. 1.

162 *Nezavisimoe voennoe obozrenie*, 2006, no. 42 (17–23 November), p. 5.

163 Ibid., 2006, no. 38 (20–26 October), p. 2.

164 According to Nikolai Pankov, in 2005 over 170,000 students were registered at 229 military faculties at civilian institutions of higher education. About 60,000 reservist officers were examined each year while only about 6,000 of these were actually conscripted. Ministry of Defence of the Russian Federation, *Vstupitelnoe slovo Nachalnika Sluzhby kadrovoi i vospitatelnoi raboty Ministerstva oborony RF, generala armii N. A. Pankova na zasedanii Press-kluba voennykh obozrevatelei rossiiskikh SMI pri Upravlenii informatsii i obshchestvennykh sviazei MO RF*, 8 September 2005. Online. Available HTTP: www.mil.ru/articles/article10956.shtml (accessed 3 October 2005). See also *Nezavisimoe voennoe obozrenie*, 2005, no. 33 (2–8 September), p. 3; and Barany, *Democratic Breakdown*, p. 117.

165 *Nezavisimoe voennoe obozrenie*, 2003, no. 3 (31 January–6 February), p. 4.

166 Ibid., p. 5; and ibid., 2006, no. 38 (20–26 October), p. 1.

167 Leijonhielm et al., *Rysk militär förmåga*, 2005, pp. 152–58. Most exercises, for example, Vostok-2005, were described as 'anti-terrorist'. However, in Vitalii Shlykov's view the Vostok-2005 exercise had 'nothing in common with the struggle against terrorism'. This was evident, if nothing else, from the units involved and the weapons and equipment used, see *Nezavisimoe voennoe obozrenie*, 2005, no. 27 (22–28 July), pp. 1, 2.

168 V. Tikhomirov, 'Reforma vnutrennykh voisk: problemy i puti ikh resheniia', *Voennaia mysl*, 2001, no. 4, pp. 2–9.

169 *Nezavisimaia gazeta*, 28 October 2002, p. 4. However, in 2005 it seemed that the Interior Troops were organized in six districts. In addition, new military-administrative units, regional commands, were to be introduced. *Nezavisimaia gazeta*, 13 July 2005, p. 3.

170 International Institute for Strategic Studies, *The Military Balance 2004/2005*, London: Oxford University Press, 2004, p. 98.

171 Blandy, *North Caucasus*.

172 In other words, the FSB would continue to conduct investigations and run its own detention prison (Lefortovo).

173 *Nezavisimaia gazeta*, 5 November 2004, p. 7.

174 *Nezavisimoe voennoe obozrenie*, 2004, no. 45 (26 November–1 December), p. 1.

175 Presidential decree no. 116, 15 February 2006. See also the Federal Law on Terrorism, no. 35-FZ, 6 March 2006.

176 *Nezavisimoe voennoe obozrenie*, 2005, no. 34 (9–15 September), p. 4. See also the statement made by Putin in the Security Council in June 2005: President of Russia, *Vstupitelnoe slovo na zasedanii Soveta Bezopasnosti 'O perspektivakh razvitiia voennoi organizatsii Rossii do 2015 goda'*, 28 June 2005. Online. Available HTTP: www.president.kremlin.ru/text/appears/2005/06/90455.shtml (accessed 7 November 2005).

177 K. Anderman, E. Hagström-Frisell and C. Vendil Pallin, *Russia–EU Security Relations: Russian perceptions and decision making*, Stockholm: FOI, February 2007, User Report, FOI-R–2243–SE, pp. 45–49.

178 See, for example, Ivanov's statement in the Federation Council, 28 October 2006, p. 1.

179 See also C. Vendil Pallin, 'Future EU–Russia relations', *RUSI Newsbrief*, 2006, vol. 26, no. 10, pp. 109–11.

180 *Nezavisimoe voennoe obozrenie*, 2007, no. 31 (14–20 September), p. 1.

181 I. Isakova, 'Russian defense reform: current trends', paper prepared for the conference 'The U.S. and Russia: Regional Security Issues and Interests', Carlisle, Pa., Strategic Studies Institute, U.S. Army War College, November 2006, p. 3.

182 According to Vitalii Shlykov, the number of companies was 1,700. Shlykov, 'The economics of defense', p. 160. In Leijonhielm et al., *Rysk militär förmåga*, 2005, p. 227, the number of companies is estimated at 1,600. The overall conclusion, however, is identical. The defence industry has not undergone any serious restructuring. See also S. Blank, 'Potemkin's treadmill: Russian military modernization', draft paper, March 2005, pp. 17–20, cited with the kind consent of the author; and S. Blank, *Rosoboroneksport: arms sales and the structure of Russian defense industry*, Carlisle, Pa.: Strategic Studies Institute, U.S. Army War College, January 2007, pp. 21–22.

183 There had been earlier, similar reform programmes for the MIC, for example in 1998: Leijonhielm et al., *Rysk militär förmåga*, 2002, pp. 178–79.

184 Shlykov, 'The economics of defense', p. 161.

185 S. Rosefielde, *Russia in the 21st Century: the prodigal superpower*, New York: Cambridge University Press, 2005, p. 94.

186 Leijonhielm et al., *Rysk militär förmåga*, 2005, pp. 246–47. On the other hand, there was also a deficit in soldiers and officers able to handle the technology that went with the new weapons and equipment. See, for example, the interview with

the commander of the Airborne Troops, Colonel-General Aleksandr Kolmakov, *Nezavisimoe voennoe obozrenie*, 2006, no. 17 (26 May–1 June), pp. 1, 3.
187 Presidential decree no. 119, 5 February 2007.
188 *Krasnaia zvezda*, 6 December 2006, p. 1.
189 Presidential decree no. 119, 5 February 2007.
190 Blank, *Rosoboroneksport*, p. 9. See also S. Blank, 'The political economy of the Russian defense sector', paper prepared for FOI Conference, 'Russian Power Structures: Present and Future Role in Russian Politics', Stockholm, 17–18 October 2007 (to be published); and Chemezov's monopoly plans for the Russian market as well, in *Nezavisimoe voennoe obozrenie*, 2007, no. 37 (26 October–1 November), p. 1.
191 M. Feshbach, 'Russian military: population and health constraints', paper prepared for FOI Conference, 'Russian Power Structures: Present and Future Role in Russian Politics', Stockholm, 17–18 October 2007 (to be published); and K. Giles, *Where Have All the Soldiers Gone? Russia's military plans versus demographic reality*, Conflict Studies Research Centre, 06/47, October 2006. Online. Available HTTP: www.defac.ac.uk/colleges/csrc/document-listings/russian/06% 2847%29KG.pdf (accessed 7 November 2007). Demographic trends also point to a decreasing ratio of ethnic Russians serving in the Armed Forces since the birth rate, especially among Russia's Muslim population, is considerably higher than that among ethnic Russians. K. Giles, *Military Service in Russia: no new model army*, Conflict Studies Research Centre, 07/18, May 2007. Online. Available HTTP: www.defac.ac.uk/colleges/csrc/document-listings/russian/ (accessed 29 October 2007), pp. 8–9.
192 *Rossiiskaia gazeta*, 14 January 2003, p. 9. The concept became an official Federal Goal Programme (*Federalnaia tselevaia programma*) in August the same year. Ministry of Defence of the Russian Federation, *Federalnaia tselevaia programma* (Government regulation no. 523, 25 August 2003). Online. Available HTTP: www.mil.ru/article5324.shtml (accessed 28 October 2005).
193 Thornton, 'Military organizations and change', pp. 456–57. See also *Kommersant daily*, 4 October 2002, p. 3; and the proposal that the Institute for the Economy in Transition published for reforming military recruitment: E. Vatolkin, E. Liuboshits, E. Khrustalev and V. Tsymbal, 'Reform of military recruitment in Russia', *Problems of Economic Transition*, 2003, vol. 46, no. 2/3, pp. 6–158.
194 Thornton, 'Military organizations and change', pp. 460–62. See also Barany, *Democratic Breakdown*, p. 129.
195 Thornton, 'Military organizations and change', pp. 460–65. See also *Nezavisimoe voennoe obozrenie*, 2007, no. 17 (26 May–1 June), pp. 1, 3; and *Nezavisimaia gazeta*, 24 August 2006, pp. 1, 4.
196 President of Russia, *Poslanie Federalnomu Sobraniiu Rossiiskoi Federatsii*, 16 May 2003. Online. Available HTTP: www.president.kremlin.ru/text/appears/2003/ 05/44623.shtml (accessed 19 April 2004).
197 President of Russia, *Stenograficheskii otchet o press-konferentsii v Kremle dlia rossiiskikh i zarubezhnykh SMI*, 20 June 2003. Online. Available HTTP: www. president.kremlin.ru/text/appears/2003/06/47449.shtml (accessed 19 April 2004).
198 *Nezavisimoe voennoe obozrenie*, 2005, no. 35 (16–22 September), p. 1. The opinon poll was conducted by the Levada Centre. L. Sedov, *Armeiskie preobrazovaniia v otrazhenii obshchestvennogo mneniia*, Levada Tsentr, 7 September 2005. Online. Available HTTP: www.levada.ru/press/2005090701.html (accessed 2 October 2005). The same trend was visible in 2002: see R. McDermott, 'Putin's military priorities: the modernisation of the Armed Forces', in Aldis and McDermott (eds), *Russian Military Reform*, p. 267.
199 The MoD claimed that the number was considerably lower than that stated by, for example, the Committee of Soldiers' Mothers. Ministry of Defence of the

Russian Federation, *Informatsiia o proisshestviiakh i prestupleniiakh v Vooruzhennykh Silakh RF.* Online. Available HTTP: www.mil.ru/articles/article10596.shtml (accessed 12 September 2005).
200 Orr, 'Reform and the Russian Ground Forces', p. 134.
201 T. Maleva, *Alternativnaia grazhdanskaia sluzhba v Rossii: byt ili ne byt?*, Carnegie Moscow Center, Briefing, 2002, vol. 4, no. 4 (April). Online. Available HTTP: www.carnegie.ru/en/pubs/briefings/4-02.pdf (accessed 4 October 2005); and Leijonhielm et al., *Rysk militär förmåga*, 2005, p. 119.
202 *Nezavisimoe voennoe obozrenie*, 2007, no. 32 (21–27 September), p. 1.
203 *Nezavisimoe voennoe obozrenie*, 2004, no. 42 (5–11 November), p. 2; Golts, *Armiia Rossii: 11 poteriannykh let*, Moscow: Zakharov, 2004, p. 91; and Ministry of Defence of the Russian Federation, *Vstupitelnoe slovo N. A. Pankova*, 8 September 2005.
204 M. Feshbach, 'Russian military'.
205 On NCOs, see Giles, *Military Service in Russia*, pp. 9–10.
206 *Rossiiskaia gazeta*, 14 January 2003, p. 9. See also 'Ravnenie na chinovnika', *Finansovyi kontrol*, 2002, no. 2, pp. 12–13.
207 *Nezavisimoe voennoe obozrenie*, 2005, no. 40 (21–27 October), pp. 1, 4.
208 *Krasnaia zvezda*, 17 November 2006, p. 1 (author's italics). If nothing else, the mortgage programme was designed to be a powerful incentive for servicemen not to leave their service until they had received housing. *Nezavisimaia gazeta*, 12 February 2007, p. 13.
209 *Rossiiskaia gazeta*, 14 January 2003, p. 9.
210 *Nezavisimoe voennoe obozrenie*, 2005, no. 36 (23–30 September), p. 1.
211 In 2003, Putin named a figure of 4 million men as 'military personnel and those equal to them in status' excluding the police force (or *militsiia*), quoted by V. Shlykov, 'The military reform and its implications for the modernization of the Russian Armed Forces', paper prepared for FOI Conference, 'Russian Power Structures: Present and Future Role in Russian Politics', Stockholm, 17–18 October 2007 (to be published).
212 Compare, for example, the numbers provided in V. Saronov, 'Critical mass: there are too many armed formations in Russia', *CDI Russia Weekly*, no. 184, December 2001. Online. Available HTTP: www.cdi.org/russia/184-6.cfm (accessed 8 November 2005). Also available in McDermott, 'Putin's military priorities', p. 261. See also H. Plater-Zyberk, *Russia's Special Forces*, Conflict Studies Research Centre, Russian Series, 05/50, September 2005. Online. Available HTTP: www.da. mod.uk/CSRC/documents/Russian/05(50)-HPZ.pdf (accessed 8 November 2005).
213 Leijonhielm et al., *Rysk militär förmåga*, 2002, pp. 95–97; and Leijonhielm et al., *Rysk militär förmåga*, 2005, pp. 104–6.
214 Even the large inflow of energy revenues could, however, prove more of a problem than a solution in the long run. The Russian economy continues to struggle with substantial structural problems – a dearth of investment, demographic decline and high levels of corruption, to mention but a few. S. Hedlund, *Will Putin Make a Difference?*, Uppsala, Sweden: Department of East European Studies, Uppsala University, Working Paper 78, August 2003, ISRN UU-ÖSTUD-AR–02/5–SE, pp. 1–11.
215 See, for example, the interview with Sergei Ivanov in N. Kalashnikova, 'Mirnoe bremia', *Itogi*, 2005, no. 15 (12 April), pp. 30–34.
216 See, for example, Baev, 'The Russian Armed Forces: failed reform attempts and creeping regionalization', in Betz and Löwenhardt (eds), *Army and State in Postcommunist Europe*, p. 28; and Barany, *Democratic Breakdown*, p. 76.
217 *Krasnaia zvezda*, 21 September 2004, pp. 1, 3. See also the website of the fund, www.nvfond.ru; and Alfa-Bank's own announcement of its generous donation of 2 million dollars, Alfa-Bank, *Alfa-Bank vydelil Obshcherossiiskomu Natsionalnomu*

Voennomu Fondu 2 mln dollarov SShA dlia pomoshchi rossiiskim voennosluzhashchim, 9 December 2004. Online. Available HTTP: www.alfabank.ru/press/news/2004/12/9/1.html (accessed 10 March 2005).

218 *Nezavisimaia gazeta*, 3 November 2005, p. 1; and Vendil Pallin, 'The Russian power ministries', p. 20.

219 Leijonhielm et al., *Rysk militär förmåga*, 2005, p. 105; and Rosefielde, *Russia in the 21st Century*, pp. 96–99.

220 Leijonhielm et al., *Rysk militär förmåga*, 2005, p. 105.

221 *Nezavisimoe voennoe obozrenie*, 2005, no. 40 (21–27 October), pp, 1, 4.

222 Blank, S., *Rosoboroneksport*, p. 34.

223 *Nezavisimoe voennoe obozrenie*, 2003, no. 1 (17–23 January), p. 3.

224 Ibid.

225 S. Rosefielde, 'Russian rearmament: motives, options and prospects', paper prepared for FOI Conference, 'Russian Power Structures: Present and Future Role in Russian Politics', Stockholm, 17–18 October 2007 (to be published).

226 M. de Haas, 'The development of Russia's security policy, 1992–2002', in Aldis and McDermott (eds), *Russian Military Reform*, p. 14.

227 Ibid., p. 15.

228 D. Betz and V. Volkov, 'A new day for the Russian army? Reforming the Armed Forces under Yeltsin and Putin', in Aldis and McDermott (eds), *Russian Military Reform*, pp. 49–50.

229 See, for example, *Nezavisimoe voennoe obozrenie*, 2002, no. 40 (15–21 November), p. 4.

230 *Rossiiskaia gazeta*, 14 January 2003, p. 9.

231 Ministry of Defence of the Russian Federation, *Aktualnye zadachy razvitiia vooruzhennykh sil Rossiiskoi Federatsii*, Moscow: Voeninform, 2003.

232 Statement by Igor Ivanovon 29 September 2004, in *Nezavisimoe voennoe obozrenie*, 2004, no. 37 (1–7 October), p. 1. See also M. de Haas, *Putin's Internal and External Security Policy*, Conflict Studies Research Centre, Russian Series, 05/05, February 2005. Online. Available HTTP: www.da.mod.uk/CSRC/documents/Russian/05%2805%29-MDH-Comp.pdf (accessed 9 November 2005), p. 12.

233 A conference on a new doctrine was arranged by the AVN at the Russian MoD on 20 January 2007.

234 *Nezavisimoe voennoe obozrenie*, 2003, no. 3 (31 January–6 February), p. 4.

235 Golts, *Armiia Rossii*, pp. 120–21.

236 Baluevskii's speech at a conference on the new military doctrine on 20 January 2007: Yu. Baluevskii, 'Teoreticheskie i metodologicheskie osnovy formirovaniia voennoi doktriny Rossiiskoi Federatsii', *Voennaia mysl*, 2007, no. 3, p. 16. Also available in Yu. Baluevskii, 'Kakoi byt novoi Voennoi doktrine Rossii?', *Rossiiskoe voennoe obozrenie*, 2007, no. 2, p. 8.

237 However, no large-scale exercises have been held in the western parts of Russia since 2001.

238 In many ways, this argument brings to mind the debate on morale versus firepower in the 1850s–1870s. See G. Persson, 'The Russian army and foreign wars 1859–1871', doctoral thesis, Government Department, London School of Economics and Political Science, 1999, pp. 90–99.

239 D. Trenin, 'Russia's security integration with America and Europe', in A. J. Motyl, B. A. Ruble and L. Shevtsova (eds), *Russia's Engagement with the West: transformation and integration in the twenty-first century*, Armonk, N.Y.: M. E. Sharpe, 2005, p. 282.

240 President of Russia, *Vstupitelnoe slovo*, 28 June 2005.

241 President of Russia, *Vystuplenie i diskussiia na Miunkhenskoi konferentsii po voprosam politiki bezopasnosti*, 10 February 2007. Online. Available HTTP: www.president.kremlin.ru/text/appears/2007/02/118097.shtml (accessed 16 October 2007).

Conclusion: presidential will, know-how and perseverance

1 A. Golts, 'Russian power structures and their impact on Russian politics regarding the upcoming elections', paper prepared for FOI Conference, 'Russian Power Structures: Present and Future Role in Russian Politics', Stockholm, 17–18 October 2007 (to be published).
2 A. Golts, *Armiia Rossii: 11 poteriannykh let*, Moscow: Zakharov, 2004, p. 141.
3 D. Betz, 'No place for a civilian? Russian defense management from Yeltsin to Putin', *Armed Forces and Society*, 2002, vol. 28, no. 3, p. 493. See also A. Kokoshin, *Strategicheskoe upravlenie: teoriia, istoricheskii opyt, sravnitelnyi analiz, zadachi dlia Rossii*, Moscow: MGIMO, ROSSPEN, 2003, p. 314.
4 I am indebted to Steven Rosefielde for this term. At a seminar at FOI in 2005, he made the observation that Russia lacked 'an autonomous economic core'.

References and bibliography

Newspapers and compilations of news and laws

BBC Summary of World Broadcasts (BBC SWB)
Kommersant daily
Krasnaia zvezda
Moskovskii komsomolets
Moscow News
Nezavisimaia gazeta
Nezavisimoe voennoe obozrenie
Pravitelstvennyi vestnik
Rossiiskaia gazeta
Rossiiskie vesti
Segodnia
Sovetskaia Rossiia
Vedomosti Sezda narodnykh deputatov SSSR

Books, articles, internet sources, etc.

Alfa-Bank, *Alfa-Bank vydelil Obshcherossiiskomu Natsionalnomu Voennomu Fondu 2 mln dollarov SShA dlia pomoshchi rossiiskim voennosluzhashchim* [Alfa-Bank assigned the All-Russian National Military Fund 2 million US dollars to support Russian servicemen], 9 December 2004. Online. Available HTTP: www.alfabank.ru/press/news/2004/12/9/1.html (accessed 10 March 2005).

Allison, G. and Zelikow, P., *Essence of Decision: explaining the Cuban missile crisis*, 2nd edn, New York: Longman, 1999.

Allison, R., 'Russia, regional conflict, and the use of military power', in S. E. Miller and D. Trenin (eds), *The Russian Military: power and policy*, Cambridge, Mass.: MIT Press, 2004, pp. 121–56.

——'The Russian Armed Forces: structures, roles and policies', in V. Baranovsky (ed.), *Russia and Europe: the emerging security agenda*, Oxford: Oxford University Press for the Stockholm International Peace Research Institute (SIPRI), 1997, pp. 165–95.

Anderman, K., Hagström-Frisell, E. and Vendil Pallin, C., *Russia–EU Security Relations: Russian perceptions and decision making*, Stockholm: Swedish Defence Research Agency (FOI), February 2007, User Report, FOI-R–2243–SE.

Arbatov, A., 'Military reform: from crisis to stagnation', in S. E. Miller and D. Trenin (eds), *The Russian Military: power and policy*, Cambridge, Mass.: MIT Press: 2004, pp. 95–119.

——'The transformation of Russia's military doctrine in the aftermath of Kosovo and Chechnya', in G. Gorodetsky (ed.), *Russia Between East and West: Russian foreign policy on the threshold of the twenty-first century*, London: Frank Cass, 2003, pp. 28–32.

——'Military reform in Russia: dilemmas, obstacles, and prospects', *International Security*, 1998, vol. 22, no. 4, pp. 83–134.

Argumenty i fakty, 'V armii i na flote' [In the army and navy], *Rossiiskoe voennoe obozrenie*, 2004, no. 6 (June), p. 50.

——*Nagrazhdenie chinovnikov ordenami za operatsiiu na Dubrovke vyzvalo protest boitsov, shturmovavshikh 'Nord-Ost'* [Decorating the officials with orders for the Dubrovka operation caused protests from the men who stormed 'Nord-Ost'], Argumenty i fakty – Press-Tsentr, 4 March 2003. Online. Available HTTP; http://news.aif.ru/news.php?id=10659 (accessed 18 April 2006).

Audit Chamber of the Russian Federation, *Schetnaia palata Rossiiskoi Federatsii kak vyshchii organ gosudarstvennogo kontrolia* [Audit Chamber of the Russian Federation as the highest organ of state control]. Online. Available HTTP: www.ach.gov.ru/about/history/sprf.php> (accessed 25 January 2005).

——Federalnyi zakon ot 1 dekabria 2004 goda No 145-FZ 'O vnesenii izmenenii v federalnyi zakon "O Schetnom palate Rossiiskoi Federatsii"' [Federal law, 1 December 2004, no.145-FZ 'On the introduction of changes to the Federal Law "On the Audit Chamber of the Russian Federation"']. Online. Available HTTP: www.ach.gov.ru/zakon/fedzakon/chapter5.php> (accessed 25 January 2005).

——Federalnyi zakon 'O Schetnom Palate Rossiiskoi Federatsii', no 4-FZ, 11 ianvaria 1995 goda [Federal law 'On the Audit Chamber of the Russian Federation', no. 4-FZ, 11 January 1995], 11 January 1995. Online. Available HTTP: www.ach.gov.ru/zakon/fedzakon/zakon.php (accessed 25 January 2005).

Baev, P. *Putin's War in Chechnya: who steers the course?*, Center for Strategic and International Studies, PONARS, Policy Memo 345, November 2004. Online. Available HTTP: www.csis.org/ruseura/ponars/policymemos/pm_0345.pdf (accessed 4 March 2005).

——'Reforming the Russian military: history and trajectory', in Yu. Fedorov and B. Nygren (eds), *Russian Military Reform and Russia's New Security Environment*, Stockholm: Swedish National Defence College, May 2003, ACTA B28, pp. 37–54.

——*Putin's Military Reform: two trajectories for the first presidency*, Oslo: Norwegian Atlantic Committee, 2001, Security Policy Library, no. 6–2001.

——'The Russian army and Chechnya: victory instead of reform?', in S. J. Cimbala (ed.), *The Russian Military into the Twenty-first Century*, London: Frank Cass, 2001, pp. 75–93.

——'The Russian Armed Forces: failed reform attempts and creeping regionalization', in J. Löwenhardt et al. (eds), *Army and State in Postcommunist Europe*, London: Frank Cass, 2001, pp. 23–42.

——*Putin's Court: how the military fits in*, Center for Strategic and International Studies, PONARS, Policy Memo 153, November 2000. Online. Available HTTP: www.csis.org/ruseura/ponars/policymemos/pm_0153.pdf (accessed 3 February 2003).

——*The Russian Army in a Time of Troubles*, London: Sage, 1996.

Baker, D. (ed.), *Jane's Space Directory 2003/2004*, Coulsdon: Jane's, 2003, pp. 602–7.

Baker, P. and Glasser, S., *Kremlin Rising: Vladimir Putin's Russia and the end of revolution*, New York: Scribner, 2005.

Baluevskii Yu., 'Kakoi byt novoi Voennoi doctrine Rossii?' [What should be the new military doctrine of Russia?], *Rossiiskoe voennoe obozrenie*, 2007, no. 2, pp. 6–10.

Baluevskii, Yu., 'Novaia rol voennogo okruga' [The new role of the military district], *Voennaia mysl*, 1999, no. 3, pp. 2–7.

——'Teoreticheskie i metodologicheskie osnovy formirovaniia voennoi doktriny Rossiiskoi Federatsii' [The theoretical and methodological basis for forming the military doctrine of the Russian Federation], *Voennaia mysl*, 2007, no. 3, pp. 14–21.

Baranets, V., *Eltsin i ego generaly: zapiski polkovnika genshtaba* [Yeltsin and his generals: notes of a colonel of the general staff], Moscow: Sovershenno sekretno, 1998.

Barany, Z., *Democratic Breakdown and the Decline of the Russian Military*, Princeton, N.J.: Princeton University Press, 2007.

——'The tragedy of the *Kursk*: crisis management in Putin's Russia', *Government and Opposition*, 2004, vol. 39, no. 3, pp. 477–503.

Barynkin, V., 'Problemy stroitelstva Vooruzhennykh Sil Rossiiskoi Federatsii na sovremennom etape' [The problems of development of the Armed Forces of the Russian Federation at the present stage], *Voennaia mysl*, 1996, no. 1, pp. 2–6.

Belin, L., *Competition Intensifies for the 'Patriotic' Vote*, Radio Free Europe/Radio Liberty (RFE/RL), 12 November 1999. Online. Available HTTP: www.rferl.org/specials/russianelection/archives/02-121199.asp (accessed 3 November 2004).

Bennett, G., *The Federal Agency of Government Communications & Information*, Conflict Studies Research Centre, C105, August 2000. Online. Available HTTP: www.csrc.ac.uk/pdfs/C105.pdf (accessed 16 October 2002).

——*The Federal Border Guard Service*, Conflict Studies Research Centre, C107, March 2002. Online. Available HTTP: www.csrc.ac.uk/pdfs/c107-gb.pdf (accessed 13 May 2002).

——*The Federal Security Service of the Russian Federation*, Conflict Studies Research Centre, C102, March 2000. Online. Available HTTP: www.csrc.ac.uk/pdfs/c102.pdf (accessed 16 October 2002).

——*The Ministry of Internal Affairs of the Russian Federation*, Conflict Studies Research Centre, C106, October 2000. Online. Available HTTP: www.csrc.ac.uk/pdfs/C106-GB.pdf (accessed 16 October 2002).

Betz, D., *Civil–Military Relations in Russia and Eastern Europe*, London: Routledge Curzon, 2004.

——'No place for a civilian? Russian defense management from Yeltsin to Putin', *Armed Forces and Society*, 2002, vol. 28, no. 3, pp. 481–504.

Betz, D. and Volkov, V., 'A new day for the Russian army? Reforming the armed forces under Yeltsin and Putin', in A. C. Aldis and R. McDermott (eds), *Russian Military Reform 1992–2002*, London: Frank Cass, 2003, pp. 41–59.

Betz, D., Löwenhardt, J. and Strachan, H., 'Conclusion', in D. Betz and J. Löwenhardt (eds), *Army and State in Postcommunist Europe*, London: Frank Cass, 2001, pp. 146–53.

Bland, D., 'Managing the "expert problem" in civil–military relations', *European Security*, 1999, vol. 8, no. 3, pp. 25–43.

——'A unified theory of civil–military relations', *Armed Forces and Society*, 1999, vol. 26, no. 1, pp. 7–26.

Blandy, C. W., *Chechnya: continued violence*, Conflict Studies Research Centre, Caucasus Series, 06/54, December 2006. Online. Available HTTP: www.defac.ac.uk/colleges/csrc/document-listings/caucasus/ (accessed 3 October 2007).

——*North Caucasus: on the brink of far-reaching destabilisation*, Conflict Studies Research Centre, Caucasus Series, 05/36, August 2005. Online. Available HTTP: www. da.mod.uk/CSRC/documents/Caucasus/05%2836%29-CWB.pdf (accessed 6 October 2005).

Blank, S., 'The political economy of the Russian defense sector', paper prepared for FOI Conference, *Russian Power Structures: Present and Future Role in Russian Politics*, Stockholm, 17–18 October 2007 (to be published).

——*Rosoboroneksport: arms sales and the structure of Russian defense industry*, Carlisle, Pa.: Strategic Studies Institute, U.S. Army War College, January 2007.

——'Potemkin's treadmill: Russian military modernization', draft paper, March 2005.

—— 'The general crisis in the Russian military', *Journal of Slavic Military Studies*, 2003, vol. 16, no. 2, pp. 1–26.

——'Valuing the human factor: the reform of Russian military manpower', *Journal of Slavic Military Studies*, 1999, vol. 12, no. 1, pp. 64–93.

——*Russia's Armed Forces on the Brink of Reform*, Royal Military Academy Sandhurst, Conflict Studies Research Centre, C97, October 1997.

Bransten, J., 'Patriotic TV channel launches, but is anyone watching?', *RFE/RL Media Matters*, vol. 5, no. 5 (24 February 2005). Online. Available HTTP: www. rferl.org/reports/mm/2005/02/5-240205.asp (accessed 28 September 2005).

'Bratstvo "Boreev"', *Rossiiskoe voennoe obozrenie*, 2007, no. 5, pp. 26–27.

Bukkvoll, T., 'Their hands in the till: scale and causes of Russian military corruption', *Armed Forces and Society*, 2007, vol. 34, no. 2.

Caiazza, A., *Mothers and Soldiers: gender, citizenship, and civil society in contemporary Russia*, New York: Routledge, 2002.

Clarke, D. L., 'Soviet military reform: a moving target', *Report on the USSR*, 1991, vol. 3, no. 47, pp. 14–19.

Colton, T., *Commissars, Commanders, and Civilian Authority: the structure of Soviet military politics*, Cambridge, Mass.: Harvard University Press, 1979.

Cooper, J., 'Society–military relations in Russia: the economic dimension', in S. Webber and S. Mathers (eds), *Military and Society in Post-Soviet Russia*, Manchester, UK: Manchester University Press, 2006, pp. 131–56.

Cornell, S., 'International reactions to massive human rights violations: the case of Chechnya', *Europe–Asia Studies*, 1999, vol. 51, no. 1, pp. 85–100.

Council on Foreign and Defence Policy, *Kratkii variant doklada SVOP: Voennoe stroitelstvo i modernizatsiia vooruzhennykh sil Rossii* [Short version of SVOP statement: military development and modernization of the armed forces of Russia], 30 March 2004. Online. Available HTTP: www.svop.ru/live/materials.asp? m_id=8481&r_id=8482 (accessed 21 April 2004).

Cronin, P., 'Perestroika and Soviet military personnel', in W. C. Green and T. Karasik (eds), *Gorbachev and His Generals: the reform of Soviet military doctrine*, Boulder, Col.: Westview Press, 1990, pp. 125–45.

Dadonov, A., 'The Russian Interior Ministry's special Internal Troop units for combating terrorism: organization, training system and the conduct of special operations', *Low Intensity Conflict and Law Enforcement*, 1997, vol. 6, no. 2, pp. 124–28.

Daucé, F., 'L'armée dans l'histoire de l'État russe contemporain' [The army in the history of the modern Russian state], *Hérodote*, 2002, no. 104, pp. 119–43.

——'Les mouvements de mères de soldats à la recherche d'une place dans la société russe' [The movement of the soldiers' mothers in search of a place in Russian society], *Revue d'études comparatives Est-Ouest*, 1997, vol. 28, no. 2, pp. 121–53.

de Haas, M., 'The development of Russia's security policy, 1992–2002', in A. C. Aldis and R. McDermott (eds), *Russian Military Reform 1992–2002*, London: Frank Cass, 2003, pp. 3–21.

——*Putin's Internal and External Security Policy*, Conflict Studies Research Centre, Russian Series, 05/05, February 2005. Online. Available HTTP: www.da.mod.uk/CSRC/documents/Russian/05%2805%29-MDH-Comp.pdf (accessed 9 November 2005).

Department for Information about Court Practice of the Military Collegium of the Supreme Court of the Russian Federation, *Voennye sudy v Rossiiskoi Federatsii* [Military courts in the Russian Federation]. Online. Available HTTP: www.supcourt.ru (accessed 22 March 2005).

Dick, C. J., 'The military doctrine of the Russian Federation', *Journal of Slavic Military Studies*, 1994, vol. 7, no. 3, pp. 481–506.

Donnelly, C., 'Civil–military relations in the new democracies', in J. Löwenhardt et al. (eds), *Army and State in Postcommunist Europe*, London: Frank Cass, 2001, pp. 7–10.

Engnér, E., *Satellituppskjutningar 2000–2002* [Satelite launches 2000–2002], Stockholm: FOI, February 2005, Internal Report, FOI-D–0208–SE.

Evangelista, M., *The Chechen Wars: will Russia go the way of the Soviet Union?*, Washington, D.C.: Brookings Institution Press, 2002.

Eyal, J., 'The tragedy of Russia: lessons unlearnt', *RUSI Newsbrief*, 2004, vol. 24, no. 9, pp. 97–98.

Facon, I., 'La réforme de l'armée russe: Enjeux et obstacles' [Reform of the Russian army: stakes and obstacles], *Le courrier des pays de l'Est*, 2002, no. 1022 (February), pp. 22–23.

Fast Scott, H. and Scott, W. F., *The Soviet Art of War: doctrine, strategy, and tactics*, Boulder, Col.: Westview Press, 1982.

——*Soviet Military Doctrine: continuity, formulation, and dissemination*, Boulder, Col.: Westview Press, 1988.

Feshbach, M., 'Russian military: population and health constraints', paper prepared for FOI Conference, *Russian Power Structures: Present and Future Role in Russian Politics*, Stockholm, 17–18 October 2007 (to be published).

Fond 'Pravo materi', *Sto is 15 tysiach: Kniga pamiati* [One hundred out of 15,000], Moscow: Izvestiia, 1992.

Foye, S., 'Manning the Russian army: is contract service a success?', *RFE/RL Research Report*, 1994, vol. 3, no. 13, pp. 36–45.

——'Rebuilding the Russian military: some problems and prospects', *RFE/RL Research Report*, 1992, vol. 1, no. 44, pp. 51–56.

——'The Soviet high command and the politics of military reform', *Report on the USSR*, 1991, vol. 3, no. 27, pp. 9–14.

Fuller, W., *Civil–Military Conflict in Imperial Russia, 1881–1914*, Princeton, N.J.: Princeton University Press, 1985.

Galeotti, M., 'Putin puts confidence in new generation of missiles', *Jane's Intelligence Review*, 2005, vol. 17, no. 2, pp. 54–55.

——'Beslan shows growing Islamist influence in Chechen war', *Jane's Intelligence Review*, 2004, vol. 16, no. 10, pp. 12–17.

——'Russia's emerging security doctrine', *Jane's Intelligence Review*, 2004, vol. 16, no. 11, pp. 46–47.

——'Emergency presence', *Jane's Intelligence Review*, 2002, vol. 14, no. 1, pp. 50–51.

——'Russia's military reforms?', *Jane's Intelligence Review*, 2000, vol. 12, no. 9, pp. 8–9.

——'Russia's phantom cuts', *Jane's Intelligence Review*, 2000, vol. 12, no. 11, pp. 8–9.

——'Russia's criminal army', *Jane's Intelligence Review*, 1999, vol. 11, no. 6, pp. 8–10.

——*The Kremlin's Agenda: the new Russia and its armed forces*, Coulsdon: Jane's Intelligence Review, 1995.

——'Russia's internal security forces: does more mean better?', *Jane's Intelligence Review*, 1994, vol. 6, no. 6, pp. 271–72.

Gareev, M., 'Struktura i osnovnoe soderzhanie novoi voennoi doktriny Rossii' [The structure and basic content of Russia's new military doctrine], *Voennaia mysl*, 2007, no. 3, pp. 2–13.

Gelman, H., *The Rise and Fall of National Security Decisionmaking in the Former USSR: implications for Russia and the Commonwealth*, Santa Monica, Calif.: RAND, 1992, R-4200-A.

General Procuracy of the Russian Federation, *Glavnaia voennaja prokurora – struktura* [The Main Military Procuracy – structure]. Online. Available HTTP: www.genproc.gov.ru/ru/military/structure/ (accessed 22 March 2005).

——*Struktura organov prokuratury Rossiiskoi Federatsii* [Structure of the procuracy organs of the Russian Federation]. Online. Available HTTP: www.genproc.gov.ru/ru/about/structure/ (accessed 22 March 2005).

Gerber, T. and Mendelson, S., *Strong Public Support for Military Reform in Russia*, Center for Strategic and International Studies, PONARS, Policy Memo 288, May 2003. Online. Available HTTP: www.csis.org/ruseura/ponars/policymemos/pm_0288.pdf (accessed 3 February 2003).

Giles, K., *Military Service in Russia: no new model army*, Conflict Studies Research Centre, , May 2007. Online. Available HTTP: www.defac.ac.uk/colleges/csrc/document-listings/russian/ (accessed 29 October 2007).

——*Where Have All the Soldiers Gone? Russia's military plans versus demographic reality*, Conflict Studies Research Centre, 06/47, October 2006. Online. Available HTTP: www.defac.ac.uk/colleges/csrc/document-listings/russian/06%2847%29KG. pdf (accessed 7 November 2007).

Godzimirski, J., *Russian National Security Concepts 1997–2000: a comparative analysis*, Security Policy Library, No. 8–2000, Norwegian Atlantic Committee, 2000. Online. Available HTTP: www.atlanterhavskomiteen.no/publikasjoner/sp/2000/8–2000_utskrift.htm (accessed 25 June 2001).

Golts, A., 'Russian power structures and their impact on Russian politics regarding the upcoming elections', paper prepared for FOI Conference, *Russian Power Structures: Present and Future Role in Russian Politics*, Stockholm, 17–18 October 2007 (to be published).

——*Armiia Rossii: 11 poteriannykh let* [Russia's army: 11 lost years], Moscow: Zakharov, 2004.

——'The social and political condition of the Russian military', in S. E. Miller and D. Trenin (eds), *The Russian Military: power and policy*, Cambridge, Mass.: MIT Press: 2004, pp. 73–94.

Golts, A. and Putnam, T., 'State militarism and its legacies: why military reform has failed in Russia', *International Security*, 2004, vol. 29, no. 2, pp. 121–58.

Government of the Russian Federation,*Dmitriev Mikhail Arkadevich*. Online. Available HTTP: www.government.gov.ru/institutions/ministries/management.html?he_id=918 (accessed 14 October 2005).

——*Federalnoe agenstvo po atomnoi energii* [Federal Agency of Atomic Energy]. Online. Available HTTP: www.government.gov.ru/institutions/ministries/details.html?he_id=988 (accessed 21 September 2005).

——*Lychagin Mikhail Ivanovich*. Online. Available HTTP: www.government.gov.ru/government/minister/index.html?he_id=1053 (accessed 1 March 2005).

——*Polozhenie o Kommissii Pravitelstva Rossiiskoi Federatsii po voenno-promyshlennym voprosam* [Statutes for the Government Commission on Military–Industrial Questions]. Online. Available HTTP: www.government.gov.ru/data/static_text.html?st_id=7791&he_id=755 (accessed 25 February 2005).

——*Sostav Kommissii Pravitelstva Rossiiskoi Federatsii po voenno-promyshlennym voprosam* [Staff of the Government Commission on Military-Industrial Questions]. Online. Available HTTP: www.government.gov.ru/data/static_text.html?st_id=7776&he_id=755 (accessed 25 February 2005).

——*Sostav Morskoi kollegii pri Pravitelstve Rossiiskoi Federatsii* [Staff of the Maritime Collegium of the Government of the Russian Federation]. Online. Available HTTP: www.government.gov.ru/data/static_text.html?st_id=7747&he_id=755 (accessed 18 February 2005).

——*Soobshchenie dlia pechati No. 1241, Postanovlenie ot 1 septiabria 2001, No. 662 'O Morskoi kollegii pri Pravitelstve Rossiiskoi Federatsii'* [Information for the press, no. 1241, Statutes, 1 September 2001, no. 662, On the Maritime Collegium of the Government of the Russian Federation]. Online. Available HTTP: www.government.gov.ru/data/news_text.html?he_id=103&news_id=3213 (accessed 18 February 2005).

Grachev, P. (ed.), *Voennaia entsiklopediia, tom 2*, Moscow: Voennoe izdatelstvo, 1994.

Granik, I., 'Gosduma svodit schety so Schetnoi palatoi' [The State Duma settles accounts with the Audit Chamber], *Kommersant daily*. Online. Available HTTP: www.kommersant.ru/doc.html?docId=549135 (accessed 21 February 2005).

Grechko, A., *Vooruzhennye sily sovetskogo gosudarstva* [The Armed Forces of the Soviet state], Moscow: Voenizdat, 1974.

Grinevsky, O., 'Disarmament: the road to conversion', in V. Genin (ed.), *The Anatomy of Russian Defense Conversion*, Walnut Creek, Calif.: Vega Press, 2001, pp. 158–207.

Guseva, D. and Gorelov, N., *Karera generala, Vremia novostei* [The career of a general: *Vremia novostei*]. Online. Available HTTP: www.vremya.ru/2004/209/4/112395.html (accessed 26 October 2005).

Hagström, E., *Integration eller sönderfall? En studie av utvecklingen av samarbetet inom OSS 1991–1997* [Integration or disintegration? A study of the development of cooperation within the CIS 1991–97], Stockholm: Swedish National Defence Research Establishment (FOA), February 1998, User Report, FOA-R–97-00728-180–SE.

Halperin, M. and Clapp, P., *Bureaucratic Politics and Foreign Policy*, 2nd edn, Washington, DC: Brookings Institution Press, 2006.

Hedlund, S., *Will Putin Make a Difference?*, Uppsala: Department of East European Studies, Uppsala University, Working Papers 78, August 2003, ISRN UU-ÖSTUD-AR–02/–SE.

Herspring, D., *The Kremlin and the High Command: presidential impact on the Russian military from Gorbachev to Putin*, Lawrence, Kan.: Kansas University Press, 2006.

——'Putin and the Armed Forces', in D. Herspring (ed.), *Putin's Russia: past imperfect, future uncertain*, Lanham, Md.: Rowman & Littlefield, 2003, pp. 155–75.

——'Putin and military reform: some first hesitant steps', *Russia and Eurasia Review* (Jamestown Foundation), 2002, vol. 1, issue 7, 10 September. Online. Available HTTP:

http://russia.jamestown.org/pubs/view/rer_001_007_001.htm (accessed 16 October 2002).

——'Russia's crumbling military', *Current History*, 1998, vol. 97, no. 621, pp. 325–28.

——*Russian Civil–Military Relations*, Bloomington: Indiana University Press, 1996.

Hudson, V., *Foreign Policy Analysis: classic and contemporary theory*, Lanham, Md.: Rowman & Littlefield, 2007.

Human Rights Watch, *Backgrounder on the Case of Kheda Kungaeva: trial of Yuri Budanov set for February 28*, 26 February 2001. Online. Available HTTP: www.hrw.org/backgrounder/eca/chech-bck0226.htm#N_4_ (accessed 3 November 2004)

——'To serve without health: inadequate nutrition and health care in the Russian armed forces', *Human Rights Watch*, 2003, vol. 15, no. 9 (D), November. Online. Available HTTP: www.hrw.org/reports/2003/russia1103/russia1103.pdf (accessed 21 January 2005).

Huntington, S., *The Common Defense: strategic programs in national politics*, New York: Columbia University Press, 1961.

——*The Soldier and the State: the theory and politics of civil–military relations*, London: Belknap Press of Harvard University Press, 1957.

Huskey, E., *Presidential Power in Russia*, Armonk, N.Y.: M. E. Sharpe, 1999.

Interfax, *PACE Will Not Monitor Elections in Chechnya–Davis*, 9 October 2005. Online. Available HTTP: www.interfax.com/17/96160/Interview.aspx (accessed 28 October 2005).

——*Russia's Strategic Missiles Guarantee Deterrence – Commander*, Interfax's interview, 3 August 2005. Online. Available HTTP: www.interfax.com/17/80995/Interview. aspx (accessed 28 October 2005).

International Institute for Strategic Studies (IISS), *The Military Balance 1991/1992*, London: Brassey's, 1992.

——*The Military Balance 1992/1993*, London: Brassey's, 1993.

——*The Military Balance 1993/1994*, London: Brassey's, 1994.

——*The Military Balance 1994/1995*, London: Brassey's, 1995.

——*The Military Balance 1995/1996*, London: Oxford University Press, 1996.

——*The Military Balance 1996/1997*, London: Oxford University Press, 1997.

——*The Military Balance 1997/1998*, London: Oxford University Press, 1998.

——*The Military Balance 1998/1999*, London: Oxford University Press, 1999.

——*The Military Balance 1999/2000*, London: Oxford University Press, 2000.

——*The Military Balance 2000/2001*, London: Oxford University Press, 2001.

——*The Military Balance 2001/2002*, London: Oxford University Press, 2002.

——*The Military Balance 2002/2003*, London: Oxford University Press, 2003.

——*The Military Balance 2003/2004*, London: Oxford University Press, 2004.

——*The Military Balance 2004/2005*, London: Oxford University Press, 2004.

——*The Military Balance 2005/2006*, London: Oxford University Press, 2005.

——*The Military Balance 2006*, London: Oxford University Press, 2006.

——*The Military Balance 2007*, London: Oxford University Press, 2007.

Isakova, I., 'Russian defense reform: current trends', paper prepared for the conference, *The US and Russia: Regional Security Issues and Interests*, Carlisle, Pa.: Strategic Studies Institute, U.S. Army War College, November 2006.

Ivanov, S. (ed.), *Voennaia entsiklopediia* [Military encyclopaedia], *tom 7*, Moscow: Voennoe izdatelstvo, 2003.

Ivanov, Yu., 'Legal, political and budgetary aspects of civilian control of the military in Russia', in J. Löwenhardt et al. (eds), *Army and State in Postcommunist Europe*, London: Frank Cass, 2001, pp. 11–22.

Jones, E., *Red Army and Society: a sociology of the Soviet military*, London: Allen & Unwin, 1985.

Jones, R. W., *Most Secret War: British scientific intelligence 1939–1945*, London: Hodder & Stoughton, 1979.

Jonsson, A., *Judicial Review and Individual Legal Activism: the case of Russia in theoretical perspective*, doctoral thesis, Uppsala, Sweden: Uppsala University, Faculty of Law and Department of East European Studies, 2005.

Kalashnikova, M., '"Ostavalos dat signal i vse by rinulos"' [You only needed to give the signal and all would dash forward], *Kommersant Vlast*, 2005, no. 12 (28 March), pp. 36–39.

Kalashnikova, N., 'Mirnoe bremia' [Peace burden], *Itogi*, 2005, no. 15 (12 April), pp. 30–34.

Kipp, J., 'War scare in the Caucasus: redefining the threat and the war on terrorism', in A. C. Aldis and R. McDermott (eds), *Russian Military Reform 1992–2002*, London: Frank Cass, 2003, pp. 234–56.

——*Russian Military Reform: status and prospects (views of a Western historian)*, Foreign Military Studies Office. Online. Available HTTP: http://call.army.mil/fmso/fmsopubs/issues/rusrform.htm (accessed 8 July 2002).

Knoph, J., *Civilian Control of the Russian State Forces: a challenge in theory and practice*, Stockholm: FOI, February 2004, User Report, FOI-R–1175–SE.

Kobrinskaya, I., 'The military reform as a social contract', Conference proceedings from Russian *Military Reform and Russia's New Security Environment*, ed. Yu. Fedorov and B. Nygren, Stockholm, Swedish National Defence College, May 2003, pp. 85–98.

Kokoshin, A., *Strategicheskoe upravlenie: teoriia, istoricheskii opyt, sravnitelnyi analiz, zadachi dlia Rossii* [Strategic command: theory, historic experience, comparative analysis and tasks for Russia], Moscow: MGIMO, ROSSPEN, 2003.

——'Defence leadership in Russia: the General Staff and strategic management in a comparative perspective', Conference proceedings from BCSIA Discussion Paper 2002–15, Kennedy School of Government, Harvard University, November 2002.

Konovalov, A., 'The changing role of military factors', in V. Baranovsky (ed.), *Russia and Europe: the emerging security agenda*, Oxford: Oxford University Press for the Stockholm International Peace Research Institute (SIPRI), 1997, pp. 196–218.

Kortunov, S. and Vikulov, S., 'Military reform and foreign policy', *International Affairs*, 1997, vol. 43, no. 6, pp. 167–77.

Kramer, M., 'The perils of counterinsurgency: Russia's war in Chechnya', *International Security*, 2004/2005, vol. 29, no. 3, pp. 5–63.

——*Civil–Military Relations in Russia and the Chechnya Conflict*, Center for Strategic and International Studies, PONARS, Policy Memo 99, December 1999. Online. Available HTTP: www.csis.org/ruseura/ponars/policymemos/pm_0099.pdf (accessed 3 February 2003).

Lambeth, B., 'Russia's wounded military', *Foreign Affairs*, 1995, vol. 74, no. 2, pp. 86–98.

Lantratov, K. and Safronov, I., 'Premer vzial v pomoshchniki generala' [The prime minister chose a general to assist him], *Kommersant daily*. Online. Available HTTP: www.kommersant.ru/doc.html?DocID=469616&IssueId=18270 (accessed 13 October 2005).

Lefebvre, S., 'The reform of the Russian air force', in A. C. Aldis and R. McDermott (eds), *Russian Military Reform 1992–2002*, London: Frank Cass, 2003, pp. 141–61.

Leijonhielm, J., 'Ryssland och hotbilden – i går, i dag och i morgon' [Russia and the threat image: yesterday, today and tomorrow], *Kungliga Krigsvetenskapsakademins Handlingar och Tidskrift*, 2005, vol. 209, no. 3, pp. 3–19.

——*Russian Military Capability in a Ten-Year-Perspective: problems and trends in 2005*, Stockholm: FOI, June 2005, FOI Memo 1396.

——*Russian Military Capability in a Ten-Year-Perspective*, Stockholm: FOI, September 2003, Strategiskt forum, no. 11.

——*Russian Military Capability in a Ten-Year-Perspective*, Stockholm: FOA, April 1999, Strategiskt forum, no. 5.

Leijonhielm, J. et al., *Rysk militär förmåga i ett tioårsperspektiv: problem och trender 2005* [Russian military capability in a 10-year perspective: problems and trends], Stockholm: FOI, June 2005, User Report, FOI-R–1662–SE.

——*Rysk militär förmåga i ett tioårsperspektiv: en förnyad bedömning 2002* [Russian military capability in a 10-year perspective: a new appraisal], Stockholm: FOI, February 2003, User Report, FOI-R–0811–SE.

——*Den ryska militärtekniska resursbasen: Rysk forskning, kritiska teknologier och vapensystem* [Russian military–technological capacity: Russian R&D, critical technologies and weapon systems], Stockholm: FOI, October 2002, User Report, FOI-R–0618–SE.

——*Rysk militär förmåga i ett tioårsperspektiv: en förnyad bedömning* [Russian military capability in a 10-year perspective: a new appraisal], Stockholm: FOA, November 2000, User Report, FOA-R–00-01758-170–SE.

——*Rysk militär förmåga i ett tioårsperspektiv* [Russian military capability in a 10-year perspective], Stockholm: FOA, May 1999, User Report, FOA-R–99-01151-170–SE.

Levada Tsentr, *Sotsialno-politicheskaia situatsiia v Rossii v sentiabre 2005 goda* [The social–political situation in Russia in September 2005], 5 October 2005. Online. Available HTTP: www.levada.ru/press/2005100506.html (accessed 7 October 2005).

Lieven, A., *Chechnya: tombstone of Russian power*, New Haven, Conn.: Yale University Press, 1998.

Litovkin, V., *Pamiati Ivana Safronova* [In memory of Ivan Safronov], RIA Novosti, 6 March 2007. Online. Available HTTP: www.rian.ru/analytics/20070306/61641899. html (accessed 25 October 2007).

Ljung, B. (ed.), *Aspects of the Kosovo Operation March–June 1999*, Stockholm: FOI, May 2001, User Report, FOI-R-0070–SE.

Lo, B., 'A people's trauma', *The World Today*, 2004, vol. 60, no. 10, pp. 5–7.

——*Vladimir Putin and the Evolution of Russian Foreign Policy*, London: Royal Institute of International Affairs, 2003.

Lobov, V., 'Voennaia reforma: istoricheskie predposylki i osnovnye napravleniia' [Military reform: historic preconditions and main directions], *Voenno-istoricheskii zhurnal*, 1991, no. 11, pp. 2–10.

Lobov, V., 'Voennoe stroitelstvo: na novom fundamente' [Military development: on new foundations], *Voennaia mysl*, 1991, no. 10, pp. 2–10.

Locksley, C., 'Concept, algorithm, indecision: why military reform has failed in Russia since 1992', *Journal of Slavic Military Studies*, 2001, vol. 14, no. 1, pp. 1–26.

Lopatin, V., 'Armiia i ekonomika' [Army and economy], *Voprosy ekonomiki*, 1990, no. 10, pp. 4–12.

Lynch, D., *'The Enemy Is at the Gate': Russia after Beslan*, Note for the PSC, IESUE/COPS(04)10, Paris: Institute for Security Studies, 2004.
——'Maneouvring with the military', *The World Today*, 1997, vol. 53, no. 11, pp. 275–77.
McDermott, R., 'Putin's military priorities: the modernisation of the armed forces', in A. C. Aldis and R. McDermott (eds), *Russian Military Reform 1992–2002*, London: Frank Cass, 2003, pp. 259–77.
McMichael, S. R., 'Military reform plan begins to take shape', *Report on the USSR*, 1991, vol. 3, no. 43, pp. 7–11.
Main, S., *Couch for the MoD or the CGS? Defence & the General Staff 2001–2004*, Conflict Studies Research Centre, Russian Series 04/09, April 2004. Online. Available HTTP: www.da.mod.uk/CSRC/documents/Russian/04%2809%29-SJM. pdf (accessed 26 October 2004).
——'The Strategic Rocket Forces, 1991–2002', in A. C. Aldis and R. McDermott (eds), *Russian Military Reform 1992–2002*, London: Frank Cass, 2003, pp. 99–123.
——*The 'Brain' of the Russian Army: the Centre for Military Strategic Research, General Staff 1985–2000*, Conflict Studies Research Centre, C101, March 2000. Online. Available HTTP: www.csrc.ac.uk/pdfs/c101-sjm.pdf (accessed 16 October 2002).
Maleva, T., *Alternativnaia grazhdanskaia sluzhba v Rossii: byt ili ne byt?* [Alternative civilian service in Russia: to be or not to be?], Carnegie Moscow Center, Briefing, 2002, vol. 4, no. 4, April. Online. Available HTTP: www.carnegie.ru/en/pubs/briefings/4–02.pdf (accessed 4 October 2005).
Mathers, J., 'Outside politics? Civil–military relations during a period of reform', in A. C. Aldis and R. McDermott (eds), *Russian Military Reform 1992–2002*, London: Frank Cass, 2003, pp. 22–40.
Mendelson, S., *Current Russian Views on US–Russian Security Relations and Military Reform*, Center for Strategic and International Studies, PONARS, Policy Memo 25, January 1998. Online. Available HTTP: www.csis.org/ruseura/ponars/ policymemos/pm_0025.pdf (accessed 3 February 2003).
Miller, S. E., 'Moscow's military power: Russia's search for security in an age of transition', in S. E. Miller and D. Trenin (eds), *The Russian Military: power and policy*, Cambridge, Mass.: MIT Press, 2004, pp. 1–41.
Ministry of Civil Defence, 'Emergency Situations and Liquidating the Consequences of Natural Disasters of the Russian Federation', *Regionalnye tsentry*. Online. Available HTTP: www.mchs.gov.ru/ministry.php?fid=1054731434674752 (accessed 22 November 2004).
Ministry of Civil Defence, 'Emergency Situations and Liquidating the Consequences of Natural Disasters of the Russian Federation', *Voiska* GO [Civil Defence Troops]. Online. Available HTTP: www.mchs.gov.ru/ministry.php?fid=1054730499538967&cid= (accessed 22 November 2004).
Ministry of Defence of the Russian Federation, *Informatsiia o proisshestviiakh i prestupleniiakh v Vooruzhennykh Silakh RF* [Information on accidents and crimes in the Armed Forces of the Russian Federation]. Online. Available HTTP: www.mil. ru/articles/article10596.shtml (accessed 12 September 2005).
——*Vstupitelnoe slovo Nachalnika Sluzhby kadrovoi i vospitatelnoi raboty Ministerstva oborony RF, generala armii N. A. Pankova na zasedanii Press-kluba voennykh obozrevatelei rossiiskikh SMI pri Upravlenii informatsii i obshchestvennykh sviazei MO RF* [Opening words by the head of the Service for Cadre and Educational Work of the

Russian Federation Ministry of Defence, Army General N. A. Pankov, at the Meeting of the Press Club for Military Correspondents of Russian Media at the Directorate for Information and Public Communication], 8 September 2005. Online. Available HTTP: www.mil.ru/articles/article10956.shtml (accessed 3 October 2005).

—— *Vstupitelnoe slovo Nachalnika Sluzhby kadrovoi i vospitatelnoi raboty Ministerstva oborony RF, generala armii N. A. Pankova na zasedanii Press-kluba voennykh obozrevatelei rossiiskikh SMI pri Upravlenii informatsii i obshchestvennykh sviazei MO RF* [Opening words by the head of the Service for Cadre and Educational Work of the Russian Federation Ministry of Defence, Army General N. A. Pankov, at the meeting of the Press Club for Military Correspondents of Russian Media at the Directorate for Information and Public Communication], 1 July 2005. Online. Available HTTP: www.mil.ru/articles/article10951.shtml (accessed 4 October 2005).

——*Vystuplenie Ministra oborony RF, S. B. Ivanova na soveshchanii rukovodiashchego sostava Vooruzhennykh Sil Rossiiskoi Federatsii* [Statement of the minister of defence of the Russian Federation S. B. Ivanov at the meeting of the senior staff of the Armed Forces of the Russian Federation], 17 November 2004. Online. Available HTTP: www.mil.ru/releases/2004/11/171230_8578.shtml (accessed 17 November 2004).

——*Vystuplenie ministra oborony Rossiiskoi Federatsii S. B. Ivanova na zasedanii Akademii voennykh nauk* [Statement of Minister of Defence of the Russian Federation S. B. Ivanov at the session of the Academy of Military Science], 24 January 2004. Online. Available HTTP: www.mil.ru/print/releases/2004/01/241203_4779.shtml (accessed 20 April 2004).

—— *Aktualnye zadachy razvitiia vooruzhennykh sil Rossiiskoi Federatsii* [Priority tasks of the development of the Armed Forces of the Russian Federation], Moscow: Voeninform, 2003.

——*Aktualnye zadachy razvitiia Vooruzhennykh Sil Rossiiskoi Federatsii* [Priority tasks of the development of the Armed Forces of the Russian Federation], 2003. Online. Available HTTP: www.mil.ru/index.php?menu_id=886 (accessed 22 October 2003).

——*Federalnaia tselevaia programma* [Federal Goal Programme] (Government Regulation no. 523, 25 August 2003). Online. Available HTTP: www.mil.ru/article5324.shtml (accessed 28 October 2005)..

——*Voennaia reforma* [Military reform]. Online. Available HTTP: www.mil.ru/index.php?menu_id=6 (accessed 3 October 2002).

Ministry of Economic Development and Trade of the Russian Federation, *Struktura Ministerstva* [Structure of the ministry]. Online. Available HTTP: www.economy.gov.ru/wps (accessed 3 March 2005).

Ministry of Finance of the Russian Federation, *Chistova Vera Yergeshevna*. Online. Available HTTP: www.minfin.ru/org_str/chistova.htm (accessed 3 March 2005).

'Minutes of State Duma of the Federal Assembly', no. 209, 7 February 2007. Online. Available HTTP://www.cir.ru/docs/duma/302/1099390?QueryID'984852&Highlight Query=984852 (accessed 19 September 2007).

Moran, J., 'Back to the future? Tolstoy and post-communist Russian military politics', *Journal of Slavic Military Studies*, 1999, vol. 12, no. 4, pp. 54–77.

Moroz, O., 'Chto budet s nashei armiei?' [What will happen to our army?], *Literaturnaia gazeta*, 30 August 2000. Online. Available HTTP: www.lgz.ru/archives/html_arch/lg34–352000/polit/art2.htm (accessed 13 May 2002).

NATO, *Slovar sovremennykh voenno-politicheskikh i voennykh terminov Rossiia– NATO* [Dictionary of modern military–political and military terms Russia– NATO], NATO, 21 June 2002. Online. Available HTTP: www.nato.int/docu/glossary/ rus/index.htm (accessed 26 September 2005).

Nikolaev, A., 'Russia's stalled military reform', *International Affairs*, 2001, vol. 47, no. 3, pp. 98–108.

——'Voennuiu reformu kavalereiskim naskokom ne provesti' [You cannot carry out military reform through cavalry attacks], *Rossiiskaia Federatsiia segodnia*, 1999, no. 4, pp. 20–22.

——'Military aspects of Russia's security', *International Affairs*, 1993, no. 10, pp. 6–9.

Nilsson, P.-O., 'Om den ryska militärreformen' [On Russian military reform], *Kungliga Krigsvetenskapsakademins Handlingar och Tidskrift*, 1997, no. 1, pp. 77–136.

Novaia Gazeta, 'Agenty vliianiia' [Agents of influence], NovaiaGazeta.ru. Online. Available HTTP: http://2004.novayagazeta.ru/nomer/2004/63n/n63n-s45.shtml (accessed 13 October 2005).

Odom, W., *The Collapse of the Soviet Military*, New Haven, Conn.: Yale University Press, 1998.

Ogarkov, N. (ed.), *Voennyi entsiklopedicheskii slovar* [Military encyclopaedic dictionary], Moscow: Voennoe izdatelstvo, 1983.

O'Hanlon, M., 'Rumsfeld's defence vision', *Survival*, 2002, vol. 44, no. 2, pp. 103–17.

Orr, M. J., 'Reform and the Russian Ground Forces, 1992–2002', in A. C. Aldis and R. McDermott (eds), *Russian Military Reform 1992–2002*, London: Frank Cass, 2003, pp. 124–40.

——*Manpower Problems of the Russian Armed Forces*, Conflict Studies Research Centre, D62, February 2002. Online. Available HTTP: www.csrc.ac.uk/frames/frames_page. htm (accessed 23 February 2005).

Paderin, A., 'Uroki otechestvennykh voennykh reform i prichiny tormozheniia voennogo reformirovaniia v kontse XX veka' [Lessons of patriotic military reforms and reasons for the braking of reforms in the late 20th century], International Scientific–Practical Conference on The Military Science, Art and Practice of Russia and Its Neighbours: Past, Present, Future, St Petersburg, 29–31 March 2005 (not published).

Pankov, N., 'Kurs – na grazhdanskii kontrol' [Towards civilian control], *Rossiiskoe voennoe obozrenie*, 2007, no. 4, pp. 6–11.

Parchomenko, W., 'The Russian military in the wake of the *Kursk* tragedy', *Journal of Slavic Military Studies*, 2001, vol. 14, no. 4, pp. 35–56.

Persson, G., 'The Russian army and foreign wars 1859–1871', doctoral thesis, Government Department, London School of Economics and Political Science, 1999.

Petrov, N., '*Siloviki* in Russian regions: new dogs, old tricks', *Journal of Power Institutions in Post-Soviet Societies*, 2005, no. 2. Online. Available HTTP: www. pipss.org/document331.html (accessed 10 May 2005).

——'Seven faces of Putin's Russia: federal districts as the new level of state-territorial composition', *Security Dialogue*, 2002, vol. 33, no. 1, pp. 73–91.

Petrov, N. and Slider, D., 'Putin and the regions', in D. R. Herspring (ed.), *Putin's Russia: past imperfect, future uncertain*, 3rd edn, Lanham, Md.: Rowman & Littlefield, 2007.

Plater-Zyberk, H., *Russia's Special Forces*, Conflict Studies Research Centre, Russian Series, 05/50, September 2005. Online. Available HTT: *www.da.mod.uk/CSRC/ documents/Russian/05(50)-HPZ.pdf* (accessed 8 November 2005).

——*Beslan: lessons learned?*, Conflict Studies Research Centre, Russian Series, 04/34, November 2004. Online. Available HTTP: www.da.mod.uk/CSRC/documents/Russian/04%2834%29-HPZ.pdf (accessed 29 November 2004).

Posen, B., *The Sources of Military Doctrine: France, Britain, and Germany between the world wars*, Ithaca, N.Y.: Cornell University Press, 1984..

President of Russia, *Zaiavlenie dlia pressy i otvety na voprosy po itogam XX sammita Rossiia-Evrosoiuz* [Statement to the press and answers to questions on the results of the 20th Russia–EU summit], 26 October 2007. Online. Available HTTP: www.president.kremlin.ru/appears/2007/10/26/2205_type63377type63380_149679.shtml (accessed 27 October 2007).

——*Stenngramma priamogo tele-i radioefira ('Priamaia linia s prezidentom Rossii')* [Minutes of direct television and radio ('Direct Line to the president of Russia')], 18 October 2007. Online. Available HTTP: www.president.kremlin.ru/appears/2007/10/18/1259_type63381type82634type146434_148629.shtml (accessed 27 October 2007).

——*Vystuplenie i diskussiia na Miunkhenskoi konferentsii po voprosam politiki bezopasnosti* [Statement and discussion at Munich Conference on Security Policy], 10 February 2007. Online. Available HTTP: www.president.kremlin.ru/text/appears/2007/02/118097.shtml (accessed 16 October 2007).

——*Stenograficheskii otchet o pervom plenarnom zasedanii Obshchestvennoi palaty Rossiiskoi Federatsii* [Minutes of the first plenary session of the Public Chamber of the Russian Federation], 22 January 2006. Online. Available HTTP: www.kremlin.ru/text/appears/2006/01/100457.shtml# (accessed 4 October 2007).

——*Vstupitelnoe slovo na zasedanii Soveta Bezopasnosti 'O perspektivakh razvitiia voennoi organizatsii Rossii do 2015 goda'* [Opening words at the meeting of the Security Council 'About the Development Prospects for the Military Organization until 2015'], 28 June 2005. Online. Available HTTP: www.president.kremlin.ru/text/appears/2005/06/90455.shtml (accessed 7 November 2005).

——*Zakliuchitelnoe slovo na soveshchanii rukovodiashchego sostava Vooruzhennykh Sil Rossii* [Closing words at the meeting for the senior staff of the Armed Forces of Russia], 17 November 2004. Online. Available HTTP: www.president.kremlin.ru/appears/2004/11/17/1845_type63378_79565.shtml (accessed 21 February 2005).

——*Stenograficheskii otchet o press-konferentsii v Kremle dlia rossiiskikh i zarubezhnykh SMI* [Minutes of press conference in the Kremlin for Russian and foreign media], 20 June 2003. Online. Available HTTP: www.president.kremlin.ru/text/appears/2003/06/47449.shtml (accessed 19 April 2004).

——*Poslanie Federalnomu Sobraniiu Rossiiskoi Federatsii* [State of the nation address to the Federal Assembly of the Russian Federation], 16 May 2003. Online. Available HTTP: www.president.kremlin.ru/text/appears/2003/05/44623.shtml (accessed 19 April 2004).

Presidential Administration, *Burutin Aleksandr Germanovich*. Online. Available HTTP: www.president.kremlin.ru/state_subj/43499.shtml (accessed 1 March 2005).

——*Kommissiia po voprosam voenno-tekhnicheskogo sotrudnichestva s innostrannymi gosudarstvami* [Commission on Questions of Military–Technological Cooperation with Foreign States]. Online. Available HTTP: www.president.kremlin.ru/state_subj/group43661.shtml (accessed 13 October 2005).

——*Soobshchenie Press-sluzhby Prezidenta Rossii* [Information from the Press Service of the President of Russia], 30 March 2004. Online. Available HTTP: www.kremlin.ru/text/news/2004/03/62552.shtml (accessed 1 March 2005).

——*Troshev Gennadii Nikolaevich*. Online. Available HTTP: www.president.kremlin. ru/state_subj/27784.shtml (accessed 14 October 2005).

Radio Free Europe/Radio Liberty, 'Interior Troops face sharp cuts', *RFE/RL Newsline*, 16 June 1998. Online. Available HTTP: www.rferl.org/newsline/1998/06/ 1-rus/rus-160698.asp (accessed 9 March 2005).

——'Yeltsin cuts Kremlin staff', *RFE/RL Newsline*, 13 February 1998. Online. Available HTTP: www.rferl.org/newsline/1998/02/130298.asp (accessed 3 November 2004).

'Ravnenie na chinovnika' [Equal to an official], *Finansovyi kontrol*, 2002, no. 2, pp. 12–13.

Renz, B., 'Media–military relations in post-Soviet Russia: who is the watchdog?', in S. Webber and S. Mathers (eds), *Military and Society in Post-Soviet Russia*, Manchester, UK: Manchester University Press, 2006, pp. 61–79.

RIA Novosti, *Putin obeshchaet usilit znachenie Genshtaba VS Rossii* [Putin promises to strengthen the importance of the General Staff of Russia's Armed Forces], RIA Novosti, 15 February 2007. Online. Available HTTP: www.rian.ru/defense_safety/ army_navy/20070215/60808273.html (accessed 26 October 2007).

Rice, C., 'The Party, the military, and decision authority in the Soviet Union', *World Politics*, 1987, vol. 40, no. 1, pp. 55–81.

Rosefielde, S., 'Russian rearmament: motives, options and prospects', paper prepared for FOI Conference, 'Russian Power Structures: Present and Future Role in Russian Politics', Stockholm, 17–18 October 2007 (to be published).

——*Russia in the 21st Century: the prodigal superpower*, New York: Cambridge University Press, 2005.

——'Back to the future? Prospects for Russia's military industrial revival', *Orbis*, 2002, vol. 46, no. 3, pp. 499–509.

Rutskoi, A., 'Voennaia politika Rossii: soderzhanie i napravlennost' [Military policy of Russia: content and direction], *Voennaia mysl*, 1993, no. 1, pp. 2–10.

Ryavec, K., *Russian Bureaucracy: power and pathology*, Lanham, Md.: Rowman & Littlefield, 2005.

Rybkin, I., *Consent in Chechnya, Consent in Russia*, London: Lytten Trading & Investment Ltd, 1998.

Safranchuk, I., *Contemporary Russian Military Journalism: achievements, problems, perspectives*, Center for Defense Information. Online. Available HTTP: www.cdi. org/program/issue/index.cfm?ProgramID=29&issueid=154 (accessed 4 April 2005).

Sakwa, R., *Putin: Russia's choice*, 2nd edn, London: Routledge, 2007.

Saronov, V., 'Critical mass: there are too many armed formations in Russia', *CDI Russia Weekly*, no. 184, December 2001. Online. Available HTTP: www.cdi.org/ russia/184-86.cfm (accessed 8 November 2005).

Savenkov, A., 'Kradut!' [They steal!], *Itogi*, 2004, no. 43 (26 October), pp. 22–26.

——'Na zashchite federalnoi sobstvennosti' [For the protection of federal property], *Finansovyi kontrol*, 2004, no. 11, pp. 42–50.

Security Council of the Russian Federation, *Sostav mezhvedomstvennoi komissii Soveta Bezopasnosti Rossiiskoi Federatsii po oboronno-promyshlennoi bezopasnosti po dolzhnostiam* [Staff of the Interdepartmental Commission of the Security Council of the Russian Federation on Defence-Industrial Security according to positions], 14 October 2002. Online. Available HTTP: www.scrf.gov.ru/documents/ mvk_oboron_2.shtml (accessed 20 October 2005).

Sedov, L., *Armeiskie preobrazovaniia v otrazhenii obshchestvennogo mneniia* [Army transformation as reflected in public opinion], Levada Tsentr, 7 September 2005. Online. Available HTTP: www.levada.ru/press/2005090701.html (accessed 2 October 2005).

Shlykov, V., 'The military reform and its implications for the modernization of the Russian Armed Forces', paper prepared for FOI Conference, 'Russian Power Structures: Present and Future Role in Russian Politics', Stockholm, 17–18 October 2007 (to be published).

——'Odin v pole ne voin' [The voice of one man is the voice of no one], *Russia in Global Affairs*, no. 3, 2007. Online. Available HTTP: www.globalaffairs.ru/numbers/26/7704.html (accessed 26 October 2007).

——'The economics of defense in Russia and the legacy of structural militarization', in S. E. Miller and D. Trenin (eds), *The Russian Military: power and policy*, Cambridge, Mass.: MIT Press, 2004, pp. 157–66.

——'Nuzhen li Rossii Generalnyi shtab? Rossiiskaia sistema vyshego voennogo upravleniia v mezhdunarodnom kontekste' [Does Russia need a general staff? The Russian system for military command in an international context], *Voennyi vestnik MFIT*, 2000, no. 7 (October).

Simons, G., *Russian Crisis Management Communications and Media Management Under Putin*, Uppsala, Sweden: Department of East European Studies, Uppsala University, January 2005, Working Papers, no. 85.

Slipchenko, V. and Shevelev, E., 'Metodologiia reformy Vooruzhennykh Sil' [Reform methodology for the armed forces], *Voennaia mysl*, 1991, no. 11–12, pp. 30–35.

Smith, M. A., *Chechnya: the political dimension*, Royal Military Academy Sandhurst, Conflict Studies Research Centre, P14, May 1995.

Sorokin, K., 'Vozrozhdenie rossiiskoi armii: blizhaishie perspektivy' [The rebirth of the Russian army: near perspectives], *Mirovaia ekonomika i mezhdunarodnye otnosheniia*, 1993, no. 1, pp. 5–17.

'"Sovet dobrykh del" nachinaet rabotu' [The 'Council of Good Things' begins work], *Rossiiskoe voennoe obozrenie*, 2007, no. 3, pp. 33–35.

State Duma of the Russian Federation, Information Channel, *O voennykh sudakh Rossiiskoi Federatsii* [On the military courts of the Russian Federation], 23 June 1999. Online. Available HTTP: www.akdi.ru/gd/proekt/079698GD.SHTM (accessed 26 April 2005).

——*Stennogramma plenarnogo zasedaniia Gosudarstvennoi Dumy RF: 13 maia 1999, dnevnoe zasedanie* [Minutes, day plenary session 13 May 1999], AKDI Ekonomika i zhizn. Online. Available HTTP: www.akdi.ru/gd/PLEN_Z/1999/s13–05_d.htm (accessed 14 November 2001).

Supreme Court of the Russian Federation, *O sudebnoi sisteme Rossiiskoi Federatsii* [On the judicial system of the Russian Federation], 31 December 1996. Online. Available HTTP: www.supcourt.ru/law1.html (accessed 22 March 2005).

Sutcliffe, P. J. and Hill, C., 'An economic analysis of Russian military reform proposals: ambition and reality', in A. C. Aldis and R. McDermott (eds), *Russian Military Reform 1992–2002*, London: Frank Cass, 2003, pp. 278–95.

Svechin, A., *Strategy*, Minneapolis, Minn.: East View Publications, 1997.

Sycheva, V., 'Osobennosti natsionalnoi bezopasnosti' [The peculiarities of national security], *Itogi*, 2004, no. 25 (22 June), pp. 16–20.

Talbott, S., *The Russia Hand: a memoir of presidential diplomacy*, New York: Random House, 2002.

Taylor, B., *The Duma and Military Reform*, Center for Strategic and International Studies, PONARS, Policy Memo 154, October 2000. Online. Available HTTP: www.csis.org/ruseura/ponars/policymemos/pm_0154.pdf (accessed 3 February 2003).

——*Putin and the Military: how long will the honeymoon last?*, Center for Strategic and International Studies, PONARS, Policy Memo 116, April 2000. Online. Available HTTP: www.csis.org/ruseura/ponars/policymemos/pm_0116.pdf (accessed 3 February 2003).

——'Russian civil–military relations after the October uprising', *Survival*, 1994, vol. 36, no. 1, pp. 3–29.

Thomas, T., '"The war in Iraq": an assessment of the lessons learned by Russian military specialists through 31 July 2003', *Journal of Slavic Military Studies*, 2004, vol. 17, no. 1, pp. 153–80.

——'Restructuring and reform in Russia's MVD: good idea, bad timing?', *Low Intensity Conflict and Law Enforcement*, 1998, vol. 7, no. 2, pp. 96–106.

——'EMERCOM: Russia's emergency response team', *Low Intensity Conflict and Law Enforcement*, 1995, vol. 4, no. 2, pp. 227–36.

Thornton, R., 'Military organizations and change: the "professionalization" of the 76th Airborne Division', *Journal of Slavic Military Studies*, 2004, vol. 17, no. 3, pp. 449–74.

Tikhomirov, V., 'Reforma vnutrennykh voisk: problemy i puti ikh resheniia' [The reform of the Interior Troops: problems and ways to solve them], *Voennaia mysl*, 2001, no. 4, pp. 2–9.

Timofeeva, O., *Prokuratura proverit Soldatskikh materei* [The procuracy investigates the Soldiers' Mothers], Izvestiia.ru, 21 October 2004. Online. Available HTTP: www.izvestia.ru/community/554982_printv (accessed 3 November 2004).

Trenin, D., 'Russia's security integration with America and Europe', in A. J. Motyl, B. A. Ruble and L. Shevtsova (eds), *Russia's Engagement with the West: transformation and integration in the twenty-first Century*, New York: M. E. Sharpe, 2005, pp. 281–94.

Troshev, G., *Chechenskii retsediv: Zapiski komanduiushchego* [Chechen relapse: notes of a commander], Moscow: Vagrius, 2003.

Troxel, T., *Parliamentary Power in Russia, 1994–2001: president vs parliament*, New York: Palgrave Macmillan, 2003.

Truscott, P., *Kursk*, London: Pocket Books, 2002.

Tsimbal, V. and Zatsepin, V., 'Reforma armii' [Army reform], *Kommersant Vlast*, 2007, no. 42 (29 October).

Tsypkin, M., 'Rudderless in the storm: the Russian navy, 1992–2002', in A. C. Aldis and R. McDermott (eds), *Russian Military Reform 1992–2002*, London: Frank Cass, 2003, pp. 162–86.

Ulfving, L., *Rysk krigskonst* [The Russian art of war], Stockholm: Swedish National Defence College, 2005.

Umbach, F., 'Zwang zur Militärreform: Die Krise der russischen Streitkräfte' [The necessity of military reform: the crisis of the Russian Armed Forces], *Internationale Politik*, 1996, vol. 51, no. 9, pp. 57–62.

Unge, W., *The Russian Military–Industrial Complex in the 1990s: conversion and privatisation in a structurally militarised economy*, Stockholm: FOA, December 2000, FOA-R–00-01702-170–SE.

van Bladel, J., 'Russian soldiers in the barracks: a portrait of a subculture', in A. C. Aldis and R. McDermott (eds), *Russian Military Reform 1992–2002*, London: Frank Cass, 2003, pp. 60–72.

Vandenko, A., 'Chelovek vo vseoruzhii' [A fully armed man], *Itogi*, 2005, no. 44 (31 October), pp. 22–26.

Vatolkin, E., Liuboshits, E., Khrustalev, E. and Tsymbal, V. 'Reform of military recruitment in Russia', *Problems of Economic Transition*, 2003, vol. 46, no. , pp. 6–158.

Vendil, C., 'The Russian Legitimation Formula, 1991–2000', doctoral thesis, Government Department, London School of Economics and Political Science, 2002.
——'The Russian Security Council', *European Security*, 2001, vol. 10, no. 2, pp. 67–94.
——*The Belovezha Accords and Beyond: delineating the Russian state*, Stockholm: FOA, May 2000, Scientific Report, FOA-R–00-01504-170–SE, pp. 25–37.
Vendil Pallin, C., 'The Russian power ministries: tool and insurance of power', *Journal of Slavic Military Studies*, 2007, vol. 20, no. 1, pp. 1–25.
——'Future EU–Russia relations', *RUSI Newsbrief*, 2006, vol. 26, no. 10, pp. 109–11.
——'Iraq war prompts debate over Russian military reform', *Jane's Intelligence Review*, 2004, vol. 16, no. 8, pp. 54–55.
Walker, C. and Orttung, R., 'No news is bad news', *Wall Street Journal Europe*, 7 September 2006, available on the Freedom House website. Online. Available HTTP: www.freedomhouse.org/template.cfm?page=72&release=411 (accessed 6 November 2007).
Webber, M., *The International Politics of Russia and the Successor States*, Manchester, UK: Manchester University Press, 1996.
Weber, M., *From Max Weber: essays in sociology*, H. H. Gerth and C. W. Mills, eds, London: Routledge, 1991.
Wheeler, M. and Unbegaun, B. (eds), *The Oxford Russian Dictionary*, Oxford: Oxford University Press, 1995.
Yasmann, V., 'The role of the security agencies in the October uprising', *RFE/RL Research Report*, 1993, vol. 2, no. 44.
Yerokhin, I., 'O razrabotke kontseptsii voennoi reformy', *Voennaia mysl*, 1991, nos 11–12, pp. 36–45.
Zherebenkov, Ye., 'Pravo na silu' [The right to use force], *Itogi*, 2002, 37 (17 September), pp. 18–22.

Index

Note: Numbers in **bold** type indicate a figure or a table.